BUCKINGHAM BURIALS

A Survey of Cemeteries in
Buckingham County
Virginia

Historic Buckingham, Inc.

WILLOW BEND BOOKS
2007

WILLOW BEND BOOKS
AN IMPRINT OF HERITAGE BOOKS, INC.

Books, CDs, and more—Worldwide

For our listing of thousands of titles see our website
at
www.HeritageBooks.com

Published 2007 by
HERITAGE BOOKS, INC.
Publishing Division
65 East Main Street
Westminster, Maryland 21157-5026

Copyright © 2007 Historic Buckingham, Inc.

Other Heritage Books in this series:

*Buckingham Burials: A Survey of Cemeteries in Buckingham County, Virginia
Volumes I and II*

Cover illustration: One of the more decorative tombstones still standing in Buckingham County is this stone for Charles H. McKinney, son of Philip W. and Nannie C. McKinney. The inscription reads:
"Our little Charlie. Charles Heath, son of P.W. & Nannie C. McKinney. Born Sept. 29, 1857: Died Dec. 7, 1859"
The child's father, Philip, served as Governor of Virginia for four years (1890-1894), the only man from Buckingham to become governor of the state.

All rights reserved. No part of this book may be reproduced or transmitted in any form or by any means, electronic or mechanical, including photocopying, recording or by any information storage and retrieval system without written permission from the author, except for the inclusion of brief quotations in a review.

International Standard Book Number: 978-0-7884-4087-X

INTRODUCTION

With the cemeteries in this volume, there are now 572 cemeteries* in Buckingham County which have been surveyed, recorded and filed. Sixty- four of these are church cemeteries, and two are community cemeteries. The balance are family cemeteries and a few single graves. In these cemeteries there are over 11,100 persons identified. And the work continues...

Unlike Volumes I and II, whose compiler was Janice J. R. Hull, this volume has cemeteries that were surveyed, researched and recorded by many people, the past and current members of the Genealogy Committee of Historic Buckingham Inc.:

Jack Bryant	Carl Henshaw	Mary Scott
Larry K. Davis	Lynne Henshaw	
Margaret Thomas	Constance Eldridge	
Martha Ellen Holmes	Robert L. Watson	Nancy Faxon
Janice J. R. Hull	Pauline Word	
Elizabeth C. Guthrie		

The information regarding persons buried in Buckingham Co., published in the three volumes, identifies the cemetery in which they are interred, gives their surname, given name, maiden name if known for married women, birth and death dates (if known), often their spouses' names when married, the inscription on the tombstone (if there is one), often the funeral home, and in many cases, additional information for genealogical research. The directions to the cemetery, the cemetery layout and description, GPS coordinates, contact person or owner of the land on which the cemetery is, are not included. This is privileged information for the descendents of the folks buried here. Any descendent may contact Historic Buckingham Inc., PO Box 152, Buckingham Va, 23921 and for the cost of printing and mailing, a complete record will be mailed to him/her. If a descendent can come to Buckingham Co. to do genealogical research, the Housewright House Museum, located on US 60 at Buckingham Court House, has the cemetery record files, and maps for finding the cemetery locations. The museum is open from April through November, Wednesday and Saturday afternoons. At other times, an appointment may be made by writing the Genealogy Committee, in care of Historic Buckingham Inc.. More information may be found at the HBI website: www.rootsweb.com/~vahb.

*The following cemeteries, which are in Volume I have been updated and included in this volume: Berkeley/Swan Family, Bryant Family on Rd. 606, Hackett Family off US 56, Jones Family #2 on Rd. 602, Benjamin W. Kitchen Family on Rd 662 (Kitchen Family-Hwy 662 in Vol. I), Rose Family on Rd. 627, Stinson-Carter-Harris Family (Old Stinson Place in Vol. I).

ACKNOWLEDGMENTS

A great deal of thanks for the work of locating the cemeteries in Volume III and/or providing information about those buried in them, goes to many residents of Buckingham County and the descendents of those interred in them, including:

At James River State Park: the Park Rangers
In the Howardsville area: David Bryant, Jackie Mann and Roland Wood
In the Glenmore area: Eva Adcock, James R. Bishop, Mildred Chambers, Claude Goode, Joyce Hartshorn, Glen Johnson, Herbert Jones, Valerie Londeree, Jackie Patterson, John N. Staton, and Mr. and Mrs. LL Self
In the Diana Mills area: Ruth Gough, Laura P. Hayes and Steve Self
In the Scottsville area: Edwin Brittle, Hazel Coles, Curtis Hedgeman, and Florine Taylor
In the Esmont area: Charlie and Maria Moseley
In the Arvonia area: Mayo Banks, Pat Clark, Trudie Nickolson, McNeal Opie, George Pankey, George Scruggs, Robin Stammer, C.D. Snoddy, Bob Toney, Steve Toney, Alene Woodson, and Rev. Woodson
In the Gladstone area: Charles Carter, Arlene Ferguson, Danny Henshaw and Otis Wiley
In the St. Joy area: John Bartee, Dorothy Bryant, Richard Bryant, Marjorie Dixon, Glen Henshaw, Mary P. Mosley, Miloyid Perkins, Ronnie Pleasants, Vernon and Janette Robertson, Evelyn K. Trakus, and Linda Seay
In the Buckingham Court House area: Willie Chambers, George Crews, Scott Crews, Elizabeth Edwards, John Wesley and Hazel Pearl Garrett, Thomas B. Hall, Anna Harris Jones,, Dorothy and John Morgan, Myrtle Morgan, Louise Swartz, Roger Ward, Esther Whorley, Margaret Whorley, and Alfred Wilson
In the Dillwyn area: Wanda A. Albrecht, Wiley Allen, Daisy Ayres, Gordon Ayres, Keith Ayres, Ruth Ayres, Chris Booker, Francis Bowles, Kathy H. Brown, Ivan "Chip" Davis, Sarah and John Davis, Mike Duncan, Glenda Harris, Catherine Kinker, Earl Lee, Pat Ragland, Mavis Sprouse,

Daniel Stanton, Patricia Stanton, John E. Staton Jr., George and Patricia Weeger, and Betty Zumbro

In the Goldhill area: Alonzo Cain, Debra Coffey, Arthur Cox, and Ollie Cox

In the Holiday Lake area: Burton Day, Evelyn Spencer Brightful, Bobbie Cook, Skip and Virginia Hoag, Nancy Lawrence, Nannie Lyon, Sherry Peak, and Thomas Watson

In the Andersonville area: Willie and Clarence Flood, Anna Miller, and Carolyn Morris

In the Willis Mountain area: Forrest Guthrie, R. Garey Hodge, Linda Johnston, and Otto Washington

Those who assisted with surveys or information about cemeteries in several areas are:

James "Rudy" Amos, Susan Auten, Kim Shumaker Clark, Elizabeth Harris, Edith Chambers Johnson, and Velma Jones

The following young people also assisted in surveying some cemeteries in Volume III:

Several full-time missionaries from the Church of Jesus Christ of Latter-day Saints

Several Buckingham Co. High-School students in the history classes of Larry K. Davis and Rudy Roethel

Several teenagers in the Young Women's program of the LDS Church.

Table of Contents

Milton Adams Family on Rd. 650 — African American 1
Adcock-Deane Family 2
   (listed in Vol. II of *Buckingham Burials* as the Jamerson-Sharp Family)
Agee Family off Rd. 631 3
Old Jacob Agee Family off Rd. 676 4
Vince Agee Family on Rd. 695 — African American 5
Alexander Hill Baptist Church — African American 6
Allen Memorial Garden-Pennington Family 7
Allen-Stanton Family on Rd. 787 — African American 9
Alvis-Booker-Coleman Family 11
Amos Family off Rd. 602 16
Amos Family on Rd. 673 19
Anderson-Word Family at Locust Grove 20
Apperson Family off US 15 22
Apperson Family on Rd. 787 22
Austin Family on Rd. 631 — African American 23
Ayres and Winfrey Families on Rd. 701 28
Ayres Family off Rd. 617 31
Ayres Grave on Rd. 678 32
Baber Family on Rd. 721 32
Baber-Turner-Wagner Family on old US 24 33
Banks Family on Rd. 676 33
Banks Family on Rd. 678 — African American 34
Banton Family off Rd. 617 34
Baptist Union Baptist Church — African American 37
Bennett Family on Rd. 653 68
Berkeley-Swan Family on Rd. 604 (update from Vol. I) 72
Boatwright Family at "Social Hall" 74
Bocock Grave at "Woodside" 76
George Bolling Family on Rd. 670 — African American 76
Booker Family off Rd. 627 77
Branch-Gunter Family on US 60 77
Bright and Morning Star Church — African American 77
Payton and Mollie Brown Family on Rd. 636 83
   — African American
Bryant Family in "Harrison's Field" 87
Bryant Family off Rd. 606 (update from Vol. 1) 87
Bryant Family off Rd. 649 105
Bryant Family on Rd. 765 105
Bryant-Stinson Family at Mt. Hermon Church 108
Burks Family off Rd. 605 111
John Burks Family off Rd. 606 111
Cabell Family in James River State Park 112
Clifford Cabell Family off Rd. 605 115
Carter Family on Rd. 607 115
Chambers Family (Caucasian) of Rd. 659 117
Chambers Family on US 20 — African American 117

George and Virgie Chambers Family on US 60 119
George Lewis Chambers Family off Rd. 671 120
 — African American
Chambers Family Slaves on Rd. 659 121
Chastain Family off Rd 732 121
Chestnut Grove Baptist Church on Rd. 673 — African American.. 121
Chief Cornerstone Baptist Church — African American 136
Claiborne Family and Slaves at "Cold Comfort" 146
Cliborne Family off the intersection of Rd. 632 and Rd. 650 148
Cobbs Family off Rd. 633 148
Coleman-Grigg Family off Rd. 722 148
Concord Baptist Church on Rd. 636 151
Cook-Williams Families on Rd. 601 — African American 175
Cottrell Family off Rd. 627 — African American 177
Cox Family at "Hickory Grove" 179
Crews Family off Rd. 649 179
Dabney Family on Rd. 615— African American 179
Dameron Family on Rd. 652 181
Joshua Davis Family off US 15 181
Davis Family at "Springfield" 183
Davis Family at "Whetstone Farm" 184
Dixon Family in James River Park 185
Dixon Family on David Creek (off US 60) 187
Drake-Gormus Family off Rd. 617 188
Dunnevant Family at "Spring Valley Stables" 189
Ebenezer Baptist Church — African American 190
Eldridge Family at "Twelve Oaks" 204
Eubanks-Hedgeman Family on US 20 — African American 206
William Evans Family at "Merioneth" 208
Farmville Christian Fellowship — Mennonite 211
Forbes Family on US 56 — African American 212
Ford Family off Rd. 652 — African American 213
Fork Union Baptist Church — African American 214
Sidney Fountain Grave on Rd. 627 231
Francisco Family at "Locust Grove" 231
Garrett Family off Rd. 699 231
Gilbert-Bagby Family at Sliders 235
R. H. Gilliam Family on Rd. 644 236
Glenmore United Methodist Church 237
Glover Family off Rd. 643 259
Goldmine Penecostal Holiness Church 261
Goode Family on Rd. 627 — African American 261
William Gormours Family on US 15 263
Nat. M. Gregory Family off Rd. 652 264
Guthrie Family at "Mt. Pleasant" off Rd. 632 265
Guthrie Slaves and Descendants at "Mt Pleasant" 266
Hackett Family off US 56 (update from Vol. I) 266
Hamner Family off Rd. 627 268
Harris Family on Rd. 617 269
Harris Family on US 15 271

Harvey Family (Sarah Harris Grave Site) off Rd. 744 273
Hocker (George Hocker) Grave off Rd. 690 273
Hodnett Family off Rd. 633 274
Holmes Grave off Rd. 607 274
Holy Trinity Baptist Church on US 15 — African American 274
J.T. Horner Grave on Rd. 668 280
Horsley Family off Rds 691 and 646 — African American 281
Jamerson-Newton Family on Rd. 778 281
Jamison-Sharp Family off Rd. 778 283
Jerusalem Baptist Church — African American 285
Johnson Family on Rd. 622 290
John H. Johnson Family on Rd. 615 — African American 292
Jones Family at "Mountain View" 299
Jones Family No. 2 on Rd. 602 300
   — African American (update from Vol. I)
Jones Family off Rd. 642 301
Jones Family on Rd. 695 — African American 301
Jones-Higgenbotham Family on Rd. 648 — African American 303
Benjamin Wickliff Kitchen Family 304
   (Update of Kitchen Family on Rd. 622 in Vol. I)
LeSueur-Call Family on Rd. 617 305
Maple Grove Penecostal Church 307
George Maxey Family off Rd. 705 313
Thomas Maxey Family on Rd. 705 314
McCraw Family at "Elysian Grove" 315
Miles Family on Rd. 655 315
Moore-Proffitt Family on Rd. 627 316
Moore-Pryer Family on Rd. 1003 318
Moorman Family on Rd. 604 318
Cleveland J. Morris Family off Rd. 791 318
Morriss Family at "Montevedio" 319
Rachel Morriss Family off Rd. 664 — African American 320
Moseley-Eldridge Slaves at "Rolfeton" 320
Mourner's Valley Baptist Church — African American 321
Mt. Olive Baptist Church — African American 331
Nativity Catholic Church 339
New Hope Baptist Church — African American 340
Newton-Moss Family off Rd. 744 352
Onion Family at Slate River Farm off Rd. 649 356
   — African American
Pankey Family at Traveler's Rest 356
Pankey Family off Rd. 607 — African American 357
Patteson-Tucker Family off Rd. 659 360
Payne Family on Rd. 750 — African American 362
Proffitt Family at James River Park 362
Radford Family off Rd. 793 — African American 362
Ragland Family on US 56 364
Reynolds Family off Rd. 607 — African American 365
Ridgeway Baptist Church on Rd. 652 — African American 367
Robertson Family and Slaves at "Stone House Farm" 374

Rose Family on Rd. 627 — African American 375
   (updated from Vol. I)
Rush Family on Rd. 691..376
Saunders Family on Rd. 612 — African American 378
Self Family on Rd. 701...378
Self Family on Rd. 722...380
Shaw Family at "Raleigh"...380
Shepherd Family at "Slate River Farm" 381
Slate Rive Baptist Church — African American.............381
Henry Smith Family on Rd. 722 — African American....392
William Smith Family on Rd. 646 393
Snoddy-Bransford Family at "Old Walter Bransford Place"...........393
Thomas Snoddy Family on Rd. 677................................395
William Snoddy Family on Rd. 653 396
Spencer Family at "Brierhook" 396
Spencer Family on Rd. 646..397
Spencer-Moseley Family at "Dixie" 397
Samuel Spencer Family off US 24 — African American................400
Spreading Oak Baptist Church — African American 402
Sprouse Family at "Sprouse's Corner"...........................418
St. Andrew's Baptist Church..419
St. Joy Baptist Church — African American..................430
Stammer Family on US 15 444
Stanton Family on Rd. 617 — African American...........444
Stevens-Alvis Family off US 60......................................449
Stevens-Alvis Slaves off US 60......................................449
Alexander Stinson Family off Rd. 754 450
Stinson-Carter-Harris Family..451
   (called "The Old Stinson Place" in Vol. I)
Henry Stinson Family off Rd. 607 452
Thomas Stinson Family off Rd. 606 455
Stout Family on Rd. 628...458
Stuart Brothers on Rd. 607...458
Swoope Family on Rd. 648 458
Taylor Family off US 15 — African American................460
Horace Taylor Family in James River State Park 461
John Taylor Family at James River State Park.............461
Taylor Family on Rd. 631 (also Moss/Meador/Pendleton Family) .462
Walker Taylor Family on Rd. 690 463
Terry Family on Rd. 811 463
Pleasant Toney Family on Rd. 745 464
Toney Slaves off Rd. 745...465
William Toney Family off Rd. 610 465
Third (3rd) Liberty Baptist Church— African American...................466
Trinity United Methodist Church 480
Turner Family on US 20 — African American................492
Union Baptist Church 492
Union Branch Baptist Church — African American......503
Union Grove Baptist Church — African American 518
Union Hill Baptist Church — African American 524

Unknown Family at "Old Pollard Place" — African American 541
Vest Family off Rd. 662 541
Matthew Via Family off Rd. 606 541
Wade Family off US 15, at Alpha 542
Wade-McFadden Family off Rd. 636 543
Watson-Perrow Family 544
Roberta Watson Grave on Rd. 640 552
West Family off Rd. 649 — African American 553
J. Y. Wheeler Grave on Rd. 652 553
Whitlow-Hardiman Familly off Rd. 1008 553
James Whorley Family on Rd. 749 554
Wiley Family off Rd. 607 — African American 556
Wilkinson Family off Rd. 610 557
Wise Family on "Dixie Hill Road" 557
Wood-Golladay Family on Rd. 605 557
Woodland Methodist Church 559
Cubie Woodson Family on US 20 — African American 582
Wooldridge Family off Rd. 662 582
Wright-Allen Family on Rd. 604 — African American 583
Charlie Wright Family on Rd. 604 – African American 584
Young-Moseley Family on Rd. 678 — African American 586
Zions Baptist Church — African American 587
Zions Grove Baptist Church — African American 614

Last Name Given Name (Maiden Name)	Date of Birth Date of Death Age at Death	Spouse	Tombstone

Milton Adams Family on Rd. 650 — African American

"Uncle Babe" | | | no

Other Info: Known to be buried here. Grave marked with fieldstones. He was the brother of Mary A. Adams also buried in this cemetery.

Adams
Eugene | | | no

Other Info: Known to be buried here. Grave marked with a wooden cross.

Adams
Jennie | 16 Sept. 1865
19 April 1936 | | yes

Other Info: She was the mother of Milton Adams Sr. also buried in this cemetery.

Adams
Mary A. | 24 Dec. 1907
(8 April 2003) | Milton Adams Sr. | yes

Other Info: Shares a headstone with her husband.

Adams
Milton Sr. | 16 Sept. 1898
26 May 1994 | Mary A. Adams | yes

Other Info: Shares a headstone with his wife.

Adams
Richard R. | 31 July 1940
18 Sept. 1975 | | yes

Other Info: He was the son of Milton Adams Sr. and Mary A. Adams also buried in this cemetery.

Hall
Boots | | Susie Adams Hall | no

Other Info: Known to be buried here-Grave marked with fieldstones.

Last Name Given Name (Maiden Name)	Date of Birth Date of Death Age at Death	Spouse	Tombstone
Hall Susie Adams		Boots Hall	no

Other Info: Known to be buried here-Grave marked with wooden cross. She was the sister of Milton Adams Sr.

Adcock-Deane Family
(listed in Vol. II of *Buckingham Burials* as the Jamerson-Sharp Family)

Adcock John		Sarah Adcock	no

Other Info: Known to be buried here.

Adcock Sarah		John Adcock	no

Other Info: Known to be buried here.

Dean William R.			yes

Inscription: Co. C, 3 VA RES, CSA

Harris William			yes

Inscription: Co. C, 4 VA RES, CSA

Jamison William J.			yes

Inscription: Co. K, 2 VA ARTY, CSA

Other Info: In this cemetery are 25 unidentified graves.

Last Name Given Name (Maiden Name)	Date of Birth Date of Death Age at Death	Spouse	Tombstone

Agee Family off Rd. 631

Agee Bettie Wood	23 Nov. 1884 16 Sept. 1950		yes

Inscription: Mother

Agee Howard W.	14 Feb. 1908 13 Aug. 1918		yes

Agee John W. (Willie)	10 Oct. 1888 16 Dec. 1943	Myrtis Louise Goin Agee	yes

Other Info: His sister, Lizzie Agee Murphy and his father, Samuel P. Agee are also buried in this cemetery. His mother was Orilla Shoemaker Agee.

Agee S. V.	7 Nov. 1940 7 Nov. 1940		yes

Inscription: Baby

Agee Samuel P.	11 Sept. 1857 15 June 1916	Orilla Shoemaker Agee	yes

Other Info: He and his wife were the parents of John W. Agee and Lizzie Agee Murphy also buried in this cemetery, and Mary Elizabeth Agee OBryant Newton, Minnie Lee Agee Newton, Christine Agee Slater and Tiny Agee Staton. Samuel P. Agee and Orilla Shoemaker Agee were married on 30 March 1882. His parents were William D. Agee and Sophia Ann Garrett Agee.

Agee Tabler	10 Jan. 1911 7 Oct. 1911		yes
Davidson Mary F.	18 Oct. 1924 24 Oct. 1924		yes
Davison John W.	17 Sept. 187_ 12 Feb. 194_		yes

Last Name Given Name (Maiden Name	Date of Birth Date of Death Age at Death	Spouse	Tombstone
Murphy Lizzie (Elizabeth) Agee	15 Nov. 1884 10 Oct. 1904		yes
Taylor Harry J.	15 March 1939 2 Nov. 1998	Edna Frances Shoemaker Taylor	yes

Inscription: Sweet Daddy

Other Info: His parents were Stafford and Agnes Agee Taylor who are also buried in this cemetery.

Taylor Stafford	13 Oct. 1887 7 Oct. 1958	(1) Laura "Dotsey" Shoemaker Taylor; (2) Agnes Agee Taylor	yes

Inscription: Gone but not Forgotten

Other Info: His mother was Lou Taylor. He and Agnes Agee Taylor were the parents of Harry J. Taylor also buried in this cemetery.

Old Jacob Agee Family off Rd. 676

Banton William J. (James)	about 1841 21 Nov. 1919	Judith Banton	yes

Inscription: Co. D, 56th VA INF, CSA

Other Info: Applied for a pension on 14 May 1900 stating that his age was 60 years.

Perrow (infant)	11 Aug. 1900		yes

Inscription: Budded on earth to bloom in heaven; Infant child of W.E. and Lizzie Perrow.

There are 6 unidentified graves in this cemetery.

Last Name	Date of Birth	Spouse	Tombstone
Given Name	Date of Death		
(Maiden Name)	Age at Death		

Vince Agee Family on Rd. 695 — African American

Agee   1926   yes
Earl   1997

   Inscription: US Navy, World War II

   Other Info: He was the father of Larry Kirk Agee, the brother of Virginia
      A. Brittle and Vincent H. Agee, and the son of Vincent Agee Sr.

Agee   no
Helen Juanita   27 Aug. 1976
                        72 years

   Other Info: Thacker Bros. Funeral Home marker

Agee   2 Sept. 1957   yes
Larry Kirk   18 Nov. 1992

   Inscription: FA, US Navy

   Other Info: His father was Earl Agee also buried in this cemetery.

Agee   no
Margie

   Other Info: Known to be buried here. Sister of Vince Agee.

Agee   4 Jan. 1924   yes
Vincent Harry   4 June 1975

   Inscription: PFC, US Army, Korea

   Other Info: He was the son of Vincent Agee Sr. also buried in this
      cemetery.

Agee   no
Vincent, Sr.

   Other Info: Known to be buried here. He was the father of Vincent H.
      Agee, Virginia Agee Brittle, and Earl Agee also buried in this
      cemetery.

Last Name Given Name (Maiden Name)	Date of Birth Date of Death Age at Death	Spouse	Tombstone
Brittle Virginia Agee	10 July 1931 6 Feb. 1979		yes

Inscription: Mother; We Love Ya

Other Info: She was the sister of Vincent H. Agee and Earl Agee, the daughter of Vincent Agee Sr. and the grandmother of Darlus Jermaine Lewis all buried in this cemetery.

Greene Ruth M.	10 Dec. 1972 63 years		no

Other Info: Thacker Bros. Funeral Home marker

Lewis Darlus Jermaine	17 Sept. 1995 17 Sept. 1995		no

Other Info: Thacker Bros. Funeral Home marker; Son of Donna Brittle Lewis and grandson of Virginia A. Brittle also buried in this cemetery.

Alexander Hill Baptist Church — African American

Harris Carrington	4 July 1962 41 years		no

Other Info: Thacker Bros. Funeral Home marker.

Harris Marshall	1968		

Other Info: unidentified funeral home marker

Harris Russell Harrison	5/25/1970		no

Other Info: Thacker Bros. Funeral Home marker

Last Name Given Name (Maiden Name)	Date of Birth Date of Death Age at Death	Spouse	Tombstone
Harris Winston	 2 Sept. 1958 62 years		no

Other Info: Thacker Bros. Funeral Home marker

Palmer Rev. G.	1834 20 May 1893		yes

Watts George	1898	 Bertha Harris Watts	no

Other Info: From records of the Jerusalem Baptist Church Cemetery survey done by Historic Buckingham Inc. He was married at age 24 on 20 August, 1922. His parents were Munci Turner and Kate Minor.

There are 22 identified graves, some marked with fieldstones, in this cemetery.

Allen Memorial Garden-Pennington Family

Allen Henry B.	1913 1980		Memorial

Inscription: In Memory Of

Allen Leonard Barnes Jr.	9 June 1921 25 Jan. 1987		Memorial

Inscription: In Loving Memory; Man of God

Allen Ruth Virginia	22 Oct. 1905 9 Feb. 1920		Memorial

Inscription: In Loving Memory of

Last Name Given Name (Maiden Name)	Date of Birth Date of Death Age at Death	Spouse	Tombstone
Loeber Mary Louis	5 April 1918 8 Nov. 1997		yes

Inscription: In Loving Memory

Other Info: She is the mother of Paul Louis, and the mother-in-law of Martha Pennington Louis.

Matney Esther Allen	4 July 1907 8 Oct. 1977		Memorial

Inscription: In Loving Memory

McPherson Bertha Anne "Bert"	10 Dec. 1922 9 April 2003		Memorial

Inscription: In Loving Memory of

Pennington Margaret Allen	9 March 1909 5 Jan. 1989	William A. Pennington	yes

Inscription: In Loving Memory; Mother, Wife, Doctor, Artist

Other Info: All of those who have memorials in this garden are the siblings of Margaret Allen Pennington.

Pennington William A.	1911 1993	Margaret Allen Pennington	yes

Inscription: In Loving Memory

Randolph Barbara Allen	18 Dec. 1918 13 Nov. 2000		Memorial

Inscription: In Loving Memory

Wills Lois Allen	9 Feb. 1903 14 May 2000		Memorial

Inscription: In Loving Memory

Last Name	Date of Birth	Spouse	Tombstone
Given Name	Date of Death		
(Maiden Name)	Age at Death		

Allen-Stanton Family on Rd. 787 — African American

Allen   1837   yes
   Jane Lou   1933/5

   Inscription: At Rest

(Bentley)   1899   no
   Froney Stanton   1959   Robert Bentley

   Other Info: Unidentified funeral home marker

Bentley   no
   Robert   Froney Stanton Bentley

   Other Info: Known to be buried here.

Johnson   2 July 1964   no
   Sammy David   23 March 1966

   Other Info: This is an above ground vault: Reids FH. He was the son
      of Henry and Helen Stanton Johnson.

Stanton   no
   Alice

   Other Info: Known to be buried here, the mother of Walter Stanton,
      who is also buried in this cemetery.

Stanton   1916   no
   Clarence Lee   1963

   Other Info: Unidentified funeral home marker

Stanton   no
   Emma

   Other Info: Known to be buried here.

Stanton   14 Feb. 1870   yes
   Houston J.   8 Sept. 1950   Mattie A. Stanton

Last Name Given Name (Maiden Name)	Date of Birth Date of Death Age at Death	Spouse	Tombstone
Stanton James A.	29 July 1943 13 Jan. 1992		Etched Fieldstone

Other Info: Has a Reids Funeral Home marker

Stanton Jennie Mae	31 May 1912 11 June 2001		no

Other Info: This is an above ground vault: Reids FH

Stanton John D.	23 Aug. 1965 5 Jan. 2000		Painted Fieldstone

Other Info: Has a Reids Funeral Home marker

Stanton John E. (Edward)			yes

Inscription: Virginia, PVT, 155 Depot Brig., 5 June 1918

Stanton Joseph E.	1917 (3 Jan.) 2005		no

Other Info: Reids Funeral Home marker; He was the brother of Russell, Clarence Lee, Vaicous, and John Edward Staton all buried in this cemetery.

Stanton Mattie A.	1884 12 Jan. 1952	Houston J. Stanton	yes
Stanton Pearl C.	9 Aug. 1917 28 June 2003		Painted Fieldstone

Other Info: Has a Reids Funeral Home marker.

Stanton Russell	1903 1999		no

Other Info: Reids Funeral Home marker

Stanton Vaicous	14 Oct. 1964		no

Other Info: Reids Funeral Home marker

Last Name Given Name (Maiden Name	Date of Birth Date of Death Age at Death	Spouse	Tombstone
Stanton Walter	15 Oct. 1909 1 Feb. 1996		no

    Other Info: This is an above ground vault: Bland & Reid FH

There are 15 unidentified graves in this cemetery, including those known to be buried here. Stanton family members report that there are many more older graves in the woods beyond the cemetery.

Alvis-Booker-Coleman Family

Alvis Prudence Branch Moseley	1810 1870		yes
Alvis William M.	24 May 1843 17 Aug. 1866		yes

    Inscription: Co. H, 2 VA Cav., CSA

    Other Info: Has a military cross as a footstone.

Alvis William W.	1 May 1808 15 May 1878		yes

    Inscription: Sgt., Co. B, 40 VA Cav., CSA

    Other Info: Has a military cross as a footstone.

Booker Edwin Marshall	15 Dec. 1904 12 Jan. 1905		yes

    Other Info: Footstone: EMB

Booker Ida Branch	7 Dec. 1902 30 April 1919		yes

    Inscription: A sunbeam from the world has vanished.

Last Name Given Name (Maiden Name	Date of Birth Date of Death Age at Death	Spouse	Tombstone
Booker Jewell Howard	7 Jan. 1922 4 April 1979	Robert Coleman Booker	yes

Other Info: Shares a headstone with her husband.

Booker John R. (Richard)	2 June 1870 21 Jan. 1952	Martha Bertha Coleman Booker	yes

Inscription: Son of Robert M. and Susanna Taylor Booker, Born Prince Edward Co., VA, Died Warwick Co., VA, Son of a Confederate Soldier. Married June 29, 1898

Other Info: Shares a headstone with his wife.

Booker John Richard III	1948 1968		yes

Other Info: Footstone: JRB

Booker John Richard Jr.	26 Feb. 1917 5 Sept. 1972	Lillian Mae Roeblad Booker	yes

Other Info: Shares a headstone with his wife.

Booker Lillian Mae Roeblad	21 Aug. 1921 18 Aug. 1972	John Richard Booker, Jr.	yes

Other Info: Shares a headstone with her husband

Booker Malcolm A. (Alvis)	19 Jan. 1915 1 April 2002		yes

Inscription: US Navy, World War II

Last Name Given Name (Maiden Name)	Date of Birth Date of Death Age at Death	Spouse	Tombstone
Booker Martha Bertha Coleman	10 Feb. 1879 5 Sept. 1970	John Richard Booker	yes

    Inscription: Daughter of Thomas E. and Ida Megginson Coleman, Born Appomattox Co., VA; Married 29 June 1898; Their children: Susie Marie, Russell Flood, Ida Branch, Edwin Marshall, Olivia Edna, George Edward, Robert Coleman, Malcolm Alvis, John Richard Jr., Wm. Alexander, Bernie Irene, Alice.

    Other Info: Shares a headstone with her husband.

Booker Robert Coleman	28 Aug. 1912 11 Aug. 1997	Jewell Howard Booker	yes

    Inscription: Son of Robert Howard Booker

    Other Info: Footstone: Robert Coleman Booker, Sgt., US Army, World War II; shares a headstone with his wife.

Christian Mary Susan Booker	19 July 1899 12 June 1978		yes

    Inscription: Children-Peggy and Katherine

Coleman Hazel Garris	16 Jan. 1900 16 March 1946	Robert Ingersol Coleman	yes

    Other Info: Footstone: Mother; Shares a headstone with her husband.

Coleman Ida Megginson	12 Aug. 1861 22 April 1881		yes

    Other Info: Footstone: IMC

Coleman Minnie Profitt	3 June 1862 14 Jan. 1936	Thomas Edwin Coleman	yes

    Other Info: Footstone: Mother; Shares a headstone with her husband.

Coleman Robert Ingersol	1 March 1896 25 July 1966	Hazel Garris Coleman	yes

    Other Info: Footstone: Father; Shares a headstone with his wife.

Last Name Given Name (Maiden Name)	Date of Birth Date of Death Age at Death	Spouse	Tombstone
Coleman Thomas Edwin	5 March 1859 24 March 1929	Minnie Profitt Coleman	yes

Other Info: Footstone: Father; Shares a headstone with his wife.

Dunn Mary Moseley	30 May 1836 12 March 1912		yes

Other Info: Footstone: MMD

Dunn Ridley B. Alvis	1831 1891		yes
Dunn William	7 July 1826 23 April 1880		yes

Inscription: Capt., Co. H., 166 VA Mil., CSA

Eubank Lucy Ann Alvis	1829 1891		yes
Eubank Mary Branch	5 June 1855 3 Nov. 1936		yes

Other Info: Footstone: MBE

Ewing Malcolm	7 April 1895 20 March 1961		yes

Inscription: Virginia, Sgt., Co. D, 317 Infantry, World War I

Ewing Olivia Booker	1906 2000		no

Other Info: Unidentified funeral home marker

Hicks Annie Coleman	1 Oct. 1888 9 March 1972	Patrick Henry Hicks	yes

Other Info: Shares a headstone with her husband.

Last Name Given Name (Maiden Name	Date of Birth Date of Death Age at Death	Spouse	Tombstone
Hicks 　Patrick Henry	10 Oct. 1900 8 Aug. 1975	Annie Coleman Hicks	yes

Other Info: Shares a headstone with his wife.

Kim 　Lee Koon	1910 1951		yes

Inscription: Killed by mankind's worse curse. Greater love hath no man than this That he lays down his life for his friends.

Other Info: Mr. Kim was a native of China and a friend of the Booker family.

Kyle 　Ida H.	30 Nov. 1854 8 May 1938		yes

Other Info: Footstone: IHK

Kyle 　Mary Wooldridge	19 April 1887 2 Feb. 1971	Robert Thomas Kyle	yes

Other Info: Footstone: Mother; Shares a headstone with her husband.

Kyle 　Robert Thomas	1 Oct. 1894 12 Dec. 1965	Mary Wooldridge Kyle	yes

Other Info: Footstone: Father; Shares a headstone with his wife.

Megginson 　Elisa Susan Alvis	1832 1863		yes

Inscription: Pocohontas 8th Generation

Slagle 　Caroline Lewis Alvis	1840 1893		yes

There are 10 unidentified graves in this cemetery.

Last Name Given Name (Maiden Name)	Date of Birth Date of Death Age at Death	Spouse	Tombstone

Amos Family off Rd. 602 — African American

Amos Arthur Reuben	15 Aug. 1916 7 Jan. 1998		yes

Inscription: Forever with the Lord

Other Info: He was the father of Malcom Alloyd Amos and Terry Daniel Amos also buried in this cemetery.

Amos Christine K.	13 May 1926 22 May 1996		yes

Inscription: Daughter and Granddaughter

Other Info: Has a Thacker Bros. Funeral Home marker.

Amos Etta	1 Feb. 1961 66 years		yes

Inscription: At Rest

Other Info: Also has an above ground vault.

Amos Henry	25 Dec. 1881 19 May 1965		yes

Other Info: Also has an above ground vault: J.E. Bell FH

Amos James	30 Nov. 1914 26 Oct. 2001 86 years		yes

Inscription: PFC, US Army, World War II

Other Info: Thacker Bros Funeral Home Marker.

Amos Katie	22 April 1938		yes

Other Info: Has an above ground vault

Last Name Given Name (Maiden Name	Date of Birth Date of Death Age at Death	Spouse	Tombstone
Amos Lovette Evelyn, Mrs.	12 May 1910 5 Jan. 1987 75 years		no

    Other Info: Thacker Bros. Funeral Home marker

| Amos
   Malcolm Alloyd | 9 Oct. 1953
15 June 1995 | | yes |

    Inscription: Loving Son and Brother

| Amos
   Terry Daniel | 21 Oct. 1956
7 Jan. 1998 | | yes |

    Inscription: Always in our Hearts

| B_____
   John Harris | 1906
19__
83 years | | no |

    Other Info: Thacker Bros. Funeral Home marker

| Bourne
   Annie Rachel Amos | 15 March 1879
8 June 1965 | | yes |

    Inscription: At Rest

| Burton
   Nannie B. | 1873
1964 | | yes |

    Inscription: In God's Care

| Chambers
   Anis | 4 July 1908
30 Aug. 1971 | | yes |

    Other Info: Has an above ground vault: Anna Amos Chambers-J.E. Bell FH

| Harris
   Queen B. | 2 Oct. 1902
15 Dec. 1977 | | yes |

    Inscription: At Rest

    Other Info: Has a J.F. Bell Funeral Home marker.

Last Name Given Name (Maiden Name)	Date of Birth Date of Death Age at Death	Spouse	Tombstone
Harris Walter Howard	1898 1962		yes

Inscription: At Rest

Massie Bessie A.			no

Other Info: Unidentified funeral home marker with one date: 16 Aug. 1965.

Rouse Virginia S.			no

Other Info: O.F. Howard Funeral Home marker with one date: 3 March 1992

Scott Coleman Lee	17 July 1925 30 Jan. 1997		yes

Inscription: US Army, World War II

Smith Allen			no

Other Info: This is an above ground vault-no other information.

Smith Clifford	28 Sept. 1917 17 March 1961		yes

Inscription: France, CPL, US Army, World War II

Smith Dorothy	1919 1982		no

Other Info: This is an above ground vault-Reids FH

Smith John Henry Sr.	3 July 1914 13 Jan. 1991		yes

Inscription: Always in our Hearts

Last Name Given Name (Maiden Name)	Date of Birth Date of Death Age at Death	Spouse	Tombstone
Smith Kyle Dwayne	23 Feb. 1983 19 March 1996		yes
Smith Mckayla Marsha	13 Sept. 1991 15 Sept. 1991		yes
Smith Rosa	1883 1967		no

Other Info: Unidentified funeral home marker

Wright Frances	15 March 1922 23 Aug. 2000		no

Other Info: This is an above ground vault: Bland-Reid FH

There are 17 unidentified graves in this cemetery.

Amos Family on Rd. 673

Amos David W.	28 Feb. 1890 2 Dec. 1933		yes

Inscription: Gone but not Forgotten

Other Info: Footstone: DWA

Amos L. W. (Lindsey Walker)	30 July 1855 5 June 1905		yes

Inscription: Be ye therefore ready

Other Info: Footstone: LWA; Son of John C. Amos and John Mary Page Amos Wallace.

Last Name Given Name (Maiden Name)	Date of Birth Date of Death Age at Death	Spouse	Tombstone
Amos Nina Belle (Stratton)	6 Nov. 1861 6 April 1932		yes

Inscription: Mother; Safe in the arms of Jesus

Other Info: Footstone: NBA
In this cemetery are 12 unidentified graves.

Anderson-Word Family at Locust Grove

Anderson James David	17 March 1811 27 Feb. 1893	Sarah Agnes Flood Anderson	yes

Other Info: Shares a family headstone with many others; Footstone: JDA

Anderson James Lewis	23 July 1847 11 Nov. 1926	Myrtie Gardner Seal Anderson	yes

Other Info: Shares a family headstone with many others.

Anderson Martha	15 July 1856		yes

Other Info: Shares a family headstone with many others; Footstone: MA

Anderson Myrtie Gardner Seal	11 March 1870 3 March 1893	James Lewis Anderson	yes

Other Info: Shares a family headstone with many others; Footstone: MSA; Daughter of James G. and Pattie W. Taylor Seal and granddaughter of Rev. William H. Taylor. She and James Lewis Anderson were married on 30 Nov. 1886

Anderson Sarah Agnes Flood	22 Aug. 1818 15 Oct. 1885	James David Anderson	yes

Other Info: Shares a family headstone with many others; Footstone: SAA

Last Name Given Name (Maiden Name	Date of Birth Date of Death Age at Death	Spouse	Tombstone

Anderson
  Sarah H.   July 1852   yes

  Other Info: Shares a family headstone with many others; Footstone: SHA

Anderson   24 Jan. 1856   yes
  William F.   23 Aug. 1863

  Other Info: Shares a family headstone with many others; Footstone: WFA

Charlton   26 April 1857   yes
  Sarah Anderson   14 July 1944

  Other Info: Shares a family headstone with many others.

Davis   26 July 1844   yes
  Rosa Anderson Gray 15 Jan. 1927

  Other Info: Shares a family headstone with many others.

Fitzgerald   16 Sept. 1853   yes
  Mary Anderson Lewis May 1915

  Other Info: Shares a family headstone with many others.

Jones   5 Feb. 1862   yes
  Lucy Anderson   8 Jan. 1954

  Other Info: Shares a family headstone with many others.

Lewis   17 July 1842   yes
  Annie Anderson   5 March 1932

  Other Info: Shares a family headstone with many others

Richardson   29 Oct. 1847   yes
Fannie Anderson Lewis 13 Aug. 1929

  Other Info: Shares a family headstone with many others; Footstone: FALR

Last Name Given Name (Maiden Name)	Date of Birth Date of Death Age at Death	Spouse	Tombstone
Word Carrie Burke Anderson	26 Nov. 1887 30 March 1972	David Malloy Word Jr.	yes

Other Info: Shares a family headstone with many others. Footstone: CBW; She was the daughter of James Lewis and Myrtie G.S. Anderson.

Word David Malloy Jr.	27 Mar. 1888 23 Oct. 1945	Carrie Burke Anderson Word	yes

Apperson Family off US 15

Apperson William J.			yes

Inscription: Co. E, 20 VA Inf, CSA

Hanes Eliza	15 April 1944 infant		no

Other Info: Known to be buried here.

Maxey Mary E.	26 Feb. 1877 30 July 1906		yes

Inscription: She was a kind and affectionate wife, a fond mother and a friend to all

The family reports that there are 2 other unmarked graves in this cemetery.

Apperson Family on Rd. 787

Apperson Calvin Talmage	1883 1944		yes

Apperson Harrison	12 Jan. 1889 21 July 1955		yes

Last Name Given Name (Maiden Name)	Date of Birth Date of Death Age at Death	Spouse	Tombstone
Apperson P. L.	21 Jan. 1882 13 April 1935		yes
Apperson S.G.	12 Feb. 1880 13 July 1942		yes

Other Info: Dunkum Funeral Home marker: Sterling Apperson, 1880-1942

Apperson Sallie F. (England)	26 Dec. 1852 19 Aug. 1933		yes

Inscription: Rest mother rest, Quiet sleep, While friends in sorrow over thee weep.

Other Info: Footstone: SFA; She was the mother of Harrison, Sterling and P.L. Apperson all buried in this cemetery. Another son, Tom Apperson is buried at Rocky Mt. Methodist Church cemetery nearby.

Austin Family on Rd. 631 — African American

Allen Rachel Austin	6 Nov. 1919 8 Nov. 1972	Robert Allen	yes

Inscription: Mother

Other Info: Her sister, Lucy Stanton is also buried in this cemetery. Her husband is buried at Mourner's Valley Baptist Church cemetery.

Anderson Annie Virginia	26 Sept. 1939 28 June 1986		yes

Inscription: Wife

Other Info: Has a Reids Funeral Home marker

Anderson Carl E.	1963 1999		no

Other Info: Reids Funeral Home marker

Last Name Given Name (Maiden Name)	Date of Birth Date of Death Age at Death	Spouse	Tombstone
Austin Abraham	1919 1985		yes

Inscription: PFC, US Army, World War II

Austin Addie M.	1912 1943		yes
Austin James			no

Other Info: Unidentified funeral home marker with no dates

Austin John Daniel	30 March 1924 8 May 1973		yes

Inscription: Virginia, PFC, US Army, World War II

Austin John S.	1891 1949		no

Other Info: Unidentified funeral home marker

Austin Kate	6 June 1946 19 April 1920		yes
Austin Laurence B.	1 Jan. 1923 15 Aug. 1985		yes

Inscription: US Navy, World War II

Austin Ordell	24 June 1945 22 Nov. 1993		yes

Inscription: In loving memory

Austin Sallie	1898 1948		no

Other Info: Unidentified funeral home marker

Last Name Given Name (Maiden Name)	Date of Birth Date of Death Age at Death	Spouse	Tombstone
Austin Sherry			no

Other Info: Unidentified funeral home marker with one date: 12 April 1966

Austin Thornhill	18 Nov. 1925 2 July 1963		yes

Inscription: Virginia, ST3, USNR, World War II

Austin Thornhill Bones	15 June 1953 3 Oct. 1987		yes

Inscription: To our beloved brother

Other Info: His mother was Lucy J. Stanton also buried in this cemetery.

Austin Virginia	29 June 1959		no

Other Info: L.C. Gray Funeral Home marker

Austin William			no

Other Info: Reids Funeral Home marker with one date: 7 April 1964

Austin William Rufus	12 May 1929 4 May 1991		yes
Ayers Beulah	17 March 1927 20 Dec. 1990	William Howard Ayers	yes

Other Info: Shares a headstone with her husband.

Ayers William H. (Howard)	8 Oct. 1924 not inscribed	Beulah Ayers	yes

Other Info: Footstone: William Howard Ayres, PFC, US Army, World War II, 8 Oct. 1924-18 Feb. 2002; Shares a headstone with his wife; Has a Reids Funeral Home marker.

Last Name Given Name (Maiden Name	Date of Birth Date of Death Age at Death	Spouse	Tombstone
Ayres Emanuel	1908 1970		no

Other Info: Reids Funeral Home marker

| Banks
   Haywood D. | 1987
2000 | | no |

Other Info: Reids Funeral Home marker; He was the grandson of Lillian Chambers also buried in this cemetery. His parents are Tracy Chambers Banks and Johnnie Banks.

| Booker
   Mary Ford |

21 years | | no |

Other Info: Unidentified funeral home marker with dates missing

| Booker
   Roger, Jr. | 1 Nov. 1943
12 Aug. 1998 |
Elsie Austin Booker | yes |

Inscription: Beloved Husband; Honey always in my heart

| Chambers
   Lillian Irene | 7 Apr. 1944
23 Nov. 1998 | | no |

Other Info: This is an above ground vault: Reids FH

| Forbes
   Hester K. | 1950
1989 | | yes |

Inscription: In loving memory

Other Info: Her mother was Lucy J. Stanton also buried in this cemetery.

| Ford
   Pearl Austin | 1912
1943 | | no |

Other Info: Dunkum Funeral Home marker

Last Name Given Name (Maiden Name)	Date of Birth Date of Death Age at Death	Spouse	Tombstone
Ford William Henry	1904 1964		no

Other Info: Unidentified funeral home marker

Gough Andrew	1927 2003		no

Other Info: Reids Funeral Home marker

Jackson Dorothy T.	8 Jan. 1935 11 May 1994		yes

Inscription: Our beloved mother; In God's Care

Other Info: Also has an above ground vault:Bland-Reid FH

Lee Pattie W.	1890 1951		yes

Other Info: Unidentified funeral home marker: Pattie Waverly Lee, d. 9 Dec. 1951, 62 years, 11 months.

Lee Robert	1900 1972		no

Other Info: Unidentified funeral home marker

Lee Robert C.	1871 1956		no

Other Info: Unidentified funeral home marker; father of Robert Lee also buried in this cemetery.

Lee ____Virginia	1947 52 years		no

Other Info: Unidentified funeral home marker

Maxie Lester J.	26 Oct. 1957 23 March 1989		yes

Inscription: Forever in our hearts

Last Name Given Name (Maiden Name)	Date of Birth Date of Death Age at Death	Spouse	Tombstone
Stanton Garfield	1927 1975		no

Other Info: Unidentified funeral home marker

Stanton Lucy J.	17 Dec. 1925 9 Feb. 1990		yes

Inscription: Our Beloved Mother

Other Info: She was the mother of Thornhill Austin, Hester Forbes, Gertrude Toole, Lillian Chambers, and Ordell Austin all buried in this cemetery.

Toole Gertrude L. Cunningham	1952 1997		yes
Woodson James P.	29 Oct. 1911 10 Feb. 1998		yes
Woodson Jennie F.	20 Nov. 1920 29 May 1989		yes
Yates Hattie B.	25 Dec. 1930 26 June, 1992		yes

There are 19 unidentified graves in this cemetery.

Ayres and Winfrey Families on Rd. 701

Ayres Betty M.	18 Oct. 1891 25 March 1958		yes

Inscription: Love lives forever; Lost to sight, to memory dear

Other Info: Footstone: Mother

Last Name Given Name (Maiden Name)	Date of Birth Date of Death Age at Death	Spouse	Tombstone
Ayres George McKenna	18 May 1868 15 May 1961		yes

Inscription: In Memory of

Ayres Hannah L.	4 March 1870 28 June 1935		yes

Inscription: A tender mother and a faithful friend

Ayres James E.			yes

Inscription: Co. A, 20 VA INF, CSA (no dates)

Ayres James Edmond	1 Feb. 1907 18 Aug. 1966		yes
Ayres Laura E.	7 Feb. 1869 1877		yes

Inscription: Asleep in Jesus

Ayres Lizzie May	15 July 1901 8 July 1998		yes
Ayres Mayo G.	14 Nov. 1876 7 Sept. 1943		yes

Inscription: Farewell until we meet again; There is no parting in heaven.

Ayres Sallie H.	10 June 1873 7 July 1879		yes

Inscription: Such is the kingdom of heaven

Ayres Sarah F.	1836 1928		yes

Inscription: She was sunshine of our home

Last Name Given Name (Maiden Name)	Date of Birth Date of Death Age at Death	Spouse	Tombstone
Ayres Willie H.	1871 1876		yes

Inscription: Gone to be an angel

B_____ MHW	1837 1855		yes
Winfrey baby	1855 1855		
Winfrey Egbert B.	21 March 1868 15 May 1891		yes

Inscription: In Memory of; Blessed are the dead who die in the Lord.

Winfrey Elisha Thornton	17 Nov. 1910 22 Dec. 1923		yes

Other Info: Has a W. A. Hartman Funeral Home marker.

Winfrey G.N.	22 Jan. 1861 19 March 1909		yes

Inscription: Loyal and true in every condition of life

Winfrey George H.	1835 1918	Judith C. R. Winfrey	yes

Inscription: At Rest

Other Info: Another headstone: Geo. H. Winfrey, Co. D, 56th VA INf, CSA; Double footstone: Geo. Hill Winfrey and his wife Judith C.R., married 1856; Parents of seven sons and four daughters.

Winfrey James Allen	4 March 1866 20 June 1944		yes
Winfrey Judith C. R.		George Hill Winfrey	no

Other Info: Double footstone: Geo. Hill Winfrey and his wife Judith C. R., married 1856; parents of seven sons and four daughters.

Last Name Given Name (Maiden Name)	Date of Birth Date of Death Age at Death	Spouse	Tombstone
Winfrey Sallie Spencer	6 June 1877 28 Dec. 1921		yes

Other Info: W.A. Harman Memorials Funeral Home marker

Winfrey Sarah Y. Holman	2 Feb. 1808 24 June 1854	William Hill Winfrey	yes

Other Info: Shares a headstone with her husband

Winfrey Susie Holman	20 May 1872 20 June 1944		yes

Winfrey William Hill	1 July 1806 23 July 1846	Sarah Y. Holman Winfrey	yes

Other Info: Shares a headstone with his wife.

Ayres Family off Rd. 617

Ayres Bettie (Dunkum)	12 Oct. 1881 29 June 1900		Etched Fieldstone

Ayres infant			no

Other Info: Parents were James and Margaret Ayres

Ayres John		Melissa Duncan Ayres	Etched Fieldstone

Ayres M.C. (Melissa Duncan)		John Ayres	Etched Fieldstone

Other Info: Daughter of Mathias Duncan

Last Name Given Name (Maiden Name)	Date of Birth Date of Death Age at Death	Spouse	Tombstone
Banton Marvin Lee	9 Sept. 1902 31 July 1940	Katie Ayres Banton	yes

Inscription: Gone but not Forgotten

Other Info: His wife was the granddaughter of John and Melissa Ayres also buried in this cemetery.

Duncan Mattias (Mathias)			Etched Fieldstone

Inscription: Memory (of)

Other Info: Father of Melissa Duncan Ayres.

There are 6 unidentified graves in this cemetery.

Ayres Grave on Rd. 678 — African American

Ayers Robert M. (McKinley)	19 Aug. 1909 17 Feb. 1985		yes

Inscription: Precious memories

Other Info: Thacker Bros. Funeral Home marker gives age at death as 75 years. His parents were Paul and Virginia Ayers buried at Mourners Valley Baptist Church cemetery.

Baber Family on Rd. 721

Baber Ida M (May).	18 May 1853 22 Oct. 1935	Joseph W. Baber	yes

Other Info: Shares a headstone with her husband. She was the daughter of James Robert Steger (1821-1846) and Clementine F. Hadnell.

Last Name Given Name (Maiden Name	Date of Birth Date of Death Age at Death	Spouse	Tombstone
Baber Joseph W. (Weldear)	30 March 1847 9 Jan. 1918	Ida M. Baber	yes

Other Info: Shares a headstone with his wife. They were married in 1869, and had 9 children: Sally W., Willie C., Clementine, Cleopatra, Julie H., Gerry, Mary A., James Ancil., and Earl W. Parents of Joseph W. were George Barber (1795-1875) and Louise B. Agee Baber (1817-?).

Baber-Turner-Wagner Family on old US 24

Hess   no
  Martha Baber

Other Info: Unidentified funeral home marker (no dates)

Turner   no
  Robert L.

Other Info: Unidentified funeral home marker (no dates)

Wagner   no
  Julie Turner

Other Info: Unidentified funeral home marker.

This cemetery has at least 9 unidentified graves.

Banks Family on Rd. 676

There are approximately 23 graves, all unmarked and unknown. The last burial is estimated to be circa 1915.

Last Name Given Name (Maiden Name)	Date of Birth Date of Death Age at Death	Spouse	Tombstone

Banks Family on Rd. 678 — African American

Banks George Franklin	25 Dec. 1888 21 Sept. 1958		yes

    Inscription: Virginia, PVT, Co. A, 407 Labor BN, OMC, World War I

    Other Info: Thacker Bros Funeral Home marker: 69 years at death.

Banks Ida	1862 7 Sept. 1935		yes

    Other Info: Mother of Octavius Banks who is buried at Ridgeway Baptist Church cemetery on Rd. 652.

Banks Mark Antonio	1965 1997 22 years		no

    Other Info: Thacker Bros. Funeral Home marker. His grandparents were Charlie and Maria Boseley

There are 3 unidentified graves in this cemetery.

Banton Family off Rd. 617

Banton Cleveland A.	18 Dec. 1883 4 Dec. 1925	Florence Banton	yes

    Other Info: Footstone: CAB; His father was Powell Banton also known to be buried in this cemetery.

Banton Florence		Cleveland Banton	no

    Other Info: Known to be buried here.

Banton infant (1)			no

    Other Info: Parents were Bessie Caul Banton and Barnard Banton.

Last Name Given Name (Maiden Name)	Date of Birth Date of Death Age at Death	Spouse	Tombstone
Banton infant (2)			no

Other Info: Parents were Bessie Caul Banton and Barnard Banton.

Banton James H.	13 Oct. 1834 1 Jan. 1890		yes

Banton Powell			no

Other Info: Known to be buried here; father of Cleveland A. Banton also buried in this cemetery.

Caul Charlie	1848 1925	Mattie Banton Caul	yes

Other Info: Shares a headstone with his wife.

Caul Mattie B. (Banton)	1871 1891	Charlie Caul	yes

Other Info: Shares a headstone with her husband

Gayle Emmet Patterson	1902 1966		no

Other Info: Unidentified funeral home marker; He was the foster child of the Patterson family who were neighbors of the Banton Family.

Maxey Charles	21 March 1923 (baby)		no

Other Info: Died as an infant. His parents were Docia B. and James A. Maxey.

Last Name Given Name (Maiden Name)	Date of Birth Date of Death Age at Death	Spouse	Tombstone
Maxey Docia B. (Banton)	27 Sept. 1883 28 Jan. 1928	James Alfred Maxey	yes

Inscription: Gone but not Forgotten

Other Info: Footstone: DBM; She and her husband were married on 25 Dec. 1913 and are the parents of James, Charles and Mabel (infants buried in this cemetery) and Hazel M. Garrett, and several other children.

| Maxey
  George (Georgia) Ann | 14 Feb. 1844
7 Dec. 1917 | James Glover Maxey | yes |

Other Info: Footstone: GAM; She and her husband were married on 24 May 1876 and were the parents of James Alfred Maxey, John Alexander Maxey, and Mary E. Maxey.

| Maxey
  James | 18 Nov. 1921
(baby) | | no |

Other Info: Died as an infant. Parents were Docia B. and James A. Maxey.

| Maxey
  James Glover | 10 June 1851
10 Feb. 1933 | Georgia Ann Banton Maxey | no |

Other Info: Known to be buried here.

| Maxey
  Mabel | 27 Sept. 1924
(baby) | | no |

Other Info: Died as an infant; parents were Docia B. and James A. Maxey.

Last Name Given Name (Maiden Name)	Date of Birth Date of Death Age at Death	Spouse	Tombstone
Taylor M. (Matthew) J. (James)	14 Oct. 1861 11 Dec. 1935	(1) Ida Miles Taylor (2) Virginia Banton Taylor	yes

Inscription: Gone but not Forgotten

Other Info: Footstone: MJT His parents were Anderson Taylor and Lucy Jane Garrett Taylor; Matthew Taylor and Ida Miles were married on 15 March 1881.

| Taylor
Virginia Banton | | Matthew James Taylor | no |

Other Info: She and her husband had : Harry, George, Henderson, Russell, Marvin, Andrew, Willie, Lucy, Callie, Louise, Estelle; They also reared John, the son of Ida Maxey Taylor and Matthew J. Taylor.

There are 20 unidentified graves in this cemetery. The names of nine of these are known.

Baptist Union Baptist Church — African American

| Agee
Charles E. | 1914
1988 | | yes |

Inscription: US Army, World War II

| Agee
Jessie E. Allen | 1913
1979 | | yes |

Inscription: Mother

Other Info: Unidentified funeral home marker: J. Edna Agee

| Agee
Lucy A | 1898
8 June 1941 | | yes |
| Allen
Archer | | | Etched Fieldstone |

Inscription: (no dates)

Last Name Given Name (Maiden Name	Date of Birth Date of Death Age at Death	Spouse	Tombstone
Allen Curtis Preston			Etched Fieldstone

Inscription: Curits Preston Allen-1930

| Allen
  Mary | | | Etched fieldstone |

Inscription: (no dates)

| Allen
  Mary B. | | | Etched Fieldstone |

Inscription: Mary B. Allen (only)

| Allen
  Preston R. | 17 April 1899
8 June 1951 | | yes |

Inscription: Father

| Allen
  Sallie Ann | 25 Nov. 1903
5 Oct. 1980 | | yes |

Inscription: Gone but not Forgotten

| Allen
  Viola E. | 3 April 1926
25 Aug. 1993 | William T. Allen | yes |

Other Info: Has an above ground vault: Reids FH

| Allen
  William Evan | | | yes |

Inscription: Dad (no dates)

| Anderson
  Alvin Early | 1922
1986 | | no |

Other Info: Has an above gorund vault:Reids FH

Last Name Given Name (Maiden Name	Date of Birth Date of Death Age at Death	Spouse	Tombstone
Anderson Annie	1887 1972		yes

Inscription: Our Mother

Anderson Annie F. Eldridge	24 Sept. 1916 3 Jan. 1979		yes
Anderson Betty Ann	1950 1995		no

Other Info: This is an above ground vault: Reids FH

Anderson C.B.	1917 1971		yes
Anderson Cary	1912 1936		yes
Anderson Charles F.	21 May 1930 10 March 1985		yes

Inscription: At Rest; Wife, with love

Anderson Edna B.	2 Sept. 1993 12 June 1973		yes

Inscription: Gone but not Forgotten

Anderson Florence G.	1920 1983		yes

Inscription: Mother

Other Info: Has a Reids Funeral Home marker

Anderson George Sam			yes (no dates)

Other Info: Has a Reids Funeral Home marker

Anderson Glenn W.	1899 1939		yes

Last Name Given Name (Maiden Name	Date of Birth Date of Death Age at Death	Spouse	Tombstone
Anderson 　Nelson T.	1943 2001		no

Other Info: Reids Funeral Home marker

Anderson 　William	1868 1936		yes
Ayers 　Ruby M.	3 Feb. 1909 8 Aug. 1981		yes
Ayres 　Catherine A.	1948 1994		no

Other Info: This is an above ground vault: Reids FH

Banks 　Charlie R.	1935 1995		no

Other Info: Has an above ground vault: Reids FH

Bartee 　Robert James	1910 1995		yes

Inscription: Loving Father

Other Info: Has a Reids Funeral Home marker.

Bartee 　Ruth Sears	2 April 1917 16 March 1983		yes

Inscription: Beloved wife and mother

Other Info: Footstone: RSB

Benders 　Elendra P.	1905 199__		no

Other Info: Reids Funeral Home marker

Bentley 　Sarah Stanton	27 Feb. 1921 7 Feb. 2002		no

Other Info: This is an above ground vault: Reids FH

Last Name Given Name (Maiden Name)	Date of Birth Date of Death Age at Death	Spouse	Tombstone
Blake Ella			Etched fieldstone

Inscription: (no dates)

Bolling Janie Mae	21 June 1916 29 Sept. 2000		yes

Inscription: In Loving Memory

Booker Celia F.	6 March 1880 6 Aug. 1939		yes

Inscription: Mother

Booker Martha C.	1854 17 Dec. 1917		yes

Other Info: Footstone: MCB

Branch Henry			Etched Fieldstone

Inscription: Henry Branch-8-1-1918

Branch Horace	1907 1985		no

Other Info: Unidentified funeral home marker

Branch Miss Virgie	3 May 1909		Etched Fieldstone

Bridges Dorothy Ann	15 Oct. 1950 14 Feb. 1998	Bobby Bridges	yes

Inscription: Beloved wife of Bobby Bridges; Forever in our hearts.

Brown Albert	1878 1968		yes

Inscription: In Memory of

Last Name Given Name (Maiden Name)	Date of Birth Date of Death Age at Death	Spouse	Tombstone
Brown Baby			Etched Fieldstone

Inscription: (no dates)

Brown Beulah P. (Peaks)	3 March 1901 20 May 1997	Junious Brown	yes

Other Info: Has an above ground vault: Reids FH; Shares a headstone with her husband.

Brown Eli	1880 1970		yes

Inscription: In Memory of

Brown Florence Winn	4 Sept. 1922 13 April 1998		yes

Inscription: Mother; Let not your heart be troubled

Other Info: Has an above ground vault: Reids FH

Brown J.G.			Etched fieldstone

Inscription: (no dates)

Brown Jennie Sears	1877 1957		yes

Inscription: Mother

Brown Jinnie	25 Dec. 1841 Apr. 1919	Sam Brown	yes

Inscription: Wife of Sam Brown

Other Info: Footstone: JB

Last Name Given Name (Maiden Name	Date of Birth Date of Death Age at Death	Spouse	Tombstone
Brown Junious	11 Aug. 1903 3 May 1992	Beulah P. Brown	yes

  Other Info: Has an above ground vault: Reids FH; Shares a headstone with his wife.

| Brown
  Lorraine | 24 Nov. 1924
6 Mar. 1947 | | yes |
| Chambers
  Sarah E. | 20 May 1921
10 July 1992 | | yes |

  Inscription: Mother

| Chennault
  Margaret F. | 1912
2002 | | no |

  Other Info: Reids Funeral Home marker

| Conyers
  Alma L. | 1921
1998 | | no |

  Other Info: Reids Funeral Home marker

| Cooper
  Wilbur | 1926
1996 | | Cement |

  Inscription: Name painted on

  Other Info: Reids Funeral Home marker gives dates

| Cox
  Clara | 1918
1988 | | no |

  Other Info: Unidentified funeral home markder

| Cox
  Guy W. | 1940
1998 | | no |

  Other Info: Reids Funeral Home marker

Last Name Given Name (Maiden Name)	Date of Birth Date of Death Age at Death	Spouse	Tombstone
Daniel Jennetta White	14 March 1891 20 March 1969		yes

Inscription: Peace, Perfect Peace

Edmonds Virginia L.	30 July 1903 5 Sept. 1927		yes

Inscription: Faithful to her trust even unto death

Other Info: Footstone: VLE

Eldridge Benjamin H.	1897 1985		yes

Inscription: PVT, US Army, World War I

Eldridge Bettie	1855 1928		yes
Eldridge Clara Herbert	24 May 1933 24 Dec. 1988		yes

Inscription: CPL, Korea

Eldridge Clarice E.	15 Aug. 1946 3 Feb. 1992		yes
Eldridge Cora B.	15 Aug. 1909 21 July 1997		yes

Inscription: Mother; Blessed quietness

Eldridge Curtis B. Sr.	6 Nov. 1934 19 Sept. 1970	Helen E. Eldridge	yes

Inscription: Beloved Husband of Helen E. Eldridge

Eldridge Dimple	1895 1974		yes

Inscription: Our Mother

Last Name Given Name (Maiden Name)	Date of Birth Date of Death Age at Death	Spouse	Tombstone
Eldridge Edward G.	1923 1964		yes
Eldridge Edward L.	13 April 1943 20 Dec. 1988		yes

Inscription: Gone but not Forgotten

Eldridge Eleanor N.	25 April 1914 16 Dec. 1990	Thomas B. Eldridge	yes

Inscription: Love Lives On

Eldridge Elisah	15 Oct. 1934 7 April 1983		yes
Eldridge Elmore Jr.	29 June 1913 15 March 1975		yes

Inscription: US Navy

Other Info: .Has an O.F Howard Funeral Home marker.

Eldridge Evelyn D.	14 Dec. 1957 31 July 1976		yes

Inscription: In Loving Memory

Other Info: Has a Reids Funeral Home marker.

Eldridge Fannie D.			no

Other Info: Dunkum Funeral Home marker with no dates.

Eldridge Fanny L.	10 May 1882 4 July 1943		yes
Eldridge George	1913 1984		no

Other Info: Unidentified funeral home marker

Last Name Given Name (Maiden Name)	Date of Birth Date of Death Age at Death	Spouse	Tombstone
Eldridge Harold Ivan	1 Nov. 1938 10 Feb. 1994		yes
Eldridge Harold W.	6 Aug. 1945 5 Jan. 1996		yes
Eldridge James Granville	1901 1986	Cora L. Eldridge	yes

Other Info: Has an above ground vault.

Eldridge James M.	1932 1975		yes

Inscription: By Wife and Children

Eldridge Katie	1914 1987		no

Other Info: Reids Funeral Home marker

Eldridge Linwood Taylor	Nov. 1934 2 Dec. 1995		no

Other Info: This is an above ground vault.

Eldridge Marshall	20 July 1931 4 April 2000	Lucille Eldridge	yes

Inscription: Married 10 Nov. 1956

Other Info: Has an above ground vault.

Eldridge Mary Anna			Etched fieldstone

Inscription: Mary Anna Eldridge C

Eldridge Morton H.	1888 1977		yes

Inscription: Our Father

Last Name Given Name (Maiden Name)	Date of Birth Date of Death Age at Death	Spouse	Tombstone
Eldridge Preston	1840 1944		yes
Eldridge Preston Simon	1917 1991	Oretha M. Eldridge	yes

Inscription: Married 20 Aug. 1942

Other Info: Has an above ground vault: Reids FH; Footstone: Dad

Eldridge Robert	10 May 1891 22 May 1951		yes

Inscription: Virginia, PVY, Co. D, 521 Engineers, World War I

Eldridge Robert Cortley	3 March 1900 3 March 1997		yes

Other Info: Has a Reids Funeral Home marker

Eldridge Robert Stanley	19 Jan. 1923 13 July 1969		yes

Inscription: New York, SGT, Us Army, World War II and Korea

Other Info: Has a Reids Funeral Home marker.

Eldridge Samuel	1947 1981		yes

Inscription: Gone but not Forgotten

Eldridge Thomas E.	2 May ___ 20 May 1989		Cement Stone
Eldridge William Elmore	15 April 1878 30 Nov. 1959		yes

Inscription: Father

Eldridge William H.			no

Other Info: O.F. Howard Funeral Home marker with no dates.

Last Name Given Name (Maiden Name)	Date of Birth Date of Death Age at Death	Spouse	Tombstone
Ford Anna E.			no

Other Info: Reids Funeral Home marker with one date: 25 Dec. 1969

| Ford
   Charlie C. | 1924
2003 | | no |

Other Info: Reids Funeral Home marker

| Ford
   Dorothy | 2 Nov. 1895
29 June 1940 | | yes |

| Ford
   George Huston | 13 Sept. 1909
21 Sept. 1981 | | yes |

Inscription: Rest in Peace

Other Info: Has a Reids Funeral Home marker.

| Ford
   George J. | 11 Jan. 1940
14 Sept. 1999 | | yes |

Inscription: Son, Father, Brother, Friend

Other Info: Has a Reids Funeral Home marker

| Ford
   R. Blanche | | | Etched fieldstone |

Inscription: (no dates)

| Gibson
   Giles E. | 8 Oct. 1888
8 Dec. 1965 | | yes |

Inscription: In memory of father

| Gibson
   Percell | 22 March 1922
17 Nov. 1965 | | yes |

Inscription: In love of my brother

Last Name Given Name (Maiden Name)	Date of Birth Date of Death Age at Death	Spouse	Tombstone
Gilliam C.	1935 1968		yes
Goode Frances Scruggs	19 July 1893 8 June 1938		Etched Fieldstone
Goss Alease R. Harvey	1920 1992		yes

Inscription: Beloved Mother

Other Info: Has a Johnson and Jenkins Funeral Home marker: Died 6 Aug. 1992, 71 years, 9 months, 13 days (FH address: 716 Kennedy St. N.W., Wash. D.C.)

Goss Donald Harvey	15 Nov. 1938 7 May 2003		no

Other Info: Has an above ground vault: Reids FH

Gray Edna			no

Other Info: Unidentified funeral home marker with one date: 9 Sept. 1958

Gregory Alfred Randolph	14 April 1932 23 May 1951		yes

Inscription: Virginia, CPL, 24 Infantry, 15 Infantry Div., Korea

Gregory Christopher C.	24 Aug. 1969 26 Feb. 1993		yes
Gregory Curtis	1962 1975		yes
Gregory Dorothy Lee	28 May 1915 15 June 1982		yes
Gregory Eugene	10 May 1926 29 Nov. 1965		yes

Last Name Given Name (Maiden Name)	Date of Birth Date of Death Age at Death	Spouse	Tombstone
Gregory Hilton	27 March 1906 27 Oct. 1989	Irene E. Gregory	yes

Inscription: Father; Married 10 March 1930

Other Info: Shares a headstone with his wife.

| Gregory
Irene E. | 10 Dec. 1911
6 June 1998 | Hilton Gregory | yes |

Inscription: Mother; Married 10 March 1930

Other Info: Shares a headstone with her husband.

| Gregory
James | 1910
1977 | | no |

Other Info: Reids Funeral Home marker

| Gregory
James Franklin | 25 Oct. 1947
9 May 1994 | | yes |

| Gregory
James T. | 1 Aug. 1915
(2000) | Jennie Mae Gregory | yes |

Other Info: Has a Reids Funeral Home marker; Shares a headstone with his wife.

| Gregory
Jennie Mae | 6 Jan. 1917
26 Dec. 1999 | James T. Gregory | yes |

Other Info: Shares a headstone with her husband. Has a Reids Funeral Home marker.

| Gregory
Junious | 1921
1995 | | no |

Other Info: Reids Funeral Home marker

| Gregory
Junious | | | no |

Other Info: Reids Funeral Home marker with no dates

Last Name Given Name (Maiden Name	Date of Birth Date of Death Age at Death	Spouse	Tombstone
Gregory Kate B.	22 Sept 1898 15 Nov. 1984		yes

Inscription: Loving Mother

| Gregory
  Leroy | 1917
1992 | | no |

Other Info: Reids Funeral Home marker

| Gregory
  Leslie | 19 Jan. 1933
23 May 1954 | | yes |

Inscription: Virginia, CPL, 24 Infantry, 13 Infantry Div., Korea

| Gregory
  Lucy W. | 1917
1995 | | no |

Other Info: Reids Funeral Home marker.

| Gregory
  Marsha | Jan. ___
1950 | | Cement Stone |

Inscription: (somewhat illegible)

Other Info: Footstone: MG

| Gregory
  Mary B. | 7 April 1934
10 Jan. 1981 | | yes |

Other Info: Has an above ground vault.

| Gregory
  Moses | 1932
1983 | | no |

Other Info: Reids Funeral Home marker

| Gregory
  Polly | 1897
1969 | | yes |

Inscription: In Memory of

| Gregory
  Randolph | 13 Nov. 1871
11 June 1963 | | yes |

Last Name Given Name (Maiden Name)	Date of Birth Date of Death Age at Death	Spouse	Tombstone
Gregory Ruby	23 March 1921 13 April 1999		yes

Inscription: Our loving sister and aunt; I'm free with Jesus

Other Info: Has a Reids Funeral Home marker

| Gregory
Stephen | 14 July 1895
29 Oct. 1983 | | yes |

Inscription: At Rest

| Gregory
Wanda Melissa | 2 Jan. 1972 | | yes |

Other Info: Has a Reids Funeral Home marker

| Gregory
William L | 14 Sept. 1946
13 Aug. 1994 | | yes |

| Harris
Baby | 14 Apr. 2003 | | yes |

Other Info: Has a Thomasson Funeral Home marker

| Harris
Gertrude E. | 1930
2002 | | yes |

Inscription: Mother

| Harris
Mr. William | 1926
2004 | | no |

Other Info: Thomasson Funeral Home marker

| Harvey
Charlie | 15 July 1893
6 July 1981 | | yes |

Inscription: Gone but not Forgotten

Last Name Given Name (Maiden Name)	Date of Birth Date of Death Age at Death	Spouse	Tombstone
Harvey Mrs. Lottie B.	5 Dec. 1895 4 Aug. 1985		yes

Inscription: Loving Mother, went to peaceful rest

Harvey Robert Len	3 Jan. 1929 13 Oct. 1972		yes

Inscription: Virginia, CPL, US Army, Korea

Jackson Essie Corrine	16 Jan. 1931 17 March 1985		yes

Inscription: In Memory with love, your family

Jackson Tonita V.	1981 1983		yes

Jen Barbra			Etched Fieldstone

Inscription: Barbra Jen and Children

Jennison Rev. Watson W.	29 Jan. 1909		yes

Inscription: Sacred to the memory of; He was an officer of Universal Brotherhood for Home Protection, and General Manager, and was a member of St. Lukes and Odd Fellows; At Rest

Other Info: Footstone: WJ

Johnson Hubert O.	5 July 1931 18 Nov. 2001		yes

Inscription: US Army, Korea

Other Info: Has a Reids Funeral Home marker.

Johnson Rosa Florine	21 Dec. 1925 4 Aug. 1989		yes

Last Name Given Name (Maiden Name)	Date of Birth Date of Death Age at Death	Spouse	Tombstone
Johnson Sallie C.	1903 1985		yes

Other Info: Has a Reids Funeral Home marker.

| Johnson
William A. | 10 Aug. 1955
27 June 1976 | | yes |

Inscription: SP4, US Army

| Jones
Allice | 1916
1988 | | no |

Other Info: Reids Funeral Home marker

| Jones
Elizabeth | 1910
2002 | | no |

Other Info: Reids Funeral Home marker

| Jones
Johnnie W. | 1915
1983 | | no |

Other Info: Reids Funeral Home marker

| Jones
Lucy A. | | | no |

Other Info: Unidentified funeral home marker with one date: 17 Sept. 1968

| Jones
Mansfield ONell | 1918
1985 | | no |

Other Info: This is an above ground vault: Reids FH

| Jones
Mary Brachett | 1922
1952 | | no |

Other Info: Reids Funeral Home marker

Last Name Given Name (Maiden Name)	Date of Birth Date of Death Age at Death	Spouse	Tombstone
Jones Richard Donald	1957 1988		no
Other Info: Reids Funeral Home marker			
Jones Samuel	1906 1990		no
Other Info: Reids Funeral Home marker			
Jones Walter	20 March 1917 7 Dec. 2002		yes
Inscription: US Army, World War II			
Jorden Maria	1911 1955		yes
Kidd Virginia Stanton	21 Aug. 1925 12 April 1992		yes
Other Info: Has a Dunkum Funeral Home marker			
Lee Curtis J.	1940 2001		no
Other Info: Reids Funeral Home marker			
Lee George Thomas	12 Oct. 1935 1 Dec. 2001 66 years		no
Other Info: Unidentified funeral home marker			
Lee Glenn A.	1966 2003		no
Other Info: Reids Funeral Home marker			
Lee Jaylah Fleming	2003		no
Other Info: Reids Funeral Home marker			

Last Name Given Name (Maiden Name)	Date of Birth Date of Death Age at Death	Spouse	Tombstone
Lewis Betty F.	29 Sept. 1914 15 Oct. 1998		yes

Inscription: Mother

Other Info: Has a Reids Funeral Home marker

Lewis Carrie Alice	20 June 1904 8 Sept. 1955		yes
Lewis Charles	1880 1953		yes
Lewis Edward	1909 1996		no

Other Info: Reids Funeral Home marker

Lewis Irvin	27 Jan. 1905 28 Jan. 1995		yes
Lewis James Irvin	15 Dec. 1943 4 Jan. 1985		yes

Inscription: At Rest

Lewis Lawrence	1912 1992		no

Other Info: E.B. Allen Funeral Home marker

Lewis S. Francis	1882 1970		yes

Other Info: Unidentified funeral home marker: Sarah F. Lewis

Lindsey Joseph	15 Aug. 1899 21 Feb. 1981	Nannie Lindsey	yes

Inscription: At Rest

Other Info: Shares a headstone with his wife.

Last Name Given Name (Maiden Name	Date of Birth Date of Death Age at Death	Spouse	Tombstone
Lindsey Nannie	28 March 1908 26 Sept. 1983	Joseph Lindsey	yes

Inscription: At Rest

Other Info: Shares a headstone with her husband.

Logan Archer	1888 1933		Cement Stone
Logan Charles Stuart, Rev.	17 Sept. 1888 23 March 1959		yes

Other Info: Footstone: Charles S. Logan, Virginia, PFC Engineers, World War I, 1888-23 March 1959

Logan E. H.			Etched Fieldstone

Inscription: 1933 (one date only)

Logan Henry			Etched Fieldstone

Inscription: (no dates)

Logan Herbert Hoover	27 Aug. 1930 12 April 1951		yes

Inscription: Virginia, PVT, 24 Infantry Div., Korea

Logan James Francis	12 Aug. 1919 1 Jan. 1991		yes
Logan Jessie P.	13 Sept. 1887 23 Feb. 1982		yes

Inscription: Mother

Logan John Wesley	7 March 1887 17 Dec. 1960		yes

Last Name Given Name (Maiden Name)	Date of Birth Date of Death Age at Death	Spouse	Tombstone
Logan 　Mary M.	25 Feb. 1876 28 July 1941		yes

　　Inscription: Mother

Logan 　Nathaniel D.	21 March 1900 28 Aug. 1948		yes
Logan 　Nellie F.	22 May 1902 8 Aug. 1973		yes
Mallory 　V. Florence White	8 Feb. 1915 14 Nov. 1990		yes
Mayo 　Mattie V.	19 April 1905 9 Jan. 1994		yes

　　Inscription: Mother; Gone but not Forgotten

McDowell 　Edna	1924 1977		yes
Mosley 　Beatchria	1921 1961		yes

　　Other Info: Has a Ranson-Smith Funeral Home marker with different
　　　spelling of name and different dates: Beatrice Moseley, 1923-1951

Norman 　C.P.	10 Nov. 1903 23 July 1936	Etched Fieldstone	
Peaks 　Arthur J.	May 1892 Aug. 1918		yes

　　Other Info: Footstone: AJP

Peaks 　Arthur R.	1933 1977		no

　　Other Info: Unidentified funeral home marker

Last Name Given Name (Maiden Name)	Date of Birth Date of Death Age at Death	Spouse	Tombstone
Peaks Ernest L.	1878 1957	Willie P. Peaks	yes

Other Info: Shares a headstone with his wife. Has a Jones Funeral Home marker.

Peaks John	8 May 1860 5 April 1905		Etched Fieldstone

Inscription: In Memory of our Father

Peaks Milton	27 June 1894 26 April 1921		Etched Fieldstone

Peaks Senobia V.	1898 1971		yes

Other Info: Footstone: SVP

Peaks Willie P.	1881 1972	Ernest L. Peaks	yes

Other Info: Shares a headstone with her husband.

Saunders Ophelia Anderson	13 July 1925 26 Jan. 2003		yes

Other Info: Has a Reids Funeral Home marker.

Scruggs Ann Mariah	25 Feb. 1801 31 Dec. 1916	W.H. Scruggs	yes

Inscription: Wife of W.H. Scruggs

Scruggs Annie E.	1920 1938		yes

Scruggs Deacon Nelson S.	1901 1997	Deaconess Elizabeth R. Scruggs	yes

Inscription: Married 16 Oct. 1952

Other Info: Has an above ground vault: Nelson S. Scruggs, 8 Oct. 1901-25 Oct. 1997

Last Name Given Name (Maiden Name)	Date of Birth Date of Death Age at Death	Spouse	Tombstone
Scruggs Dolores Ann	17 Nov. 1951 9 Jan. 1961		yes
Scruggs G. Willard	1887 1943		yes
Scruggs John A.	30 Sept. 1888 1 Sept. 1929		Etched Fieldstone
Scruggs Nancy A.	1832 1918	Alex Scruggs	yes

Inscription: Wife of Alex Scruggs

Scruggs Sarah S.	1892 1957		yes
Scruggs Virginia	1924 2000		no

Other Info: Reids Funeral Home marker

Sears Eddie Winn	28 Sept. 1871 27 July 1960		yes
Sears Emmitt	5 May 1885 19 April 1947		yes

Inscription: We will meet again

Sears James W.	9 March 1889 2 April 1957		yes
Sears James Wesley	8 Jan. 1915 14 June 1986		yes

Inscription: TEC 5, US Army, World War II

Other Info: Has a Reids Funeral Home marker.

Last Name Given Name (Maiden Name)	Date of Birth Date of Death Age at Death	Spouse	Tombstone
Sears Joseph	28 April 1919 17 March 1986		yes

Other Info: Has a Reids Funeral Home marker.

Sears Lottie	1893 1940		yes
Sears Lucy Ann	6 Aug. 1877 13 May 1957		yes

Inscription: Mother

Sears Maggie Walker	21 July 1913 8 Feb. 2002		yes

Other Info: Has a Bland-Reid Funeral Home marker.

Sears Robert M.	2 Oct. 1878 2 Sept. 1985		yes
Sears William Fredrick	8 Oct. 1925 1 Nov. 1971		yes

Inscription: STM3, US Navy, World War II

Stanton Alvin V.	1937 1956		yes

Other Info: Has an L.C. Gray Funeral Home marker with the death date as 8 July 1956

Stanton Blanche C.	26 Dec. 1932 12 July 1987		yes

Inscription: Rest in Peace

Other Info: Has a Reids Funeral Home marker.

Stanton Eddie Mack	1897 1987		no

Other Info: Has an above ground vault: Reids FH

Last Name Given Name (Maiden Name	Date of Birth Date of Death Age at Death	Spouse	Tombstone
Stanton Evelyn A.	7 Sept. 1907 24 Aug. 1993		yes
Stanton Godfrey P.	24 March 1914 18 Oct. 1982		yes

Inscription: Rest in Peace

Other Info: Has an above ground vault: Reids FH

Stanton James E.	1923 1983		yes
Stanton Lacy Ann	9 May 1906 26 Jan. 1972		yes

Inscription: Mother

Stanton Nona Allen			Etched Fieldstone
Stanton Norvell	1902 1964		yes
Stanton Ollie L.	27 Nov. 1927 22 May 1994		yes

Inscription: The Lord is my Shepherd

Stanton Ressie	3 June 1910 23 Feb. 1989		yes
Stanton W.	1913 1974		yes
Swann Lee	1920 1996		no

Other Info: Reids Funeral Home marker

Swann Willie P.	1922 1987		no

Other Info: This is an above ground vault: Reids FH

Last Name Given Name (Maiden Name	Date of Birth Date of Death Age at Death	Spouse	Tombstone
Taylor E. Ruth	14 July 1912 12 Nov. 1995		yes

Inscription: Mother; In God's Care

Other Info: Unidentified funeral home marker: Eddie Ruth Taylor

Taylor Ophelia Booker	1889 1943	Leon B. Taylor Sr.	yes

Inscription: In Memory of; Beloved wife of Leon B. Taylor Sr.; At Rest

Thomas Elizabeth	10 March 1891 24 July 1976		yes
Turner Hollis O.	23 July 1926 4 July 2003		no

Other Info: This is an above ground vault: Reids FH

Vowels Mary Lee	26 Jan. 1894 27 Dec. 1956		yes

Inscription: Gone but not Forgotten

Vowels Thelma C.	23 March 1906 7 Feb. 1986		yes
Watkins Baby (1)			yes

Inscription: (no dates)

Watkins Baby (2)			yes

Inscription: (no dates)

Watkins Julia	24 Jan. 1957		yes

Inscription: Rest in Peace

Last Name Given Name (Maiden Name	Date of Birth Date of Death Age at Death	Spouse	Tombstone
Watkins Maggie Elizabeth	18 June 1903 6 March 2001		yes
Watkins Mattie	1878 1932		yes
Watkins Spencer "Buster"	1 Jan. 1885 14 May 1965		yes
Watkins T. Spencer	1904 1964		yes

Inscription: At Rest

Wells Henry	23 April 1868 21 Dec. 1953		yes
Wells Theodore	31 July 1900 6 Aug. 1918		yes

Inscription: In sad but loving memory of our son; Sleep on dear son and take your rest. I loved you well but Jesus loves you best, your sad and loving mother.

Other Info: Footstone:TW

White Arthur Benjamin	18 June 1946 9 June 1998		yes

Inscription: SP4, US Army, Vietnam

Other Info: Has a Thomasson Funeral Home marker.

White Bobbie	1940 2000		yes

Other Info: Has a Thomasson Funeral Home marker

White Dora	3 March 1901 19 April 2003		yes

Inscription: In God's Care

Last Name Given Name (Maiden Name	Date of Birth Date of Death Age at Death	Spouse	Tombstone
White Eveline	1908 1996		no

Other Info: Reids Funeral Home marker

| White
   Grace P. | 1923
1980 | | no |

Other Info: Reids Funeral Home marker

| White
   H. A. | | | Etched fieldstone |

Inscription: (no dates)

| White
   John | | | no |

Other Info: Unidentified funeral home marker with one date: 16 March 1967

| White
   Leitha | | | Etched Fieldstone (no dates) |

| White
   Mary Edna | 1911
1997 | | no |

Other Info: Reids Funeral Home marker

| White
   Shadrick M. | 4 Dec. 1886
4 July 1937 | | yes |

Inscription: Peace, Perfect Peace

| White
   Vivian Shadrach | 2 March 1919
15 Jan. 1960 | | yes |

Inscription: Maryland, SK3, USNR, World War II

| White
   William H. | 1912
1998 | | yes |

Other Info: Has a Reids Funeral Home marker.

Last Name Given Name (Maiden Name	Date of Birth Date of Death Age at Death	Spouse	Tombstone
Wilkins Odessa J.	1928 1987		no

Other Info: Reids Funeral Home marker

| Wilson
  Nellie L. | 1947
1993 | | no |

Other Info: E.B. Allen Funeral Home marker

| Winn
  Harold Raymond | 22 April 1919
11 Sept. 1988 | | yes |

Inscription: US Navy, World War II

| Winn
  James Randolph | 14 April 1921
10 March 1971 | | yes |

Inscription: Virginia, TEC5, 777 Med. San. Co., World War II

| Winn
  Lillian J. | 1883
1956 | | yes |

Inscription: Mother; Her memory is blessed

| Winn
  Thomas | 16 Aug. 1880
30 Aug. 1947 | | yes |

| Wood
  Carrie | 1932
1971 | | no |

Other Info: Reids Funeral Home marker

| Wood
  Westa Winn | 21 July 1917
6 May 1999 | | yes |

Inscription: Mother; Vessel of honor, the world needs more people like you.

| Woodson
  Baby | 1995 | | no |

Other Info: Reids Funeral Home marker

Last Name Given Name (Maiden Name	Date of Birth Date of Death Age at Death	Spouse	Tombstone
Woodson Elbert	22 Feb. 1953 24 Sept. 1996		yes

Inscription: Now Cometh Eternal Rest

Other Info: Has a Reids Funeral Home marker

Woodson Gpa Elbert			Etched Fieldstone
Woodson John Early	1922 1988		yes

Inscription: US Navy, World War II

Woodson Olivia Susan	1873 1961		Etched Fieldstone

Inscription: Gma

Other Info: Unidentified funeral home marker gives the name and dates.

Woodson Wayne	1968 1987		no

Other Info: Reids Funeral Home marker

Woodson William	1924 1975		no

Other Info: Reids Funeral Home marker

Woodson Willie Ann	5 April. 1897 24 Oct. 1997		yes

Inscription: Have faith in God; Mother

There are 191 unidentified graves in this cemetery. Tradition has it that some of these are slaves buried here before Emancipation, and that this ground was donated to the church after that time to be continued as a cemetery.

Last Name Given Name (Maiden Name)	Date of Birth Date of Death Age at Death	Spouse	Tombstone

Bennett Family on Rd. 653

Bartee Lola L. J.	8 Dec. 1935 27 Aug. 1987		yes

    Inscription: Sleep in Peace

    Other Info: Has an E.B. Allen Funeral Home marker.

Bartee Robert L	1955 1993		yes
Bennett George W.	1893 1961		yes

    Inscription: At Rest

Bennett James Edward	1897 1968		yes

    Inscription: At Rest

Carey Betty E.	1886 1970		yes

    Inscription: Gone but not Forgotten

Dudley Mattie Mosley	18 July 1950 2 June 1987		yes

    Inscription: Your memory is dear to us.

Griffin Harry Lee	1935 1981		yes

    Inscription: Beloved Son

Griffin James W.	1937 1983		yes

    Inscription: Beloved Son

Last Name Given Name (Maiden Name	Date of Birth Date of Death Age at Death	Spouse	Tombstone
Griffin Kiah D.	1950 1985		yes

Inscription: Our Beloved Husband and Father

Other Info: Unidentified funeral home marker: 1960-1983 (different dates on headstone)

Jackson Amos M.	21 June 1918 20 April 1975		yes

Inscription: TEC 5, US Army, World War II

Kyle John Edward Jr.	16 Feb. 1966 26 Feb. 1989		yes
Kyle Tonia Renee	1969 1981		yes
Miles Grerrial	Aug. 1988 Nov. 1988		no

Other Info: E.B. Allen Funeral Home marker

Morgan Emmett	1911 1944		yes

Inscription: Now Cometh Eternal Rest

Other Info: Has an Amlar-Curtis Funeral Home marker.

Morris Marvin A.	6 April 1971 14 Aug. 1974		yes
Moseley Daniel	2 Feb. 1901 25 Aug. 1998		yes

Inscription: PVT, US Army, World War II

Last Name Given Name (Maiden Name)	Date of Birth Date of Death Age at Death	Spouse	Tombstone
Mosley Charity Perkins	1894 1977		yes

Inscription: Gone but not Forgotten

Other Info: Footstone: CPM

Mosley Christopher O"Neal	4 Sept. 1968 29 Jan. 1991		yes

Inscription: We Love You

Mosley Clarance	1938 1977		yes

Mosley Daniel P.			no

Other Info: E. B. Allen Funeral Home marker with no dates

Mosley Grace B.	1946 1996		no

Other Info: Unidentified funeral home marker

Mosley Harry	1948 1995		yes

Inscription: SP4, US Army, Vietnam

Other Info: Has an E.B. Allen Funeral Home marker

Mosley John E. Jr.	22 July 1916 4 June 1991		yes

Inscription: Rest in Peace

Mosley John Ed.	5 July 1899 9 July 1947		yes

Other Info: Footstone: JEM

Last Name Given Name (Maiden Name	Date of Birth Date of Death Age at Death	Spouse	Tombstone
Mosley Margaret	1915 1984		yes

   Inscription: Now Cometh Eternal Rest

Mosley Mildred Lee	7 Sept. 1917 24 June 1993		yes

   Inscription: At Rest

Mosley Mormon	10 May 1930 14 Aug. 1960		yes

   Inscription: Virginia, A1C, US Air Force

Mosley Richard A.	1939 1996		yes

   Inscription: Rest in Peace

   Other Info: Has an E.B. Allen Funeral Home marker

Mosley Rosa	8 Feb. 1921 19 Aug. 2000		no

   Other Info: This is an above ground vault: Bland-Reid FH

Mosley Ruben Sr.	1908 1970		yes
Mosley Rulan Jr.	1940 1961		yes
Mosley Sandra G.	1959 1996		yes

   Inscription: At Rest

   Other Info: E. B. Allen Funeral Home marker: Sandra Mosley, 1957-1996 (birth year is different on the headstone)

Last Name Given Name (Maiden Name)	Date of Birth Date of Death Age at Death	Spouse	Tombstone
Mosley Stephen	1 June 1912 12 April 1957		yes

Inscription: Your memory is dear to us

Other Info: Footstone: Father

Mosley Stephen J.	15 Sept. 1944 6 Oct. 1997		no

Other Info: This is an above ground vault: Henry Funeral Chapel, Washington DC

Mosley Sylvester Ross	1929 1978		yes

Inscription: At Rest

Other Info: Footstone: SRM

Mosley Thomas Ed.	1941 1961		yes

Berkeley-Swan Family on Rd. 604
(update from Vol. I)

Berkeley Edward Elias	1883 1970		yes
Berkeley Thomas Alfred	1888 1972		yes
Kidd Corine S.	30 Jan. 1923 21 June 2001	J. V. Kidd	yes

Inscription: In Loving Memory

Kitchen Alma Ethelle Swan	13 Sept. 1899 17 Mar. 1994	Johnnie Denton Kitchen	yes

Inscription: Wife of Johnnie Denton Kitchen, daughter of Frederick Winston Swan Sr. and Cora Lee Berkeley.

Last Name Given Name (Maiden Name	Date of Birth Date of Death Age at Death	Spouse	Tombstone
Shannon Joseph E.	18 June 1920 7 May 1997	Violet K. Shannon	yes

Inscription: In Loving Memory; Father

| Shannon
  Violet K. | 27 Aug. 1923
5 Aug. 1997 | Joseph E. Shannon | yes |

Inscription: In Loving Memory; Mother

| Swan
  Alexander Hugh | 12 July 1904
9 May 1971 | Marie Ann Davis Swan | yes |

Inscription: At Rest

Other Info: Shares a headstone with his wife.

| Swan
  Carrie Ragland | 26 July 1898
23 Jan. 1988 | William Wilson Swan | yes |

Other Info: Shares a headstone with her husband.

| Swan
  Cora Berkeley | 17 July 1872
17 March 1969 | Frederick Winston Swan Sr. | yes |

Inscription: Mother; wife of Frederick Winston Swan Sr.; Gone but not Forgotten

| Swan
  Frederick W. Jr. | 26 Feb. 1896
6 Nov. 1988 | Melva Kitchen Swan | yes |

Inscription: In Loving Memory

Other Info: Shares a headstone with his wife.

| Swan
  Marie Ann Davis | 13 July 1903
23 Nov. 1969 | Alexander Hugh Swan | yes |

Inscription: At Rest

Other Info: Shares a headstone with her husband.

Last Name Given Name (Maiden Name)	Date of Birth Date of Death Age at Death	Spouse	Tombstone
Swan Melva Kitchen	8 Sept. 1899 6 Feb. 1986	Frederick W. Swan Jr.	yes

Inscription: In Loving Memory

Other Info: Shares a headstone with her husband

Swan William Wilson	2 Nov. 1893 20 Oct. 1969	Carrie Ragland Swan	yes

Other Info: Shares a headstone with his wife.

Throckmorton Richard Lee	24 Sept. 1933 11 Sept. 2001	Shirley Swan Throckmorton	yes

Boatwright Family at "Social Hall"

Boatwright E. L.	30 March 1816 18 Sept. 1860	Thomas Boatwright	yes

Inscription: In Memory of

Other Info: Footstone: ELB; Shares a headstone with her husband

Boatwright Mary Alice	22 Feb. 1852 24 Nov. 1922	Walter Leake Boatwright	yes

Other Info: Footstone: MAB Shares a headstone with her husband.

Last Name Given Name (Maiden Name	Date of Birth Date of Death Age at Death	Spouse	Tombstone
Boatwright 　Thomas	1 April 1798 15 April 1891	E.L. Boatwright	yes

Inscription: In Memory of

Other Info: Footstone: TB; Shares a headstone with his wife.

Boatwright 　Walter Leake	24 Oct. 1853 20 April 1922	Mary Alice Boatwright	yes

Other Info: Footstone: WLB Shares a headstone with his wife.

Boatwright 　William Thomas	8 July 1884 24 June 1885		yes

Inscription: Son of MA and WL Boatwright; A lamb that binds us to heaven

Other Info: Footstone: WTB

Layne 　George F.	15 Sept. 1826 23 June 1884	Mary V. Boatwright Layne	yes

Other Info: Footstone: GFL

Layne 　Mary V. (Boatwright)	13 April 1837 2 Feb. 1917	George F. Layne	yes

Inscription: None knew thee but to love thee

Other Info: Footstone: MVL; sister of Walter L. Boatwright also buried in this cemetery.

Putney 　Lucie J.	25 April 1813 3 Oct. 1885		yes

Inscription: Asleep in Jesus

Other Info: Footstone: LJP

Last Name Given Name (Maiden Name)	Date of Birth Date of Death Age at Death	Spouse	Tombstone
Putney 　W. R. MD	26 March 1834 21 Nov. 1901		yes

　　　Inscription: Therefore be ye also ready: For such an hour as ye think not, the Son of Man cometh.

| Putney
　William Robert | | | yes |

　　　Inscription: CSA (no dates)

| Taylor
　A. M. | 19 July 1846
22 July 1910 | | yes |

　　　Inscription: I put on righteousness and it clotheth me.

　　　Other Info: Footstone: AMT

There are 15 unidentified graves in this cemetery.

Bocock Grave at "Woodside"

| Bocock
　Octavia Rose Gantt 1913 | | Nicholas Flood Bocock | no |

　　　Other Info: According to the records of Rev. Barrell of Maysville Presbyterian Church, she was buried here on 3 April 1913. The location of the grave has been lost. She was the 8th child of John Weems Gantt.

George Bolling Family on Rd. 670 — African American

| Love
　Orin Michael Sr. | 16 May 1970
18 July 2003 | | |

　　　Other Info: SPC US Army

Last Name Given Name (Maiden Name)	Date of Birth Date of Death Age at Death	Spouse	Tombstone
Underwood Willie James	4 July 1931 26 Feb. 2001	 Eleanor Octavia Underwood	yes

Other Info: Shares a headstone with his wife.

Booker Family off Rd. 627

Booker C.	 13 Sept. 1912		yes

Other Info: Footstone: At Rest

There are 3 unidentified graves in this cemetery.

Branch-Gunter Family on US 60

Branch Steven Douglas	7 Nov. 1958 13 March 1983		yes

Inscription: There's a new name written down in Glory; In my distress I cried unto the Lord and He heard me. Ps 120:1

Gunter Thomas W.	17 March 1916 5 June 1983	 Mamie Burks Gunter	yes

Inscription: Father; Married 22 Aug. 1938

Bright and Morning Star Church — African American

Bolden Alsenda M.	7 Nov. 1938 7 June 1979		yes

Inscription: Mother; On our minds, the memories stay, Until in heaven we'll join her someday.

Last Name Given Name (Maiden Name	Date of Birth Date of Death Age at Death	Spouse	Tombstone
Bolden Charlotte M.	12 Nov. 1900 9 Feb. 1984	James Bolden	yes

Inscription: Our Beloved Mother; Rest in Peace

Other Info: Has an above ground vault.

Bolden Emily J.	3 Dec. 1943 29 July 1986		yes

Inscription: Rest in Peace

Other Info: Has also, an above ground vault: Emily June Bolden, 1943-1986; Reids FH

Bolden Ethel B.	1910 2004		no

Other Info: Reids Funeral Home marker

Bolden Nannie Louise	12 April 1920 15 Sept. 1941		yes
Booker Cary A.	1898 1978		yes

Inscription: World War I

Booker John W.	12 May 1929 13 March 1984		yes

Inscription: In Memory of

Other Info: Has a Reids Funeral Home marker

Booker Maggie R.	27 Feb. 1902 3 Nov. 1987		yes

Inscription: At Rest

Last Name Given Name (Maiden Name	Date of Birth Date of Death Age at Death	Spouse	Tombstone
Booker Rosella Elizabeth	16 May 1937 17 Jan. 1998		yes

Inscription: Rest in Peace

Other Info: Has a Reid's Funeral Home marker

Collier Renee	13 Nov 1963 23 March 2004		yes

Inscription: Her Love Lives On

Other Info: Reids Funeral Home marker gives these dates: 1964-2004

Corbin Letcher Wade	1909 1998		yes

Inscription: Mother

Other Info: Reids Funeral Home marker gives the following: Letcher B. Corbin, 1910-1998.

Gray Annie E.	16 Feb. 1892 3 Feb. 1978		yes

Inscription: Rest in Peace

Gregory Fannie D.	28 March 1918 19 April 1981	George W. Gregory	yes

Inscription: Mother

Other Info: Has also, an above ground vault; Shares a headstone with her husband.

Gregory George W. Sr.	7 May 1906 4 Jan. 1998	Fannie D. Gregory	yes

Inscription: Father

Other Info: Has also, an above ground vault: Reids FH

Last Name Given Name (Maiden Name)	Date of Birth Date of Death Age at Death	Spouse	Tombstone
Gregory George Wesley Jr.	24 June 1941 16 Sept. 1998		no

Other Info: This is an above ground vault; Reids FH

Gregory Kevin D.	20 Mar. 1967 6 June 1998		yes
Harris Christine	1942 1984		no

Other Info: Reids Funeral Home marker

Harris Joe			no

Other Info: Has an LC Gray Funeral Home marker with one date: 17 Feb. 1956.

Harris Joseph			no

Other Info: Has a Reids Funeral Home marker with one date: 27 April 1965

Hudson Sarah Wade	1907 1998		yes

Inscription: Aunt

Other Info: Has a Reids Funeral Home marker.

Jones Lillian L.	8 Nov. 1890 none inscribed	Peter F. Jones	yes

Other Info: Shares a headstone with her husband.

Jones Peter F.	11 March 1888 5 Sept. 1961	Lillian L. Jones	yes

Other Info: Footstone: Father; LC Gray Funeral Home marker: Bishop P.F. Jones; Shares a headstone with his wife.

Last Name Given Name (Maiden Name)	Date of Birth Date of Death Age at Death	Spouse	Tombstone
Moody Elizabeth Simms	1925 1969		no

    Other Info: E.B. Allen Funeral Home marker

Parker Bahi R. M., Mrs.	26 April 1955 19 Aug. 1986		yes
Simms Elder James	1893 1980	Lillian B. Simms	yes

    Other Info: Has an EB Allen Funeral Home marker: Shares a headstone with his wife.

Simms Lillian B.	1905 1988	Elder James Simms	yes

    Other Info: Has an EB Allen Funeral Home marker; Shares a headstone with her husband.

Swan Gary S.	1 June 1959 13 March 1996		yes

    Other Info: Shares a headstone with Renaldo Swan.

Swan Renaldo	29 Sept. 1965 9 Aug 2003		yes

    Other Info: Shares a headstone with Gary S. Swan

Swann Edith P.	2 May 1920 14 Oct. 1995		yes

    Inscription: Mother: We loved you but God loved you best.

Tyree Baby Boy	1961 1961		no

    Other Info: Unidentified funeral home marker

Tyree Daniel Benjamin	20 Oct. 1917 12 July 2004		no

    Other Info: This is an above ground vault: Bland and Reid FH

Last Name Given Name (Maiden Name)	Date of Birth Date of Death Age at Death	Spouse	Tombstone
Tyree Doris B.	21 Sept. 1921 25 Nov. 1996		no

Other Info: This is an above ground vault: Reids FH

Tyree Vera Wade	1900 1935		yes

Inscription: Rest in Peace

Wade Beverly Louis	22 Feb. 1905 14 May 1993	Mary Etta Wade	yes

Inscription: Wed July 16, 1933

Other Info: Has a Reids Funeral Home marker; Shares a headstone with his wife.

Wade John Matthew	25 March 1897 8 Oct. 1943		yes

Inscription: Now Cometh Eternal Rest

Wade Martha	1870 1943		yes

Inscription: In Memory of Mother; At Rest

Wade Mary Etta	16 June 1909 20 Dec. 1995	Beverly Louis Wade	yes

Inscription: Wed July 16, 1933

Other Info: Shares a headstone with her husband.

Wade Mary Etta			no

Other Info: Unidentified funeral home marker with name only.

Wade Matt	1865 1941		yes

Inscription: In Memory of Father; At Rest

Last Name Given Name (Maiden Name)	Date of Birth Date of Death Age at Death	Spouse	Tombstone
Woodson Mary P.	1 Nov. 1888 20 June 1968	Van D. Woodson	yes

Other Info: Shares a headstone with her husband.

Woodson Van D.	13 May 1880 18 Sept. 1932	Mary P. Woodson	yes

Other Info: Shares a headstone with his wife. This cemetery has 12 unidentified graves.

Payton and Mollie Brown Family on Rd. 636 — African American

Brown Bee	11 Sept. 1887 9 April 1971		yes
Brown David D.	26 Dec. 1938 18 Nov. 1973		yes

Inscription: My Dad

Other Info: Allen Funeral Home marker gives birth year as 1939. Family reports the birth year was 1939.

Brown Edna Johnson	1890 1918		yes

Inscription: At Rest

Brown Frances Zenith Penn			yes

Inscription: Now Cometh Eternal Rest

Other Info: One date is inscribed: 19 March 1921; Has an E.B. Allen Funeral Home marker

Brown Hester F.	22 Feb. 1896 8 March 1967		yes

Last Name Given Name (Maiden Name)	Date of Birth Date of Death Age at Death	Spouse	Tombstone
Brown Joe L.	1 June 1933 13 Aug. 1952		yes

Inscription: Virginia, PFC, 245 Med. Tank BN, Korea

| Brown
  Martha | 1884
1967 | | no |

Other Info: Unidentified funeral home marker

| Brown
  Mollie | 18 March 1851
14 Sept. 1933 | Payton Brown | yes |

Inscription: At Rest

| Brown
  Norman | 7 March 1907
2 Aug. 1977 | | yes |

Inscription: PFC, Us Army, World War II

| Brown
  Payton | 18 April 1834
28 June 1913 | Mollie Brown | yes |

Inscription: Rest in Peace

| Brown
  Payton Jerome | 1917
1969 | | no |

Other Info: Known to be buried here.

| Brown
  Payton, Jr. | 1888
1920 | | yes |

| Brown
  Robert D. Sr. | 5 Sept. 1917
12 June 1977 | | yes |

Inscription: Gone but not Forgotten

| Brown
  Robert T. Milton | 6 March 1917
27 March 1978 | | yes |

Inscription: PVT, US Army, World War II

Last Name Given Name (Maiden Name)	Date of Birth Date of Death Age at Death	Spouse	Tombstone
Brown Tommy	1922		no

Other Info: Unidentified funeral home marker

Brown William Ernest			no

Other Info: Fieldstones only; known to be buried here.

Brown William Russell	23 Aug. 1928 1 Sept. 1986		yes

Other Info: Has an E.B. Allen Funeral Home marker.

Callaghan Alice Celeste	1937 1999		no

Other Info: Unidentified funeral home marker

Clark Rosby D.	2 April 1908 25 May 1956	Vernell B. Clark	yes

Other Info: Has an L.C. Gray Funeral Home marker. Shares a headstone with his wife.

Clark Vernell B.	7 Jan. 1914 3 July 1978	Rosby D. Clark	yes

Other Info: Has an L.C. Gray Funeral Home marker; Shares a headstone with her husband.

Dade Clarence F.	1907 1992	Minnie E. Dade	yes

Inscription: At Rest

Other Info: Shares a headstone with his wife.

Last Name Given Name (Maiden Name)	Date of Birth Date of Death Age at Death	Spouse	Tombstone
Dade Minnie E.	1912 1994	Clarence F. Dade	yes

Inscription: At Rest

Other Info: Shares a headstone with her husband.

Jackson Minnie B.	2 June 1896 26 April 1992		yes

Inscription: At Rest

Nicholas Alice B.	1882 or 1892 1913		no

Other Info: Unidentified funeral home marker

Nicholas Ossie B.	1896 1933		no

Other Info: Unidentified funeral home marker

Nicholas Wash	1944		

Other Info: Unidentified funeral home marker with birth year missing.

Nicholas William Earnest	1973		no

Other Info: Known to buried here

Perry Lizzie B.			no

Other Info: Illegible funeral home marker-known to be buried here.

Smith Helen W.	1910 1970		no

Other Info: Allen Funeral Home marker

Last Name Given Name (Maiden Name	Date of Birth Date of Death Age at Death	Spouse	Tombstone
Wright Mary B.			no

Other Info: Known to be buried here.

Bryant Family in "Harrison's Field"

Bryant Martin Harrison	10 Jan. 1858 13 Feb. 1862		yes

Inscription: Farewell dear parents---(illegible)

Bryant Nannie	April 1932 or 1942		no

Other Info: Unidentified funeral home marker. She was the last to be buried in this cemetery.

There are 24 unidentified graves in this cemetery. They are likely the families of William Martin Bryant and Powell Bryant.

Bryant Family off Rd. 606 (update from Vol. 1)

Amos Thomas Lee	5 Sept. 1912 17 Oct. 1974		yes

Inscription: PFC, US Army

Bates Carl Edward	1916 1988		no

Other Info: Whitten Funeral Home marker

Booth Richard T. (Tamaridge)	12 (or 19) Dec. 1920 20 Aug. 1984	 Irene Bryant	yes

Other Info: Has a Dunkum Funeral Home marker. He was the grandfather of Brandon S. Kear also buried in this cemetery.

Last Name Given Name (Maiden Name)	Date of Birth Date of Death Age at Death	Spouse	Tombstone
Bryant Allen Hoover	1929 2001		no

Other Info: Robinson Funeral Home marker

Bryant Annie Elizabeth (Tyree)	1870 1939	William David Bryant (2)	no

Other Info: Unidentified funeral home marker. Her parents were Benjamin and Susan Stinson Tyree.

Bryant B. (Benjamin) Franklin	5 Nov. 1921 25 Sept. 1983		yes

Inscription: At Rest

Other Info: Dunkum Funeral Home Marker: Benjamin Franklin Bryant. His parents were Howard Elliott and Maude Ellis Burks Bryant.

Bryant Baby Girl	1984		yes

Other Info: Has a Dunkum Funeral Home marker. Her parents are Curtis and Dale Bryant.

Bryant Bessie Bryant	29 April 1893 11 June 1953	Luther Harry Bryant	yes

Other Info: Footstone: BBB She shares a headstone with her husband. Her parents were William David and Annie Tyree Bryant.

Bryant Bettie R.	1886 1958	Clifford Bryant	no

Other Info: Sheffield Funeral Home marker; She and her husband were the parents of Elsie Bryant Ross also buried here.

Bryant Calvin David	1922 2002		no

Other Info: Dunkum Funeral Home marker

Last Name Given Name (Maiden Name)	Date of Birth Date of Death Age at Death	Spouse	Tombstone
Bryant Carrington C.	1905 1980		yes

Inscription: Brother; At Rest

Other Info: His parents, William W. and Mary Ida Bryant, and sister Viola B. Stinson are also buried in this cemetery.

Bryant Catherine Elizabeth Bryant	5 April 1853 12 April 1921	William David Bryant(1)	yes

Other Info: Shares a headstone with her husband. Footstone: CEB. Her parents were James and Elizabeth Stinson Bryant. She and her husband were the parents of Neely F. Stinson also buried in this cemetery.

Bryant Curtis Elliott	22 June 1928 14 July 1990	Dale Bryant	yes

Inscription: Rest in Peace

Other Info: He and his wife were the parents of Baby Girl Bryant buried next to him. His parents were Howard E. and Maude Ellis Bryant.

Bryant Damarcus L. (Mark)			no

Other Info: Known to be buried here; son of David M. and Lucy Via Bryant also buried in this cemetery.

Bryant David M.	(Dec. 1834)	Lucy Via Bryant	yes

Inscription: Lyneman's VA Infantry, CSA

Other Info: His parents were Powell and Martha Eagle Bryant.

Bryant Ella Jane	24 June 1876 31 May 1951		yes

Other Info: Daughter of David M. and Lucy Via Bryant.

Last Name Given Name (Maiden Name	Date of Birth Date of Death Age at Death	Spouse	Tombstone
Bryant 　Ellen Dian(e)	7 June 1943 12 July 1943		yes
Bryant 　Emory Houston	1907 197_		no

　　Other Info: Virginia Funeral Home marker; His parents were John Tilden Bryant and Lillie Bryant also buried in this cemetery.

Bryant 　Evelyn N.	10 March 1921 10 April 1921		yes
Bryant 　Floyd W.	1881 1949	Nannie Vest Bryant	yes

　　Other Info: His parents, William David and Catherine Bryant and he and his wife's children, Roy Lee, Evelyn N., Minnie Frances, Lonie B. Sorrells, and the baby born in 1923 are all buried in this cemetery.

Bryant 　G. (George) Clemon	1927 1987		no

　　Other Info: Robinson Funeral Home marker

Bryant 　Harry William	31 Oct. 1913 17 Feb. 1947		yes

　　Inscription: Virginia, PVT, 83 DIV Artillery, World War II

Bryant 　Howard Elliott	3 Jan. 1897 20 May 1986	(1)Maude Ellis Burks Bryant	yes

　　Inscription: We will meet in heaven.

　　Other Info: Footstone: HEB; Has a Robinson Funeral Home marker. His parents, William David (2) and Annie Tyree Bryant, are all buried in this cemetery.

Last Name Given Name (Maiden Name	Date of Birth Date of Death Age at Death	Spouse	Tombstone
Bryant Hubbard M. (Matthew)	3 Jan. 1953	Lillie Stinson Bryant	yes

Other Info: Son of William D. and Catherine Bryant also buried in this cemetery.

| Bryant
Irving Leslie | 10 May 1912
20 Oct. 1962 | | yes |

Inscription: Virginia, PVT, Co. D, 33 INF, TNG BN, World War II

Other Info: His mother was Ella Jane Bryant also buried in this cemetery.

| Bryant
John Tilden | Nov. 1876 | Lillie Bryant Bryant | no |

Other Info: Known to be buried here. His parents were William David and Catherine Bryant

| Bryant (infant)
Joseph Tavern | | | yes |

Inscription: Infant

Other Info: His parents were Howard E. and Maude Burks Bryant also buried in this cemetery.

| Bryant
Lafayette | 1841
1864 | | yes |

Inscription: In Memory of PVT; Co H., 49th VA INF., CSA

| Bryant
Lillie Bryant | 1884 | John Tilden Bryant | no |

Other Info: Known to be buried here; daughter of James and Ann Gunter Bryant.

Last Name Given Name (Maiden Name)	Date of Birth Date of Death Age at Death	Spouse	Tombstone
Bryant Lillie S. (Stinson)	10 May 1890 13 July 1968	Hubbard Matthew Bryant	yes

Other Info: Her parents were George and Letitia Via Stinson. She and her husband were the parents of G. Clemon, Raymond M., Allen H., Harry William and Calvin David Bryant also buried in this cemetery.

Bryant Lucy A.	1861(or 1851) 1917	Thomas C. Bryant	no

Other Info: Unidentified funeral home marker; Her parents were David and Lucy Via Bryant. She and her husband were the parents of Luther Harry Bryant, also buried here.

Bryant Lucy Via	May 1838 (Grave marked by fieldstones) 1902	David M. Bryant	no

Other Info: Known to be buried here. She was the daughter of Matthew and Sally Carter Via.

Bryant Luther Harry	20 Aug. 1885 6 Aug. 1952	Bessie Bryant Bryant	yes

Other Info: Footstone: LHB; He shares a headstone with his wife.

Bryant Mary Ida (Bryant)	9 Oct. 1883 17 Feb. 1955	William Wilson Bryant	yes

Inscription: Although She Sleeps, Her memory lives on.

Other Info: Footstone: MIB. Her parents were William David and Catherine Bryant.

Bryant Mary Via	10 May 1845 17 Sept. 1920	Powhatan Bryant	yes

Other Info: Her parents were Matthew and Sally Carter Via.

Last Name Given Name (Maiden Name)	Date of Birth Date of Death Age at Death	Spouse	Tombstone
Bryant Maude Ellis (Burks)	2 May 1900 5 Nov. 1958	Howard Elliott Bryant	yes

Inscription: Till we meet in heaven

Other Info: Footstone: Mother. Her parents were Clifford and Martha Burks.

Bryant Maude Isabell			yes (no dates)

Inscription: Daughter

Other Info: Her parents were Howard E. and Maude Burks Bryant.

Bryant Minnie Frances	12 July 1914 1915		yes

Bryant Nannie Vest	15 Aug. 1886 2 Dec. 1971	Floyd W. Bryant	yes

Bryant Otis Reid	5 Apr. 1914 29 Apr. 1976	Edna Mae Storm Bryant Thacker	yes

Inscription: SSGT, US Army, World War II

Other Info: His parents were William W. and Mary Ida Bryant.

Bryant Powhatan		Mary Via Bryant	yes

Inscription: Co. H, 49 VA INF, CSA

Other Info: His parents were Powell and Martha Eagle Bryant.

Bryant Raymond M.	16 June 1918 12 May 1988	Lorine Stinson Bryant	yes

Inscription: Father; Gone but not forgotten

Other Info: He and his wife were the parents of Ellen Diane Bryant also buried here.

Last Name Given Name (Maiden Name)	Date of Birth Date of Death Age at Death	Spouse	Tombstone
Bryant Roy Edward	1912 1976		no

Other Info: Dunkum Funeral Home marker

Bryant Roy Lee	28 Nov. 1920 10 July 1923		yes

Bryant Ruby	(1920) (resembles a lightening rod-no name or dates) (child)		yes

Other Info: Known to be buried here. Her parents are Russell and Minnie Burks Bryant

Bryant Samuel T. (infant)			yes (no dates)

Other Info: Son of Sam and Louise Bryant.

Bryant Thomas C.	1858 1917	Lucy A. Bryant	no

Other Info: Unidentified funeral home marker; His parents were James and Elizabeth Stinson Bryant.

Bryant William Cullen	1920 1953		yes

Other Info: His parents were Howard E. and Maude Burks Bryant.

Bryant William David (1)	Oct. 1858 31 July 1918	Catherine Elizabeth Bryant Bryant	yes

Other Info: Shares a headstone with his wife. Footstone: WDB His parents were David and Lucy Via Bryant.

Bryant William David (2)	1870 1946	Annie Elizabeth Tyree Bryant	no

Other Info: Unidentified funeral home marker. His parents were Powhatan and Mary Frances Bryant also buried in this cemetery.

Last Name Given Name (Maiden Name)	Date of Birth Date of Death Age at Death	Spouse	Tombstone
Bryant William Wilson ("Tete")	26 Aug. 1879 (15 May 1951)	Mary Ida Bryant Bryant	yes

Inscription: Gone but not Forgotten

Other Info: His parents were James and Ann Gunter Bryant.

Carter Bill		Mary Carter	no

Other Info: Known to be buried here. He and his wife were the first ones buried in this cemetery.

Carter Mary		Bill Carter	no

Other Info: Known to be buried here.

Cliborne Leonard C.	11 Oct. 1940 28 May 1959		yes

Other Info: Footstone: Leonard Carol Cliborne, born 1940, died 1959; His parents were Leonard T. and Lucy Jones Cliborne also buried here.

Cliborne Leonard T.	1919 1953	Lucy Jones Cliborne	yes

Inscription: Gone to a brighter home

Other Info: He and his wife are the parents of Leonard Carol Cliborne also buried in this cemetery.

Eagle Rhonda Kay	18 Nov. 1962 9 Feb. 1981		yes

Inscription: Daughter

Last Name Given Name (Maiden Name)	Date of Birth Date of Death Age at Death	Spouse	Tombstone
Floyd 　Vincent Daniel	10 Nov. 1995 (infant)		yes

　Inscription: Our Baby; Little Ones to Him Belong

　Other Info: His great-grandparents are Howard Bryant and Maude Burks Bryant. His grandmother is Rhonda Kay Eagle.

| Ford
　Thelma Stinson | 1915
1994 | | no |

　Other Info: Dunkum Funeral Home marker.

| Gunter
　Bruce | 14 June 1922
24 Oct. 1981 | | yes |

　Inscription: At Rest

| Hackett
　Andrew L. | 1856
1943 | | yes |

　Other Info: Parents were James J. and Mary E. Raker Hackett.

| Howell
　Ester (Via) | 29 Sep 1899
5 March 1975 | | yes |

　Other Info: Parents were John L. and Jenny Vest Via.

| Hutchings
　Carl E. Bates | 15 June 1944
5 May 2002 | | yes |

　Inscription: Precious Lord Take my Hand

　Other Info: Has a Whitten Funeral Home marker. He went by the name of Shorty Daniels, a guitar player in the Loretta Lynn band. His brother was Harry A. Sorrells and his father was Carl Edward Bates also buried in this cemetery.

| Jones
　Geneva Ella | 19 June 1926
25 April 1927 | | yes |

　Other Info: Shares a headstone with her siblings, Martha Lee and James Elmo Jones.

Last Name Given Name (Maiden Name	Date of Birth Date of Death Age at Death	Spouse	Tombstone
Jones Hal Coolidge	29 April 1928 21 Oct. 1960		yes

Inscription: Virginia, PVT, Co. C, 800 Mil Police BN, World War II

Other Info: Footstone has the identical information as the headstone.

Jones James Elmo	27 Jan. 1934 18 Mar. 1934		yes

Other Info: Shares a headstone with his sisters, Martha Lee, and Geneva Ella Jones.

Jones John L (Letch)	1887 1960	Lucy B. (Blanche Bryant)	yes

Other Info: Footstone: JLJ; He shares a headstone with his wife. His parents were Bill and Fanny Jones who are buried in a Jones Family Cemetery.

Jones Leo L.	1912 1941		yes

Inscription: We will meet again.

Jones Lucy B. (Blanche Bryant)	1893 1963	John Letch Jones	yes

Other Info: Footstone: LBJ; Shares a headstone with her husband. They were the parents of Hal Coolidge, Martha Lee, James Elmo, Geneva Ella Jones, Leo L. and William Claude Jones all buried in this cemetery. They are also the parents of Lucy Jones Cliborne. Her parents were William David and Catherine Bryant.

Jones Martha Lee	16 March 1935 16 March 1935		yes

Other Info: Shares a headstone with siblings, James Elmo and Geneva Ella Jones.

Last Name Given Name (Maiden Name)	Date of Birth Date of Death Age at Death	Spouse	Tombstone
Jones William Claude	8 (or 18) Dec. 1923 24 Feb. 1988		yes

Inscription: PFC, US Army, World War II

Other Info: Fieldstone: WCJ

| Kear
Brandon S. | 12 Oct. 1978
27 Oct. 1996 | | yes |

Inscription: The Lord watch between me and thee when we are absent one from another.

Other Info: He has a Gould Funeral Home marker. His grandparents are Richard T. and Irene Bryant Booth.

| Kidd
Troy Lee | 1967
1967 | | no |

Other Info: Unidentified funeral home marker. He was the son of Wilson and Cathleen Kidd.

| Macagay
Alejandro (Alec) | 15 Aug. 1896
8 Feb. 1984 | Ressie C. Macogay | yes |

Inscription: MATT I, US Navy, World War I

Other Info: His birth nation is the Phillipines.

| Macogay
Ressie C.(Stinson) | 1914
1986 | Alejandro Macogay | yes |

Inscription: No more pain

Other Info: Has a Dunkum Funeral Home marker; Her parents were Willie and Neely Bryant Stinson.

| Mays
Bland W. | 15 Jan. 1902
7 April 1976 | Nannie Tyree Mays | yes |
| Mays
Nannie Tyree | 12 Oct. 1907
30 June 1967 | Bland W. Mays | yes |

Last Name Given Name (Maiden Name)	Date of Birth Date of Death Age at Death	Spouse	Tombstone
McFadden Alfred McKinley	6 Nov. 1906 3 July 1977	Jane Kidd McFadden	yes

Inscription: PFC, US Army

McFadden Jane Kidd	1912 1986	Alfred McKinley McFadden	yes

Other Info: Her parents were Virginius and Alice Via Kidd.

Rakes Billy			no

Other Info: Known to be buried here.

Ross Elsie Bryant	23 Sept. 1914 Aug. 1980		yes

Inscription: Our Precious Mother

Other Info: Footstone: Mother

Sorrells Harry A.	1945 1998		no

Other Info: Whitten Funeral Home marker. He was the adopted son of Jesse and Lonie Sorrells. His biological brother, Carl E. Bates Hutchings and his biological father, Carl Edward Bates are also buried in this cemetery.

Sorrells Jesse James	1915 1966	Lonie Bryant Sorrells	no

Other Info: Dunkum Funeral Home marker

Sorrells Lonie B. (Bryant)	1904 1976	Jesse James Sorrells	no

Other Info: Whitten Funeral Home marker. She and her husband were the adopted parents of Harry A. Sorrells also buried in this cemetery, and his sister.

Last Name Given Name (Maiden Name)	Date of Birth Date of Death Age at Death	Spouse	Tombstone
Sorrentino William Etta (Stinson)	1918 1997		yes

Inscription: Gone But Not Forgotten

Other Info: Her parents were Willie and Neely Bryant Stinson, also buried in this cemetery. She was born just after her father died. Even though she was girl, they named her after him.

Stinson Charles T.	1910 2002	Gertrude Stinson	yes

Other Info: Has a Dunkum Funeral Home marker. He and his wife were the parents of Charles T. Junior Stinson, also buried in this cemetery.

Stinson Charles (T.) Junior	1940 2001		yes

Other Info: Has a Dunkum Funeral Home marker.

Stinson Christopher Don	6 Oct. 1977 25 Oct. 1977		yes

Inscription: Son

Other Info: His parents are Odessa R. and Linda Bryant Stinson.

Stinson Elliot Lee	19 May 1906 20 Dec. 1970		yes

Inscription: Virginia, PVT, US Army, World War II

Other Info: His parents were Robert Lee Stinson and Minnie Elizabeth Bryant Stinson also buried in this cemetery.

Last Name Given Name (Maiden Name)	Date of Birth Date of Death Age at Death	Spouse	Tombstone
Stinson Ester Mae (Stinson)	9 Dec. 1908 14 Sept. 1998	Lloyd W. Stinson	yes

Inscription: Gone but not Forgotten

Other Info: Footstone: Mother; She was the daughter of George W. and Sarah Via Stinson. She and her husband were the parents of James and Mary (infants buried in the Thomas Stinson Cemetery), Lloyd Earl, Garland P, and Leslie M. Stinson all buried in this cemetery.

Stinson Garland P.	8 July 1941 25 July 2002		yes
Stinson George Curfit	5 April 1929 11 Feb. 2002	Letitia Via Stinson	yes

Other Info: He and his wife were the parents of Tom M. Stinson.

Stinson George (W.)	1 Jan. 1879 29 Dec. 1948	Sarah Elizabeth Via Stinson	yes

Other Info: He and his wife were the parents of Thelma Stinson Ford and Mamie Florence Stinson also buried in this cemetery. His parents were George and Letitia Via Stinson.

Stinson Gertrude	1919 2004	Charles T. Stinson Sr.	no

Other Info: Has an unidentified funeral home marker

Stinson Leslie Mitchell	2 Aug. 1934 9 Jan. 1991		yes
Stinson Lloyd Earl	30 Oct. 1931 12 Nov. 2003		yes
Stinson Lloyd W.	10 June 1906 12 Sept. 1975	Ester Mae Stinson Stinson	yes

Inscription: Gone but not Forgotten. Footstone: Father

Last Name Given Name (Maiden Name)	Date of Birth Date of Death Age at Death	Spouse	Tombstone
Stinson Mamie (Florence)	15 July 1906 25 Sept. 1982		yes

Other Info: Has a Dunkum Funeral Home marker.

| Stinson
Minnie (Elizabeth) Bryant | 5 March 1873
2 June 1958 | Robert Lee Stinson | yes |

Other Info: Footstone: Mother She shares a headstone with her husband. Her parents were David Bryant and Lucy Via Bryant also buried in this cemetery.

| Stinson
Neely F. (Cornelia) | 1896
1962 | (1) Willie Stinson,
(2) Tom. M. Stinson | yes |

Inscription: May They Rest in Peace

Other Info: She was the daughter of William David and Catherine Bryant.

| Stinson
Odessa Reid | 19 Feb. 1944
24 Jan. 1980 | Linda Bryant Stinson | yes |

Inscription: Father

Other Info: His parents were Riley and Viola Bryant Stinson.

| Stinson | 10 March 1901
21 Dec. 1977 | | yes |

,QVFULSWLRQ ,Q* RGIV&DUH

Other Info: So of Thomas M. and Rosa Bell Stinson.

| Stinson
Robert Lee | 26 Nov. 1865
3 Nov. 1938 | Minnie Elizabeth Bryant Stinson | yes |

Other Info: Footstone: Father; He shares a headstone with his wife. He was the son of Robert Jackson Stinson and Martha Bryant Stinson.

| Last Name | Date of Birth | Spouse | Tombstone |
| Given Name | Date of Death | | |
(Maiden Name	Age at Death		

Stinson   23 Sept. 1880   yes
    Sarah (Elizabeth Via) 5 April 1955

    Other Info: Her parents were John L and Jenny Vest Via. Her sister,
       Ester Howell is also buried in this cemetery.

Stinson   7 Oct. 1972   yes
    Shane Douglas   11 Oct. 1972

    Inscription: Our Baby

    Other Info: His parents are Odessa R. and Linda Bryant Stinson.

Stinson   1876   yes
    Tom. M. (Thomas Matthew) 1960   (1)Rosa Bell Stinson
                                                   (2)Neely F. Bryant Stinson

    Inscription: May they rest in peace

    Other Info: Shares a headstone with his second wife.

Stinson   6 Sept. 1907   yes
    Viola B. (Bryant)   16 Feb. 1985

    Inscription: Mother

    Other Info: Has a Dunken FH Marker

Stinson   1894   yes
    Willie   1918   Neely Bryant Stinson

    Inscription: Gone but not Forgotten

    Other Info: His parents were James Wesley and Nancy Eagle Stinson.

Stinson   5 March 1912   yes
    Wilton D.   18 May 1998

    Inscription: PVT, US Army, World War II

    Other Info: Has a Dunkum Funeral Home marker; His parents were
       Willie Stinson and Neely F. Stinson also buried in this cemetery.

Last Name Given Name (Maiden Name)	Date of Birth Date of Death Age at Death	Spouse	Tombstone
Thacker Edna Mae (Storm Bryant)	2 June 1936 16 July 2000	(I) Otis Reid Bryant (2) Wesley F. Thacker	yes

Inscription: Gone but never forgotten

Other Info: Has a Dunkum Funeral Home marker; Her parents were William Etta Stinson Storm and Bill Storm.

Thacker Wesley F.	1942 2002	Edna Mae Storm Bryant Thacker	no

Other Info: Dunkum Funeral Home marker

Tyree Earl L.	1920 1947		no

Other Info: Known to be buried here.

Tyree Echo L.	1882 1967	Hattie Stinson Tyree	no

Other Info: Browning Funeral Home marker.

Tyree Hattie S.(Stinson)	1880 1956	Echo L. Tyree	no

Other Info: Browning Funeral Home marker; Her parents were James Wesley and Nancy Eagle Stinson. She and her husband were the parents of: Nannie Tyree Mays, Earl L. Tyree and Ruby Tyree all buried in this cemetery.

Tyree Ruby	child		no

Other Info: Known to be buried here.

Last Name Given Name (Maiden Name	Date of Birth Date of Death Age at Death	Spouse	Tombstone

Bryant Family off Rd. 649

| Bryant
   Mary Susan |
29 Apr. 1941
73 years | | no |

Other Info: J.C. Dunkum and Bro. Funeral Home marker

| Bryant
   William |
2 Aug. 1934
67 years, 2 mo., 2 days | | no |

Other Info: J.C. Dunkum and Bro. Funeral Home marker

| Bryant
   William R. | 4 Oct. 1895
31 July 1920 | | yes |

Inscription: His toils are past, his work is done; He fought the fight; The victor won.

Other Info: Footstone: WRB

There are 4 unidentified graves in this cemetery.

Bryant Family on Rd. 765

| Bryant
   Annie E. | 23 July 1902
4 July 1988 | | yes |

| Bryant
   Edmonia, Mrs. | 1876
1945 | | yes |

Inscription: At Rest

Other Info: Footstone: EMB

| Bryant
   Herbert Carroll | 7 June 1906
March 1935 | | yes |

Last Name Given Name (Maiden Name	Date of Birth Date of Death Age at Death	Spouse	Tombstone
Bryant Hiawatha	8 March 1901 26 Oct. 1959		yes

Inscription: Virginia, PVT, 16 Co., Coast Artillery, World War I

Other Info: Footstone: Hiawatha Bryant, 8 March 1901, 26 Oct. 1959

Bryant Joe W.	1902 1973		Painted slate stone

Other Info: Robinson Funeral Home marker: Joe William Bryant, 1902

Bryant John Everett	20 April 1931 9 Aug. 1998		yes

Other Info: Has a Dunkums Funeral Home marker.

Bryant John H.	22 April 1934 5 May 1958		yes

Inscription: VA, MM3, USNR

Bryant John R.	4 Aug. 1905 3 July 1961		yes

Inscription: At Rest

Other Info: Unidentified funeral home marker: John Robert Bryant, 1905-1961

Bryant Lizzie R.	6 July 1911 14 Jan. 1985		yes

Inscription: At Rest

Other Info: Whitten Funeral Home marker: Lizzie Pearl Bryant, 1911-1985

Bryant Maggie Bell	4 Nov. 1874 12 July 1947		yes

Inscription: At Rest

Last Name Given Name (Maiden Name)	Date of Birth Date of Death Age at Death	Spouse	Tombstone
Bryant Mary Stanley			yes-no dates
Bryant Nellie Duree	1919 1992		Painted slate stone

Other Info: Robinson Funeral Home marker: Nellie Durie Bryant, 1919-1992

Bryant Peter A.	1875 1965		yes

Inscription: At Rest

Other Info: Footstone: Father

Bryant Robert Lee			yes-no dates
Bryant Sam C.	1877 1960		yes
Bryant William N.	13 Jan. 1920 17 Apr. 1997		yes

Inscription: PVT, US Army, World War II

Other Info: Has a Dunkums Funeral Home marker

Chidester Duke A.	1895 1939	Mamie B. Chidester	yes

Other Info: Shares a headstone with his wife.

Chidester Mamie B.	1898 1938	Duke A. Chidester	yes

Other Info: Shares a headstone with her husband.

Day Willie Ann			yes-no dates

Last Name Given Name (Maiden Name)	Date of Birth Date of Death Age at Death	Spouse	Tombstone
Ragland Estelle B.	4 June 1913 20 June 1988		yes

Inscription: At Rest

Other Info: Footstone: Mother

Ragland James Thomas Clyde, Brother	28 Jan. 1944 Feb. 1996		yes

Ragland Lewis D.	25 May 1906 1 Jan. 1981		yes

Other Info: Footstone: Father

Ragland Louise B.	1915 1939		yes

Other Info: Footstone: Mother

Vanderpool Alice B.	5 Sept. 1931 24 Dec. 1996		

There are 4 unidentified graves in this cemetery.

Bryant-Stinson Family at Mt. Hermon Church

Bryant Annie E.	2 July 1885 11 Aug. 1935	Crawford D. Bryant	yes

Inscription: Gone but not forgotten

Other Info: Footstone: Mother; Shares a headstone with her husband.

Bryant Arlene Shelor	15 Feb. 1926 1 July 1989		yes

Other Info: Footstone: Wife and Mother, with love -James, Carol, Calvin and Kyle; Has a Whitten Funeral Home marker.

Last Name Given Name (Maiden Name)	Date of Birth Date of Death Age at Death	Spouse	Tombstone
Bryant Crawford D.	24 Oct. 1888 27 Dec. 1967	Annie E. Bryant	yes

Inscription: Gone but not forgotten

Other Info: Footstone: Father; Shares a headstone with his wife.

Bryant David C.	17 March 1923 17 Nov. 1979		yes

Inscription: PVT, US Army, World War II

Other Info: Footstone: Father

Bryant Edna Rose	8 May 1898 19 April 1976		yes

Inscription: In memory of our precious mother

Other Info: Footstone: ERB

Bryant George Thomas	3 June 1916 27 May 1961		yes

Inscription: Virginia, PVT, Co. F, 355 Engr, GS Regt, World War II

Bryant Gilbert A.	5 Nov. 1930 24 Nov. 1930		yes

Inscription: Our beloved baby

Bryant James Camden	26 Oct. 1931 11 June 1999		yes

Other Info: Has a Dunkums Funeral Home marker.

Bryant Lucy A.	6 Feb. 1929 13 April 1998		yes

Other Info: Has a Dunkum Funeral Home marker

Last Name Given Name (Maiden Name	Date of Birth Date of Death Age at Death	Spouse	Tombstone
Bryant Percy Hilbert	11 Oct. 1893 10 April 1971		yes

  Inscription: Virginia, PVT, 168 Infantry, 42 Division, World War I

  Other Info: Footstone: PHB Has a Dunkum Funeral Home marker: Percy Hilbert Bryant, 1894-1971 (birth year is different on headstone).

| Bryant
  Susie Dunning | 25 Aug. 1927
16 April 1988 | | yes |

  Inscription: Our loving mother

  Other Info: Footstone: Mother

| Ragland
  Betty S. | 23 July 1897
3 Dec. 1945 | | yes |

| Stinson
  Eva Roberta | 1930
1992 | | yes |

  Other Info: Has a Dunkum Funeral Home marker: Shares a headstone with Gloria E. Stinson.

| Stinson
  Gloria E. | 1951
1992 | | yes |

  Other Info: Has a Dunkum Funeral Home marker; Shares a headstone with Eva Roberta Stinson.

| Stinson
  Mary Bryant | 1888
1988 | | no |

  Other Info: Dunkum Funeral Home marker

| Stinson
  Paul Jefferson | 1900
1980 | | no |

  Other Info: Dunkum Funeral Home marker

Last Name Given Name (Maiden Name)	Date of Birth Date of Death Age at Death	Spouse	Tombstone
Stinson Wert	1923 1997		yes

Other Info: Has a Dunkum Funeral Home marker

Burks Family off Rd. 605

Bryant P. Alexander	13 April 1894 27 April 1968		yes

Other Info: Footstone: PAB

Burks Al Gould	8 Oct. 1935 26 March 1968		yes

Inscription: At Rest

Burks Albert Crews	24 March 1883 21 Sept. 1948	Elsie Bryant Burks	yes

Other Info: Shares a headstone with his wife.

Burks Elsie Bryant	31 March 1909 12 Oct. 2001	Albert Crews Burks	yes

Other Info: Shares a headstone with her husband.

There are 2 unidentified graves in this cemetery.

John Burks Family off Rd. 606

Burks			no

Other Info: Wife of John Burks.

Burks John A.			yes (no dates)

Inscription: Corp., Co. B, 25 VA INF, CSA

Last Name Given Name (Maiden Name)	Date of Birth Date of Death Age at Death	Spouse	Tombstone
Jones Tom			no

Other Info: Known to be buried here.

There are 26 unidentified graves in this cemetery.

Cabell Family in James River State Park

Antrim R. E. (Eldridge)	9 Oct. 1940 9 Sept. 1992	P. H. (Patricia) White	yes

Other Info: Shares a headstone with his wife.

Cabell Arthur Preston	5 Nov. 1893 9 Dec. 1949		yes

Inscription: Daddy

Other Info: Footstone: APC

Cabell Elizabeth Thorton, Mrs.	11 Feb. 1904		yes

Inscription: Entered into Eternal Rest Feb. 11, 1904

Cabell Evalee (Wright)	14 Feb. 1870 14 Feb. 1945		yes

Inscription: Mom

Other Info: Footstone: ELC

Cabell Hammett Lawton	29 Oct. 1900 1 Dec. 1939		yes

Other Info: Footstone: HLC; He was the son of Winston Cabell.

Cabell John S. "Sam"	29 Oct. 1913 30 Dec. 1987		yes

Last Name Given Name (Maiden Name)	Date of Birth Date of Death Age at Death	Spouse	Tombstone
Cabell Josie			no

  Other Info: Known to be buried here. She was the sister of Winston Cabell.

Cabell Marcia J.	21 June 1946 3 May 1979		yes
Cabell Margaret L.	10 Dec. 1904 10 Sept. 1981		yes
Cabell Marion Winston	28 April 1864 7 Oct. 1942		yes

  Inscription: Dad

  Other Info: Footstone: MWC

Cabell Marion Winston	28 Nov. 1932 22 April 1939		yes

  Inscription: Son of W.M. and V.L. Cabell; In Heaven

Cabell Nannie C.			no

  Other Info: Known to be buried here. She was the daughter of Winston Cabell.

Cabell Thomas E.	3 July 1903 9 Aug. 1973		yes
Cabell Virginia L.	14 Feb. 1914 8 May 1982		yes

  Inscription: Mom

  Other Info: Footstone: VLC

Last Name Given Name (Maiden Name)	Date of Birth Date of Death Age at Death	Spouse	Tombstone
Cabell William M.	4 Sept. 1898 19 July 1957		yes

Inscription: Dad

Other Info: Footstone: WMC; Has also, a US Vet. marker.

Clarke Alice C.	1896 1971		no

Other Info: Joseph W. Bliley Funeral Home marker

White Edmund Palmer	30 June 1933 20 March 1988		yes

Inscription: Our love goes with you and our souls wait to join you.

White Henry A. Jr. "Jiddy"	11 Sept. 1931 22 Feb. 1989		yes

Inscription: Daddy; In God's Care

Other Info: Has a Robinson Funeral Home marker.

White Henry A. Sr. "John Henry"	7 Oct. 1905 8 May 1970		yes

White Laura Campbell	10 May 1905 25 Feb. 1982		yes

Inscription: Mom

White P. (Patricia) H.	21 June 1940 3 June 1993	R. E. (Eldridge) Antrim	yes

Other Info: Shares a headstone with her husband.

Last Name	Date of Birth	Spouse	Tombstone
Given Name	Date of Death		
(Maiden Name)	Age at Death		

Clifford Cabell Family off Rd. 605

Cabell
Clifford
    17 Aug. 1810
    18 Sept. 1871   Margaret Couch Anthony Cabell   yes

Other Info: Shares a headstone with his wife and daughter, Lucy. He and his wife were married 5 Dec. 1833.

Cabell
Lucy Galt
    8 Jan 1852
    28 Feb. 1856   yes

Inscription: Daughter of Clifford and Margaret C. Cabell.

Other Info: Shares a headstone with her parents.

Cabell
Margaret C. (Couch Anthony)
    5 Jan. 1811
    29 Oct. 1882   Clifford Cabell   yes

Inscription: His Wife

Other Info: Shares a headstone with her husband and daughter, Lucy. According to family records she was born in Jan. 1814. The homeplace was named "Fernley". Other children born to Clifford and Margaret Cabell were: Evelyn Carter Byrd, Mary Washington, Alice Winston, and Clifford Cabell.

Carter Family on Rd. 607

Carter
Charles Jesse   Maude Carter   yes (no dates)

Other Info: His father was George P. Carter, and the grandfather of the present owner of the Carter Farm, Charles J. Carter Sr.

Last Name Given Name (Maiden Name	Date of Birth Date of Death Age at Death	Spouse	Tombstone
Carter G. L.			yes

Inscription: 4 - 3 - 1906 (one date)

Other Info: This is the grave of a child. He is the brother of Charles J. Carter Sr., present owner of the Carter farm.

| Carter
George P. | 17 Sept. 1851
16 April 1911 | | yes |

Other Info: He was the father of Charles Jesse Carter.

| Carter
James Eddie | 15 Nov. 1860
20 July 1909 | Kate Moorman Carter | yes |

| Carter
Kate Moorman | 17 Feb. 1860
26 June 1920 | James Eddie Carter | yes |

Other Info: She and her husband were the parents of Moorman Harry Carter and Minnie Carter Harris.

| Carter
Martha A. | 21 Aug. 1821
3 July 1889 | Patrick B. Carter | yes |

| Carter
Maude | | Charles Jesse Carter | yes (no dates) |

Other Info: She and her husband are the grandparents of Charles Carter Sr., present owner of the Carter Farm.

| Carter
Moorman Harry | 24 Dec. 1891
16 Sept. 1970 | | yes |

Inscription: Rest in Peace

Other Info: His parents were Kate Moorman Carter and James Eddie Carter. He was the nephew of Charles Jesse Carter. Minnie Carter Harris was his sister.

| Carter
Patrick B. | 9 May 1816
14 Jan. 1887 | Martha A. Carter | yes |

Last Name Given Name (Maiden Name)	Date of Birth Date of Death Age at Death	Spouse	Tombstone
Harris Minnie Carter	13 Jan. 1890 12 Sept. 1915		yes

This cemetery has 13 unidentified graves.

Chambers Family (Caucasian) of Rd. 659

Chambers Elizabeth M.	1805 1839		yes
Chambers John	1760 1815	yes	

Other Info: This information is from the WPA 1937 survey. There is only a broken pedestal now to mark the grave.

Chambers Martha	1763 1805	yes	

Other Info: Footstone: MC

Chambers Susan E.	1830 1832	yes	
Henson Irene	28 Sept. 1860 26 Oct. 1862	yes	

Inscription: Daughter of J. Walter and Pattie Henson; I am going to my home in heaven.

Other Info: The tombstone is now partially illegible. The birth and death month and day are not decernable. These were taken from the WPA 1937 survey.

Chambers Family on US 20 — African American

Chambers Darrell Foster			no

Other Info: Reids Funeral Home marker with one date: 18 Nov. 1969

Last Name Given Name (Maiden Name)	Date of Birth Date of Death Age at Death	Spouse	Tombstone
Chambers David E.	1955 1976		no

Other Info: Reids Funeral Home marker; His father was David Ervin Chambers also buried in this cemetery.

Chambers David Ervin	6 Aug. 1928 31 Jan. 1973		yes

Inscription: Virginia, CPL, US Army, Korea

Chambers Dorothy K.	1933 1988		no

Other Info: Reids Funeral Home marker

Chambers Fannie M.			no

Other Info: Reids Funeral Home marker with one date:_-13-1968

Chambers James Ceasar	4 June 1923 28 Mar. 2000		yes

Inscription: US Army, World War II

Chambers Joe Nathan	1920 1991		yes

Inscription: US Army, World War II

Other Info: He was the grandfather of Vinton Marcell Chambers also buried in this cemetery.

Chambers Nathan			no

Other Info: Reids Funeral Home marker with one date: _-4-1966

Last Name Given Name (Maiden Name)	Date of Birth Date of Death Age at Death	Spouse	Tombstone
Chambers Vinton Marcell (Bennie)	11 Feb. 1968 3 April 1997		no

Other Info: This is an above ground vault: Reids FH; He was a twin. His parents are Rev. Joe and Katie Chambers; His grandfather was Joe Nathan Chambers also buried in this cemetery.

Chambers Willie Moses Sr.	19 May 1913 26 Dec. 2000		no

Other Info: This is an above ground vault: Reids FH

Perkins Robert Toney	15 Aug. 1920 23 Oct. 1998		yes

Inscription: US Army, World War II

Other Info: Has a Reids Funeral Home marker.

Toney Angie P.	1900 1983		no

Other Info: Reids Funeral Home marker

Toney Thomas A.	8 May 1887 23 Feb. 1915		yes

Inscription: Virginia, PVT, 153 Depot Brig.

There are 4 unidentified graves in this cemetery.

George and Virgie Chambers Family on US 60 — African American

Chambers George		Virga (Virgie) Spencer Chambers	no

Other Info: Known to be buried here. He and his wife were married 19 Aug. 1903.

Last Name Given Name (Maiden Name)	Date of Birth Date of Death Age at Death	Spouse	Tombstone
Chambers Virga (or Virgie) (Spencer)		George Chambers	no

Other Info: Known to be buried here.

| Chambers Matilde | | Wilber Chambers | no |

Other Info: Known to be buried here. She was the sister of George Chambers.

George Lewis Chambers Family off Rd. 671 — African American

| Chambers Agnes Moseley | 1878 | George Lewis Chambers | no |

Other Info: Known to be buried here. Her parents were Jake and Ella Moseley.

| Chambers George Lewis | 1866 | Agnes Moseley Chambers | no |

Other Info: Known to be buried here. His parents were Gilbert and Willie Chambers. He and his wife were married 28 March 1894.

| Chambers unnamed female infant 1916 | 1916 1 day | | no |

Other Info: Known to be buried here. She was the daughter of Lewis Eli and Mary Lee Stanton Chambers and the granddaughter of George Lewis Chambers.

There are 5 unmarked graves in this cemetery, including those known to be buried here.

Last Name Given Name (Maiden Name)	Date of Birth Date of Death Age at Death	Spouse	Tombstone

Chambers Family Slaves on Rd. 659

There are at least 4 graves, none with identification. This cemetery is across the field and north of the Chambers Family cemetery.

Chastain Family off Rd 732

| Chastain
Rene | 24 June 1741
1824
83 years | | no |

Other Info: Known to be buried here.

There are approximately 30 unidentified graves in this cemetery, most marked with fieldstones.

Chestnut Grove Baptist Church on Rd. 673 — African American

| Agee
Thelma M. | 8 May 1900
9 Sept. 1995 | | yes |

Other Info: Has a Reids Funeral Home marker.

| Banks
Arvis L. | 20 Nov. 1939
17 Dec. 1969 | | yes |

| Banks
Charlie | 1898
1979 | | no |

Other Info: Reids Funeral Home marker

| Banks
David | | | no |

Other Info: Reids Funeral Home marker

Last Name Given Name (Maiden Name)	Date of Birth Date of Death Age at Death	Spouse	Tombstone
Banks J. Archie			yes

Inscription: 21 Feb. 1938 (one date only)

Banks Richard	23 Feb. 1918 13 Aug. 1990		yes

Inscription: US Navy, World War II

Other Info: Manning Funeral Home marker

Banks Swan	7 Sept. 1907 28 Jan. 1949		yes

Inscription: Gone but not Forgotten

Booker Charlie J.	1895 1970		yes

Inscription: In Memory of

Booker Henry	22 Jan. 1842 11 April 1912		yes

Inscription: My Trust is in God: Footstone: H.B.

Booker Mildred	1869 1942		no

Other Info: J. C. Dunkum Bros. Funeral Home marker

Booker Ruby J.	1906 1973		yes

Inscription: At Rest

Bowling Frank Thomas	15 July 1931 22 June 1996		yes

Inscription: US Air Force, Korea

Last Name Given Name (Maiden Name	Date of Birth Date of Death Age at Death	Spouse	Tombstone
Bowling Jennie M.	1935 1978		no

Other Info: Reids Funeral Home marker

Bradley James	12 Oct. 1872 27 Apr. 1930		yes

Inscription: Jesus Loved of thee, But We Loved Thee Best

Bradley Ogden M.	3 July 1907 26 Dec. 1995		yes
Bradley William	1900 1978		no

Other Info: Reids Funeral Home marker

Carson Samuel R.	1927 2000 72 years		no

Other Info: Above ground vault: Colbert FH; Funeral Home marker gives dates as: B. 3-27-27, D. 2-5-00

Chambers Bettie	1865 1928		yes

Inscription: A Tender Mother and Faithful Friend

Chambers Reuben	1856 1918		yes

Inscription: Our Father

Chatman Cornelia (Chambers)	1885 1930		yes
Collins Hattie	22 June 1915 3 Oct. 1993		no

Other Info: Vault: Manning FH

Last Name Given Name (Maiden Name)	Date of Birth Date of Death Age at Death	Spouse	Tombstone
Cooper Naomi E.	1929 2001		no

Other Info: Above ground vault: Colbert FH

Fountain W.H. (or C.)			yes

Inscription: US Navy, Cook

Other Info: Tombstone has fallen forward and is difficult to read.

Hanley Beatrice	1913 1972		no

Other Info: unidentified funeral home marker

Harris Garland	1856 17 Oct. 1916		yes

Inscription: In Memory Of

Hemley Willie A.	 57 years	 Jack Hemley	yes

Inscription: Nov. 21, 1920; The Rose May Fade, Then Die, But Flowers Memorial Bloom on High

Henley Rannie	2 Aug. 1895 19 Aug. 1954		yes

Inscription: Virginia, PVT, Co. C, 812 Pioneer Inf., World War I

Home Mary Anne (Jones)	21 June 1943 17 Sept. 1997		yes
Hughes Angie	1896 19_1		no

Other Info: Dunkum Funeral Home marker

Last Name Given Name (Maiden Name)	Date of Birth Date of Death Age at Death	Spouse	Tombstone
Hughes Bernice	1920 1983		yes
Hughes Carey J.	30 May 1920 27 March 1995		yes

Inscription: PFC, US Army, World War II

| Hughes
  Ethel | 1912
1989 | | no |

Other Info: Manning Funeral Home marker

| Hughes
  James Hasten Sr. | 1922
1989 | | no |

Other Info: This inscription is on a vault-Reids Funeral Home

| Hughes
  Lucy | 1887
1971 | | no |

Other Info: Reids Funeral Home marker

| Hughes
  Pattie M. J. | 3 Nov. 1925
30 Dec. 1997 | | no |

Other Info: This inscription is on a vault-O.P. Chiles Funeral Home.

| Jacobs
  Ephraim E. | 17 March 1895
26 Oct. 1967 | | yes |

Inscription: Georgia, SGT, US Army, World War I

| Johnson
  Edna | 21 Feb. 1900
14 July 1915 | | yes |

Inscription: Daughter of Love, Thou Art Gone to Thy Rest

| Johnson
  James Alex | 28 July 1921
21 Dec. 2000 | | yes |

Inscription: US Army, World War II

Last Name Given Name (Maiden Name)	Date of Birth Date of Death Age at Death	Spouse	Tombstone
Johnson Jeff	10 Mar. 1856 17 May 1923		yes

Inscription: Father let thy Grace be Given That we Meet in Heaven

Johnson Susie	26 Feb. 1923		yes
Johnson William	26 Feb. 1923		yes
Johnson Willie C.	15 May 1895 2 Oct. 1956		yes
Jones Annie K.	6 Feb. 1917 1 Jan. 1993		yes

Inscription: Loved One

Other Info: Headstone erected by W.A. Harman Memorials, Charlottesville, VA

Jones Bettie	5 May, 1904		Etched fieldstone
Jones Ella			no

Other Info: Reids Funeral Home marker

Jones Frank Sr.	20 Jan. 1896 6 May 1984		yes

Other Info: F. M. Chiles Funeral Home marker gives birth year as 1898.

Jones Jewel	15 Aug. 1895 17 Feb. 1963		yes
Jones Mary V. (Bradley)	1 Sept. 1899 1 Dec. 1945		yes

Last Name Given Name (Maiden Name)	Date of Birth Date of Death Age at Death	Spouse	Tombstone
Jones Matthew Sr., Deacon	15 April 1924 19 Sept. 1991		yes

Inscription: In Loving Memory of His Wife and Family

Other Info: Has an above ground vault-Reid's FH

Jones Nellie	1 Oct. 1921 29 June 1999		no

Other Info: Above ground vault: Reids FH

Jones William W.	10 Feb. 1858 20 Oct. 1927		yes

Inscription: His Record is on High

King James I. Sr.	1905 1988		no

Other Info: unidentified funeral home marker

King Macy R.			no

Other Info: Reids Funeral Home marker

King Rebecca (Lee)	1948 1986		no

Other Info: Thacker Bros. Funeral Home marker

Lee Lenora	1915 1940		no

Other Info: Reids Funeral Home marker

Malory Robert	2 July 1895 3 Feb. 1955		yes

Inscription: Virginia, PVT, 155 Depot Brigade, World War I

Last Name Given Name (Maiden Name)	Date of Birth Date of Death Age at Death	Spouse	Tombstone
Mason Betty A.			yes

Inscription: (name only); Footstone-Betty A. Mason

Other Info: Footstone: Betty A. Mason; Reids Funeral Home marker gives the dates as 1880-1972

| Mason
   Clarence | 1880
1951 | | yes |
| Matthews
   Leonard W. | 4 May 1910
6 Sept. 1971 | | yes |

Inscription: PFC, 477 Infantry, World War II

| Matthews
   Virginia W. | 16 Feb. 1903
20 June 1993 | | yes |

Inscription: Rest in Peace, Aunt from Snooks

| Maxey
   Philip Brooks | 7 June 1910
8 Dec. 1983
73 years | | no |

Other Info: Thacker Bros. Funeral Home marker

| Maxie
   Nellie | 1910
1986 | | no |

Other Info: Reids Funeral Home marker

| Maxie
   Reuben | 1 Jan. 1885
9 Mar. 1987 | | yes |
| Maxie
   Ruben | 1912
1983 | | no |

Other Info: unidentified funeral home marker

| Miller
   Anna H. | 21 June 1898
4 Sept. 1966 | | yes |

Inscription: Mother

Last Name Given Name (Maiden Name	Date of Birth Date of Death Age at Death	Spouse	Tombstone
Miller 　Maggie H.	1917 2000		no

　Other Info: Reids Funeral Home marker

| Miller
　Theoplus | 1935
1972 | | no |

　Other Info: Reids Funeral Home marker

| Miller
　Thomas | 1905
1974 | | no |

　Other Info: Reids Funeral Home marker

| Miller
　Vernon V. Sr. | 6 Mar. 1934
13 Sept. 1997 | | yes |

　Other Info: Above ground vault: Reids Funeral Home

| Monroe
　Alberta J. | 5 March 1917
27 May 1989 | | yes |

| Mosley
　Richard | 1898
1968 | | no |

　Other Info: unidentified funeral home marker

| Moss
　Eddie | 1854 | | yes |

　Other Info: The rest of the inscription is illegible.

| Nash
　Beatrice | 19 Oct. 1916
6 July 1997 | | yes |

　Inscription: Always in Our Hearts

　Other Info: The same name and dates are inscribed on a vault-Reids Funeral Home.

Last Name Given Name (Maiden Name)	Date of Birth Date of Death Age at Death	Spouse	Tombstone
Nash Henry	1915 1988		yes

Inscription: PFC, US Army, World War II

Nash Lizzie	1920 1983		yes

Inscription: Rest in Peace

Nash Sallie (Hughes)	30 May 1950 54 years		no

Other Info: Dunkum Funeral Home marker

Pierce Mildred	Dec. ___ 51 years, 5 months		no

Other Info: Illegible funeral marker

Redwood Frances	28 July 1891 20 May 1979		yes

Inscription: Daughter

Other Info: Shares a headstone with her parents.

Redwood James T.	6 April 1894 31 May 1915		Etched fieldstone

Inscription: He was a member of U.V.

Redwood Lucian W.	7 Oct. 1858 19 Jan. 1921	Mary E. Redwood	yes

Inscription: Father; Footstone-not inscribed

Other Info: Shares a headstone with his wife and daughter.

Last Name Given Name (Maiden Name	Date of Birth Date of Death Age at Death	Spouse	Tombstone
Redwood Mary E.	10 Aug. 1871 8 Feb. 1962	Lucian W. Redwood	yes

Inscription: Mother; Footstone-not inscribed

Other Info: Shares a headstone with her husband and daughter.

Redwood Matilda	16 Dec. 1838 29 Dec. 1899		yes

Inscription: At Rest

Scott Bettie	29 Jan. ____ 17 Feb. 1889		yes

Inscription: In Memory Of

Other Info: Tombstone has broken.

Scott Donald Alan	1957 1963		yes
Scott Judie	1881 28 Oct. 1953		yes
Scott Louise E.	10 July 1913 31 May 1994		yes

Inscription: Mother; Though you have taken your journey home, your loving memory lingers on; Rest in Peace, Your Children

Other Info: Dunkum Funeral Home marker

Scott Noel	1873 27 Feb. 1934		yes
Scott Ralph Edward	1919 1983		yes

Inscription: PFC, US Marine Corps, World War II

Last Name Given Name (Maiden Name)	Date of Birth Date of Death Age at Death	Spouse	Tombstone
Scott Rebecca C.	12 Aug. 1873 11 Oct. 1964		yes

Inscription: Sleep on Mother. We all Love You, But God Loved You Best, Because He Took You Home to Rest.

Scott Robert H.	1899 29 June 1929		yes
Scott Robert Lee	1920 1991		yes

Inscription: US Army, World War II

Scott William Howard Taft	15 April 1909 7 Jan. 1969		yes

Inscription: Brother and Uncle, Rest in Peace

Other Info: Dunkum Funeral Home marker

Smith Daniel	12 Oct. 1900		Etched fieldstone
Smith Louisa	March 1861 23 July 1924		yes
Stanton Jenniom	15 Aug. 1887 2 Aug. 1908		Etched fieldstone
Stanton Leslie	6 Sept. 1907 25 Apr. 1988		yes

Inscription: US Army, World War II

Tigger Wiss	19 Oct. 1895		Etched fieldstone
Tindall John E.	24 Nov. 1922 1 Jan. 1957		yes

Last Name Given Name (Maiden Name)	Date of Birth Date of Death Age at Death	Spouse	Tombstone
Toney Samuel Lee	1888 1973		no

Other Info: Doyne-Burger Funeral Home marker

Tutwyler Robert Lee	2 July 1949 25 July 1998		yes

Inscription: God Doesn't Make Mistakes; You Are Gone But Not Forgotten; Your Wife, Children and Grandchildren

Other Info: Reids Funeral Home marker

Watkins Leslie R.	17 Aug. 1904 10 May 1968		yes

Inscription: CPL 20. 20 QM Truck Co. A.U.N., World War II

Watts Fountain	1852 1935		yes
Watts Willie A.	1865 1989		yes
Wheeler Nudie (Henley)	28 Dec. 1928 20 Nov. 1985		yes

Inscription: Mother, Rest in Peace

White Mary M.	9 Oct. 1917 19 Dec. 1984		yes
Williams Annie D. (Daisy)	1898 18 March, 1968		yes
Williams Ervin Sr.	6 Nov. 1919 22 July 2001		no

Other Info: Reids Funeral Home marker

Last Name Given Name (Maiden Name)	Date of Birth Date of Death Age at Death	Spouse	Tombstone
Williams George W.	8 June 1910 16 June 1962		yes

Inscription: Virginia, TEC 5, US Army, World War II

Other Info: Chiles Funeral Home

Williams James	10 July 1888 3 Feb. 1968		yes

Inscription: Virginia, PFC, 3 BN, 510 Engineers, World War I

Williams Jesse	19 Jan. 1914 8 Feb. 1988		yes

Other Info: Headstone erected by W.A. Hartman Memorials, Charlottesville.

Williams Lee E.	14 Aug. 1857 29 Oct. 1928		yes

Inscription: Absent Not Dead

Williams Lucy H.	3 Aug. 1926 8 June 1999		no

Other Info: This inscription is on a vault; O.P. Chiles Funeral Home.

Williams Maria	1893 1978		yes
Williams Mary			yes

Other Info: Tombstone has sunk into the ground, so dates are not visible

Williams Monroe	13 April 1917 29 March 1997		yes

Other Info: Has a Dunkum Funeral Home marker.

Last Name Given Name (Maiden Name	Date of Birth Date of Death Age at Death	Spouse	Tombstone
Williams Percy	20 June 1913 22 May 1982		yes

Inscription: PFC, US Army, World War II

| Woodson
  Cardozau Jr. | 1959
2000 | | no |

Other Info: Reid's Funeral Home marker

| Woodson
  Catherine E. | 14 March 1909
22 July 1985 | | yes |
| Woodson
  Chambers C. | 10 Nov. 1899
24 Jan. 1978 | | yes |

Inscription: At Rest

| Woodson
  Corine | 14 Oct. 1917
18 Jan. 1995 | | no |

Other Info: Above ground vault: Our Precious Mother, Bobby, Billy and Larry; Manning FH

| Woodson
  Elvira | 1 July 1851
12 Oct. 1912 | | yes |

Inscription: She Owned a Part in Christ. She was one of the Founders of the Brotherhood and was Treasurer (Eastern Star symbol on tombstone).

| Woodson
  Henry E. | 1921
1988 | | no |

Other Info: Manning Funeral Home marker

| Woodson
  Janet Evelyn | 14 Oct. 1930
22 July 1999 | | yes |

Inscription: TSGT, US Air Force, Vietnam

Other Info: This is the daughter of Catherine E. Woodson.

Last Name Given Name (Maiden Name)	Date of Birth Date of Death Age at Death	Spouse	Tombstone
Woodson Lettie M.	1895 1970		no

Other Info: Smith Funeral Home marker

Woodson Lillie L.	6 Aug. 1900 9 Aug. 1979		no

Other Info: Above ground vault: In Loving Memory of our Mother, Rest in Peace

Woodson Norman E.	30 May 1908 13 April 1988		yes
Woodson Ressie	20 June 1920 18 April 1994		no

Other Info: Above ground vault: Manning FH

Woodson Silvira	1904 1985		no

Other Info: This inscription is on a vault-Reids FH

Wooldridge A. L.	 3 May 1953		no

Other Info: Chiles Funeral Home marker.

There are 35 visible graves that are not identified, either by illegible funeral markers, uninscribed or broken tombstones or no markers. There may be many more unmarked graves in this cemetery.

Chief Cornerstone Baptist Church — African American

Anderson Charles T.	1910 1967		no

Other Info: Dunkums Funeral Home marker

Last Name Given Name (Maiden Name)	Date of Birth Date of Death Age at Death	Spouse	Tombstone
Anderson James, Deacon	1871 1947		yes
Ayers David E.	12 Feb. 1893 20 Dec. 1971		yes
Ayers Layman			no
Other Info: unidentified funeral home marker			
Ayers Lorenzo	1948		no
Other Info: unidentified funeral home marker			
Ayres Gracie V.	5 Oct. 1892 2 July 1990		yes
Ayres James C. Jr.	10 Jan. 1964 28 Oct. 1964		yes
Ayres Luther	1920 1976		yes
Inscription: TEC 5, US Army, World War II			
Ayres Ray.	7 Nov. 1936 12 Dec. 1992		yes
Inscription: US Army, Korea			
Ayres Walker	1891 1981		yes
Inscription: Gone But Not Forgotten			
Banks Rosa Lee (Ayers)	27 April, 1936 8 May 1993		yes
Other Info: Has a Reids Funeral Home marker			

Last Name Given Name (Maiden Name)	Date of Birth Date of Death Age at Death	Spouse	Tombstone
Booker Billy W.			no

Other Info: unidentified funeral home marker

Booker Bobby	197_		no

Other Info: Reids Funeral Home marker

Booker Charles			no

Other Info: unidentified funeral home marker gives one date: 1943

Booker Ernest O.	1928 6 Oct 1968		yes

Other Info: unidentified funeral home marker

Booker Hobert	21 July 1969		no

Other Info: Reids Funeral Home marker

Booker James	15 Nov. 1996		no

Other Info: Known to be buried here

Booker Kate	1903 1940		yes

Booker Lynwood J.	19 April 1962 2 Sept. 1979		yes

Other Info: Reids Funeral Home marker

Booker Mary Frances	1951 1986		yes

Other Info: Dunkums Funeral Home marker

Last Name Given Name (Maiden Name)	Date of Birth Date of Death Age at Death	Spouse	Tombstone
Booker Minnie Lee	1902 1941		yes

   Inscription: Mother

| Booker
   Pearl L. (Lee) | | | no |

   Other Info: unidentified funeral marker gives one date:1938

| Booker
   Shirley (Swann) | 8 Aug 1938
5 Aug 2002 | | yes |

   Inscription: Loving Wife and Mother

   Other Info: E. B. Allen Funeral Home marker

| Booker
   Whitley | 1 Mar. 1889
9 Dec. 1962 | | yes |

   Other Info: Name on unidentified funeral marker is Wirley Booker.

| Brown
   Emma | | | no |

   Other Info: unidentified funeral home marker

| Brown
   Jonah | 1977
2002 | | no |

   Other Info: Bland-Reid Funeral Home marker

| Brown
   Lillian Elizabeth | 1886
1965 | | no |

   Other Info: unidentified funeral home marker

| Brown
   Ollie | | | no |

   Other Info: unidentified funeral home marker

Last Name Given Name (Maiden Name)	Date of Birth Date of Death Age at Death	Spouse	Tombstone
Brown Perch	1958		no

Other Info: unidentified funeral home marker

Brown Willie L.	1934 1983		no

Other Info: unidentified funeral home marker

Cain Alice			no

Other Info: Known to be buried here; dates not known.

Cain David			no

Other Info: Dunkum Funeral Home marker

Cain Isiah	1898 1960		no

Other Info: unidentified funeral home marker

Cain Warren	21 March 1958		no

Other Info: unidentified funeral home marker

Cain Wirt	1888 1976		no

Other Info: Reids Funeral Home marker

Gregory Deacon Emmett	1892 1986	Elizabeth Gregory	yes

Inscription: US Army, World War I

Other Info: Reids Funeral Home marker

Last Name Given Name (Maiden Name)	Date of Birth Date of Death Age at Death	Spouse	Tombstone
Edmonds Joseph R.	2 May 1904 26 Jan. 1977	Mattie Ruth Edmonds	yes

Inscription: Dad, We Love You

Edmonds Mattie Ruth	10 July 1920 20 Mar. 1972	Joseph R. Edmonds	yes

Inscription: Mother, We Love You

Epps Natalie	1931 2001		no

Other Info: Reids Funeral Home marker

Gray James Wesley	12 Sept. 1897 15 Feb. 1981		yes

Inscription: US Army, World War I

Gray Sue	4 Nov. 1888 22 Nov. 1966		yes

Inscription: Beloved Wife and Mother

Gregory Alexander	1871 1942		yes

Other Info: Cement Stone-illegible; Dunkums Funeral Home marker.

Gregory Annie			yes

Other Info: Cement stone-difficult to read; unidentified funeral marker gives the name only

Gregory Clarence	30 June 1918 27 Dec. 1977		yes

Inscription: US Army, World War II

Last Name Given Name (Maiden Name	Date of Birth Date of Death Age at Death	Spouse	Tombstone
Gregory Elizabeth	1967	Deacon Emmett Gregory	no

Other Info: Has an above ground vault.

| Gregory
Lucy | | | yes |

Other Info: Cement tombstone-difficult to read; unidentified funeral marker gives the name only

| Gregory
Moses | 1908
2000 | | no |

Other Info: Oliver & Egglestone Funeral Home marker

| Gregory
Sarah Jane | 1883
1943 | | yes |

Other Info: Cement Stone-illegible; Dunkums Funeral Home marker.

| Gregory
Willie | | | yes |

Other Info: Cement Stone-difficult to read; unidentified funeral marker gives the name only

| Gregory
Edkie | 5 Jan. 1959
53 years 0 months 3 days | | yes |

Other Info: Cement Stone with Dunkum Funeral Home marker imbedded in it.

| Harris
Clifton P. | 1934
1997 | | yes |

Inscription: Beloved Husband and Brother

| Harris
Leon N. | 25 June 1896
17 Sept. 1985 | | yes |

Inscription: US Army, World War I

Last Name Given Name (Maiden Name)	Date of Birth Date of Death Age at Death	Spouse	Tombstone
Kidd Ida C.	1877 19__		no

Other Info: unidentified funeral home marker

Kidd Joe			no

Other Info: unidentified funeral home marker gives one date: 1956

Kidd Tom L.	22 Aug. 1967		no

Other Info: unidentified funeral marker

Lee Myrest A.	1925 2001		no

Other Info: Oliver & Eggleston Funeral Home marker

Logan Estelle L.	1889 1976	Mack. A. Logan	yes

Other Info: Shares a headstone with her husband; Reids Funeral Home marker gives birth year as 1890.

Logan Mack A. (Alfred)	1879 1962	Estelle L. Logan	yes

Other Info: Shares a headstone with his wife; Funeral marker gives birth year as 1875

Marshall Maude	8 Dec. 1903 29 Oct. 1991		yes

Inscription: In Loving Memory; Mother, Grandmother

Mitchell Jean	1925 1992		yes

Inscription: US Army

Last Name Given Name (Maiden Name	Date of Birth Date of Death Age at Death	Spouse	Tombstone
Moseley Minnie (Ayers)	17 Aug. 1907 6 Feb. 1987		yes

Inscription: In Memory of My Mother

| Porter
   Garry A. | 23 Feb. 1990
18 April 1990 | | yes |

Inscription: Son, Grandson

| Stephans
   Georgia Ann (Swann) | 1916
1975 | | no |

Other Info: Reids Funeral Home marker

| Swann
   Eddie | | | no |

Other Info: Funeral marker gives one date: 1956

| Swann
   Eliza V | 1911
1933 | | no |

Other Info: Reids Funeral Home marker

| Swann
   James E. | 1922
1970 | | no |

Other Info: unidentified funeral home marker

| Swann
   Janie | 1953 | | no |

Other Info: Known to be buried here.

| Swann
   Linwood J. | 31 Oct. 1911
21 Aug. 1976 | | yes |

Inscription: Beloved Husband and Father

| Swann
   M. Effie | 14 Dec. 1918
12 Dec. 1977 | | yes |

Last Name Given Name (Maiden Name	Date of Birth Date of Death Age at Death	Spouse	Tombstone
Swann Virginia			no

Other Info: Lightfoot Funeral Home marker gives one date: 4 Dec. 1925

Thompson James Drew	14 Feb. 1910 14 Feb. 2001		yes

Inscription: US Navy, World War II

Tyree Alexander	15 March 1895 6 Aug. 1972		yes

Inscription: Gone But Not Forgotten

Tyree Alexander A.	17 July 1920 12 June 1986		yes

Inscription: TEC 5, US Army, World War II

Tyree Charlie	1 May 1914 20 Sept. 1967		yes

Inscription: PVT, US Army, World War II

Tyree Daniel	1894 1974		no

Other Info: Known to be buried here

Tyree Dolly	1855		no

Other Info: unidentified funeral home marker

Tyree James Edward	4 June 1931 9 April 1982		yes

Inscription: CPL, Signal Corps, US Army, Korea

Last Name Given Name (Maiden Name)	Date of Birth Date of Death Age at Death	Spouse	Tombstone
Tyree 　John E., Rev.	10 June 1898 16 Dec. 1974		yes

　　Inscription: Rest in Peace

Tyree 　Josie W.	8 Sept 1898 14 March 1996		yes

　　Inscription: Rest in Peace

Tyree 　Maude	1910 1983		

　　Other Info: unidentified funeral home marker

Tyree 　Percy Phillip	18 March 1922 23 Sept. 1993		yes

　　Inscription: Rest in Peace

Tyree 　Zenobia	1867 1944		yes
Wade 　Louise (Tyree)	22 July 1903 29 Aug. 1992		yes

　　Inscription: Rest in Peace

There are 6 unidentified graves in this cemetery.

Claiborne Family and Slaves at "Cold Comfort"

Claiborne 　Garnett			no

　　Other Info: Known to be buried here. She was the daughter of Martha
　　E. Scruggs Claiborne and Temple Irving Claiborne.

Last Name Given Name (Maiden Name	Date of Birth Date of Death Age at Death	Spouse	Tombstone
Claiborne Laura Garnett	8 Aug. 1821 29 July 1901	Thomas O. Claiborne	no

Other Info: Known to be buried here. She was the mother of Temple Irving Claiborne. Her headstone has been removed to Browns Chapel cemetery. The dates here are from that stone.

Claiborne Martha E. Scruggs	20 June 1844 14 Nov. 1902	Temple Irving Claiborne	no

Other Info: Known to be buried here. Her headstone has been removed to Browns Chapel cemetery. The dates given here are from the stone at Browns Chapel.

Claiborne Temple I. (Irving)	18 Jan. 1844 20 Sept. 1916	Martha E. Scruggs Claiborne	yes

Inscription: Corp., Co. A, 22nd Infantry, CSA

Other Info: He also has a headstone at Browns Chapel cemetery. He is listed as a Sgt. on that headstone. The dates recorded here came from the headstone at Browns Chapel. There are no dates on the military stone.

Claiborne Thomas O.	16 March 1809 26 Feb. 1892	Laura Garnett Claiborne	no

Other Info: Known to be buried here. His headstone has been removed to Browns Chapel cemetery. The dates recorded here are from that stone. He was the father of Temple Irving Claiborne.

There are several unnamed slaves buried in this cemetery.

Last Name	Date of Birth	Spouse	Tombstone
Given Name	Date of Death		
(Maiden Name)	Age at Death		

Cliborne Family off the intersection of Rd. 632 and Rd. 650

Cliborne	11 May, 1781		yes
John	8 Aug. 1851		

Inscription: There is rest in heaven.

There are 2 or more unidentified graves in this cemetery. The WPA Survey of the 1930s reported this as the John Claiborne cemetery.

Cobbs Family off Rd. 633

Cobbs	4 Jan. 1895		yes
Early	15 Jan. 1968		

Inscription: Virginia, US Army, World War I

Cobbs			yes
John	20 June 1932		

Inscription: Virginia, PVT, 369 INF., 93 Div.

There are 5 unidentified graves in this cemetery.

Coleman-Grigg Family off Rd. 722

Coleman	8 March 1908		yes
Elizabeth Duryee	7 April 1977	Cyril Moseley Coleman	

Inscription: Wife of Cyril Moseley Coleman

Bailey	1957		yes
infant	1957		

Other Info: Buried next to Patricia C. Bailey.

Bailey	15 Oct. 1936		yes
Patricia Coleman	1 Oct. 1964		

Last Name	Date of Birth	Spouse	Tombstone
Given Name	Date of Death		
(Maiden Name	Age at Death		

Coleman   no
                                       Tom Fitzgerald Coleman

Other Info: Known to be buried here, the wife and infant child of Tom Fitzgerald Coleman

Coleman   (6 June) 1866   yes
     Annie A. (Amanda Gregory) (27 May) 1946   Frank Walker
                                                 Coleman

Other Info: Shares a headstone with her husband.

Coleman   22 Nov. 1919   yes
    Clayton M.   6 Nov. 1937

Other Info: He was the son of Wm. Lancaster and Emma Coleman.

Coleman   12 May 1895   yes
    Cyril Moseley   7 Dec. 1968   Elizabeth Duryee
                                               Coleman

Inscription: Served in World War I, 1917-1919

Coleman   no
    Eliza Moseley   William Henry Coleman

Other Info: Known to be buried here. Grave marked with fieldstones.

Coleman   6 Nov. 1905   yes
    Frank R.   4 Oct. 1987   Marian V. Coleman

Other Info: Footstone: Frank R. Coleman, SGT, US Army, World War II (same dates as on headstone). He shares a headstone with his wife.

Coleman   (4 Dec.) 1859   yes
    Frank W. (Walker)   (17 June) 1918   Annie Amanda Gregory
                                              Coleman

Other Info: Shares a headstone with his wife. Footstone: FWC

Coleman   1 Feb. 1915   yes
    Gladys Coleman   20 June 2001

Last Name Given Name (Maiden Name	Date of Birth Date of Death Age at Death	Spouse	Tombstone
Coleman Irene Walker	9 Dec. 1903 11 Sept. 1904		yes

Inscription: Infant

Coleman Marian V.	21 Nov. 1909 4 March 1987	Frank R. Coleman	yes

Other Info: Footstone: Marion v. Coleman, Beloved Mother (same dates as on headstone). She shares a headstone with her husband.

Coleman Marshall	(9 Sept. 1889) (11 Aug. 1918)		yes

Inscription: Supply Co. 317 Inf., USA

Other Info: He was killed in France in World War II. He was the brother of Thomas Braxton Coleman also buried in this cemetery.

Coleman Thomas Braxton	1 Aug. 1897 19 Dec. 1991		yes

Other Info: Footstone: Thomas B. Coleman, PVT, US Army, World War II (same dates as on tombstone).

Coleman William Henry	1887	Eliza Moseley Coleman	Etched Fieldstone: WHC

Other Info: Known to be buried here.

Davis Virginia Coleman	23 June 1891 28 July 1988		Tri-family stone
Grigg Edward Marshall	20 June 1929 8 Aug. 1977		yes

Inscription: Go placidly amid the noise and haste desiderata.

Grigg Julian			no

Other Info: Grave marked with a wooden cross. He was the son of Julian A. and Nellie Coleman Grigg.

Last Name Given Name (Maiden Name	Date of Birth Date of Death Age at Death	Spouse	Tombstone
Grigg 　Julian A.	25 April 1897 12 June 1984	Nellie Coleman Grigg	Tri-family stone

Inscription: AEF France, A of O Germany, 1918-1919

Other Info: He and his wife were the parents of Edward M. Grigg and Julian Grigg (ashes) also buried in this cemetery.

| Grigg
　Nellie Coleman | 19 May 1901
7 Sept. 1967 | Julian A. Grigg | Tri-family stone |

Other Info: Nellie was the sister of Thomas Braxton Coleman also buried in this cemetery.

| Grigg
　Rodney Duane | 6 July 1965
1 Jan. 1974 | | yes |

Inscription: Here rest a fine boy, our beloved son, El Tigre

| Moseley
　Charles | 27 Feb. 1775
9 Jan. 1842 | Jane Walker Moseley | no |

Other Info: May be buried here.

| Moseley
　Jane Walker | 18 Jan. 1786
16 Jan. 1874 | Charles Moseley | no |

Other Info: May be buried here.

There are 9 unmarked graves in this cemetery, including the 4 known to be or may be buried here.

Concord Baptist Church on Rd. 636

| Allen
　Edith Webb | 30 Nov. 1902
29 Dec. 1991 | | yes |
| Allen
　Jack W. | 7 Nov. 1921
11 Dec. 1977 | | yes |

Inscription: SGT, US Army, World War II

Last Name Given Name (Maiden Name)	Date of Birth Date of Death Age at Death	Spouse	Tombstone
Allen Sanford Philip	8 May 1926 17 Feb. 1999	Mary Ellen Lydia Allen	yes

Inscription: Married 17 Dec. 1948; In Loving Memory

Other Info: Footstone: Sanford Philip Allen, COX, US Navy, World War II (same dates as are on headstone)

Allen Sweden Cyrus	23 Nov. 1898 2 Dec. 1983		yes
Baldwin Infant Daughter	26 Sept. 1959 26 Sept. 1959		yes

Inscription: Infant Daughter of Samuel L. and Rebecca B. Baldwin

Other Info: Footstone: Daughter

Ballowe Beatrice C.	5 April 1903 14 Jan. 1994	Benjamin F. Ballowe	yes

Inscription: Mother

Other Info: Shares a headstone with her husband.

Ballowe Benjamin F.	4 Sept. 1902 15 Jan. 1986	Beatrice C. Ballowe	yes

Inscription: Father

Other Info: Shares a headstone with his wife.

Barr Rutha	6 Aug. 1895 26 Sept. 1973	William C. Barr	yes

Other Info: Footstone: RB; Shares a headstone with her husband.

Barr William C.	3 March 1889 7 Feb. 1951	Rutha Barr	yes

Other Info: Footstone: WCB; Shares a headstone with his wife.

Beasley Carl C.	16 Jan. 1906 30 Sept. 1948		yes

Last Name Given Name (Maiden Name	Date of Birth Date of Death Age at Death	Spouse	Tombstone
Beasley Eliza Webb	14 Oct. 1872 30 Sept. 1950		yes
Beasley Frank E.	8 Jan. 1910 8 Oct. 1984		yes
Beasley John Webb	15 May 1897 17 April 1971		yes
Beasley Julian Henry	8 Jan. 1908 3 Aug. 1960		yes
Beasley Kemper M.	1 April 1904 30 May 1984	Ellen I. Beasley	yes
Beasley L. Earl	24 Jan. 1912 12 Sept. 2003		yes

Inscription: CPL, US Army, World War II

Beasley Lena Mae	5 March 1897 12 June 1979		yes
Beasley Linda Dianne	28 Dec. 1948 8 Jan. 1949		yes

Inscription: Daughter of W.H. and Ruth Beasley

Other Info: Footstone: Daughter

Beasley Priscilla Ann	27 Nov. 1939 16 Oct. 1963		yes
Beasley Ruth Dunkum	3 April 1902 11 Feb. 1983	William Houston Beasley	yes

Inscription: The Light of God Surpasseth all Understanding

Other Info: Footstone: Mother; Shares a headstone with her husband.

Beasley Sylvester V.	18 Jan. 1868 25 Aug. 1951		yes

Last Name Given Name (Maiden Name	Date of Birth Date of Death Age at Death	Spouse	Tombstone
Beasley W. H.		Ruth Beasley	no

Other Info: Footstone only: WHB

Beasley William Houston	17 Sept. 1901 1 May 1960	Ruth Dunkum Beasley	yes

Inscription: The Light of God Surpasseth all Understanding

Other Info: Footstone: Father; Shares a headstone with his wife.

Bersch Jacob C.	14 Sept. 1890 10 Feb. 1954		yes

Inscription: Asleep in Jesus

Bersch Peter O.	3 May 1882 16 April 1929		yes

Inscription: Gone but not Forgotten

Other Info: Footstone: POB

Bracey Betty Hix	6 Oct. 1918 6 May 2001		yes
Bracey Lucille Cox	29 Aug. 1923 29 Jan. 1970		yes
Bracey M. Virginia	15 Nov. 1916 13 May 1970		yes
Bracey Mary Cox	17 May 1896 22 March 1991		yes
Bracey Thomas Hix	16 March 1886 6 July 1936		yes

Last Name Given Name (Maiden Name	Date of Birth Date of Death Age at Death	Spouse	Tombstone
Brown Lonnie P.	31 Dec. 1902 26 or 28 March 1989		yes

  Inscription: HA 2, US Navy, World War I

  Other Info: Also included in a Brown multi-family stone.

| Brown
  Nannie Barker | 15 March 1905
10 June 1991 | | Multi-family stone |

  Inscription: God's Faithful Servants

| Brown
  Tearle Preston | 16 Feb. 1924
11 March 2002 | | Multi-family stone |

  Inscription: In His service

  Other Info: Footstone: Tearle P. Brown, PHM3, US Navy, World War II (same dates as on headstone)

| Carr
  Alma F. | 29 June 1918
2 Oct. 1997 | Robert P. Carr | yes |

  Inscription: Better to die a poor man whose ways are blamelss, than a rich man whose ways are perverse.

  Other Info: Shares a headstone with her husband.

| Carr
  Deanna J. | 27 Feb. 1941
1 March 1985 | Ronnie P. Carr | yes |

  Inscription: Married Dec. 7, 1962; I have fought a good fight, I have finished my course, I have kept the faith.

| Carr
  Infant Baby | 18 Aug. 1951
20 Aug. 1951 | | yes |

| Carr
  Mark Anthony | 7 Aug. 1964
27 Nov. 1969 | | yes |

  Inscription: Son of Ronnie and Deanna Carr

Last Name Given Name (Maiden Name)	Date of Birth Date of Death Age at Death	Spouse	Tombstone
Carr Robert P.	27 Jan. 1911 15 Oct. 1991	Alma F. Carr	yes

Inscription: Better to die a poor man whose ways are blameless, than a rich man whose ways are perverse

Other Info: Shares a headstone with his wife.

Chapman Hezzie	16 Jan. 1898 26 Nov. 1948		yes
Chapman Morris R.	1 July 1920 28 Aug. 1973		yes

Inscription: Virginia, TEC5, US Army, World War II

Chapman Sarah Ann	25 Nov. 1873 24 Dec. 1957		yes
Chapman William H.	24 Dec. 1854 29 Nov. 1924		yes
Chapman William McKinley	26 Oct. 1896 26 June 1980		yes
Christian Frances Ann	1970 1970		yes

Inscription: Baby

Other Info: Footstone: Daughter

Clabo Pinkney L.	16 June 1897 26 April 1983	Viola H. Clabo	yes

Other Info: Shares a headstone with his wife.

Clabo Viola H.	29 March 1897 11 Dec. 1993	Pinkney L. Clabo	yes

Other Info: Shares a headstone with her husband.

Last Name Given Name (Maiden Name)	Date of Birth Date of Death Age at Death	Spouse	Tombstone
Coleman Ami Lynn	20 March 1977 8 April 1983		yes

Inscription: In God's care; In our hearts

Coleman Benjamin Bryan	20 Sept. 1980		yes

Inscription: Infant son of Glynn and Linda Coleman

Coleman Dollie Woodall	17 Dec. 1879 15 July 1937		yes
Crump Carl T.	1926 1965		yes

Inscription: Rest in Peace

Crump Carrie B.	2 Dec. 1889 (not inscribed)	Lewis B. Crump	yes

Inscription: Married 27 April 1920

Other Info: Shares a headstone with her husband.

Crump James G.	8 April 1927 4 May 1988	Viva S. Crump	yes
Crump Lewis B.	2 Sept. 1900 25 Feb. 1962	Carrie B. Crump	yes

Inscription: Married 27 April 1920

Other Info: Shares a headstone with his wife.

Crump Luther H.	23 May 1908 31 Oct. 1955	Vera T. Crump	yes

Inscription: To live in hearts we leave behind, is not to die.

Other Info: Footstone: LHC; Shares a headstone with his wife.

Last Name Given Name (Maiden Name)	Date of Birth Date of Death Age at Death	Spouse	Tombstone
Crump Mamie Woodall	11 July 1922 15 Aug. 2001	William David Crump	yes

Other Info: Shares a headstone with her husband.

Crump Martha M.	1898 1971	W. Harvey Crump	yes

Other Info: Shares a headstone with her husband.

Crump Vera T.	3 March 1909 25 Aug. 1998	Luther H. Crump	yes

Inscription: To live in hearts we leave behind, is not to die.

Other Info: Shares a headstone with her husband.

Crump W. Harvey	1897 1973	Martha M. Crump	yes

Other Info: Shares a headstone with his wife.

Crump William Calvin	1 Jan. 1943 2 Jan. 1943		yes

Inscription: Asleep in Jesus

Crump William David	15 July 1918 6 April 1992	Mamie Woodall Crump	yes

Other Info: Shares a headstone with his wife.

Davis Ashby Grigg	1878 1952		yes

Davis Etta Mae	1878 1944		yes

Dedmond Grace D.	17 Sept. 1905 24 Feb. 1996	John E. Dedmond	yes

Other Info: Shares a headstone with her husband.

Last Name Given Name (Maiden Name)	Date of Birth Date of Death Age at Death	Spouse	Tombstone
Dedmond John E.	25 Oct. 1899 4 April 1975	Grace D. Dedmond	yes

Other Info: Shares a headstone with his wife.

Dedmond John E. Jr.	June 23, 1926 23 Oct. 1997		yes

Dedmond Roger Dale	7 July 1964 12 Feb. 1967		yes

Inscription: Son

Dickinson Ronald L.	16 Aug. 1950 6 April 1999	Willimar M. Crump Dickinson	yes

Inscription: The Lord is my Shepherd; In God's Care

Dudley Gladys L.	9 April 1935 4 July 1997		yes

Inscription: Mother

Dunkum Gladys Bersch	22 Aug. 1897 15 Aug. 1975		yes

Dunn Kathleen Stiles	19 June 1934 13 Feb. 1983	Nim Bennie Dunn	yes

Inscription: Lived, Laughed and Loved

Other Info: Footstone: Mother: Jr., Susan, Candy

Dunn Nim Bennie	8 Nov. 1933 18 Sept. 2000	Kathleen Stiles Dunn	yes

Inscription: Rest in Peace

Other Info: Footstone: Nim Bennie Dunn, BM1, US Navy, Korea (same dates as on tombstone); Shares a headstone with his wife.

Falls Laythan M.	26 June 1918 12 April 2001	Ruby D. Falls	yes

Last Name Given Name (Maiden Name)	Date of Birth Date of Death Age at Death	Spouse	Tombstone
Fender Robbie P.	1905 1989	Walter S. Fender	yes

Other Info: Shares a headstone with her husband.

Fender Walter S.	1905 1989	Robbie P. Fender	yes

Other Info: Shares a headstone with his wife.

Fulcher J. Rosser	11 Nov. 1901 4 Jan. 1997		yes

Inscription: In Loving Memory

Fulcher Mary Jamerson	10 July 1906 17 Sept. 2000		yes

Inscription: In Loving Memory

Gibson Naomi Lou	19 Dec. 1923 14 March 2002		yes

Gilliam Alice E.	4 March 1854 17 March 1932		yes

Inscription: Daughter of John Wilson and Martha Gilliam; The circle is broken, one spot is forsaken, one bud from the tree of our friendship is shaken.

Gilliam Arnold C.	2 April 1913 26 Oct. 1988		yes

Inscription: Our Uncle Jack

Gilliam John Henry			yes

Other Info: There is one date on the headstone: 2 Jan. 1919.

Last Name Given Name (Maiden Name)	Date of Birth Date of Death Age at Death	Spouse	Tombstone
Gilliam Nannie Duncan			yes

Other Info: There is one date on the headstone: 2 May 1918.

Gills Earl Irving	19 Feb. 1920 26 April 1926		yes
Gills Ella Wilson	28 March 1917 8 Nov. 1920		yes
Gills Harriet W.	15 May 1847 28 Jan. 1919	John H. Gills	yes

Inscription: Wife of John H. Gills; She was a kind and affactionate wife, a fond mother and a friend to all.

Gills Henry W.	1884 1974	Leona D. Gills	yes

Other Info: Shares a headstone with his wife.

Gills Hugh Andrews	28 March 1887 30 May 1964	Ida M. Gills	yes
Gills Ida M.	(not inscribed) 5 Feb. 1918	Hugh Andrews Gills	yes

Inscription: Wife of H.A. Gills; Thy life was beauty, truth, goodness and love.

Gills Irene Leona	22 Sept. 1910 9 Oct. 1994		yes
Gills John H.	13 April 1835 16 June 1918	Harriet W. Gills	yes

Inscription: VA CAV, CSA

Gills John W.	4 Sept. 1881 31 July 1930		yes

Inscription: His words were kindness, his deeds were love, his spirit humble, he rests above.

Last Name Given Name (Maiden Name	Date of Birth Date of Death Age at Death	Spouse	Tombstone
Gills Leona D.	1890 1956	Henry W. Gills	yes

Other Info: Footstone: LDG Shares a headstone with her husband.

Gills Lillie Roxie	20 Aug. 1913 27 Jan. 1988		yes
Griffith Archie Ray	 Oct. 2002		no

Other Info: Unidentified funeral home marker

Griffith Erma E. Deal	29 July 1896 25 Aug. 1938	 John Leroy Griffith	yes

Inscription: A tender mother and faithful wife

Other Info: Footstone: Mother

Griffith Grace E.	1900 1941	 Noah C. Griffith	yes

Other Info: Shares a headstone with her husband.

Griffith John Leroy	20 Nov. 1891 16 Oct. 1963	 Erma E. Deal Griffith	yes
Griffith Noah C	1898 1946	 Grace E. Griffith	yes

Other Info: Shares a headstone with his wife.

Harvey Alice Lowe	27 June 1884 5 May 1957		yes
Harvey Mary A.	Feb. ___ Apr. ___		yes, broken
Harvey Mary Alice	26 April 1918 8 Feb. 1920		yes

Last Name Given Name (Maiden Name)	Date of Birth Date of Death Age at Death	Spouse	Tombstone
Harvey 　Richard Eddie	25 June 1886 13 July 1939		yes
Hayes 　James Colbert	1854 1940	Martha A. Hayes	yes

Other Info: Shares a headstone with his wife.

Hayes 　Mack	28 Dec. 1879 25 April 1952		yes
Hayes 　Martha A.	1856 1942	James Colbert Hayes	yes

Other Info: Shares a headstone with her husband.

Hill 　Myrtle Chapman	21 Feb. 1913 15 April 1999		yes
Hix 　Bessie Susan	1910 1922		yes
Hix 　Hilda Baldwin	1902 1987		yes
Hix 　Susie Garnett	1870 1965		yes
Hix 　Thomas Bocock	1864 1946		yes
Hix 　Thomas Cook	1905 1985		yes
Hooper 　Benjamin A.	1848 1922	Mary H. Hooper	yes

Other Info: Footstone: BAH; Shares a headstone with his wife.

Hooper 　Mary H.	1861 1926	Benjamin A. Hooper	yes

Other Info: Footstone: MHH; Shares a headstone with her husband.

Last Name Given Name (Maiden Name	Date of Birth Date of Death Age at Death	Spouse	Tombstone
Hopkins Fannie Lowe	27 Oct. 1892 8 Jan. 1973		yes
Hopkins Jake C.	16 Nov. 1892 28 July 1966		yes

Inscription: Virginia, PVT, US Army, World War I

Harvey Roy William	17 Feb. 1913 25 Dec. 1925		yes
Jamerson Charles H.	28 March 1922 18 July 1994	Florence E. Jamerson	yes

Other Info: Footstone: Charles H. Jamerson, US Army, World War II (same dates as are on the headstone).

Johnson Clyde T.			yes

Other Info: Footstone: Clyde T. Johnson, SSGT, US Army, World War II, 5 Oct. 1920, 20 May 1993

Johnson Edgar M. Jr.	18 Feb. 1933 6 July 1995		yes

Inscription: He flew, he surfed, he caved, he played bluegrass music, he loved and he was loved.

Kelsey Elizabeth A.	1839 1925		yes
Kelsey Frank E.	1873 1960		yes
Kelsey Grace C.	1871 1955		yes
Kirby Fred	20 Feb. 1898 30 June 1978		yes
Kirby Maggie Moss	15 Aug. 1908 31 May 1993		yes

Last Name Given Name (Maiden Name	Date of Birth Date of Death Age at Death	Spouse	Tombstone
Kirby Odell J.	26 Sept. 1928 20 Oct. 2002		yes

Inscription: US Army, Korea

| Kirby
    Robert Woodford | 20 Nov. 1929
19 April 1991 | | yes |

Inscription: AN, US Navy

| Love
    Fulton R. | 30 March 1876
18 April 1927 | | yes |

Inscription: No pain, no grief, no anxious fear can reach our loved one sleeping here.

Other Info: Footstone: FRL

| Lowe
    Josephine B. | 1874
1962 | | yes |

| Lowe
    Mary S. | 6 April 1851
21 July 1923 | | yes, broken |

Other Info: Footstone: MSL

| Lowe
    Robert Lee | 1872
1933 | | yes |

| Lowe
    W.M.H. | 1841
1928 | | yes |

Inscription: He was beloved of God and man.

Other Info: Footstone: WMHL

| Manis
    Aubry Lee | 29 Aug. 1956
10 Nov. 1984 | | yes |

| Manis
    David A. | 1900
1974 | | yes |

Last Name Given Name (Maiden Name)	Date of Birth Date of Death Age at Death	Spouse	Tombstone
Marks Addie G.	12 May 1890 1 April 1959		yes

Inscription: Buck

Marks Alfred M.	1875 1913		yes
Marks Alice O.	26 Feb. 1886 13 May 1970	George W. Marks	yes

Other Info: Shares a headstone with her husband.

Marks George W.	4 Sept. 1887 3 Feb. 1961	Alice O. Marks	yes

Other Info: Shares a headstone with his wife.

Marks Jesse V.	1850 1924	Mary C. Marks	yes

Other Info: Shares a headstone with his wife.

Marks Mary C.	1852 1925	Jesse V. Marks	yes

Other Info: Shares a headstone with her husband.

McLaughlin Louise Gills	7 June 1912 9 Oct. 2001		yes
Meyer Ward Alker	17 June 1912 7 Jan. 1989		yes
Morgan Howard D.	24 Feb. 1913 30 April 2003	Myrtle Dixie J. Morgan	yes

Inscription: Gone but not forgotten; Father

Other Info: Footstone: Howard D.M. My trust is in God; Shares a headstone with his wife.

Last Name Given Name (Maiden Name)	Date of Birth Date of Death Age at Death	Spouse	Tombstone
Morgan Myrtle Dixie J.	18 Sept. 1916 10 June 1991	Howard D. Morgan	yes

Inscription: Gone but not forgotten; Mother

Other Info: Footstone: Myrtle D.J.M., Forever honour'd and forever mourn'd; Shares a headstone with her husband.

Mottley Alexander S.	1922 1873		yes

Inscription: Cox, US Navy, World War II, Korea

Orange Frank B.	1904 1961		yes
Orange Lawrence H.	19 Sept. 1917 14 April 1976		yes
Orange Lula C.	1915 1990		yes
Orange Octavis	1870 1942		yes
Orange Robert A.	14 Feb. 1909 10 May 1956	Vola B. Orange	yes

Inscription: Earth has no sorrow that heaven cannot heal

Orange Ruth L.	16 Nov. 1916 7 Aug. 1965		yes
Orange Susie F.	1880 1959		yes
Parott Lawrence G.	1922 1946		yes
Parott Patsy Ann	1943 1946		yes

Other Info: Footstone: PAP

Last Name Given Name (Maiden Name	Date of Birth Date of Death Age at Death	Spouse	Tombstone
Patterson Dorothy V.	28 May 1937 26 Dec. 1987		yes

Inscription: 20 years and forever

Patterson Fern C.	24 July 1931 2 Dec. 1974		yes

Inscription: MSG, US Army

Penick W. Price	2 Sept. 1858 6 Jan. 1925		yes

Inscription: An honest man's the noblest work of God.

Other Info: Footstone: WPP

Proffitt Vernard C.	20 March 1913 7 June 1990		yes
Rafferty Asa Menville	27 June 1900 27 Oct. 1969		yes

Inscription: In Loving Memory; Husband and Father

Rafferty Floyd Everett	26 July 1926 4 June 1991		yes

Inscription: BM2, US Navy, World War II-Korea

Rafferty Nellie Wooten	11 July 1903 11 May 1980		yes

Inscription: In Loving Memory; Wife and Mother

Rafferty Riley F	2 Oct. 1928 30 April 1990		yes

Inscription: US Navy, Korea

Last Name Given Name (Maiden Name)	Date of Birth Date of Death Age at Death	Spouse	Tombstone
Rafferty Tom	14 Aug. 1940 8 March 1993		yes

Inscription: HTR; Dad, my best friend, rest in peace.

Other Info: Footstone: Henry T. Rafferty, 1940-1993; Has a Nelsen Funeral Home marker.

Ramey John Edward	28 Sept. 1929		

Inscription: yes

Reynolds Linwood A.	1882 1944		yes

Other Info: Footstone: LAR

Runion Margaret Barbara Jean	1943 1992		yes

Inscription: Thy Kingdon Come

Rutledge Sue Gilliam			yes

Other Info: There is one date on the headstone: 16 July 1917.

Scott J. Estelle Gills	1923 1987		yes

Inscription: Beloved Mother and Grandmother

Senger Rickey Dexter	4 June 1958 27 March 2001		yes

Inscription: In God's Care

Senger Ronald W.	23 Oct. 1952 7 Jan. 1995		yes

Last Name Given Name (Maiden Name)	Date of Birth Date of Death Age at Death	Spouse	Tombstone
Silby D. Branch	23 June 1893 28 Aug. 1966		yes

Inscription: A Loving Father

Other Info: Footstone: DBS

Silby Martha B.	3 Sept. 1901 15 Jan. 1965		yes

Inscription: A Kind Wife and Mother

Simpson Patricia Ann	11 Oct. 1950 14 Oct. 1950		yes

Inscription: Daughter of W.I. and Elizabeth Simpson

Other Info: Footstone: Daughter

Simpson Robert Lee	2 Aug. 1951 3 Aug. 1951		yes

Inscription: Son of W.I. and Elizabeth Simpson

Other Info: Footstone: Son

Skinner Lorraine V.	22 Aug. 1931 4 Jan. 1996	Milton L. Skinner	yes

Smith Edward D.	12 March 1920 14 May 2004	Arbie E. H. Smith	yes

Steele Earl A.	18 Jan. 1886 30 Nov. 1977		yes

Sterne Alice C.	17 April 1899 25 June 1987	James M. Sterne	yes

Other Info: Shares a headstone with her husband.

Sterne James M.	16 Sept. 1875 7 Sept. 1958	Alice C. Sterne	yes

Other Info: Shares a headstone with his wife.

Last Name Given Name (Maiden Name)	Date of Birth Date of Death Age at Death	Spouse	Tombstone
Townsend Ardean C.	6 April 1912 5 Dec. 1994	Evert James Townsend	yes

Other Info: Shares a headstone with her husband.

Townsend C. Howard	23 Jan. 1913 26 June 2001	Vaden Dare Townsend	yes
Townsend Cora T. Norwood	7 Sept. 1898 23 Aug. 1996	James Sherman Townsend	yes

Other Info: Shares a headstone with her husband

Townsend Evert James	21 April 1906 9 May 1984	Ardean C. Townsend	yes

Other Info: Shares a headstone with his wife.

Townsend Homer H.	1937 2001	Margie M. Townsend	yes

Inscription: Married 25 Feb. 1954

Other Info: Shares a headstone with his wife.

Townsend Homer Michael	22 Feb. 1956 31 Dec. 1986		yes
Townsend James Sherman	7 Aug. 1891 19 Sept. 1949	Cora T. Norwood Townsend	yes

Other Info: Footstone: JST; Shares a headstone with his wife.

Townsend John W. Jay	1927 2000	Katherine T. Townsend	yes

Other Info: Footstone: John W. Townsend Jr., US Army Air Forces, 4 June 1927, 21 June 2000; Shares a headstone with his wife.

Last Name Given Name (Maiden Name	Date of Birth Date of Death Age at Death	Spouse	Tombstone
Townsend John Wesley	22 July 1880 23 Sept. 1940	Rosa Hayes Townsend	yes

Inscription: Married: 26 May 1903

Other Info: Shares a headstone with his wife.

Townsend Katherine T.	1933 1955	John W. Jay Townsend Jr.	yes

Other Info: Footstone: KTT; Shares a headstone with her husband.

Townsend Margie M.	1935 1984	Homer H. Townsend	yes

Inscription: Married 25 Feb. 1954

Other Info: Shares a headstone with her husband.

Townsend Melvin C.	27 Dec. 1912 26 April 1989	Ruth T. Townsend	yes

Other Info: Shares a headstone with his wife.

Townsend Rosa Hayes	29 May 1884 23 July 1964	John Wesley Townsend	yes

Inscription: Married: 26 May 1903

Other Info: Footstone: Mother; Shares a headstone with her husband.

Townsend Ruth T.	17 March 1915 26 June 1976	Melvin C. Townsend	yes

Other Info: Shares a headstone with her husband.

Townsend Troy L.	24 Feb. 1920 19 Jan. 1974		yes

Underwood Lacie	9 April 1992 9 April 1992		yes

Inscription: Infant Daughter of Jim and Susan Underwood.

Last Name Given Name (Maiden Name	Date of Birth Date of Death Age at Death	Spouse	Tombstone
Warner Mildred M.	3 Feb. 1928 28 Sept. 1996	Calvin R. Warner	yes

Inscription: In Loving Memory; Mother

| Wilkerson
   Floyd N. | 2 April 1879
25 May 1959 | Annie S. Wilkerson | yes |

Inscription: All things change-but God remains

Other Info: W. A. Harman Memorials, Charlottesville Va; Footstone: Father; Shares a headstone with his wife.

| Wilkerson
   Annie S. | 10 Feb. 1899
4 June 1995 | Floyd N. Wilkerson | yes |

Inscription: All things change-but God remains.

Other Info: W.A. Hartman Memorials, Charlottesville VA; Footstone: Mother; Shares a headstone with her husband.

| Wilkerson
   Herbert. P. | 24 Aug. 1926
22 April 2003 | Berta W. Wilkerson | yes |

| Wilkerson
   J. Robert | 19 March 1875
9 Jan. 1941 | | yes |

Inscription: To Him we trust a peace is given among the saints with Christ in heaven.

| Wilkerson
   Ray Porter | 3 Dec. 1884
10 Jan. 1959 | | yes |

Inscription: Earth has no sorrow, that heaven cannot heal.

Last Name Given Name (Maiden Name)	Date of Birth Date of Death Age at Death	Spouse	Tombstone
Wilkerson Sallie E.	1 July 1854 2 Feb. 1940	F. M. Wilkerson	yes

Inscription: Wife of F.M. Wilkerson; Rest, Mother, Rest in quiet sleep, while friends in sorrow o're thee weep.

Williams Elizabeth B.	4 Dec. 1920 3 April 2000	Benjamin C. Williams	yes

Inscription: In God's Care

Witt Edward Samuel	19 Sept. 1891 15 Dec. 1977		yes
Witt Goodwin Byrd	11 Dec. 1892 19 Nov. 1965		yes
Woodall Charles E.	6 Aug. 1915 29 March 1993		yes

Other Info: Footstone: Charles Edward Woodall, PFC, US Army, World War II (same dates as are on the headstone)

Woodall George W.	1888 1974		no

Other Info: Unidentified funeral home marker

Woodall Judith Ann	1872 1945		yes
Woodie R. Alfred	April 1918 2 Jan. 1992	Hazel T. Woodie	yes

Inscription: Wed: April 13, 1940

Other Info: Footstone: Father

Woodie Thomas W.	30 Jan. 1949 2 June 2003		yes

Other Info: Footstone: Son

Last Name Given Name (Maiden Name	Date of Birth Date of Death Age at Death	Spouse	Tombstone
Woolridge A. Lyle	1907 1973	Bessie C. Woolridge	yes

Inscription: Rest in Peace

Other Info: Shares a headstone with his wife.

Woolridge Bessie C.	1904 1991	A. Lyle Woolridge	yes

Inscription: Rest in Peace

Other Info: Shares a headstone with her husband.

Wooten Anna P.	7 Sept. 1923 18 May 2001	Shirley L. Wooten	yes

Inscription: Married: 2 Sept. 1944; In Loving Memory

Other Info: Shares a headstone with her husband.

Wooten Shirley L.	22 July 1923 1 May 2003	Anna P. Wooten	yes

Inscription: Married: 2 Sept. 1944; In Loving Memory

Other Info: Shares a headstone with his wife.

Cook-Williams Families on Rd. 601 — African American

Austin Virginia L.	23 May 1928 26 June 1999		yes

Other Info: Has a Reids Funeral Home marker.

Cook Elizabeth	22 Jan. 1931 12 Mar. 1996		yes

Cook Floyd W.	1932 1999		no

Other Info: Reids Funeral Home marker

Last Name Given Name (Maiden Name	Date of Birth Date of Death Age at Death	Spouse	Tombstone
Cook Ida W.	1898 1993		yes

Other Info: Has an E.B. Allen Funeral Home marker.

Kassim Ida Cook	2 Feb. 1955 10 June 1989 34 years		yes

Other Info: Has a Reids Funeral Home marker.

Lee Donald	 31 Dec. 1969		yes
William Virginia H.	31 Dec. 1900 8 Oct. 1989		yes

Other Info: Has an E.B. Allen Funeral Home marker.

Williams Birthiar, Rev.	12 March 1894 29 April 1984		yes

Inscription: Rest in Peace

Williams Charles E.	24 Jan. 1933 April 1983		yes
Williams Jack	1902 1989		yes

Other Info: Has an E.B. Allen Funeral Home marker.

Williams James			no

Other Info: Unidentified funeral home marker with no dates.

Williams Mary			no

Other Info: Unidentified funeral home marker with no dates.

Last Name Given Name (Maiden Name	Date of Birth Date of Death Age at Death	Spouse	Tombstone
Williams Sallie A.			Painted slate

Other Info: No dates on slate stone.

Cottrell Family off Rd. 627 — African American

Braxton ————	66 years		no

Other Info: Unidentified funeral home marker with one date: 19 Feb. 1937

Cottrell Edward			no

Other Info: Known to be buried here.

Cottrell George Melvin	24 Aug. 1924 17 Oct. 1993		yes

Inscription: US Army, World War II

Cottrell Isaiah			no

Other Info: Known to be buried here. His brothers, James, Major and Edward are buried in this cemetery.

Cottrell James	about 1951-1952	Martha Cottrell	no

Other Info: Illegible funeral home marker-known to be buried here. His brothers, Isaiah, Major and Edward Cottrell are also buried in this cemetery.

Cottrell Major			no

Other Info: Known to be buried here.

Last Name Given Name (Maiden Name	Date of Birth Date of Death Age at Death	Spouse	Tombstone
Cottrell 　Martha	about 1951-1952	James Cottrell	no

　　Other Info: Known to be buried here. She and her husband are the great grandparents of Valerie Londeree.

| Cottrell
　Paul B. | 11 Dec. 1950 | | no |

　　Other Info: Unidentified funeral home marker.

| Cottrell
　Paul Burley | 5 Dec. 1926
21 June 1965 | | yes |

　　Inscription: Virginia, PVT, US Army, World War II

| Cottrell
　Paul D. | 11 Dec. 1956
68 years | | no |

　　Other Info: Thacker Bros Funeral Home marker

| Kenny
　Lily Mae Turner | 1939
30 April 1968
30 years | | no |

　　Other Info: Thacker Bros. Funeral Home marker

| Londeree
　Paul A.(Arthur) | 1940
1983 | Rosa L. Londeree | yes |

　　Other Info: Thacker Bros. Funeral Home marker: Paul Arthur Londeree, 11 Dec. 1940, 2 June 1983, age 42. He and his wife are the parents of Valerie Londeree.

| Londeree
　Rosa L. | 1943
2002 | Paul Arthur Londeree | no |

　　Other Info: Reids Funeral Home marker.

| Randolph
　Lucy | 11 Oct. 1952 | | no |

　　Other Info: A.D. Price Funeral Home marker

Last Name Given Name (Maiden Name	Date of Birth Date of Death Age at Death	Spouse	Tombstone
Williams Edna Cottrell	1920 1990		no

Other Info: Thacker Bros Funeral Home marker. She is the grandmother of Valerie Londeree.

| Williams
   Ellis |
11 May 1962 | | no |

Other Info: Thacker Bros. Funeral Home marker

There are 9 unidentified graves in this cemetery.

Cox Family at "Hickory Grove"

| Cox
   Matthew Joel | 20 Jan. 1853
29 Dec. 1922 | | yes |

Inscription: Father let thy grace be given that we may meet in heaven.

There are 5 unidentified graves marked with fieldstones in this cemetery.

Crews Family off Rd. 649

| Crews
   (2 infants-twins) | 1948
1948 | | no |

Other Info: There is one grave with 2 infants, whose parents are George Edward and Elizabeth Stegar Crews.

Dabney Family on Rd. 615 — African American

| Dabney
   Alex | 1913
1975 | | no |

Other Info: This is an above ground vault:Bruce and Stiff FH

Last Name Given Name (Maiden Name	Date of Birth Date of Death Age at Death	Spouse	Tombstone
Dabney Decker	24 Mar. 1873 10 Feb. 1973	Helen Dabney	yes

Inscription: Blessed is the dead that dieth in my name henceforth; they shall rest from thier labor.

Other Info: West Funeral Home marker: Decker Dabney, 1979-1973 (birth year is different on headstone).
Shares a headstone with his wife.

Dabney Helen	20 March 1888 25 April 1988	Decker Dabney	yes

Inscription: Blessed is the dead that dieth in my name henceforth, they shall rest form their labor.

Other Info: Shares a headstone with her husband; Has a Bruce and Stiff Funeral Home marker.

Dabney William E.	22 Jan. 1918 1 April 1954		yes

Inscription: West Virginia, TEC 5, 224 OM, Laundry Platoon, World War II

Garrett Rickey L.	12 Nov. 1953 11 Feb. 1992		no

Other Info: This is an above ground vault: Chinn FH

Jackson Ella Mae	9 May 1910 27 Oct. 1989		yes

Inscription: Our Mother; Asleep in Jesus

Other Info: Has a Reid's Funeral Home marker.

Last Name	Date of Birth	Spouse	Tombstone
Given Name	Date of Death		
(Maiden Name	Age at Death		

Dameron Family on Rd. 652

Dameron   8 Dec. 1873   yes
   Clementine B.   12 Nov. 1965

   Other Info: She was the mother of Robert and Sallie Dameron buried in this cemetery. She has one other son, Joe Dameron.

Dameron   no
   Miss Sallie   6 Nov. 1956
                      10 years, 11 months

   Other Info: Thacker Bros. Funeral Home marker.

Dameron   12 Nov. 1900   yes
   Robert B.   6 Oct. 1967

There is one grave in this cemetery with an illegible funeral marker.

Joshua Davis Family off US 15

Davis   yes
   A.B.

   Inscription: None knew thee but to love thee.

   Other Info: Footstone: A.B. Davis, 18 Aug. 1882, 22 Oct. 1923

Davis   30 April 1904   yes
   Bernard L.   13 July 1928

   Inscription: The Lord is my shepherd; Father let thy grace be given, that we may meet in heaven.

Davis   21 July 1872   yes
   Carrie E.   8 March 1957

   Other Info: Footstone: CED

Last Name Given Name (Maiden Name)	Date of Birth Date of Death Age at Death	Spouse	Tombstone
Davis Joshua	13 June 1828 19 May 1898 70 years		yes

    Inscription: In Memory of; Born in Cornwall County, England; One precious to our hearts has gone. The voice we loved is stilled. The place made vacant in our home, can never more be filled.

    Other Info: Footstone: JD He was a postmaster of the Dillwyn PO when it was located about a mile northwest of the present town of Dillwyn. The post office was in his home.

Davis Joshua Lee	13 July 1855 28 Oct. 1936		yes
Davis Mamie A.	23 July 1902 11 July 1903		yes

    Inscription: Daughter of T.H. and Rosa E. Davis; A precious one from us has gone, a voice we love is stilled. A place is vacant in our home, which never can be filled.

Davis Mary E.	24 Nov. 1832 26 Dec. 1912		yes

    Inscription: In Memory of; One precious to our hearts has gone. The voice we loved is stilled. The place made vacant in our home, can never more be filled.

Davis Robert N.	3 Oct. 1869 31 Oct. 1935		yes

    Inscription: Asleep in Jesus

    Other Info: Footstone: RND

Davis Travis H.	3 Feb. 1863 19 June 1907		yes

    Inscription: Dearest Travis, thou hast left us and our loss we deeply mourn; But in heaven we hope to meet you, where no sorrow will be known.

    Other Info: Footstone: THD

Last Name Given Name (Maiden Name)	Date of Birth Date of Death Age at Death	Spouse	Tombstone
LeSueur Margaret Ann	18 May 1860 1 June 1940		yes

Inscription: At Rest

Other Info: MAL

An article in a local paper some years ago by Genevieve Agee reported that there were 80-100 unmarked graves surrounding the fenced in area that has the marked graves of the Joshua Davis family, and these were descendents of Joshua Davis. Presently there are no indications that there are other graves in the immediate area of this family cemetery.

Davis Family at "Springfield"

Davis Caroline (Wood)	27 Oct. 1823 16 May 1913	J. H. Davis	yes

Other Info: She shares a headstone with her husband.

Davis Eugene	13 Sept. 1893 15 July 1897		yes

Other Info: He was the son of Jefferson Davis.

Davis J. H. (John H.) "Jack"	19 Feb. 1819 20 Jan. 1891	Caroline Wood Davis	yes

Other Info: He and his wife were the parents of Jefferson Davis. He and his wife share a headstone.

Davis Jefferson	14 Jan. 1859 18 April 1902		yes

Other Info: His parents were J.H. and Caroline Davis.

Last Name Given Name (Maiden Name)	Date of Birth Date of Death Age at Death	Spouse	Tombstone

Davis Family at "Whetstone Farm"

Davis Aubrey Mitchell	14 March 1910 1 Dec. 1965		yes

Inscription: Virginia, SSgt, 896 AAA, AW BN, World War II

Davis Eugene	28 Nov. 1919 22 June 1970		yes

Inscription: Virginia, S1, US Navy, World War II

Other Info: His parents were Gertrude and Thomas. J. Davis also buried in this cemetery.

Davis Gertrude Price	7 Feb. 1883 17 Sept. 1969	Thomas Jefferson Davis	yes

Other Info: She and her husband share a headstone. They were the parents or in-laws of all the others buried in this cemetery.

Davis Gordon Langhorn	24 July 1912 7 Jan. 1981		yes

Other Info: He is the father of Gordon Langhorn Jr. and Jimmy Davis.

Davis Herman Foster	29 Oct. 1914 15 Dec. 1974	Margaret Davis	yes

Inscription: Buried at sea in international waters

Other Info: He and his wife are the parents of Benzie Davis.

Davis Julian Rein	19 April 1922 Oct. 1923		yes

Inscription: Son

Last Name Given Name (Maiden Name	Date of Birth Date of Death Age at Death	Spouse	Tombstone
Davis Robert Earland	9 May 1907 10 June 1993	Doris Robertson Davis	yes

Other Info: He was the son of Gertrude and Thomas J. Davis. He and his wife are the parents of Betty Earland Davis Parnell, Randel Craig Davis, DeeDee Davis Uwinski, and Michelle Davis Taylor.

Davis Thomas Jeff Jr.	21 Aug. 1908 7 March 1959	Lucille Mitchell Davis	yes

Inscription: Son

Other Info: He and his wife are the parents of William Davis.

Davis Thomas Jefferson	14 Nov. 1879 7 Nov. 1965	Gertrude Price Davis	yes

Other Info: He and his wife share a headstone.

Gordon Stuart D.	11 Jan. 1917 22 Aug. 1985	Rosemary Davis Gordon	yes

Inscription: PI2, US Navy, World War II

Other Info: His wife is the daughter of Gertrude and Thomas J. Davis. Stuart and Rosemary Gordon are the parents of Lantz and Wayne Gordon.

Savage Ulysses S. Jr.	7 Dec. 1922 25 Jan. 1986	Iris Davis Savage	yes

Inscription: 1st Lt., US Army, World War II

Other Info: His wife is the daughter of Gertrude and Thomas J. Davis. Ulysses and Iris Savage are the parents of Terry and Kim Savage.

Dixon Family in James River Park

Dixon Alice L.	24 Jan. 1872 21 Dec. 1926		yes

Inscription: In memory of; A tender mother and a faithful friend

Last Name Given Name (Maiden Name)	Date of Birth Date of Death Age at Death	Spouse	Tombstone
Dixon Amanda C.	15 Sept. 1825 5 June 1888	Madison P. Dixon	yes

Inscription: My mother

Other Info: Footstone: ACD

| Dixon
John Henry | 29 Sept. 1918
28 Nov. 1983 | | yes |

Inscription: 36 year railroad man

Other Info: Footstone: 1st Lt., US Army, World War II, 29 Sept. 1918, 28 Nov. 1983. Has a Robinson Funeral Home marker.

| Dixon
John Madison | 24 Feb. 1893
5 Jan. 1983 | | yes |

Other Info: Has a Robinson Funeral Home marker.

| Dixon
Lloyd Allen | 24 Dec. 1925
20 March 1937 | | yes |

Inscription: Son of J.M. and Ruth Dixon; Earth has no sorrow that heaven cannot heal.

Other Info: Footstone: LAD

| Dixon
Madison P. | 18 March 1823
12 May 1887 | Amanda C. Dixon | yes |

Inscription: My father

Other Info: Footstone: MPD

| Dixon
Mary Atkins | 11 Sept. 1925
11 Sept. 1925 | | yes |
| Dixon
Montague Uriah | 26 Aug. 1904
14 Sept. 1948 | | yes |

Inscription: Dying is but going home.

Last Name Given Name (Maiden Name	Date of Birth Date of Death Age at Death	Spouse	Tombstone
Dixon Ruth A. Ewers	1900 1966	John M. Dixon	yes

Inscription: In memory of; wife of John M. Dixon

Other Info: Whitten Funeral Home marker: Anna Ewers Dixon, 1900-1966

Williams James Terry Dixon "Toby"	1 March 1964 1 Aug. 1986		yes

Inscription: I leave behind my dreams to live, in my eternal love for you all. To die is but to come home.
He has left us now, but he still lives on, in the glorious light of another dawn. Be comforted then with this thought each day. He is not dead-he is just away! Footstone: Toby-By the example of his forefathers, Toby gave his life for his fellow man.

Dixon Family on David Creek (off US 60)

Dixon Geneva			no

Other Info: Known to be buried here, as is her daughter.

Dixon John Tery	28 July 1850 17 March 1890		yes

Inscription: Brother, Gone but not Forgotten

Other Info: Footstone: JTD

Dixon Mary A.	28 Feb. 1825 7 Nov. 1907	W.N. Dixon	yes

Inscription: No pain, no grief, anxious fear, can reach our loved ones sleeping here.

Other Info: Footstone: MAD She and her husband share a headstone.

Last Name Given Name (Maiden Name)	Date of Birth Date of Death Age at Death	Spouse	Tombstone
Dixon W. N.	22 Oct. 1817 4 Sept. 1898	Mary A. Dixon	yes

Inscription: No pain, no grief, anxious fear, can reach our loved ones sleeping here.

Other Info: Footstone: WND   He and his wife share a headstone.

There are 6 unidentified graves in this cemetery.

Drake-Gormus Family off Rd. 617

Drake George Howard			no

Other Info: Known to be buried in this cemetery. His mother was Ida Virginia Garrett Drake also buried in this cemetery.

Drake Ida Virginia Garrett	1926		no

Other Info: Known to be buried in this cemetery.

Gormus Judy Walden	1883 1927		no

Other Info: Grave marked by fieldstones only.

Gormus Wesley	1852 1961		no

Other Info: Grave marked by fieldstones. Some family members question his birth date.

Taylor B. L.	 29 May 1915		yes

Inscription: Member of P.G. Patterson Bible Class

Last Name Given Name (Maiden Name)	Date of Birth Date of Death Age at Death	Spouse	Tombstone
Wise M. Gormus			Etched fieldstone

There are at least 23 unidentified graves in this cemetery.

Dunnevant Family at "Spring Valley Stables"

Clairborne Dolly Price			no

Other Info: Known to be buried here. Mother of Lossin C. Clairborne. Her husband is also probably buried here, as also is a slave named Bessie.

Clairborne Lossin C.	30 May 1898 28 April 1914		yes

Inscription: My darling boy

Dunnevant Ann Ranson		Samuel A. Dunnovant	no

Other Info: Known to be buried here.

Dunnevant Irene			no

Other Info: Known to be buried here. Daughter of Samuel A. and Ann Ranson Dunnevant.

Dunnevant Johnny			

Other Info: Known to be buried here.

Dunnovant Samuel A.		Ann Ranson Dunnevant	yes

Inscription: Co. K, 4 VA Cav. CSA

Last Name Given Name (Maiden Name	Date of Birth Date of Death Age at Death	Spouse	Tombstone
Price Cal			no

Other Info: Known to be buried here. Brother of Dolly Price Clairborne.

| Price
Sarah E. | 1 Jan. 1834
9 Mar. 1916 | | yes |

Inscription: Asleep in Jesus

There are 18 unidentified graves in this cemetery.

Ebenezer Baptist Church — African American

| Adams
Annie | 4 Feb. 1951 | | no |

Other Info: Information is from church records.

| Allen
Agnes | 24 Jan. 1918 | | no |

Other Info: Information is from church records.

| Allen
Charles Sr. | 17 July 1936 | | no |

Other Info: Information is from church records.

| Allen
Martha Ann | 29 Dec. 1930 | | no |

Other Info: Information is from church records.

| Allen
Willie Sue | 27 June 1923 | | no |

Other Info: Information is from church records.

Last Name Given Name (Maiden Name	Date of Birth Date of Death Age at Death	Spouse	Tombstone
Armistead Annie	1905 1972		no

Other Info: unidentified funeral home marker

Austin Jimmy	13 April 1951		no

Other Info: Information is from church records.

Austin Laura	11 July 1949		no

Other Info: Information is from church records.

Ayers Mark S.	1973 1973		no

Other Info: Reids Funeral Home marker

Ayers Nathan	14 Jan. 1921		no

Other Info: Information is from church records.

Ayers Noner	22 Nov. 1922		no

Other Info: Information is from church records.

Ayers Robert	26 March 1922		no

Other Info: Information is from church records.

Ayers Sarah	22 Jan. 1952		no

Other Info: Information is from church records.

Ayers Tempy	13 June 1913		no

Other Info: Information is from church records.

Last Name Given Name (Maiden Name	Date of Birth Date of Death Age at Death	Spouse	Tombstone
Ayers Wesley	12 Jan. 1917		no

Other Info: Information is from church records.

Bells Ned	3 Nov. 1936		no

Other Info: Information is from church records.

Booker Amanda E.	6 March 1909 15 Jan. 1997		yes

Booker Charles	9 May 1920		no

Other Info: Information is from church records.

Briddle Maude			no

Other Info: John McNeil Funeral Home marker-1015 Main St., St. Joseph MO

Brown Calvin Coolage	Jan. 1945		no

Other Info: Information is from church records.

Brown Charles V.	6 Jan. 1910 6 July 1973		yes

Inscription: Precious Memory

Brown Lewis	17 June 1947		no

Other Info: Information is from church records.

Carter John, Deacon	26 March 1913		no

Other Info: Information is from church records.

Last Name Given Name (Maiden Name	Date of Birth Date of Death Age at Death	Spouse	Tombstone
Carter Rachel	15 July 1915		no

Other Info: Information is from church records.

Carter Susie	11 July 1915		no

Other Info: Information is from church records.

Cattrell James, Rev.	2 Feb. 1952		no

Other Info: Information is from church records.

Chambers Emma H.	1854 12 Dec. 1925		no

Other Info: Cinderblock wall around the grave. Church records give death date as 12 Dec. 1924

Chambers Gilbert, Deacon	20 Apr. 1921		no

Other Info: Information is from church records.

Chambers Joseph	14 Nov. 1924		no

Other Info: Information is from church records.

Chambers Martha	26 Aprl. 1931		no

Other Info: Information is from church records.

Chambers Minnie	26 Jan. 1939		no

Other Info: Information is from church records.

Last Name Given Name (Maiden Name	Date of Birth Date of Death Age at Death	Spouse	Tombstone
Chambers Peggie	 17 March 1925		no

Other Info: Information is from church records.

Chambers Peter	 2 Jan. 1967		no

Other Info: unidentified funeral home marker

Cobbs Malinda	 26 Jan. 1918		no

Other Info: Information is from church records.

Coleman Earnest	1920 1990		no

Other Info: Reids Funeral Home marker

Dean Fannie	 7 April 1919		no

Other Info: Information is from church records.

Dean James, Rev.	 15 March 1930		no

Other Info: Information is from church records.

Diggs Emma	2 April 1949		no

Other Info: Information is from church records.

Douglas Mariah	 28 July 1941		no

Other Info: Information is from church records.

Dyer Chris, Deacon	 23 Feb. 1918		no

Other Info: Information is from church records.

Last Name Given Name (Maiden Name	Date of Birth Date of Death Age at Death	Spouse	Tombstone
Dyer Manervia	8 April 1936		no

Other Info: Information is from church records.

Dyer Vence	8 Jan. 1926		no

Other Info: Information is from church records.

Eldridge Annie Florence	31 May 1936		no

Other Info: Information is from church records.

Forbes Kate	9 Oct. 1948		no

Other Info: Information is from church records.

Forrest W. M., Rev.	20 Oct. 1950		no

Other Info: Information is from church records.

Goolsby Alice	20 April 1872 20 June 1915		no

Other Info: Cinderblock wall around the grave.

Gough Annie V. (Virginia)	14 Sept. 1922 23 July 1969	Warren Harden Gough	yes

Inscription: Mother

Gough Frances	25 Aug. 1950		no

Other Info: Information is from church records.

Last Name Given Name (Maiden Name	Date of Birth Date of Death Age at Death	Spouse	Tombstone
Gough Herbert S.	1958 1995 38		no

Other Info: Thacker Bros. Funeral Home marker

Gough Lloyd D.	28 April 1955 20 Sept. 1985		yes

Gough Warren Harden	10 March 1921 8 Sept. 1968	Annie V. Gough	yes

Inscription: Father

Gough Wilson E.	1959 2001		no

Other Info: unidentified funeral home marker

Harris Annie L.	7 Aug. 1951		no

Other Info: Information is from church records.

Harris Maggie	10 March 1916		no

Other Info: Information is from church records.

Hill George Ellis	8 April 1892 15 March 1953	Rosa L. Hill	yes

Inscription: Virginia, PVT, 3 Co., 1 DEV BN, World War I

Hill Judie	23 Nov. 1913		no

Other Info: Information is from church records.

Hill Rosa L.	1900 1970	George Ellis Hill	yes

Inscription: We Miss You

Last Name Given Name (Maiden Name	Date of Birth Date of Death Age at Death	Spouse	Tombstone
Holeman James	1855 1942		no

Other Info: J. C. Dunkum Bros. Funeral Home marker

| Holeman Mollie | 8 May 1948 | | no |

Other Info: Information is from church records.

| Johnson Arzie D. (Dyer) | 1902 1993 | Clarence E. Johnson | yes |

| Johnson Clarence E. | 22 March 1902 23 March 1992 | Arzie Dyer Johnson | yes |

| Johnson Jaquin C. | 1999 2000 | | no |

Other Info: Reids Funeral Home marker

| Johnson Kyle | 28 July 1926 | | no |

Other Info: Information is from church records.

| Jones Bessie Ann | 31 Oct. 1916 | | no |

Other Info: Information is from church records

| Jones Emma Perkins | 1891 (or 6) 1990 (or 1996) | | no |

Other Info: Thacker Bros. Funeral Home marker; Emma Perkins Jones was the aunt of Mary C. Perkins and Lilly Perkins Peterson.

| Jones Fannie L. | 1918 1982 | | no |

Other Info: Reids Funeral Home marker

Last Name Given Name (Maiden Name	Date of Birth Date of Death Age at Death	Spouse	Tombstone
Jones Hattie	6 Oct. 1949		no
Other Info: Information is from church records			
Jones James	30 Nov. 1965		no
Other Info: unidentified funeral home marker			
Jones Lawrence	30 July 1952		no
Other Info: Information is from church records.			
Jones Pocahantas	20 Aug. 1928		no
Other Info: Information is from church records.			
Jones Sopha	16 Feb. 1926		no
Other Info: Information is from church records.			
Jones Wilmare, Deacon	22 June 1954		no
Other Info: Information is from church records.			
Lee Ella	6 April 1949		no
Other Info: Information is from church records.			
Lee Kate	23 June 1921		no
Other Info: Information is from church records.			
Lee Pollie	12 March 1951		no
Other Info: Information is from church records.			

Last Name Given Name (Maiden Name)	Date of Birth Date of Death Age at Death	Spouse	Tombstone
Marshall Bessie L.	1901 1987	Charlie Marshall	yes

Other Info: Shares a headstone with her husband.

Marshall Charlie	1900 1984	Bessie L. Marshall	yes

Other Info: Shares a headstone with his wife.

Marten Frances	20 Jan. 1922		no

Other Info: Information is from church records.

Palmore Ollie	1937		no

Other Info: Information is from church records.

Patterson Mary	14 March 1914		no

Other Info: Information is from church records.

Patterson Mary Jane	19 July 1930		no

Other Info: Information is from church records.

Patterson Sam, Deacon	8 May 1922		no

Other Info: Information is from church records.

Perkins Alice V.	May 1865 5 Sept. 1927		yes

Inscription: Faithful to her trust even unto death

Other Info: Alice V. Perkins was the mother of Toliver Perkins and George W. Perkins.

Last Name Given Name (Maiden Name)	Date of Birth Date of Death Age at Death	Spouse	Tombstone
Perkins George W.	Oct 1893 30 Nov. 1919		yes
Perkins Jack	 17 Feb. 1913		no

Other Info: Information is from church records.

Perkins Kittie	 29 March 1915		no

Other Info: Information is from church records.

Perkins Louise V.	10 April 1930 13 Feb. 2002	 James F. Perkins	yes
Perkins Mary C.	17 Dec. 1933 21 Nov. 1995 61 years		yes

Inscription: Believer in Acts 2:38

Other Info: Mary C. Perkins was the sister of Lilly Perkins Peterson.

Perkins Mattie B.	1903 1946	 Toliver Perkins	yes
Perkins Mollie	 9 Feb. 1936		no

Other Info: Information is from church records.

Perkins Toliver	9 Aug. 1894 4 March 1963	 Mattie B. Perkins	yes

Inscription: Virginia, PVT, Co. A, 41 Labor BN QMC, World War I

Peterson Lilly Perkins	1919 1994		no

Other Info: Thacker Bros. Funeral Home marker

Last Name Given Name (Maiden Name	Date of Birth Date of Death Age at Death	Spouse	Tombstone
Randolph Jannie	20 July 1930		no

  Other Info: Information is from church records.

| Lee
  G. M., Rev. | 23 Nov 1889
4 July 1965 | | yes |

| Lee
  William E., Rev. | 21 Feb. 1948 | | no |

  Other Info: Information is from church records.

| Saunder
  Emily | 2 Feb. 1913 | | no |

  Other Info: Information is from church records.

| Saunders
  Lelia | 6 April 1914 | | no |

  Other Info: Information is from church records.

| Saunders
  Lucy | 17 Aug. 1930 | | no |

  Other Info: Information is from church records.

| Smith
  Courtney | 30 April 1934 | | no |

  Other Info: Information is from church records.

| Solomon
  Charlotte Louise Perkins | 29 Aug. 1951
19 May 1985 | | yes |

  Inscription: Daughter

| Taylor
  Walter | 15 Aug. 1902
12 July 1986 | | yes |

  Other Info: Thacker Bros. Funeral Home marker

Last Name Given Name (Maiden Name	Date of Birth Date of Death Age at Death	Spouse	Tombstone
Toney David A., Deacon	19 July 1917		no
Other Info: Information is from church records.			
Toney Jane	1 Sept 1914		no
Other Info: Information is from church records.			
Toney Joseph Lee, Rev.	23 Feb. 1943		no
Other Info: Information is from church records.			
Toney Julia (Price)	29 Aug 1918		no
Other Info: Information is from church records.			
Toney Pearl M.	1900 1974		yes
Tony Jessie E.	27 July 1970		no
Other Info: unidentified funeral home marker			
Tucker Grant	20 Feb. 1920		no
Other Info: Information is from church records.			
Turner Barry M.	1972 1973		no
Other Info: unidentified funeral home marker; Funeral home marker gives the birth date as 1971			
Turner Caroline	16 Oct. 1968	Walker Turner	no

Last Name Given Name (Maiden Name	Date of Birth Date of Death Age at Death	Spouse	Tombstone
Turner Ellen	10 March 1916		no

Other Info: Information is from church records

| Turner
  James "Casey" | 12 June 1970
2 Feb. 2002 | | yes |

Inscription: Always in our Hearts

Other Info: His parents are Moses and Cornelius Turner who are buried at Mourner's Valley Baptist Church cemetery.

| Turner
  James H. | 1921
2001 | | no |

Other Info: Reids Funeral Home marker

| Turner
  James H. (Henry) | 1921
2001 | | no |

Other Info: Reids Funeral Home marker; His parents are Moses and Cornelius Turner who are buried at Mourner's Valley Baptist Church cemetery.

| Turner
  Mary (Willis) | 2 Aug. 1934 | | no |

Other Info: Information is from church records.

| Turner
  Michael | 1957
1976 | | no |

Other Info: unidentified funeral home marker; Michael Turner was the son of James H. Turner and the uncle of Barry M. Turner.

| Turner
  Walker | 19 Aug. 1938 | | no |

Other Info: Information is from church records.

Last Name Given Name (Maiden Name	Date of Birth Date of Death Age at Death	Spouse	Tombstone
Warner 　John H.	1916 1999	(1) Fannie L. Jones Warner, (2) Louise A. Warner	no

Other Info: Reids Funeral Home marker

Warner 　Louise A	16 Feb. 1932 14 Dec. 1979	John H. Warner	yes

Inscription: Mother

Other Info: Reids Funeral Home marker

Warner 　Mariah L.	1937 2000		no

Other Info: Reids Funeral Home marker

White 　Mariah	22 Dec. 1933		no

Other Info: Information is from church records.

Woodson 　Ernest	26 April 1931		no

Other Info: Information is from church records.

Eldridge Family at "Twelve Oaks"

Eldridge 　Jessie Dorothy Elizabeth Greenwood	25 Dec. 1906 29 Jan. 1991	Memorial stone John Eldridge Jr.	

Other Info: She was born in Canada. Upon her death and at her request, she was cremated and some of her ashes were distributed in the Pacific near where her husband died.

Last Name Given Name (Maiden Name)	Date of Birth Date of Death Age at Death	Spouse	Tombstone
Eldridge John	1864 1951	Lillian Eldridge	yes

Other Info: He was the grandson of Rolfe Eldridge Jr. who is buried at "Rolfeton". He and his wife were the parents of (Lt. Cdr) John Eldridge Jr.

Eldridge John Jr.	10 Oct. 1903 2 Nov. 1942	Jessie Dorothy Elizabeth Greenwood Eldgridge	Memorial Stone

Inscription: Lt. Cdr.

Other Info: He died "at sea" during World War II. His body was not recovered. In 1943, a ship, which was a destroyer escort, was commissioned the USS Eldridge in his memory. It was christened by his wife. Sometime in the 1950s it was decommissioned and given to the Greek Navy.

Eldridge Lillian	1877 1946	John Eldridge	yes

Other Info: She and her husband were the parents of (Lt. Cdr.) John Eldridge Jr.

Eldridge Wm. Rolfe	6 Nov. 1911 29 Mar. 1931		yes
Moorman Antoinette Wise Spencer "Nettie"	1872 1946	Henry H. Moorman	no
Moorman Henry H.	1872 1936	Antoinette Wise Spencer Moorman	yes

Inscription: At Rest

Other Info: His sister, Lillian Eldridge is also buried here.

Last Name	Date of Birth	Spouse	Tombstone
Given Name	Date of Death		
(Maiden Name	Age at Death		

Eubanks-Hedgeman Family on US 20 — African American

Eubanks   4 April 1951   yes
    Phyllise Hutcherson 15 Feb. 1970   Terry M. Eubanks

    Other Info: Shares a headstone with her husband.

Eubanks   10 Aug. 1963   yes
    Terry M.   7 June 1984   Phyllise Hutcherson
                                                              Eubanks

    Inscription: Brother

    Other Info: He and his wife share a headstone.

Hedgeman
    Bennie   Polly Hedgeman

    Other Info: Known to be buried here. A freed slave; He and his wife
       are the grandparents of Rev. Curtis Hedgeman.

Hedgeman   no
    Calvin

    Other Info: Known to be buried here.

Hedgeman   no
    Charlie Bennie   1 March 1954
                             69 years

    Other Info: Thacker Bros. Funeral Home marker

Hedgeman   14 June 1899   yes
    Fannie R.   4 Jan. 1969   John E. Hedgeman

    Inscription: Mother

Last Name Given Name (Maiden Name	Date of Birth Date of Death Age at Death	Spouse	Tombstone
Hedgeman John E.	1891 1976	Fannie R. Hedgeman	yes

Inscription: CPL, US Army, World War I

Other Info: He and his wife are the parents of William, Charlie, and Calvin Hedgeman, also buried in this cemetery, and Curtis Hedgeman.

Hedgeman Polly		Bennie Hedgeman	no

Other Info: Known to be buried here-a freed slave; She and her husband are the grandparents of Rev. Curtis Hedgeman.

Hedgeman William MacArthur	1941 2002 60 years		no

Other Info: Thacker Bros. Funeral Home marker

Washington Amanda Hedgeman	15 Sept. 1936 11 March 1987 50 years		no

Other Info: Thacker Bros. Funeral Home marker

Washington infant			no

Other Info: Known to be buried here; the infant son of Amanda H. Washington.

Washington Samuel			no

Other Info: Thacker Bros. Funeral Home marker with one date: 21 Jan. 1956

Last Name Given Name (Maiden Name	Date of Birth Date of Death Age at Death	Spouse	Tombstone
Washington Tony	 4-5 years		no

Other Info: Known to be buried here. He was the son of Amanda H. Washington who is also buried in this cemetery.

There are 16 unidentified graves in this cemetery.

William Evans Family at "Merioneth"

Baker Eliza Y.	 9 Sept. 1830 24 years		no

Inscription: departed this life Sept. 9, 1830 in the 24th year of her age.

Other Info: This is a vault which sits entirely above ground.

Brown Capt. L.	28 May 1780 2/8 Nov. 1850		yes

Inscription: Erected by his widow

Other Info: The tombstone was missing in the cemetery survey done in 2001. It was reported in 3 earlier surveys.

Evans Martha	 6 March 1810 43rd or 13th		yes

Inscription: In Memory of; who died the 6th of March 1810 in the 43rd (or 13th) year of her age.

Evans Mary, Mrs.	2 Feb. 1765 28 Aug. 1810		yes

Inscription: In Memory of

Evans Thomas H.	10 Oct. 1825 7 Oct. 1829		yes

Last Name Given Name (Maiden Name)	Date of Birth Date of Death Age at Death	Spouse	Tombstone
Evans William	1756 1840		no

Other Info: Known to be buried here. He was a Col. in the Revolutionary War. He named his home in Buckingham Co. after an ancestral home in the British Isles. He was born in Burks Co., PA. His children were: Pamelia E. Wyche, Elizabeth E. Hobson, Martha E. Bonsell, Virginia E. Bagby, America E. Allen, James Evans and William M. Evans who was the administrator of the estate.

Gannaway Catharine S.	12 Oct. 1797 22 Jan. 1827 30 years		yes

Inscription: In Memory of; (died) in the 30th year of her age

Gannaway John	1 Oct. 1778 9 Sept. 1838 60 years		yes

Inscription: In Memory of; (died) in the 60 (th) year of his age.

Gannaway Martha H.	19 March 1820 8 March 1825 5 years		yes

Inscription: In Memory of; (died) in the 5th year of her age.

Glover Mary J.	15/16 Aug. 1795 25 June 1839		yes

Inscription: In Memory of

Other Info: Footstone: MJG

Grigg Edward	about 1793 6 July 1860	Harriet H. Grigg	no

Other Info: Known to be buried here.

Last Name Given Name (Maiden Name	Date of Birth Date of Death Age at Death	Spouse	Tombstone
Grigg Harriet H.	3 April (or Aug.) 1837 36 year	Edward Grigg	no

Inscription: (died) in the 36th year of her age

Other Info: This is a vault which sits entirely above ground.

| Grigg
    Peter S. | 23 June 1833
25 Nov. 1855 | | yes |

Other Info: The tombstone was missing in the cemetery survey done in 2001. Reported in 3 earlier surveys.

| Grigg
    Philip N. | 24 May 1864 | | no |

Other Info: He was the son of Edward and Harriet H. Grigg; Died of wounds incurred in the battle at Drewry's Bluff, Civil War.

| Hendrick
    Edith Irene | 7 May 1781
11 March 1840 | | no |

Inscription: Sacred

Other Info: This is a vault which sits entirely above ground.

| Hendrick
    Elijah H. | 19 Aug. 1779
9 April 1820
41 years | | yes |

Inscription: In Memory of; died the 9th of April 1820 in the 41st year of his age.

There are 18 unidentified graves including 5 persons known to be buried who have no stones or markers.

Last Name	Date of Birth	Spouse	Tombstone
Given Name	Date of Death		
(Maiden Name	Age at Death		

Farmville Christian Fellowship — Mennonite

Miller	3 Jan. 1934		yes
John Dan	25 Feb. 1998	Marie Miller	

Inscription: For to me to live as Christ, and to die is gain. Phil. 1:21

Other Info: Has a Shorter Funeral Home marker.

Miller	12 March 1951		yes
Ruth Eichorn	1 Sept. 2002	Monroe Miller	

Inscription: A tender mother and faithful friend; (on back-Blessed are the pure in heart For they shall see God.)

Other Info: Has a Shorter Funeral Home marker.

Shetler	10 Dec. 1977		yes
James	19 Nov. 1986		

Inscription: Safe in the hands of Jesus. Son of Uria(h) and Rachel Shetler.

Swartz	13 Jan. 1937		yes
Edith T. (Troyer)	28 Apr. 1977	Noah Swartz	

Troyer	1913		yes
Amanda	1991	Ezra Troyer	

Inscription: In Loving Memory

Other Info: She and her husband were the parents of Edith T. Swartz and Clara J. Yoder also buried in this cemetery.

Yoder	6 March 1933		yes
Clara J.	11 Jan. 1979	Elvin Yoder	

Last Name Given Name (Maiden Name	Date of Birth Date of Death Age at Death	Spouse	Tombstone

Forbes Family on US 56 — African American

Abril Lucy F. G.	6 Sept 1897 16 Dec. 1955		yes

Other Info: Footstone: LFGA

Forbes Alfred	1867 1946		yes
Forbes Bertha M.	7 July 1908 5 Jan. 1947		yes

Other Info: Footstone: BMF

Forbes Oscar Reed	12 Dec. 1945 56 years, 9 mos., 13 days.		no

Other Info: Dunkum Funeral Home marker

Forbes Sallie	1866 1948		yes
Forbes Susanna B.	1868 1908		yes
Forbes Susie O.			no

Other Info: Unidentified funeral home marker with one date: 8 May 1968

Gillispie Melvin			no

Other Info: Unidentified funeral home marker with one date: 5 Jan. 1966

Last Name	Date of Birth	Spouse	Tombstone
Given Name	Date of Death		
(Maiden Name	Age at Death		

Ford Family off Rd. 652 — African American

Coles
   Mary   no

Other Info: Wharton-Savage Funeral Home marker with no dates.

Ford
   Diamond   no

Other Info: Wharton-Savage Funeral Home marker with no dates.

Ford
   Elizabeth, Miss   24 July 1970   no
                                    98 years

Other Info: Thacker Bros. Funeral Home marker.

Ford
   Emma L., Mrs. (Chambers) 21 Aug. 1965   no
                                                       Grover Harrison Ford
                                76 years

Other Info: Thacker Bros Funeral Home marker

Ford   no
   Grover Harrison   30 June 1954   Emma L. Chambers Ford
                                  80 years

Other Info: Thacker Bros. Funeral Home marker

Ford
   Johnnie   no

Other Info: Wharton- Savage Funeral Home marker with no dates

Last Name Given Name (Maiden Name	Date of Birth Date of Death Age at Death	Spouse	Tombstone
Ford M. Eva	1879 1959		yes

    Inscription: In Memory of; Mother of Rev. L.L. Ford; Gone but not Forgotten

    Other Info: She was also the mother of Grover H. Ford, her youngest child, who also is buried in this cemetery.

| Ford
   Maria | | | no |

    Other Info: Wharton-Savage Funeral Home marker with no dates

| Ford
   Phillip | | | no |

    Other Info: Wharton-Savage Funeral Home marker with no dates.

| Ford
   Rosa Wright | | | no |

    Other Info: Wharton-Savage Funeral Home marker with no dates

| Ford
   Roslyn | | | no |

    Other Info: Wharton-Savage Funeral Home marker with no dates.

| Ford
   William "Will" | | | no |

    Other Info: Thacker Bros Funeral Home marker with no dates. Other members of the Ford family are buried in the Spreading Oak Baptist Church cemetery nearby.

Fork Union Baptist Church — African American

| Agee
   Amanda (Allen) | Dec. 1913
April 1954 | | yes |

Last Name Given Name (Maiden Name	Date of Birth Date of Death Age at Death	Spouse	Tombstone
Agee Caesar Alexander	17 April 1921 6 Nov. 1982		yes

    Inscription: CPL, World War II

    Other Info: Has an above ground vault

| Agee
    Charlie | 1888
1973 | Lelia Agee | yes |

    Other Info: Shares a headstone with his wife.

| Agee
    Floyd Arthur | 12 July 1912
9 Nov. 1999 | | yes |

    Inscription: PVT, US Army, World War II

    Other Info: Reids Funeral Home marker

| Agee
    Lelia | 1894
1978 | Charlie Agee | yes |

    Other Info: Shares a headstone with her husband

| Agee
    Norman Daniel | 3 Oct. 1927
18 May 1998 | | yes |

    Inscription: US Army

    Other Info: Reids Funeral Home marker

| Agee
    Randolph | 21 May 1919
29 June 1975 | | yes |

    Inscription: PVT, US Army, World War II

| Allen
    Helen B. | 1921
1978 | | yes |
| Allen
    Zack Sr. | 1902
1971 | | yes |

Last Name Given Name (Maiden Name	Date of Birth Date of Death Age at Death	Spouse	Tombstone
Bartee Bruce	1909 2000		no

Other Info: Reids Funeral Home marker

| Bartee
  Laureen G. | 1913
1945 | | no |

Other Info: Has an above ground vault.

| Bethel
  Earl E. | 19 Oct. 1926
24 Aug. 1993 | | yes |

Inscription: PVT, US Army, World War II

| Bolling
  Thomas | 1903
1993 | | yes |

Inscription: Rest in Peace

| Booker
  Lou | 1867
1937 | | no |

Other Info: Dunkum Funeral Home marker

| Bradby
  Nannie (Brown) Davis | 1 Oct. 1915
17 April 1990 | | yes |

| Bradley | | | no |

Other Info: Two unmarked graves-known to be buried here: 2 members of the Bradley family.

| Bradley
  A. P. |
8 March 1964 | | no |

Other Info: unidentified funeral home marker

| Branch
  Charles Henry | 19 July 1915
5 June 1949 | | yes |

Inscription: Virginia, PFC, 578 ORD AM Co., World War II

Last Name Given Name (Maiden Name)	Date of Birth Date of Death Age at Death	Spouse	Tombstone
Branch Clara	11 August 1962		no

Other Info: L. C. Gray Funeral Home marker

Brown Bessie G.	1939 2001		no

Other Info: Reids Funeral Home marker

Brown David	1881 1883	Lucy Jones Brown	yes

Inscription: Faithful unto Death

Other Info: Shares a headstone with his wife.

Brown Kenneth Maurice	20 June 1955 8 Aug. 1978		yes

Inscription: SP4, US Army

Brown Lucy (Jones)	1883 1961	David Brown	yes

Inscription: Faithful unto Death

Other Info: Shares a headstone with her husband.

Brown Phillip Matthew	1 Sept. 1908 9 July 1946		yes

Inscription: Staff Sgt, 364 Engrs, World War II

Brown William	1940 2001		no

Other Info: Reids Funeral Home marker

Brown William A.	1910 1990		yes

Inscription: PFC, US Army, World War II

Last Name Given Name (Maiden Name	Date of Birth Date of Death Age at Death	Spouse	Tombstone
Carey Antoinette M.	1981 1999		yes

Inscription: Daughter

Other Info: Reids Funeral Home marker

| Carey
    Calvin Joe | 1964
2000 | | no |

Other Info: E. B. Allen Funeral Home marker

| Carey
    Edna E., Mrs. | 15 Aug. 1925
16 Apr. 1980 | | no |

Other Info: Reids Funeral Home marker

| Carey
    John H. Sr. | 2 Nov. 1910
29 Dec. 2000 | Martha D. Carey | yes |

Other Info: Above ground vault: Reids FH; Shares a headstone with his wife.

| Carey
    Martha D. | 30 June 1917
1 Feb. 2001 | John H. Carey Sr. | yes |

Other Info: Above ground vault: Reids FH; Shares a headstone with her husband.

| Carey
    Robert | 16 April 1962
83 years | | no |

Other Info: unidentified funeral home marker

| Carey
    Tom | 3 Dec. 1907
16 Nov. 1979 | | yes |

Inscription: Now Cometh Eternal Rest

| Carey
    William | 30 May 1966 | | no |

Other Info: unidentified funeral home marker

Last Name Given Name (Maiden Name)	Date of Birth Date of Death Age at Death	Spouse	Tombstone
Carey William E.	1942 1997		yes

Inscription: Husband

Other Info: Reids Funeral Home marker

| Chambers
   Ella W. | 16 Feb. 1895
12 June 1972 | James G. Chambers | yes |

Inscription: Thy Kingdom Come

Other Info: Shares a headstone with her husband.

| Chambers
   George W. | 1913
1998 | | no |

Other Info: unidentified funeral home marker

| Chambers
   James G. | 18 March 1881
15 Jan. 1957 | Ella W. Chambers | yes |

Inscription: Thy Kingdom Come

Other Info: Shares a headstone with his wife.

| Chambers
   Josh | 1 Nov. 1903
21 Dec. 1978 | Eliza Chambers | yes |

| Chambers
   Martha C. | 22 Feb. 1924
15 Oct. 1999 | | no |

Other Info: Above ground vault: Reids FH

| Chambers
   Monroe | 4 July 1894
14 Dec. 1974 | | yes |

Inscription: PVT, US Army

| Chatman
   Glover Jr. | | | yes |

Other Info: Cremation-plaque gives name only

Last Name Given Name (Maiden Name	Date of Birth Date of Death Age at Death	Spouse	Tombstone
Cunningham Andrew			no

Other Info: Reids Funeral Home marker states: Merchant Marines; no dates

| Cuttino
   George, Jr. | 1930
1991 | | yes |

Inscription: US Army, Korea

Other Info: Reids Funeral Home marker

| Davis
   Bessie | 1899
1982 | | no |

Other Info: unidentified funeral home marker

| Davis
   Duane T. | 20 Dec. 1977
3 Jan. 1997 | | yes |

Inscription: Loving Son and Brother

Other Info: Above ground vault: Duane Thomas Davis, 1977 - 1997, Reids FH

| Davis
   Isiah | 9 Dec. 1909
3 July 1940 | | yes |

Inscription: Our Loving Brother, Sisters: Laura and Ruth

| Davis
   Lillie | 1883
1951 | Walter Davis | yes |

Inscription: From the Children

Other Info: Shares a headstone with his wife.

| Davis
   Virginia G. | 29 June 1914
4 Nov. 1980 | | yes |

Last Name Given Name (Maiden Name)	Date of Birth Date of Death Age at Death	Spouse	Tombstone
Davis 　Virginia Mary	1937 1952		yes

Inscription: Gone but not Forgotten

Davis 　Walter	1885 1953	Lillie Davis	yes

Inscription: From the Children

Other Info: Shares a headstone with her husband.

Day 　Mary F. (Johnson)	7 May 1909 20 Oct. 1995		yes

Inscription: Rest in Peace

Dryer 　Rebecca C.	1913 1999		no

Other Info: Reids Funeral Home marker

Fitzgerald 　F.	1892 1982		yes

Other Info: Also has a Reids Funeral Home marker

Fitzgerald 　Mar	1893 1982		yes

Other Info: Reids Funeral Home marker

Forbes 　Alfred J.	16 May 1904 10 May 1979		yes

Inscription: Rest in Peace

Other Info: Has an above ground vault.

Forbes 　Penelope L.	5 June 1910 17 March 1998		yes

Inscription: Wife, Rest in Peace

Last Name Given Name (Maiden Name	Date of Birth Date of Death Age at Death	Spouse	Tombstone
Fuller Daisy (Davis)	9 July 1929 28 Jan 1999		yes

Inscription: Much Loved

Other Info: Reids Funeral Home marker

| Garrett
    Anderson Wert | 23 July 1911
30 Sept. 1999 | | yes |

Inscription: TEC 5, US Army, World War II

| Garrett
    Arthur W. | 24 April 1907
2 May 1971 | | yes |

Inscription: PFC, US Army, World War II

| Garrett
    Barbara Ann | 22 Feb. 1959
14 Sept. 1959 | | yes |

Inscription: Asleep in Jesus

Other Info: Funeral Marker gives birthdate as 6 Feb. 1959, and death date as 14 Aug. 1959

| Garrett
    John Ed | 16 July 1877
24 Dec. 1936 | | yes |

Inscription: Father, At Rest

| Garrett
    John Wesley | 9 July 1917
28 Dec. 1994 | | yes |

Inscription: US Navy, World War II

| Garrett
    Mary E. | 26 Sept. 1906
7 Mar. 1979 | | yes |

Inscription: Rest in Peace

| Garrett
    Robert A. Sr. | 11 Dec. 1922
2 Sept. 1988 | | yes |

Inscription: Asleep in Jesus

Last Name Given Name (Maiden Name	Date of Birth Date of Death Age at Death	Spouse	Tombstone
Garrett Sarah E.	3 Jan. 1888 11 June 1958		yes

Inscription: At Rest

| Gillispie
  Emma C. | 29 June 1930
3 July 2000 | | no |

Other Info: Above ground vault: Bruce and Stiff FH

| Glover
  Bessie N. | 1900
1958 | | no |

Other Info: Reids Funeral Home marker

| Glover
  Frank Eugene | 10 Feb. 1929
16 Jan. 1993 | | yes |

| Glover
  George A. | 1936
2000 | | yes |

Other Info: Reids Funeral Home marker

| Glover
  Howard Jr. | | | no |

Other Info: Reids Funeral Home marker: dates are illegible

| Glover
  Howard Jr. | | | no |

Other Info: Known to be buried here

| Glover
  Howard Sr. | | | no |

Other Info: Known to be buried here.

| Glover
  John | 1946
1990 | | no |

Other Info: Reids Funeral Home marker

Last Name Given Name (Maiden Name)	Date of Birth Date of Death Age at Death	Spouse	Tombstone
Governor Augustine E. (Fields)	9 June 1901 23 March 1958	Onizene A. Governor	yes

Inscription: Rest in Peace

Green James R.	11 Nov. 1918 11 Oct. 1975		yes

Inscription: PVT, US Army, World War II

Hudgins James Edward	31 Dec. 1898 28 Dec. 1981	Sallie Ann Hudgins	yes

Inscription: In Loving Memory

Other Info: Shares a headstone with his wife.

Hudgins Sallie Ann	17 Nov. 1907 14 Jan. 1980	James Edward Hudgins	yes

Inscription: In Loving Memory

Other Info: Shares a headstone with her husband.

Johnson Abraham Jr.	22 Jan. 1916 27 Feb. 1980	Mary S. Johnson	yes

Inscription: To God We Entrust

Johnson Lucille	28 July, 1940 19 April, 1999		no

Other Info: Reids Funeral Home marker

Johnson Mary S.	3 Feb. 1918 21 June 1981	Abraham Johnson, Jr.	yes

Inscription: To God We Entrust

Last Name Given Name (Maiden Name	Date of Birth Date of Death Age at Death	Spouse	Tombstone
Johnson Thomas L.	1911 1988		no

Other Info: Parks Funeral Home marker (out of state); Thomas L. Johnson was the brother of Abraham Johnson, Jr.

Jones Charles (Chuck)	1899 1987		no

Other Info: unidentified funeral home marker

Jones Clara	 25 Oct. 1941		yes

Inscription: Blessed are the Dead in the Lord

Jones Eddie Nathaniel	18 June 1913 29 Jan. 1996		yes

Inscription: US Navy, World War II

Jones Lawrence P. E.	1944 1978	 Mildred Branch Jones	yes

Inscription: Father; married 19 June 1965

Other Info: Shares a headstone with his wife.

Jones Lelia B.	1939 1998		yes

Inscription: Loving Mother and Grandmother

Jones Mildred (Branch)	1947 1976	 Lawrence P.E. Jones	yes

Inscription: Mother; married 19 June 1965

Other Info: Shares a headstone with her husband.

Jones Sarah	 1 August 1956		no

Other Info: L. C. Gray Funeral Home marker

Last Name Given Name (Maiden Name	Date of Birth Date of Death Age at Death	Spouse	Tombstone
Lewis Alene A.	21 Oct. 1913 8 July 1990	Emmitt L. Lewis	yes

Inscription: Thy Kingdom Come

| Lewis
    Hilda J. | 6 June 1937
8 May 1994 | | no |

Other Info: Reids Funeral Home marker

| Lewis
    John O. | 1893
1973 | | yes |

Inscription: Gone but not Forgotten

| Lyle
    Pattie | 1905
1980 | | yes |

Inscription: At Peace

| Mays
    Elisha | | | no |

Other Info: unidentified funeral home marker with no dates

| Mays
    Lucille (Agee) | 23 Dec. 1910
11 May 1991 | Willie A. Mays | yes |

Other Info: Shares a headstone with her husband.

| Mays
    Milicent C. | 1896
1994 | | no |

Other Info: unidentified funeral home marker

| Mays
    Riley | | | no |

Other Info: Known to be buried here.

| Mays
    W. I. E. | 1927
1945 | | yes |

Last Name Given Name (Maiden Name	Date of Birth Date of Death Age at Death	Spouse	Tombstone
Mays 　Walter			

　　Other Info: Known to be buried here.

Mays 　Willie A.	23 Nov. 1907 14 April 1988	Lucille Agee Mays	yes

　　Other Info: Shares a headstone with his wife.

Miller 　Virginia W.	1886 1968		yes

　　Inscription: At Rest

　　Other Info: Unidentified funeral home marker: Virginia L. Miller, died
　　　　June 27, 1968

Monroe 　Raymond K.	1929 1949		yes

Oliver 　Carrie (Jones)	1889 1987	Hugh Oliver	yes

　　Other Info: Shares a headstone with her husband.

Oliver 　Chapman	31 Oct 1958		yes

　　Other Info: L. C. Gray Funeral Home marker

Oliver 　Chatman J. Sr.	17 Nov. 1913 22 Dec. 1983		yes

　　Inscription: PFC, US army, World War II

Oliver 　Henry R.	1910 1974		yes

　　Inscription: Our Brother

Last Name Given Name (Maiden Name	Date of Birth Date of Death Age at Death	Spouse	Tombstone
Oliver Herbert	16 Jan. 1915 13 July 1998		yes

Inscription: US Army, World War II, Purple Heart

Oliver Hugh	1887 1971	Carrie Jones	yes

Other Info: Shares a headstone with his wife. Has a Reids Funeral Home marker.

Oliver John Thomas	27 Aug. 1911 9 Jan. 1991		yes

Inscription: Have Faith in God

Other Info: Reids Funeral Home marker

Oliver Lawrence Calvin	18 Jan. 1922 10 Dec. 1991		yes

Inscription: In Loving Memory

Oliver Mary A.	12 Sept. 1908 22 Jan. 1979		yes
Oliver Minnie S.	21 Nov. 1913 19 Oct. 1988		yes

Inscription: Mother

Oliver Nannie	1890 1968		yes

Inscription: Our Mother

Oliver Thelma T.	14 May 1907 21 Feb. 1990		yes
Peaks Effie, Mrs.	18 Jan. 1993		yes

Last Name Given Name (Maiden Name)	Date of Birth Date of Death Age at Death	Spouse	Tombstone
Peaks John	14 Jan. 1978		yes

Inscription: American Veteran

Other Info: Wm. N. Bland Funeral Home marker

Perkins Annie	June 1893 22 March 1953		yes
Perkins Catherine (Daniel)	27 May 1897 19 Dec. 1974		yes
Porter Lawton Charles	16 Sept. 1932 14 April 1996		yes

Inscription: SSG, US Army, Korea, Vietnam

Seay Bernard	1902 1973	Grace E. Seay	yes
Seay Linwood	1924 1987		yes

Inscription: PFC, US Army, World War II

Simms Laura			no

Other Info: C. M. Robinson Funeral Home marker

Terrell Elizabeth J.	8 June 1891 22 Feb. 1968		yes

Inscription: The Rose May Fade, The Lily Die, But the Flowers Immortal Bloom on High.

Williams Evelyn M.	7 Aug. 1931 9 April 2000		yes
Wilson Adelaide	1883 1966		yes

Inscription: At Rest

Last Name Given Name (Maiden Name	Date of Birth Date of Death Age at Death	Spouse	Tombstone
Woodson Charlie E. Sr.	1925 2000		no

Other Info: Reids Funeral Home marker

| Woodson
   Lillian W. (Saunders) | 8 Oct. 1935
11 Jan. 1992 | | yes |

Inscription: Children's names (on back of headstone): Gary, Carolyn, Shawn, William, Gloria, James, Doretha, Lydia

| Woodson
   Marques | 1995
1995 | | yes |

| Woodson
   Ruby (Carey) | 22 Sept. 1903
9 Oct. 1988 | | yes |

Inscription: Beloved Mother

Other Info: Reids Funeral Home marker

| Woodson
   Sarah Irene | 24 April 1930
3 Oct. 1953 | | yes |

Inscription: Mother, at Rest

Other Info: Unidentified funeral home marker gives death date as 8 Oct. 1958

| Yates
   F. D., Rev. | 4 March 1898
9 Dec. 1976 | | yes |

Inscription: Blessed are the Dead, Rest From Their Labors-Rev. 14:13
Vault: Rev. F. D. Yates, 1898-1976

There are approximately 30 visible graves which have not been identified in this cemetery.

Last Name	Date of Birth	Spouse	Tombstone
Given Name	Date of Death		
(Maiden Name)	Age at Death		

Sidney Fountain Grave on Rd. 627

| Fountain | 20 May 1890 | | yes |
| Sidney | 23 Oct. 1966 | | |

Inscription: Air Service, World War I

Francisco Family at "Locust Grove"

| Francisco | | | no |
| male child | | | |

Other Info: Known to be buried here, the son of Peter Francisco, the Revolutionary War hero.

Garrett Family off Rd. 699

Banton	12 June 1885		yes
Belle (Godsey Newton)	21 March 1987	(1) James Alfred Newton	
		(2) Emmett Elwood Banton	

Other Info: Has a Dunkum Funeral Home marker.

| Banton | | | yes |
| Charles (Lafayette) | | Isabelle Garrett Banton | |

Inscription: Co. B, 20 VA INF, CSA (no dates)

| Banton | 1897 | | yes |
| Emmett Elwood | 1979 | Belle Godsey Newton Banton | |

Inscription: PFC, US Army, World War I

Last Name Given Name (Maiden Name	Date of Birth Date of Death Age at Death	Spouse	Tombstone
Banton John R.	18 March 1856 29 March 1925	Mary Marie Garrett Banton	yes

Inscription: May he rest in peace.

Other Info: Footstone: JRB

Banton Lattie A.	10 March 1898 31 March 1915	Etched Fieldstone	
Banton Mary Lou	14 Oct. 1903 16 Aug. 1932		yes
Banton Mattie	16 June 1903 24 Jan. 1972		yes
Banton Susie R.			yes

Inscription: (no dates)

| Banton
  Walker E. | 18 April 1870
7 Feb. 1930 | Christina Rebecca
Garrett | yes |
| Childress
  Emmett L. | 2 Sept. 1896
4 March 1956 | | yes |

Inscription: Virginia, PVT, Co. C, 130 ENG BN, World War I

| Childress
  Fannie B. | 29 May 1879
19 May 1953 | | yes |
| Childress
  Jackson | 5 Oct. 1900
11 July 1973 | | yes |

Inscription: Rest in Peace

Other Info: Has a Dunkum Funeral Home marker; He was the son of Joseph Childress, also buried in this cemetery.

Last Name Given Name (Maiden Name	Date of Birth Date of Death Age at Death	Spouse	Tombstone
Childress 　Joseph	16 Dec. 1861 10 May 1936		yes

　　Other Info: He was the father of Jackson Childress also buried in this cemetery.

| Childress
　Virginia A. | 2 May 1895
28 Nov. 1915 | | yes |

　　Inscription: No pains, no cries, no anxious fear can reach our loved one sleeping here.

　　Other Info: Footstone: VAC

| Garrett
　Aubrey Rolf | 1 Dec. 1908
19 Nov. 1971 | | yes |
| Garrett
　Ella O'Bryant | 13 Oct. 1887
25 Sept. 1953 | George Rolf Garrett | yes |

　　Inscription: In my Father's House are many Mansions.

　　Other Info: Shares a headstone with her husband.

| Garrett
　George Rolf | 12 Nov. 1879
29 Jan. 1953 | Ella O'Bryant Garrett | yes |

　　Inscription: In my Father's House are Many Mansions

　　Other Info: Shares a headstone with his wife.

| Garrett
　Geo. Washington | 14 March 1836
29 March 1895 | Louisa W. Gormus Garrett | yes |

　　Other Info: CSA, 21st Va. Inf. Co. E. He was the father of Annie L. Moss also buried in the cemetery.

| Garrett
　Landon Levi Sr. | 28 May 1919
18 March 1993 | | yes |
| Garrett
　Larry Melvin | 30 Sept. 1922
(2) Aug. 1923 | | yes |

Last Name Given Name (Maiden Name	Date of Birth Date of Death Age at Death	Spouse	Tombstone
Garrett Louisa Walker Gormus	3 Aug. 1843 19 July 1917	Geo. Washington Garrett	no

Other Info: Known to be buried here. Her parents were Augustus and Rebecca Whitlo Gormas also buried in this cemetery.

Garrett Roy Garland	12 June 1914 30 Aug. 1991		yes

Other Info: Footstone: Roy Garland Garrett, PFC, US Army, World War II (same dates as are on the headstone)

Gormas Augustus	27 July 1832 18 July 1913		yes

Inscription: His toils are past, his work is done. He fought the fight, the victory won.

Other Info: Footstone: A.G.

Gormas Rebecca Whitlo		Augustus Gormas	no

Other Info: Known to be buried here.

Moss Annie L. (Lillian) (Garrett)	20 Feb. 1877 13 April 1909	W.R. Moss	yes

Inscription: In Memory of; Married W.R. Moss Nov. 16, 1893

Other Info: Her parents were Geo. Wash. Garrett and Louisa G. Garrett

Moss Fitzhugh Lee	19 April 1898 11 May 1899		yes

Moss William Reeves	15 June 1871 10 Dec. 1955	Annie L. Garrett Moss	no

Other Info: Known to be buried here.

Newton George R.	18 June 1901 14 Feb. 1904		yes

Last Name Given Name (Maiden Name)	Date of Birth Date of Death Age at Death	Spouse	Tombstone
Newton Willie M. "Jack in the Box"	1919 2000		yes

    Other Info: Has a Dunkum Funeral Home marker

Vaughan Lucille Garrett	12 Aug. 1912 6 March 1986		yes

Gilbert-Bagby Family at Sliders

Bagby 2 infants			no

    Other Info: Known to be buried here, 2 infant daughters of William R. Bagby (also buried in this cemetery) and Nannie Sue Perrow Bagby.

Bagby William Riley	Nov. 1852 20 May 1906	Nannie Sue Perrow Bagby	yes

    Inscription: Father

    Other Info: His parents were Josiah J. and Judith Albina G. Bagby. His mother is also buried in this cemetery.

Gilbert Joseph C.	8 Jan. 1894		Etched fieldstone

    Inscription: JCG

Gilbert Judith Albina (Elbinah)	about 1825 31 May 1895	Josiah J. Bagby	yes

    Inscription: Dau. of Humphrey and Paulina Gilbert

    Other Info: At the head of the grave of Judith A. Gilbert is an etched fieldstone: JAB, 31 May 1895. The tombstone is at the foot of her grave (on the back of the William Riley Gilbert stone). She was his mother. He is buried at her feet.

Last Name Given Name (Maiden Name	Date of Birth Date of Death Age at Death	Spouse	Tombstone
Gilbert Leanna F.	Etched fieldstone: LFG Died 14 May 1879 14 May 1879		
Gilbert Sophia Jane	about 1881-1886		no

Other Info: Known to be buried here. She was the sister of Leanna F. Gilbert also buried in this cemetery.

Gilbert William P.	Jan. 1820 (10) Sept. 1886		yes

Inscription: PVT, Company E, 11th VA Inf., CSA

Other Info: Has an etched fieldstone: WPG, Deceased 10 Sept. 1886.

R. H. Gilliam Family on Rd. 644

Gilliam Ann Steger	Nov. 1844 19 Feb. 1934	Robert Hendricks Gilliam	no

Other Info: Known to be buried here.

Gilliam Robert Hendricks "Big Bob"	21 March 1915	Ann Steger Gilliam	yes

Inscription: CSA

Other Info: Military tombstone placed in 1999.

Gilliam Robert Isham "Little Bob"	2 May 1882 17 Oct. 1913		no

Other Info: Known to be buried here. His parents were Robert H. and Ann Steger Gilliam.

Gilliam Sidney	infant		no

Other Info: Known to be buried here. He was the grandson of Robert H. and Ann Steger Gilliam.

Last Name Given Name (Maiden Name)	Date of Birth Date of Death Age at Death	Spouse	Tombstone
Gilliam 　Sidney Branch	9 April 1873 4 April 1888		no

Other Info: Known to be buried here. His parents were Robert H. and Ann Steger Gilliam.

Gilliam 　Susan Ellen	(12 July 1873) 22 March 1955 81 years 8 months, 10 days		no

Other Info: Unidentified funeral home marker. Her parents were Robert H. and Ann Steger Gilliam.

Glenmore United Methodist Church

Adcock 　Albert Thomas	23 June 1932 8 March 1989	Dorothy Taylor Adcock	yes

Inscription: In My Fahters House Are Many Mansions.

Other Info: He and Dorothy Taylor Adcock were the parents of Buford S. and Ray Murphy Adcock.

Adcock 　Betty B. (Ballowe)	22 Mar. 1923 13 Mar. 1995	Tucker R. Adcock Sr.	yes

Inscription: Mother

Other Info: Shares a headstone with her husband.

Adcock 　Buford S.	4 June 1924 28 Feb. 1985		yes

Inscription: CPL, US Army, World War II

Adcock 　Daniel M.	10 April 1927 19 July 1968		yes

Inscription: PVT, US Army, Korea

Last Name Given Name (Maiden Name	Date of Birth Date of Death Age at Death	Spouse	Tombstone
Adcock George			no

Other Info: Name is on a brass marker at grave site. He is the brother of Walker Adcock., also buried in this cemetery.

| Adcock
James Willis Sr. | 4 Jan. 1937
12 Feb. 2001 | | yes |

| Adcock
Lindsey | | | no |

Other Info: Name is on a brass marker at grave site.

| Adcock
Minnie | | Walker Adcock | no |

Other Info: Name is on a brass marker at grave site.

| Adcock
Morton B. | 7 March 1881
29 Dec. 1953 | | yes |

Other Info: Footstone: Husband

| Adcock
Ray Murphy | 20 Feb. 1939
25 July 1997 | Delores Baker Adcock | yes |

| Adcock
Sarah A. (Adcock) | 4 Feb. 1897
24 Dec. 1962 | Willis L. | yes |

Other Info: Shares a headstone with her husband.

| Adcock
Tucker R. Sr. | 8 March 1919
12 July 1990 | Betty Ballowe Adcock | yes |

Inscription: Father

Other Info: Shares a headstone with his wife.

| Adcock
Walker | | Minnie Adcock | no |

Other Info: Name is on a brass marker at grave site.

Last Name Given Name (Maiden Name	Date of Birth Date of Death Age at Death	Spouse	Tombstone
Adcock Willis L.	11 Sept. 1893 29 March 1964	Sarah (Adcock) Adcock	yes

Other Info: Shares a headstone with his wife. They were the parents of Daniel M. Adcock, James Willis Adcock Sr., and Pearl Adcock Hackett.

Ballowe Charles E.	12 May 1908 12 Feb. 1983	Ruby Duncan Ballowe	yes

Inscription: Forever in our Hearts

Other Info: He was the sibling of Norman E. Ballowe and Margie B. Wallace.

Ballowe Norman E.	1932 1960		yes

Beasley Bertha Ragland	22 June 1896 14 Oct. 1960	Emmett W. Beasley	yes

Other Info: Footstone: Mother; Shares a headstone with her husband.

Beasley Calwell W.	27 Nov. 1916 5 Feb. 1995		yes

Inscription: Fl, US Navy

Other Info: His parents were Emmett W. and Bertha Ragland Beasley.

Beasley Ella (Ragland)		Robert L. Beasley	no

Other Info: This is a brass plate inscribed with name only to mark the grave site. She was the sister of Joseph Ragland.

Beasley Emmett W.	20 May 1891 7 June 1961	Bertha Ragland Beasley	yes

Inscription: No Parting in Heaven

Other Info: Footstone: Father; Shares a headstone with his wife.

Last Name Given Name (Maiden Name)	Date of Birth Date of Death Age at Death	Spouse	Tombstone
Beasley Etta May	8 Nov. 1891 13 Aug. 1968	Thomas Beasley	yes

Other Info: Shares a headstone with her husband.

Beasley Melvin Carl	14 April 1930 17 Dec. 1961		yes

Inscription: Virginia, BM2, US Navy

Beasley Robert Gene	2 May 1960 1 July 1989		yes
Beasley Robert L.		Ella Ragland Beasley	no

Other Info: This is a brass plate inscribed with name only to mark the grave site.

Beasley Ruby M.			no

Other Info: This is a brass plate inscribed with name only to mark the grave site.

Beasley Thomas	21 June 1888 4 July 1971	Etta May Beasley	yes

Other Info: Shares a headstone with his wife.

Bragg Edwin D.	14 May 1861 15 June 1945	Mary E. Ragland Bragg	yes

Other Info: Shares a headstone with his wife.

Bragg J. Russell	26 Aug. 1903 16 Aug. 1984	Jennie R. Bragg	yes

Inscription: Wedding Date: 4 Aug. 1934

Other Info: Shares a headstone with his wife.

Last Name Given Name (Maiden Name)	Date of Birth Date of Death Age at Death	Spouse	Tombstone
Bragg Jennie R.	21 May 1915 5 Nov. 2001	J. Russell Bragg	yes

Inscription: Wedding Date: 4 Aug. 1934

Other Info: Shares a headstone with her husband

Bragg Mary E. (Ragland)	11 March 1869 15 Nov. 1910	Edwin D. Bragg	yes

Other Info: Shares a headstone with her husband. She was the sister of Connie Ragland Londeree.

Brown Alma A.	2 July 1900 20 Aug. 1964	George Brown	yes

Brown Annie E. (Elizabeth) (Ragland)	24 April 1911 1 Nov. 2000	Elliott S. Brown	yes

Other Info: Shares a headstone with her husband. She was the daughter of Thomas and Alice Ragland and the sister of Lula Ragland Garland.

Brown Elliott S.	17 May 1893 6 March 1972	Annie Elizabeth Ragland Brown	yes

Other Info: Shares a headstone with his wife.

Bryant Clifford Earl	16 Nov. 1926 1 Feb. 1999	Lillie Byrd Bryant	yes

Inscription: A Good Man

Other Info: His parents were Grace Farrish Bryant and Harry Bryant

Bryant Emma Londeree	30 Oct. 1914 2 April 2000	Harry Willard Bryant	yes

Inscription: Mother

Other Info: Shares a headstone with her husband. Her parents were Charles L. and Connie B. Londeree.

Last Name Given Name (Maiden Name	Date of Birth Date of Death Age at Death	Spouse	Tombstone
Bryant Grace Farrish	20 March 1904 5 Jan. 1993	Harry Bryant	yes

Other Info: Shares a headstone with her husband.

Bryant Harry	5 Aug. 1905 12 Oct. 1991	Grace Farrish Bryant	yes

Other Info: Shares a headstone with his wife.

Bryant Harry Willard	29 Sept. 1916 8 July 1976	Emma Londeree Bryant	yes

Inscription: Father

Other Info: Shares a headstone with his wife. His parents were Ralph E. and Sallie R. Bryant.

Bryant James Ralph "Jimmie"	13 Sept. 1952 5 Nov. 1992	Judy Bryant	yes

Inscription: Father; He was an inspiration to us all.

Other Info: He was the son of Harry Willard Bryant and Emma Londeree Bryant.

Bryant Ralph Eldridge	23 Oct. 1888 3 Dec. 1968	Sallie Ragland Bryant	yes

Other Info: Shares a headstone with his wife.

Bryant Sallie (Ragland)	27 July 1888 5 Oct. 1963	Ralph Eldridge Bryant	yes

Other Info: Shares a headstone with her husband.

Burcher Earl B.	1909 1985		yes

Last Name Given Name (Maiden Name)	Date of Birth Date of Death Age at Death	Spouse	Tombstone
Camden Rebecca A. Miller	13 Nov. 1858 21 Aug. 1924	Walter T. Camden	yes

Other Info: Shares a headstone with her husband. She was the sister of Susannah Walker Miller, also buried in this cemetery.

Camden Walter T.	30 Jan. 1860 18 Feb. 1926	Rebecca A. Miller Camden	yes

Other Info: Shares a headstone with his wife.

Daniel Myrtle Miller	15 May 1895 16 April 1964	Thomas Dabney Daniel	yes

Other Info: Shares a headstone with her husband.

Daniel Thomas Dabney	14 Oct. 1890 6 March 1950	Myrtle Miller Daniel	yes

Other Info: Military Footstone: Virginia, PVT, Co. F, 5th Bn, Repl. Tr. Center, Camp Lee, VA, World War I; Shares a headstone with his wife.

Duncan Rosa B. (Ballowe)	21 April 1911 1 Nov. 2000		yes

Other Info: Shares a headstone with Ernest D. Palmore and Tyler M. Duncan.

Duncan Tyler M.	6 Oct. 1916 17 July 1981		yes

Other Info: Shares a headstone with Ernest D. Palmore and Rosa B. Duncan.

Eanes Edward L.	1885 1946	Pearl M.	yes

Other Info: Shares a headstone with his wife. They are the parents of Oliver, Fred, Lynn, Helen, Lena, Ruby and Edward Eanes.

Last Name Given Name (Maiden Name	Date of Birth Date of Death Age at Death	Spouse	Tombstone
Eanes Fred T.	23 Jan. 1926 18 Aug. 1993	Sylvia Ann (Miller) Eanes	yes

Inscription: S1 US Navy, World War II

| Eanes
  Oliver W. | 20 Mlay 1915
14 June 1973 | | yes |

Inscription: Virginia, PVT, US Army, World War II

Other Info: Also has a military footstone which has the same inscription.

| Eanes
  Pearl M. | 1890
1979 | Edward L. Eanes | yes |

Other Info: Shares a headstone with her husband.

| Eanes
  Sylvia Ann (Miller) | 16 Sept. 1931
23 Dec. 1999 | Fred. T. Eanes | yes |

Inscription: Mama Ann

| Farrish
  Joyce (Bryant) | 18 Dec. 1937
22 Dec. 1997 | Shirley D. Farrish | yes |

Inscription: Married 4 Feb. 1956

Other Info: She was the daughter of Harry W. and Emma Londeree Bryant.

| Gregory
  Clinton H. | 18 May 1874
28 Jan. 1966 | Cora L. Gregory | yes |

Other Info: Shares a headstone with his wife.

| Gregory
  Cora L. | 18 Sept. 1879
3 Nov. 1955 | Clinton H. Gregory | yes |

Other Info: Shares a headstone with her husband.

Last Name Given Name (Maiden Name	Date of Birth Date of Death Age at Death	Spouse	Tombstone
Hackett Barbara (A.) R. (Ragland)	16 May 1939 6 Jan. 2000	Dennis M. Hackett	yes

Inscription: Married 12 Jan. 1957; With all my love

Other Info: She shares a headstone with her husband; Her parents were Garland and Louise Ragland also buried in this cemetery.

Hackett Dennis M.	14 Oct. 1935 6 Jan. 2000	Barbara A. Ragland Hackett	yes

Inscription: Married Jan. 12, 1957, with all my love.

Other Info: Shares a headstone with his wife; Family records show the birth year as 1933; His parents were Thomas Edmund Hackett and Bessie Wade Hackett.

Hackett Edmund W. (Word)	24 April 1929 29 Dec. 1981	Pearl Adcock Hackett	yes

Inscription: CPL, US Army, Korea

Other Info: His parents were Thomas E. Hackett and Bessie Wade Hackett.

Hackett Henry	3 June 1936 19 Sept. 1987		yes

Inscription: Brother

Hackett Otis Lee	3 Oct. 1934 20 Oct. 2004	Shirley Astroth Hackett	yes

Other Info: He was the brother of Henry Hackett (1936-1987).

Hackett Pearl Adcock	15 May 1929 5 Sept. 1995	Edmund W. Hackett	yes

Harris Edith Miller	27 Sept. 1904 28 Mar. 1998	Francis Tilden Harris	yes

Other Info: Shares a headstone with her husband.

Last Name Given Name (Maiden Name	Date of Birth Date of Death Age at Death	Spouse	Tombstone
Harris Francis Tilden	10 Sept. 1906 1 Jan. 1977	Edith Miller Harris	yes

Other Info: Footstone: Father; Shares a headstone with his wife.

Johnson James R.	22 March 1905 19 May 1980	Nellie V. Ross Johnson	yes

Other Info: Shares a headstone with his wife.

Johnson Nellie V. (Ross)	13 Sept. 1911 24 Dec. 2001	James R. Johnson	yes

Other Info: Shares a headstone with her husband.

Jones Minnie J. (Stinson)	1854 1904	William A. Jones	yes

Other Info: Shares a headstone with her husband and his 2nd wife.

Jones Nora J. (Steger)	1879 1948	William A. Jones	yes

Other Info: Shares a headstone with her husband and his first wife.

Jones William A.	1855 1913	(1) Minnie J. Stinson Jones, (2) Nora J. Steger Jones	yes

Other Info: Shares a headstone with both his wives.

Leebrick Elsie I. Ballowe	13 Feb. 1886 10 Sept. 1946	William Henry Leebrick	yes

Other Info: Footstone: E.B.L.

Leebrick William Henry	18 Oct. 1883 14 Dec. 1954	Elsie I. Ballowe Leebrick	yes

Other Info: Footstone: W.H.L.

Last Name Given Name (Maiden Name	Date of Birth Date of Death Age at Death	Spouse	Tombstone
Londeree Charles L.	22 Sept. 1849 17 Feb. 1926	Connie B. Ragland Londeree	yes

Other Info: Shares a headstone with his wife.

Londeree Connie B. (Ragland)	25 Sept. 1884 29 July 1962	Charles L. Londeree	yes

Other Info: Shares a headstone with her husband. They were the parents of Evelyn Vernell Ragland and Emma Londeree Bryant.

Londeree Lillie L. (Adcock)			no

Other Info: This is a brass plate inscribed only with the name to mark the grave site.

Londeree Luther E.			no

Other Info: This is a brass plate inscribed with name only to mark the grave site. His parents were Charles L. and Connie B. Londeree.

Londeree Massie C. (Cabell)	16 March 1893 4 May 1967		yes

Inscription: Virginia, PVT, US Army, World War I

March Edward			no

Other Info: This is a brass plate inscribed with name only to mark the grave site.

Maxey Mary P.	15 April 1904 28 Jan. 1990	William Jennings Maxey	yes
Maxey William Jennings	15 Dec. 1895 8 June 1978	Mary P. Maxey	yes

Last Name Given Name (Maiden Name	Date of Birth Date of Death Age at Death	Spouse	Tombstone
Miles Clara Bragg	30 Sept. 1890 18 Apr. 1978	 Thomas J. Miles	yes

Other Info: Footstone: C.B.M.; Shares a headstone with her husband.

| Miles
   Edward Jackson Jr. | 5 Aug. 1943
14 May 1944 | | yes |

Inscription: Our Darling; A Little bud of Love to Bloom with God Above

Other Info: He was the son of Mabel Ragland Miles and Kenneth Wayne Miles.

| Miles
   James Cook | 15 Apr. 1921
25 Oct. 1999 |
Louise Stanley Miles | yes |

Inscription: In Loving Memory; Married 9 Nov. 1957, With All My Love

Other Info: Shares a headstone with his wife. He was the son of Clara Bragg Miles and Thomas J. Miles.

| Miles
   Kenneth Wayne | 25 March 1950
24 June 1994 |
Mabel Ragland Miles | yes |

| Miles
   Louise Stanley | 25 Nov. 1938
Oct. 2005 |
James Cook Miles | yes |

Other Info: Shares a headstone with her husband.

| Miles
   Lucy D. | 3 Nov. 1854
15 Sept. 1929 | | yes |

| Miles
   Mabel Ragland | 27 Nov. 1924
5 April 1997 |
Kenneth Wayne Miles | yes |

| Miles
   Thomas J. | 1867
1943 |
Clara Bragg Miles | yes |

Other Info: Footstone: T.J.M.; Shares a headstone with his wife.

| Miller
   Agnes W. (Williams) | 2 Jan. 1886
5 Dec. 1961 |
William T. Miller | yes |

Other Info: Shares a headstone with her husband.

Last Name Given Name (Maiden Name	Date of Birth Date of Death Age at Death	Spouse	Tombstone
Miller Flossie Self	20 Feb. 1898 6 Oct. 1985		yes
Miller Frank W.	26 Dec. 1885 10 May 1960		yes
Miller Jake R.	25 July 1899 13 Sept. 1930		yes
Miller John G.	28 Oct. 1853 8 Dec. 1922		yes

Inscription: To Know Him is to Love Him

Other Info: Footstone: J. G. M.; John G., Jake R. and William T. Miller were all brothers. Edith Miller Harris was their sister.

Miller Joseph D. (Jack)	22 July 1919 18 Dec. 1973		yes

Other Info: Joseph D. Miller was the foster child of William T. and Agnes W. Miller.

Miller Mary E. Jones	17 Aug. 1856 1 May 1935	Thomas E. Miller	yes

Other Info: Shares a headstone with her husband and son.

Miller Mary Lucy	10 Dec. 1860 3 Jan. 1955		yes
Miller Percy Ross	12 Sept. 1876 16 March 1939		yes

Other Info: Shares a headstone with his parents.

Miller Susannah Walker	9 Nov. 1981 9 Aug. 1936		yes

Last Name Given Name (Maiden Name	Date of Birth Date of Death Age at Death	Spouse	Tombstone
Miller 　Thomas E.	3 Nov. 1847 5 Oct. 1906	Mary E. Jones	yes

Other Info: Shares a headstone with his wife and son.

| Miller
　William S. | 20 April 1896
12 Feb. 1967 | | yes |

Inscription: Virginia, Wagoner, 401 Engr. Pon Park, World War I

| Miller
　William T. | 3 March 1884
8 Oct. 1967 | Agnes Williams Miller | yes |

Other Info: Shares a headstone with his wife.

| Moon
　Fitch | | Virginia Moon | no |

Other Info: Name is on a brass marker at grave site.

| Moon
　Virginia | | Fitch Moon | no |

Other Info: Name is on a brass marker at grave site.

| Nash
　Elizabeth H. | 24 June 1856
27 Feb. 1907 | H. A. Nash | yes |
| Palmore
　Ernest D. | 18 June 1905
6 Oct. 1959 | | yes |

Inscription: He was the sunshine of our home.

Other Info: Footstone: Father; His name, birthdate, and death date are also inscribed on the neighboring headstone which is shared with Rosa Duncan and Tyler Duncan.

| Palmore
　Kelsey Ann | 6 April 1999 | | yes |

Inscription: Daughter of J.D. and Betty, Our Angel

Last Name Given Name (Maiden Name)	Date of Birth Date of Death Age at Death	Spouse	Tombstone
Palmore Sadie R. (Ragland)	2 July 1929 30 Oct. 1994	Ernest D. Palmore Jr.	yes

Inscription: Forever in Our Hearts

Patterson Joseph Watson	31 Aug. 1885 23 Oct. 1950		yes

Other Info: Son of G. W. and Marcia B. Patteson.

Patteson G. W.	26 July 1838 11 April 1918	Marcia B. Patteson	yes
Patteson Marcia B.	26 Dec. 1856 1 June 1941	G. W. Patteson	yes

Inscription: Mother

Ragland Albert Thomas	17 Jan. 1930 9 April 1974		yes

Other Info: Footstone: Albert T. Ragland, PFC, US Army, (same dates as are on the headstone)

Ragland Alice			yes

Other Info: Headstone is broken; dates are missing.

Ragland Alice V.	19 June 1873 5 Apr. 1910	Thomas H. Ragland	yes
Ragland Annie S.		James H. Ragland	no

Other Info: This is a brass plate inscribed with name only to mark the grave site.

Ragland C. Walker	1 April 1877 12 April 1952	Nora E. Ragland	yes

Other Info: Shares a headstone with his wife.

Last Name Given Name (Maiden Name	Date of Birth Date of Death Age at Death	Spouse	Tombstone
Ragland Charles L.	29 May 1890 16 Nov. 1976	Lelia P. Ragland	yes

Inscription: Precious Lord Take My Hand

Other Info: Shares a headstone with his wife.

Ragland Christine B.	20 Sept. 1922 13 July 1961	Tucker Ragland	yes
Ragland Emma Mildred	28 July 1875 21 June 1952	Thomas Edward Ragland	yes

Other Info: Footstone: Mother

Ragland Evelyn Vernell (Londeree)	30 Dec. 1914 22 Sept. 1931		yes

Inscription: She was the sunshine in our home.

Other Info: Footstone: E.V.R. She was the daughter of Charles L. and Connie R. Londeree.

Ragland Francis Jackson Jr.	20 Oct. 1967 11 Oct. 2004		yes

Other Info: Has a Henry Funeral Home marker. He was the son of Francis Jackson Ragland Sr, and Dorothy Adcock Ragland.

Ragland Frank H.	2 Aug. 1932 9 July 1980		yes

Inscription: CPL, US Army, Korea

Ragland Garland	3 April 1885 18 March 1974	(1) Lula Ragland Ragland (2) Louise Ragland	yes

Other Info: Shares a headstone with his wives.

Ragland Gwyndline Hope	9 Nov. 1966 25 Dec. 1968		yes

Last Name Given Name (Maiden Name)	Date of Birth Date of Death Age at Death	Spouse	Tombstone
Ragland Henryetta		Joseph Ragland	no

Other Info: Brass marker with name inscribed on it to mark the grave site.

Ragland Infant son of Louise and Garland Ragland	1933 1933		yes

Ragland James H.		Annie S. Ragland	no

Other Info: This is a brass plate inscribed with name only to mark the grave site.

Ragland John Willard	25 July 1958 14 May 1993		yes

Ragland Joseph		Henryetta Ragland	no

Other Info: This is a brass marker with the name inscribed to mark the grave site.

Ragland Judy Staton	23 Nov. 1894 14 Oct. 1971	Sam Ragland	yes

Other Info: Shares a headstone with her husband.

Ragland Lelia P.	11 Feb. 1894 19 Oct. 1980	Charles L. Ragland	yes

Inscription: Precious Lord Take My Hand

Other Info: Shares a headstone with her husband.

Ragland Louise	13 July 1913 17 Aug. 1981	Garland Ragland	yes

Other Info: Shares a headstone with her husband and his first wife. They are the parents of Barbara Ragland Hackett.

Last Name Given Name (Maiden Name	Date of Birth Date of Death Age at Death	Spouse	Tombstone
Ragland Lula (Ragland)	11 Feb. 1895 14 March 1928	Garland Ragland	yes

Other Info: Shares a headstone with her husband and his second wife.

Ragland Mary E.	21 April 1921 Oct. 1921		yes
Ragland Mary Pearson Rosen	28 Apr. 1875 5 March 1932		yes
Ragland Nora E.	24 Aug. 1882 20 May 1952	C. Walker Ragland	yes

Other Info: Shares a headstone with her husband.

Ragland Sam	8 Oct. 1896 5 Oct. 1969	Judy Staton Ragland	yes

Other Info: Shares a headstone with his wife.

Ragland Sam Jr.	20 Dec. 1926 28 Sept. 1978		yes

Inscription: SGT, US Army, World War II

Other Info: His parents were Sam Ragland and Judy Staton Ragland.

Ragland Thomas Edward (Eddie)	28 Jan. 1889 9 Feb. 1970	Emma Mildred Ragland	yes
Ragland Thomas H.	11 April 1871 3 July 1927	Alice V. Ragland	yes
Ragland Thomas Jr.			yes

Other Info: No dates on the headstone-died as an infant. He was the son of Thomas H and Alice V. Ragland.

| Last Name | Date of Birth | Spouse | Tombstone |
| Given Name | Date of Death | | |
(Maiden Name)	Age at Death		

Robert   14 Oct. 1959   yes
    Mary Miles   1 June 1997

Inscription: Gone but not Forgotten

Other Info: Nickname was Merdie. She was the daughter of Mabel Ragland Miles and Kenneth Wayne Miles.

Robertson   26 Feb. 1925   yes
    John Boatwright   13 Jan. 1979   Marion Gregory
                                                      Robertson

Inscription: To live in hearts we leave behind is not to die.

Other Info: Shares a headstone with his wife. They are the parents of John Wayne Robertson.

Robertson   16 Dec. 1952   yes
    Kathryn (Schroders) 28 Feb. 1997   John Wayne Robertson

Robertson   28 March 1958   yes
    Kenneth L.   3 Sept. 1993

Inscription: Sgt., US Air Force

Other Info: He is the son of Thomas J. and Louise A. Robertson.

Robertson   9 Dec. 1932   yes
    Marion Gregory   18 March 2004   John Boatwright
                                                     Robertson

Other Info: Shares a headstone with her husband.

Robertson   5 April, 1900   yes
    Meta Staton   28 Feb. 1971   Tubal Cane Robertson

Other Info: She and her husband were the parents of William Lewis Robertson and John Boatwright Robertson.

Robertson   24 Feb. 1928   yes
    Thomas J.   3 Dec. 1995   Louise A.

Other Info: Footstone: Husband and Devoted Father

Last Name Given Name (Maiden Name)	Date of Birth Date of Death Age at Death	Spouse	Tombstone
Robertson Tubal Cain	13 July 1882 21 April 1965	Meta Staton Robertson	

Other Info: He and his wife were the parents of William Lewis Robertson and John Boatwright Robertson.

Robertson William Lewis	1923 1944		yes

Inscription: Gone but not Forgotten

Rosen Louis Tate	28 Dec. 1912 26 July 1988		yes
Rosser Ella Staton	1878 1953		yes
Rosser Julia	19 March 1901 17 May 1974		yes

Inscription: Now Cometh Eternal Rest

Rosser Roy	28 Dec. 1905 17 Nov. 1978		yes

Inscription: Now Cometh Eternal Rest

Rosser Samuel Fletcher	1867 1941		yes

Inscription: Gone But Not Forgotten

Sargent Endia (Moss)	15 Jan. 1900 15 May 1922		yes

Inscription: A Precious one From us is Gone, A Voice we Loved is Still, A Place is Vacant in our Home, Which Never can be Filled.

Sargent Fannie S.	14 July 1874 31 July 1937		yes

Inscription: Mother

Other Info: Mother of George Sargent

Last Name Given Name (Maiden Name	Date of Birth Date of Death Age at Death	Spouse	Tombstone
Sargent George Archer	5 July 1898 14 Jan. 1949		yes
Snoddy Robert Harold	21 Oct. 1926 31 July 1990		yes
Spencer Bennie L.	27 Aug. 1903 25 May 1995	Louise Jones Spencer	yes
Other Info: Shares a headstone with his wife.			
Spencer Louise (Jones)	14 Aug. 1906 26 Apr. 1975	Bennie L Spencer	yes
Other Info: Shares a headstone with her husband.			
Staton Ben			no
Other Info: This is a brass plate inscribed with name only to mark the grave site.			
Staton Catmbay			no
Other Info: This is a brass plate inscribed with name only to mark the grave site.			
Staton Drusilla			no
Other Info: This is a brass plate inscribed with name only to mark the grave site.			
Staton Irving F.	13 Feb. 1905 15 Dec. 1974	Ruth B. Staton	yes
Other Info: Shares a headstone with his wife.			
Staton Ruth B.	28 June 1902 24 Dec. 2001	Irving F. Staton	yes
Other Info: Shares a headstone with her husband.			

Last Name Given Name (Maiden Name)	Date of Birth Date of Death Age at Death	Spouse	Tombstone
Staton Walter			no

Other Info: This is a brass plate inscribed with name only to mark the grave site.

Tyree Roger Dale "Bubby" Jr.	3 Nov. 1981 26 Nov. 1999		yes

Inscription: If tears could build a stairway, and memories a lane, I'd walk right up to heaven, and bring you home again.

Walker William Glenn Sr.	25 July 1908 13 April 1985		yes

Inscription: Love Lifted Me; The Lord is my Shepherd

Wallace Margie B. (Ballowe)	27 Dec. 1920 14 Sept. 1980		yes

Inscription: Her Memory is Blessed.

Wright Joseph Spencer	22 Nov. 1900 16 Oct. 1960	Nettie Burnley Wright	yes

Other Info: Shares a headstone with his wife.

Wright Nettie Burnley	12 Feb. 1909 7 July 1984	Joseph Spencer Wright	yes

Other Info: Shares a headstone with her husband.

Wright Olanda Ambrose	20 Sept. 1875 10 Oct. 1939	Ollie Printess Wright	yes
Wright Ollie Printess	16 March 1963	Olanda Ambrose Wright	yes

Last Name	Date of Birth	Spouse	Tombstone
Given Name	Date of Death		
(Maiden Name)	Age at Death		

Glover Family off Rd. 643

Glover   1853   yes
   Ann E. (Elizabeth) (Flood)   (27 March) 1923   Richard
                                                           Asbury Glover

   Other Info: Shares a headstone with her husband. Footstone: AEG
     She and her husband were married: 8 March 1880.

Glover   18 June 1853   no
   Anthony Dibrell   2 May 1855

   Other Info: Known to be buried here, the son of Stephen Anthony and
     Rebecca Susan Glover.

Glover   28 April 1895   no
   Charles Benjamin   April 1895

   Other Info: Known to be buried here, the son of Richard Asbury and
     Ann Elizabeth Glover.

Glover   14 Sept. 1863   no
   Hallie Spencer   27 Oct. 1912

   Other Info: Known to be buried here, the daughter of Stephen Anthony
     and Rebecca Susan Glover.

Glover   2 Jan. 1851   no
   James David   23 Aug. 1908

   Other Info: Known to be buried here, the son of Stephen Anthony and
     Rebecca Susan Glover

Glover   6 June 1858   no
   Joseph Walter Spriggs   22 Nov. 1923

   Other Info: Known to be buried here, the son of Stephen Anthony and
     Rebecca Susan Glover.

Last Name Given Name (Maiden Name)	Date of Birth Date of Death Age at Death	Spouse	Tombstone
Glover Louis Thomas	20 July 1861 23 Dec. 1916		no

Other Info: Known to be buried here, the son of Stephen Anthony and Rebecca Susan Glover.

| Glover
    Mary J. Flood | | Edward Lee Glover | no |

Other Info: Known to be buried here.

| Glover
    Rebeccca Susan Anderson | 15 April 1825
28 May 1887 | Stephen Anthony Glover | no |

Other Info: Known to be buried here. There is a fieldstone in the cemetery etched: Mrs. RSG

| Glover
    Richard A. (Asbury) Glover | (1 March) 1848
(30 March) 1913 | Ann Elizabeth Flood | yes |

Other Info: Shares a headstone with his wife. Footstone: RAG His parents were Stephen Anthony and Rebecca Susan Glover.

| Glover
    Richard Monroe | 21 May 1886
1889 | | no |

Other Info: Known to be buried here, the son of Richard Asbury and Ann Elizabeth Glover.

| Glover
    Sarah Elizabeth | 14 Aug. 1849
1 Nov. 1926 | | yes, broken |

Other Info: She was the daughter of Stephen Anthony and Rebecca Susan Glover.

| Glover
    Stephan A. (Anthony) | (10 Dec. 1824)
(21 Jan. 1890) | Rebecca Susan Anderson Glover | yes |

Inscription: Co. K, 4 VA CAV., CSA

Other Info: He and his wife were married on 6 Jan. 1847.

Last Name Given Name (Maiden Name	Date of Birth Date of Death Age at Death	Spouse	Tombstone
Glover twins	 a few days		no

Other Info: Known to be buried here, the children of Joseph Walter Spriggs Glover.

Goldmine Penecostal Holiness Church

Gunther Janie S.	1881 1967		yes

Inscription: Mother

Gunther John W.	1868 1948		yes

Jamerson Maggie G.	14 Feb. 1911 8 June 1999		yes

Inscription: Doll Baby

Jamerson William Oscar	20 Oct. 1913 4 Nov. 2001		yes

Other Info: Dunkum Funeral Home marker.

Gunther R. W. "Buster"	1906 1947		yes

Goode Family on Rd. 627 — African American

Goode Berta	 about 1937	 James Goode	no

Other Info: Known to be buried here. She was the grandmother of Claude Goode Sr.

Last Name Given Name (Maiden Name	Date of Birth Date of Death Age at Death	Spouse	Tombstone
Goode Claude Jr.	25 April 1955 13 July 1996		yes

    Other Info: Has a Thacker Bros. Funeral marker. He was the brother of Thomas B. Goode also buried in this cemetery.

Goode Effie Rip	in the 1960s		no

    Other Info: Known to be buried here. She was the mother of Claude Goode Sr.

Goode infant male	in the 1960s		no

    Other Info: Known to be buried here.

Goode James	in the 1940s	Berta Goode	no

    Other Info: Known to be buried here. He was the grandfather of Claude Goode Sr.

Goode Thomas B.	30 April 1962 10 Aug. 1997 35 years		yes

    Other Info: Has a Thacker Bros. Funeral Home marker. He was the brother of Claude Goode Jr. also buried in this cemetery. Their father is Claude Goode Sr.

Law Kenneth Jr.	25 June 1961 8 Sept. 2002 41 years		yes

    Inscription: SP4, US Army

    Other Info: Has a Thacker Bros. Funeral Home marker

Taylor _____			no

    Other Info: Known to be buried here.

Last Name Given Name (Maiden Name	Date of Birth Date of Death Age at Death	Spouse	Tombstone

William Gormours Family on US 15

Gormours Pattie Childress		William G. Gormours	no

  Other Info: Known to be buried here.

Gormours Sarah J.	1830-1832 after 1880	William Gormours Sr.	no

  Other Info: Known to be buried here.

Gormours William G.	20 Nov 1842-1849 28 Nov. 1924	Pattie Childress Gormours	yes

  Inscription: CSA

  Other Info: Footstone: WG

Gormous William Sr.	1826-1830 after 1880	Sarah J. Gormours	no

  Other Info: Known to be buried here.

Harris		Georgia Gormours Harris	no

  Other Info: Known to be buried here.

Harris Georgia Gormours	1873	_____Harris	no

  Other Info: Known to be buried here, the daughter of William G. and
    Pattie Gormours.

Simmons child			no

  Other Info: Known to be buried here, the child of Betty Harris Simmons
    and the grandchild of Georgia Gormours Harris.

Last Name Given Name (Maiden Name	Date of Birth Date of Death Age at Death	Spouse	Tombstone
Simmons Betty Harris			no

Other Info: Known to be buried here. She is the daughter of Georgia Gormours Harris.

There are 3 unidentified graves in this cemetery.

Nat. M. Gregory Family off Rd. 652

Foster C. D.	4 July 1833 8 Jan. 1920	Mary A. Foster	yes

Inscription: He was ever ready to do any good work.

Other Info: Footstone: CDF

Foster Ewell J.	1870 1936		yes

Inscription: May he rest in peace.

Other Info: Footstone: EJF

Foster Mary A.	22 June 1844 26 Mar. 1921	C. D. Foster	yes

Inscription: She hath cone what she could.

Other Info: Footstone: MAF

Gregory Laura Foster	1873 1942	Nathaniel Marshall Gregory	yes

Gregory Nathaniel Marshall		Laura Foster Gregory	yes

Other Info: His tombstone has a military bronze plaque-World War I. His parents were Nat. Lancaster Gregory and Virginia Marshall Saunders Gregory.

Last Name Given Name (Maiden Name	Date of Birth Date of Death Age at Death	Spouse	Tombstone
Gregory Orville Bell	1905 1961		yes
Gregory Tillman Arthur	1909 1944		yes

Other Info: His parents were Annie Brizendine Gregory and Millard Gregory.

Haislip Foster S.	1906 1933		yes

Inscription: Dying is but going home.

Other Info: He was the nephew of Laura and Nat. M. Gregory.

Guthrie Family at "Mt. Pleasant" off Rd. 632

Guthrie Elizabeth Coleman		William Guthrie Jr.	no

Other Info: Known to be buried here.

Guthrie J. J. (John James)	(4 Nov. 1817) (March 1892)	Martha Goodman Guthrie	yes

Inscription: Co. C, 3rd VA REG, CSA

Guthrie` Martha Goodman		John James Guthrie	no

Other Info: Known to be buried here. She and her husband were married 3 April 1839. They were the parents of 12 children, some buried in this cemetery in unidentified graves.

Guthrie William Jr. "Buck"	24 Sept. 1781 4 Dec. 1848	Elizabeth Coleman Guthrie	no

Other Info: Known to be buried here.

Last Name Given Name (Maiden Name	Date of Birth Date of Death Age at Death	Spouse	Tombstone
Spencer Bettie G. (Shepherd Guthrie-"Kish")	25 Dec. 1837 16 Nov. 1876	 John James Spencer	yes

Inscription: In Memory of; Mother; Mother dear we miss you. Since to heaven you have gone. You prayed God bless your children and bring them to the Throne. We know that you are happy and that God answers prayer. We mourn our loss dear mother, and will try and meet you there.

Other Info: The stone was erected by M.R. Jones-Arvonia

There are 17 unidentified graves in this cemetery.

Guthrie Slaves and Descendants at "Mt Pleasant"

Hill Kindora	21 Aug. 1894 2 Jan. 1916		yes

Inscription: Meet Me in Heaven

There are 19 unidentified graves in this cemetery

Hackett Family off US 56 (update from Vol. I)

Hackett Bessie W. (Wade)	20 Dec. 1894 13 Jan. 1973	 Thomas Edmund Hackett	yes

Other Info: Shares a headstone with her husband. Her parents were Jessie D. and Mary Godsey Wade.

Hackett Calvin E.	12 April 1941 31 July 1950		yes

Inscription: Son of Princey and Ann Hackett; Asleep in Jesus.

Last Name Given Name (Maiden Name	Date of Birth Date of Death Age at Death	Spouse	Tombstone
Hackett John Preston	1827 1903	Sarah Elizabeth (Dolan or Stark) Hackett	yes

Other Info: His parents were Thomas Hackett (born 1789, died 31 Sept. 1960) and Elizabeth M. Tate Pool Hackett (born 1784, died 14 April 1862)

Hackett Mary Elizabeth Word	1852 1907	Willis Walker Hackett	yes

Other Info: Her parents were Thomas Harrison Word (born 1813, died 1860s) and Marrie P. Caroline Word (born 1824, died 1898). She married Willis W. Hackett on 17 Sept. 1873.

Hackett Princey	1889 1897		no

Other Info: Known to be buried here. He was the son of Willis W. and Mary Elizabeth Word Hackett.

Hackett Princey A.	16 April 1919 23 Feb. 1945	Ann Hackett	yes

Inscription: Virginia, PFC, 1276 ENGR, CMBT BM, 102 DIV, World War II

Other Info: He was killed in action. His parents were Thomas E. and Bessie W. Hackett also buried in this cemetery.

Hackett Sarah Elizabeth "Eliza" (Dolan or Stark)	1829 1907	John Preston Hackett	yes

Other Info:

Hackett Thomas E. (Edmund)	4 June 1886 22 June 1978	(1) Annie Blade Hackett (2) Bessie Wade Hackett	yes

Other Info: He shares a headstone with his second wife. His parents were Willis Walker and Mary Elizabeth Word Hackett.

Last Name Given Name (Maiden Name)	Date of Birth Date of Death Age at Death	Spouse	Tombstone
Hackett Willis J.	20 Dec. 1894 13 Jan. 1973		no

Other Info: Known to be buried here. He was the son of Thomas E. and Bessie W. Hackett also buried in this cemetery.

Hackett Willis Walker	1850 1919	Mary Elizabeth Word Hackett	yes

Other Info: His parents were JP and Sarah E. Hackett also buried in this cemetery.

Layne Nannie C. Hackett	16 May 1879 27 June 1947	James E. Layne "Jim"	yes

Other Info: Her sister, Nettie H. Wood and their parents, Willis Walker and Mary Elizabeth Word Hackett are also buried in this cemetery.

Wood Nettie Lue Hackett	10 Aug. 1894 29 Feb. 1916	Ollie A. Wood	yes

Inscription: Wife of O. A. Wood; Gone but not Forgotten

Hamner Family off Rd. 627

Baber Wyatt Somers			yes

Other Info: There is only one date on the tombstone: 25 Dec. 1882

Hamner Annie Putney	15 Feb. 1888 29 July 1888		yes
Hamner Ila H. Jones	4 Aug. 1868 8 Jan. 1892		yes

Inscription: Mother

Hamner Manoah S.	20 Sept. 1845 5 April 1865		yes

Inscription: PVT, Co. E, 21 VA INF, CSA

Last Name Given Name (Maiden Name	Date of Birth Date of Death Age at Death	Spouse	Tombstone
Hamner Sarah Morris	Sept. 1820 (not inscribed)	Walter Leland Hamner	yes

Other Info: Shares a headstone with her husband.

| Hamner
   Walter Leland | 1817
25 Sept. 1885 | Sarah Morris Hamner | yes |

Other Info: Shares a headstone with his wife.

| Hamner
   William Edward | 19 March 1850
20 June 1920 | | yes |

Inscription: Father

| Hamner
   Wyatt LeLand | 16 Nov. 1843
(not inscribed) | | yes |

Inscription: Confederate Soldier

| McCary
   Amanda Hamner | 25 Aug. 1852
20 Feb. 1935 | Graven Payton McCary | yes |

Other Info: Shares a headstone with her husband.

| McCary
   Graven Payton | 1837
13 April 1921 | Amanda Hamner McCary | yes |

Inscription: Confederate Soldier

Other Info: Shares a headstone with his wife.

Harris Family on Rd. 617

| Duncan
   Bernice Esther | 30 Oct. 1899
22 Aug. 1904 | | yes |

Inscription: Daughter of W.A. and M.R. Duncan; Precious one from us has gone, a voice we loved is stilled; a place is vacant in our home, which never can be filled.

Last Name Given Name (Maiden Name	Date of Birth Date of Death Age at Death	Spouse	Tombstone
Duncan infant son	1 June 1915 1 June 1915		yes

Inscription: Infant son of Will and M.R. Duncan; Them also which sleep in Jesus, will God bring with him. 1 Thess. 4:14

Duncan Percy A.	1 Nov. 1912 8 July 1913		yes

Inscription: God gave, He took, He will rest one, He doeth all things well.

Other Info: Footstone: PAD

Garrison George W.	5 July 1852 15 May 1917	Rosa Harris Garrison	yes

Inscription: A light from our household has gone; A voice we loved is stilled; A place is vacant in our hearts that never again will be filled.

Other Info: Footstone: GWG; He was the son-in-law of A. B. and Willie A. Harris.

Harris A. B. (Alexander Benjamin)	4 April 1842 15 June 1911	Willie Anna England Harris	yes

Inscription: It was hard indeed to part with thee, but Christ's strong arm supported us.

Other Info: Footstone: Alex. B. Harris, Co. F, 20 VA INF, CSA

Harris Bennie B. (Benjamin Beadle)	15 Nov. 1874 25 Dec. 1943	(1) Mary J. Harris (2) Marion Catherine Collier Harris (Katie C. Harris)	yes

Other Info: His parents were A.B. and Willie A. Harris also buried in this cemetery.

Last Name Given Name (Maiden Name	Date of Birth Date of Death Age at Death	Spouse	Tombstone
Harris Robert W.	9 Oct. 1883 28 April 1907		yes

Inscription: Son of A.B. and Willie A. Harris; Dearest Robert, thou hast left us and our loss we deeply mourn, but in heaven we hope to meet you where (no) sorrow will be known.

Other Info: Footstone: RWN

| Harris
    Willie A. | 10 May 1846
10 Dec. 1930 | Alexander Benjamin
Harris | yes |

Inscription: Her spirit smiles from that bright shore, and sweetly whispers weep no more.

There are 3 unidentified graves in this cemetery.

Harris Family on US 15

| Collier
    Sam | | | no |

Other Info: Known to be buried here. He was the father of Katie C. Harris.

| Harris
    David H. | | | yes |

Inscription: Cook Chemical Warfare Service, 1 April 1923

| Harris
    Edwin A. | 4 Jan. 1912
24 July 1920 | | yes |

Other Info: He was the son of Benjamin Beadle and Katie C. Harris.

| Harris
    infant | | | no |

Other Info: Known to be buried here. His father was Isiah Harris.

| Last Name | Date of Birth | Spouse | Tombstone |
| Given Name | Date of Death | | |
(Maiden Name	Age at Death		

Harris   28 Nov. 1846   yes
     James W.   25 Dec. 1896   Mary J. Harris

     Inscription: Since thou cans't no longer stay, to cheer me with thy love-I hope to meet with thee again in yon bright world above.

     Other Info: Footstone: JWH

Harris   28 Feb. 1877   yes
     Katie C. (Marion Catherine Collier)   25 July 1955
                                          Benjamin Beadle Harris

     Other Info: Footstone: Mother. Her children were Raymond Beadle, Collier Caswell, Aileen Jeannette, James Wesley and Edwin A. Harris

Harris   no
     Kenneth Ayres   infant

     Other Info: Known to be buried here. His parents were Jack and Aileen Ayres Harris.

Harris   19 Aug. 1820   yes
     Mary J. "Mollie"   7 July 1892   (1) James W. Harris
                                            (2) Benjamin Beadle Harris

     Inscription: In Memory of; A precious one from us has gone, a voice we loved is still; a place is vacant in our home, which never can be filled.

Harris   no
     Willie Cleveland   about 1930

     Other Info: Known to be buried here. She was the daughter of James W. and Mary J. (Mollie) Harris.

Jamerson   10 April 1901   yes
     Frances   28 Nov. 1927

     Inscription: At Rest; We will meet again; Gone but not Forgotten

Last Name Given Name (Maiden Name)	Date of Birth Date of Death Age at Death	Spouse	Tombstone
Jamerson John D.	1875 1936	Roberta Harris Jamerson	yes

Inscription: Father

Other Info: He and his wife were the parents of Mary N. LeSueur, and Frances Jamerson also buried in this cemetery.

Jamerson Roberta H. (Harris)	2 May 1874 19 April 1960	John D. Jamerson	yes
LeSueur Mary N. (Nowlin)	13 Dec. 1900 16 May 1987		yes

Other Info: She was the daughter of John and Roberta Harris Jamerson.

There are 13 unidentified graves in this cemetery.

Harvey Family off Rd. 744

Harris Sarah	 5 April 1940		no

Other Info: Dunkum Funeral Home marker. There is another grave beside this one, with no identification.

George Hocker Grave off Rd. 690

Hocker George Walker	1879 1961		no

Other Info: Unidentified funeral marker

Last Name	Date of Birth	Spouse	Tombstone
Given Name	Date of Death		
(Maiden Name	Age at Death		

Hodnett Family off Rd. 633

Hodnett	1710		no
John	about 1799	Lucy (Lucia) Brooks Hodnett	

Other Info: Known to be buried here. His parents were John and Anne Eyres Hodnett who were married in 1702, Diocese of Cork and Rossm, Ireland.

Hodnett	about 1710		no
Lucy (Lucia) Brooks	during the Rev. War	John Hodnett	

Other Info: Known to be buried here. She was born in Ireland. Her parents were Peter and Katherine Gartree Brooks who were married 8 June 1709 in Co. Limerick, Ireland.

Hodnett	1 May 1737		no
Philip	17 March 1822		

Other Info: Known to be buried here. He was the son of John and Lucy Brooks Hodnett.

Holmes Grave off Rd. 607

Holmes	1917		no
Herbert A.	1991		

Other Info: This is an above ground vault:West FH. The Holmes family, from New York, resided for a time in a dwelling near the grave. The rest of the family returned to New York after Mr. Holmes passed away.

Holy Trinity Baptist Church on US 15 — African American

Anderson	27 Aug. 1897		yes
Joshua	28 Feb. 1981		

Last Name Given Name (Maiden Name)	Date of Birth Date of Death Age at Death	Spouse	Tombstone
Anderson Joshua Jr.	31 Jan. 1927 4 Jan. 1984		yes

Inscription: US Army, World War II

Other Info: Has an above ground vault: Joshua Anderson Jr., 1927-1983, Reids FH

| Anderson
Ulyssses W. | 3 July 1931
5 Aug. 2001 | | yes |

Other Info: Has a Reids Funeral Home marker

| Anderson
Wilbur Grant | 1933
1992 | | yes |

Inscription: TSgt, US Air Force

Other Info: Has an above ground vault: Wilbur G. Anderson, Sept., 1913-12 Nov. 1992 (birth year is different from tombstone)-Reids FH

| Banks
Pearline R. | 1947
1982 | | no |

Other Info: Has an above ground vault: Bland-Reid FH

| Booker
Florence T. | 5 May 1898
26 April 1980 | | yes |

Inscription: At Rest

Other Info:

| Dozier
Hamlet M. | 23 April 1895
18 April 1923 | | yes |

Inscription: At rest with angels above

Other Info: Footstone: HMD

Last Name Given Name (Maiden Name	Date of Birth Date of Death Age at Death	Spouse	Tombstone
Dudley Rosa	1901 1989		yes

Inscription: We love you

| Eldridge
    Bernice | 1923
2000 | | no |

Other Info: Bland-Reid Funeral Home marker

| Eldridge
    Carrie Jones | 1909
1993 | | no |

Other Info: Has an above ground vault: Reids FH

| Eldridge
    Rolfe E., Dea. | 12 Dec. 1906
23 May 2000 | | no |

Other Info: Has an above ground vault: Bland-Reid FH

Goodwin Emily	1904 1929		yes
Gray Charlie	13 Jan. 1960		yes, broken
Gray Eligah	15 Oct. 1894 14 March 1979		yes

Inscription: Our Precious Father

| Gray
    Rose | 1951
2001 | | no |

Other Info: Bland-Reid Funeral Home marker

| Gray
    Sallie B. | 31 Jan. 1918
11 Jan. 1999 | | yes |

Inscription: Mother; May the work I've done speak for me.

Other Info: Has a Bland-Reid Funeral Home marker: Sallie W. Gray
    (different middle initial from tombstone).

Last Name Given Name (Maiden Name	Date of Birth Date of Death Age at Death	Spouse	Tombstone
Hamlin Clara	1903 1993		no

Other Info: E.B. Allen Funeral Home marker

Harvey Clarence Lee	1920 2001		no

Other Info: Dunkum Funeral Home marker

Hollind Mattie	 30 March 1965	 Frank Hollind	yes

Inscription: Wife of Frank

Johnson Ellen W.	17 Oct. 1882 21 Aug. 1968		yes

Jones Charlie	15 Aug. 1866 9 May 1947		yes

Inscription: Father; Life's work well done, He rests in peace.

Jones Sarah	1 Dec. 1851 5 Dec. 1923		yes

Inscription: In memory of; She believeth and sleeps in Jesus

Other Info: Footstone: SJ

Jones Winston	15 Nov. 1895 25 Sept 1918		yes

Inscription: Born Buckingham Co., VA, Died Camp Dix, N.J.

Other Info: Footstone: WJ

Murray Hallie G.	1875 1959		yes

Other Info: Footstone: HGM

Last Name Given Name (Maiden Name	Date of Birth Date of Death Age at Death	Spouse	Tombstone
Spencer Eugene T.	25 Jan. 1918 6 Dec. 1984	Pocahontas Spencer	yes

Inscription: US Navy, World War II

Other Info: His parents were Samuel and Minnie W. Spencer.

Trent Wales W.	24 Dec. 1937 3 Jan. 1961		yes

Walker Burum E.	1882 1969	Mittie W. Walker	yes

Other Info: Footstone: Father; Shares a headstone with his wife.

Walker Mittie W.	1872 1958	Burum E. Walker	yes

Other Info: Footstone: Mother; Shares a headstone with her husband.

Washington Emily	10 March 1851 13 Jan. 1929		yes

Inscription: Dear Mother, Beloved by all

Washington Ethel L. (Jones)	24 Oct. 1893 17 Oct. 1998	U.S. Washington Sr.	yes

Inscription: The Lord is my Shepherd

Other Info: Shares a headstone with her husband; Has an E.B. Allen Funeral Home marker.

Washington James	1887 1946		yes

Inscription: At Rest

Washington Robert	11 Feb. 1889 9 April 1963		yes

Inscription: At Rest

Last Name Given Name (Maiden Name	Date of Birth Date of Death Age at Death	Spouse	Tombstone
Washington Thomas	8 Sept. 1925 13 April 1975		yes

   Inscription: Cpl, Army Air Force, World War II

   Other Info: Has an above ground vault: Thomas Washington, 1925-1975

Washington Thomas	18 July 1848 9 March 1917		yes

   Inscription: Gone to Rest, His memory still lives

   Other Info: Footstone: TW

Washington U. S. Sr.	3 June 1895 1 July 1978	Ethel L. Washington	yes

   Inscription: US Army, 1918-1919; The Lord is my Shepherd

   Other Info: Shares a headstone with his wife.

Williams Hollister Lamont	21 July 1954 15 Oct. 1976		yes

   Inscription: PVT, US Army, Vietnam

   Other Info: Has an above ground vault: Hollister L. Williams, 1954-1976

Williams James A.	1920 1990		yes

Williams Odell Raymond	10 Dec. 1926 28 April 1980		yes

   Inscription: US Air Force

   Other Info: Has an above ground vault: Odell R. Williams, 1918-1980 (different birth year from tombstone)

Last Name Given Name (Maiden Name	Date of Birth Date of Death Age at Death	Spouse	Tombstone
Woodson Robert W.	11 Oct. 1901 14 May 1969		yes

Inscription: At Rest

| Woodson
  Russell B. | 1940
2001 | | no |

Other Info: Oliver and Eggleston Funeral Home marker

| Woodson
  Willie Brown B. | 24 Dec. 1883
30 Oct. 1968 | | yes |
| Wright
  Richard | 1942
1970 | | yes |

Inscription: Son

Other Info: He is the son of Mary E. Wright.

| Wright
  Salomon | 1915
1983
66 years | | no |

Other Info: Reids Funeral Home marker

There are 25 unidentified graves in this cemetery.

J.T. Horner Grave on Rd. 668

| Horner
  J. (John) T. | 1861
1879 | | yes |

Inscription: By M.L. Horner

Other Info: His parents were Thomas J. and Mary E. Horner. According to county death records he was a white, male, unmarried, age 18 years.

Last Name Given Name (Maiden Name)	Date of Birth Date of Death Age at Death	Spouse	Tombstone

Horsley Family off Rds 691 and 646 — African American

Horsley
    Alvin   about 1936

    Other Info: Known to be buried here.

Horsley   no
    Daniel   about 1956   Mattie Horsley

    Other Info: Known to be buried here. His brother, Alvin, and wife,
        Mattie are also buried in this cemetery.

Horsley   no
    Mattie   about 1971   Daniel Horsley

    Other Info: Known to be buried here.

Jamerson-Newton Family on Rd. 778

Huddleston   17 May 1908   Multi-family stone
    Roberta Jamerson 9 March 1984

Huddleston   12 Jan. 1888   yes
    Rosa L. (Jamerson) 2 Sept. 1970

    Inscription: Mother; At Rest

Jamerson   2 Nov. 1893   Multi-family stone
    Calvin Marshall "Boo" 2 Sept. 1976

Jamerson   30 June 1898   Multi-family stone
    Daniel Wallace   29 Sept. 1979

Last Name Given Name (Maiden Name)	Date of Birth Date of Death Age at Death	Spouse	Tombstone
Jamerson Evie J. (Jame)	8 Aug. 1885 5 July 1966		yes

Inscription: At Rest

Jamerson Harry	June 1904 25 June 1955	Multi-family stone	
Jamerson P. S. (Poindexter)	28 May 1828 30 May 1910		yes

Inscription: PVT, Co. B, 25 VA INF, CSA

Other Info: He was the father of Sallie J. Thomas, and Matilda J. Newton also buried in this cemetery.

Jamerson Pocahontas Fariss "Pokey"	6 April 1868 2 Jan. 1927	Multi-family stone Thomas Jackson Jamerson	

Other Info: She is buried at the Fariss Family Cemetery.

Jamerson Robert Samuel	2 April 1892 1 Sept. 1973	Multi-family stone	
Jamerson Thomas Jackson "Tommy"	11 Sept. 1862 22 Aug. 1949	Multi-family stone Pocahontas Fariss Jamerson	

Other Info: A large multi-family stone has been erected by the great granddaughter of Tommy and Pokey Jamerson: By love they are remembered and in memory they live, by Kathy (Huddleston Brown)-Aug. 2001. He was the nephew of P. S. Jamerson, and he and his wife were the parents of Evie, Rosa J. Huddleston, Robert, Calvin, Daniel, Harry, Roberta Huddleston and Willie Early Jamerson, all buried in this cemetery. He and his wife also had Bossieux Jackson Jamerson (30 June, 1889-17 July 1969) and Thomas Edgar Jamerson (20 Feb. 1896-10 Feb. 1978).

Jamerson Willie Early	17 Aug. 1910 14 June 1978	Multi-family stone	

Last Name Given Name (Maiden Name	Date of Birth Date of Death Age at Death	Spouse	Tombstone
Newton Ella D.	24 March 1897 20 Nov. 1944		yes
Newton John E.	20 Aug. 1856 4 May 1925	Matilda Jamerson Newton	yes

Other Info: Shares a headstone with his wife.

| Newton
   Lillian R. | 9 Feb. 1885
20 July 1886 | Multi-family stone | |

Other Info: She was the daughter of John E and Matilda J. Newton.

| Newton
   Matilda J. (Jamerson) | 1 Aug. 1868
3 May 1958 | John E. Newton | yes |

Other Info: Shares a headstone with her husband.

| Thomas
   Sallie Jamerson | 3 May 1866
20 March 1903 | Multi-family stone | |

Jamison-Sharp Family off Rd. 778

| Jamerson
   Jennie (Virginia Sharp) | 2 Dec. 1837
22 Jan. 1890 | | etched fieldstone |
| Jamison
   Margaret | about 1835 | | no |

Other Info: Known to be buried here.

| Jamison
   Richard B. (Beverly) | | | yes |

Inscription: Co. K, 2 VA ARTY, CSA

Last Name Given Name (Maiden Name	Date of Birth Date of Death Age at Death	Spouse	Tombstone
Jamison Thomas P.			yes

    Inscription: 25 BN, VA INF, CSA

    Other Info: He was the grandson of Tom and Mary Ann Mann Sharp also buried in this cemetery.

Mann Lucy	1767 26 ___1856		etched fieldstone

    Other Info: She was the mother of Mary Ann Mann Sharp, also buried in this cemetery.

Sharp George F.	about 1828 1910		yes

    Inscription: Co. K, 2 VA ARTY, CSA

    Other Info: He was the son of Tom and Mary Ann Mann Sharp, also buried in this cemetery.

Sharp John Berry	about 1825 about 1859		no

    Other Info: Known to be buried here.

Sharp Mary Ann Mann	about 1801 about 1865	Thomas H. Sharp	no

    Other Info: Known to be buried here.

Sharp Thomas H. "Old Man Tom Sharp"	about 1793 about 1874	Mary Ann Mann Sharp	no

    Other Info: Known to be buried here. There is a fieldstone with THS etched on it.

Last Name Given Name (Maiden Name	Date of Birth Date of Death Age at Death	Spouse	Tombstone
Sharp Thomas Russell	about 1853		no

Other Info: Known to be buried here.

There are slaves known to be buried in a portion of this cemetery.
There are at least 34 unidentified graves in this cemetery.

Jerusalem Baptist Church — African American

Austin Nettie Mundy	1939 1996		no

Other Info: Unidentified funeral home marker

Austin Thomas E.	1 Sept. 1928 13 Oct. 2003		yes

Inscription: US Army, World War II

Other Info: Has a Bland-Reid Funeral Home marker.

Austin Willie Lewis	1 Jan. 1932 13 March 1994		yes

Inscription: CPL, US Army, Korea

Brown Alma W.	7 June 1899 11 Jan. 1993		yes
Chambers Robert Burton	11 May 1911 5 Feb. 1994		yes

Inscription: US Army, World War II

Cosby Mary M.	1882 1941	William C. Cosby	yes
Cosby William C.	1872 1954	Mary M. Cosby	yes

Last Name Given Name (Maiden Name	Date of Birth Date of Death Age at Death	Spouse	Tombstone
Gray Baby	1951 1951		yes
Gray Elise (Logan)Shelton	24 March 1913 6 Feb. 2001	(1)Allen Harvey Shelton (2) Lucius Cary Gray	yes

Other Info: Bland-Reid Funeral Home marker

Gray Lucius Cary	1907 1974	Elise Logan Shelton Gray	yes

Other Info: This is a memorial. Mr. Gray is buried in a cemetery in Powhatan County, Va.

Harris Americus B.	26 Sept. 1909 12 Jan. 1991	George Frank Harris	yes

Other Info: Shares a headstone with her daughter.

Harris Marcia J.	20 Feb. 1943 13 Feb. 1947		yes

Other Info: Shares a headstone with her mother; Footstone-Daughter of GF, AB

Hemmings Willa Jones	29 March 1907 19 July 1991		yes

Other Info: Her parents were Lottie and John C. Jones Sr.

Jones Carl Ray	12 Nov. 1923 12 July 1985	Beatrice J. Jones	yes

Jones John C. Jr.	3 Dec. 1999		yes

Other Info: Joseph Jenkins, Jr. Funeral Home marker. His parents were Lottie and John C. Jones Sr.

Jones John C. Sr.	5 May 1878 5 Aug. 1965	Lottie P. Jones	yes

Other Info: Shares a headstone with his wife.

Last Name Given Name (Maiden Name	Date of Birth Date of Death Age at Death	Spouse	Tombstone
Jones 　Lottie P.	25 Dec. 1888 15 June 1977	John C. Jones Sr.	yes

　Other Info: Shares a headstone with her husband.

| Jones
　Rolf Leon Sr. | 1928
1993 | Mary Shelton Jones | yes |

　Other Info: Footstone: TEC 5, US Army, Korea, (born) 20 Aug. 1929, (died) 5 Sept. 1993

| Kerr
　William J., Rev. | 1894
1988 | | yes |

　Inscription: Dedicated to the Memory of Rev. William J. Kerr-by student members, colleagues and friends-Oct. 29, 1989

| Lee
　Laura E. (Cosby) | 30 Nov. 1907
27 Jan. 1993 | | yes |

　Other Info: Her parents were William and Mary Cosby.

| Logan
　George William | 1887
1968 | Rosa Nellie Logan | yes |

　Other Info: Shares a headstone with his wife. They are the parents of Elise S. Gray.

| Logan
　John E. | 5 March 1929
29 July 1982 | | yes |

　Inscription: PFC, US Army, Korea

| Logan
　Mary Austin | 26 March 1900
5 March 1970 | | yes |

| Logan
　N. Christine | 1 July 1925
20 March 2000 | Carrington J. Logan | yes |

　Inscription: Married: Feb. 21, 1944

　Other Info: Above ground vault: Reid's FH

Last Name Given Name (Maiden Name	Date of Birth Date of Death Age at Death	Spouse	Tombstone
Logan Rosa Nellie	1888 1841	George William Logan	yes

Other Info: Shares a headstone with her husband.

| Morris
   Gladys E. | 21 Oct. 1916
9 May 1999 | Harry Morris | yes |

| Parker
   Annie Shelton | 10 Sept. 1909
16 July 1995 | | yes |

Inscription: Devoted Mother and Grandmother

| Shelton
   Allen | 1880
1960 | Matilda Coleman Shelton | yes |

Other Info: Shares a headstone with his wife and baby son. He is the brother of Edward L. Shelton and Annie Shelton Parker.

| Shelton
   Allen Harvey | 1906
1939 | Elise Shelton who later married Lucius Cary Gray | yes |

| Shelton
   Desmonia | 1853
1919 | King Shelton | yes |

Other Info: Shares a headstone with her husband.

| Shelton
   Edward | 1903
1904 | | yes |

Other Info: Shares a headstone with his parents.

| Shelton
   Edward L. | 1879
1970 | Willie M. Shelton | yes |

Other Info: Shares a headstone with his wife.

| Shelton
   Evelyn E. | 13 July 1922
17 Oct. 1992 | Mack L. Shelton | yes |

Other Info: Shares a headstone with her husband.

Last Name Given Name (Maiden Name	Date of Birth Date of Death Age at Death	Spouse	Tombstone
Shelton 　James E.	1911 1985		yes

　　Other Info: Reids Funeral Home marker

Shelton 　John Jasper Jr.	5 July 1949 10 Sept. 1994	Tanya Austin Shelton	yes

　　Inscription: Our Beloved Buster

　　Other Info: Footstone: MSGT., US Air Force, Vietnam; Air Force
　　　Commendation Medal

Shelton 　King	1849 1886	Desmonia Shelton	yes

　　Other Info: Shares a headstone with his wife.

Shelton 　Mack L.	6 July 1922 16 Jan. 2000	Evelyn E. Shelton	yes

　　Other Info: Footstone: Mack Lenwood Shelton, US Navy, World War II
　　　(gives same dates as on headstone). Shares a headstone with his
　　　wife.

Shelton 　Matilda Coleman	1882 1929	Allen Shelton	yes

　　Other Info: Shares a headstone with her husband and baby son.

Shelton 　Willie M.	1889 1980	Edward L. Shelton	yes

　　Other Info: Shares a headstone with her husband.

Smith 　George E.	21 April 1943 1 Nov. 1982		yes

Watts 　Bertha E. (Harris)	20 Aug. 1896 29 May 1987	George Watts	yes

　　Other Info: Married 20 Aug. 1922

Last Name	Date of Birth	Spouse	Tombstone
Given Name	Date of Death		
(Maiden Name)	Age at Death		

Johnson Family on Rd. 622

Bransford   1854   yes
   Abraham Moseley   1937   Janie Lonkard Bransford

   Other Info: Shares a headstone with his daughter. He was the brother of Nannie Bransford Johnson, and the father of Jessie Bransford Rupp and Bessie Bransford Norvell also buried in this cemetery.

Bransford   26 April 1861   yes
   Wm. S. (William Samuel)   9 Feb. 1891

   Inscription: In Memory of: (died) From injuries received While faithfully discharging his duty. In God we trust.

   Other Info: He was the brother of Nannie Hill Bransford Johnson also buried in this cemetery. She was married to William Johnson, the 5th child of Thomas and Frances Johnson.

Johnson   7 June 1852   yes
   Alice W. (Walker)   28 Nov. 1868

   Inscription: Daughter (6th child) of Thos. and Frances C. Johnson

   Other Info: Footstone: AWJ

Johnson   23 July 1884   no
   Edmond Hubbard   29 Dec. 1909

   Other Info: Known to be buried here. He was the son of William Thomas and Nanny Hill Bransford Johnson.

Johnson   18 May 1812   yes
   Frances C. (Bryant)   27 March 1869   Thomas Johnson

   Inscription: In Memory of; Wife of Thos. Johnson

   Other Info: Shares a headstone with her husband. Footstone: FCJ

Last Name Given Name (Maiden Name	Date of Birth Date of Death Age at Death	Spouse	Tombstone
Johnson George H.	1 May 1842 1 Sept. 1862		yes

Inscription: Son (4th child) of Thos. and Frances C. Johnson; Died of wounds received in battle at Malvern Hill, July 2, 1862

Other Info: Footstone: GHJ

Johnson Judith Frances (Fannie)	13 June 1885 26 Oct. 1923		no

Other Info: Known to be buried here, the daughter of William Thomas and Nanny Hilll Bransford Johnson.

Johnson Nannie Hill (Bransford)	22 Feb. 1857 2 Feb. 1925	William Thomas Johnson	yes
Johnson Thomas	11 March 1798 7 June 1875	Frances C. Bryant Johnson	yes

Inscription: In Memory of

Other Info: Shares a headstone with his wife. Footstone: TJ

Johnson William T. (Thomas)	26 July 1850 19 July 1897	Nannie Hill Bransford Johnson	yes

Inscription: Thou grief it gives, tis much thee best, to sorrow, thy will be done. He was the 5th child of Thomas and Frances Johnson.

Johnson William Thomas	18 Sept. 1880 6 April 1898		no

Other Info: Known to buried here. His parents were William Thomas and Nanny Hill Bransford Johnson also buried in this cemetery.

Norvell Bessie Bransford	25 Dec. 1900 10 Jan. 1927	Bernard Norvell	yes

Other Info: Her parents were Abraham Moseley and Janie Lonkard Bransford.

Last Name Given Name (Maiden Name	Date of Birth Date of Death Age at Death	Spouse	Tombstone
Rupp Jessie Bransford	1903 1958	 William Rupp	yes

Other Info: Shares a headstone with her father, Abraham Moseley Bransford. Her mother was Janie Lonkard Bransford.

Yancey George G.	20 June 1825 6 Sept. 1882	 Sallie (Elizabeth) Johnson Yancey	yes

Inscription: In Memory

Other Info: Shares a headstone with his wife.

Yancey Sallie (Elizabeth Johnson)	5 July 1845 30 Dec. 1902	 George G. Yancey	yes

Inscription: In Memory

Other Info: Shares a headstone with her husband. She was the second child of Thomas and Frances C. Johnson, also buried here. She and her husband were married on 2 March 1867.

John H. Johnson Family on Rd. 615 — African American

Brown Emma Lee Johnson	1884 1935		no

Other Info: Known to be buried here.

Haskins Robert		Virginia Johnson Haskins	no

Other Info: Known to be buried here.

Haskins Virginia Johnson		Robert Haskins	no

Other Info: Known to be buried here. She was the daughter of John H. and Allie Johnson.

Last Name Given Name (Maiden Name	Date of Birth Date of Death Age at Death	Spouse	Tombstone
Hollaway Elsie J.	1917 2002		no
Other Info: Dunkum Funeral Home marker			
Hollaway William O.	1911 1987		no
Other Info: Dunkum Funeral Home marker			
Johnson Abbey Elizabeth		Willis Johnson	no
Other Info: Known to be buried here.			
Johnson Abbington		Frances Johnson	no
Other Info: Known to be buried here. His parents were John H. and Allie Johnson.			
Johnson Albert		Amsia Johnson	no
Other Info: Known to be buried here. He was the son of John H. and Allie Johnson			
Johnson Allie (Alley)		John H. Johnson	no
Other Info: Known to be buried here and the mother of many buried in this cemetery.			
Johnson Amsia		Albert Johnson	no
Other Info: Known to be buried here.			
Johnson Angelina	1846		no
Other Info: Known to be buried here. She was the daughter of Washington and Judith E. Johnson.			

Last Name Given Name (Maiden Name	Date of Birth Date of Death Age at Death	Spouse	Tombstone
Johnson 　Beatrice			no

Other Info: Unidentified funeral home marker with no dates.

| Johnson
　Charlie | 1894 | | no |

Other Info: Known to be buried here. His parents were Chatman and Sarah Johnson.

| Johnson
　Charlotte T. | | John Johnson | no |

Other Info: Known to be buried here.

| Johnson
　Chatman | | (1) Emily Johnson
(2) Sarah Johnson | no |

Other Info: Known to be buried here. He was the son of John H. and Allie Johnson.

| Johnson
　Clarence | 1921
1984 | Mandie Johnson | no |

Other Info: Dunkum Funeral Home marker

| Johnson
　Ed | 1877
1951 | | no |

Other Info: Unidentified funeral home marker.

| Johnson
　Emily | | Chatman Johnson | no |

Other Info: Known to be buried here. She and her husband were married in 1866.

| Johnson
　Frances | | Abbington Johnson | no |

Other Info: Known to be buried here.

Last Name Given Name (Maiden Name	Date of Birth Date of Death Age at Death	Spouse	Tombstone
Johnson Georgiana Daniel	1938		no

Other Info: Known to be buried here.

Johnson John		Charlotte T. Johnson	no

Other Info: Known to be buried here. He was the son of John H. and Allie Johnson.

Johnson John H. "Jack"		Allie (Alley) Johnson	no

Other Info: Known to be buried here. He was caucasian, and the father of many of those buried here.

Johnson Judith E.		Washington Johnson	no

Other Info: Known to be buried here.

Johnson Lacy Irene	6 Feb. 1901 21 Mar. 1978		yes

Inscription: We will meet again

Other Info: Dunkum Funeral Home marker: Lacy Thornhill Johnson

Johnson Maria		Napoleon Johnson	no

Other Info: Known to be buried here.

Johnson Maria		Royal Johnson	no

Other Info: Known to be buried here.

Last Name Given Name (Maiden Name	Date of Birth Date of Death Age at Death	Spouse	Tombstone
Johnson Nancy	1846		no

Other Info: Known to be buried here. She was the daughter of Albert and Amsia Johnson.

Johnson Napoleon		Maria Johnson	no

Other Info: Known to be buried here. He was the son of John H. and Allie Johnson.

Johnson Ollie Stuart	1905 1962		no

Other Info: Unidentified funeral home marker

Johnson Prince			no

Other Info: Unidentified funeral home marker with no dates.

Johnson Royal		Maria Johnson	no

Other Info: Known to be buried here. His parents were John H. and Allie Johnson.

Johnson Sadie	1936		no

Other Info: Known to be buried here.

Johnson Sarah		Chatman Johnson	no

Other Info: Known to be buried here. She and her husband were married in 1890.

Johnson Sasha	1867		no

Other Info: Known to be buried here. Her parents were Chatman and Emily Johnson.

Last Name Given Name (Maiden Name	Date of Birth Date of Death Age at Death	Spouse	Tombstone
Johnson Washington		Judith E. Johnson	no

  Other Info: Known to be buried here; the son of John H. and Allie Johnson.

| Johnson
  William A. | 1854 | | no |

  Other Info: Known to be buried here. He was the son of Albert and Amsia Johnson.

| Johnson
  William A. | | | no |

  Other Info: Unidentified funeral home marker with no dates

| Johnson
  William Abner | 1886
1937 | | no |

  Other Info: Known to be buried here.

| Johnson
  William James | 1844 | | no |

  Other Info: Known to be buried here. He was the son of Washington and Judith E. Johnson.

| Johnson
  William Jr. | | | no |

  Other Info: Unidentified funeral home marker with no dates.

| Johnson
  Willis | 1869 | | no |

  Other Info: Known to be buried here. His parents were Chapman and Emily Johnson.

Last Name Given Name (Maiden Name	Date of Birth Date of Death Age at Death	Spouse	Tombstone
Johnson Willis		Abbey Elizabeth Johnson	no

Other Info: Known to be buried here. His parents were John H. and Allie Johnson.

| Moss
  Emma M. | 1924
2000 | | no |

Other Info: Dunkum Funeral Home marker

| Moss
  Fabe Henderson | 1927
1972 | | no |

Other Info: Dunkum Funeral Home marker

| Pankey
  Alice | | | no |

Other Info: Unidentified funeral home marker

| Pankey
  Andrew | | | no |

Other Info: Unidentified funeral home marker with no dates.

| Pankey
  Jane Johnson | | Robert S. Pankey | no |

Other Info: Known to be buried here. She was the daughter of John H. and Allie Johnson.

| Pankey
  Robert S. | | Jane Johnson Pankey | no |

Other Info: Known to be buried here.

| Thornhill
  Carlton | 1916
1997 | | no |

Other Info: Dunkum Funeral Home marker

Last Name Given Name (Maiden Name	Date of Birth Date of Death Age at Death	Spouse	Tombstone
Wright John Willis	14 Aug. 1888 21 Oct. 1965		yes

Inscription: Virginia, PFC, 505 Engr, SVC BN, World War I

Wright Robert	19 Oct. 1946		no

Other Info: Known to be buried here. Father of Gladys Wright Daniel and grandfather of Robert Daniel.

Jones Family at "Mountain View"

Jones Clifford			yes

Inscription: Co. A, 44 VA INF, CSA

Jones Cora Lee	15 Aug. 1867 4 Aug. 1948		no

Other Info: Unidentified funeral home marker

Jones Edna Tucker	26 July 1885 13 Feb. 1923	James Christian Jones	yes

Inscription: Prepare to meet us in heaven.

Other Info: Shares a headstone with her husband.

Jones Elbert Jr.			no

Other Info: Known to be buried here.

Jones Elbert Sr.	(adult)		no

Other Info: Known to be buried here. He was the father of Elbert Jones Jr. also buried in this cemetery.

Last Name Given Name (Maiden Name	Date of Birth Date of Death Age at Death	Spouse	Tombstone
Jones James Christian	20 May 1882 14 June 1951	Edna Tucker Jones	yes

Inscription: Prepare to meet us in heaven.

Other Info: Shares a double stone with his wife.

Jones Leon Winston Jr.	2 June 1918 4 June 1921		no

Other Info: Known to be buried here.

Jones Margaret Elizabeth "Peg"	2 Aug. 1920 28 Dec. 1922		no

Other Info: Known to be buried here.

Jones Mary Ann	10 Oct. 1916 4 Jan. 1920		no

Other Info: Known to be buried here.

Kyle James C.			yes

Inscription: 1 Lt., Co. E, 21 VA INF, CSA

Jones Family No. 2 on Rd. 602 — African American (update from Vol. I)

Jones Lilyan D.	20 Dec. 1913 21 Feb. 1988	Thomas E. Jones Jr.	yes

Other Info: Shares a headstone with her husband.

Jones Thomas E. Jr.	5 Sept. 1914 14 Dec. 1982	Lilyan D. Jones	yes

Other Info: Shares a headstone with his wife.

Last Name Given Name (Maiden Name	Date of Birth Date of Death Age at Death	Spouse	Tombstone

Jones Family off Rd. 642

Holman 　Hartwell J. (James)	1844 (27 Feb.)1863		yes

　　Inscription: PVT, Co. A., 57 VA INF, CSA

　　Other Info: His parents were Tandy and Judith Spencer Holman. He was born at "Oakland", located in Buckingham Co.

Jones 　Taswell			yes

　　Inscription: Co. C., 25 VA INF, CSA

Jones 　Wiley			yes

　　Inscription: Co. D., VA ARTY, CSA

There are 23 unidentified graves in this cemetery.

Jones Family on Rd. 695 — African American

Coles 　Robert A.	27 June 1940 29 May 1976	Hazel Jones Coles	yes
Jones 　Charlie Samuel		Claudia V. Jones	no

　　Other Info: Unidentified funeral home marker. He and his wife were the parents of George, Christine Wicks, Annie Rush, Estelle Jones, and a male child all buried in this cemetery, and Hazel Jones Coles.

Jones 　Claudia V.	1892 4 Oct. 1956 60 years	Charlie Samuel Jones	yes

　　Inscription: Mother

　　Other Info: Has a Thacker Bros. Funeral Home marker.

Last Name Given Name (Maiden Name	Date of Birth Date of Death Age at Death	Spouse	Tombstone
Jones Estelle	(child)		no

Other Info: Known to be buried here.

| Jones
   George | 1940-1942 | | no |

Other Info: Unidentified funeral home marker.

| Jones
   (male child) | | | no |

Other Info: Known to be buried here, the son of Charles and Claudia Jones.

| Jones
   Martha Ann | 25 Feb. 1921
3 Dec. 1986 | | yes |

Inscription: Mother

Other Info: Has a Thacker Bros. Funeral Home marker.

| Jones
   Rosa Ann | 1940
1980s | | no |

Other Info: Known to be buried here. She was the niece of Hazel Jones Coles.

| Rush
   Annie L. (Jones) | 12 May 1931
13 Oct. 1994
(63 years) | | yes |

Other Info: Has a Thacker Bros. Funeral Home marker.

| Wicks
   Christine M. (Jones Anderson) | 25 Dec. 1918
28 Feb. 1997
(78 years) | | yes |

Inscription: Beloved Mother

Other Info: Has a Thacker Bros. Funeral Home marker.

Last Name	Date of Birth	Spouse	Tombstone
Given Name	Date of Death		
(Maiden Name	Age at Death		

Jones-Higgenbotham Family on Rd. 648 — African American

Anderson   no
   King   29 Nov. 1959

   Other Info: L.C. Gray Funeral Home marker

Anderson   1889   no
   Hobhouse   1942

   Other Info: Dunkum Funeral Home marker

Higgenbotham   6 May 1909   yes
   Mrs. Nelson T. (Mary Nelson Trent) 31 Jan. 1993

   Other Info: Has a Reids Funeral Home marker.

Higgenbothan   1905   no
   Sidney E.   1978

   Other Info: Unidentified funeral home marker

Jones   23 April 1878   yes
   M. A.   25 Dec. 1943
                   65 years

   Inscription: Asleep in Jesus

Trent   no
   Julie

   Other Info: Reids Funeral Home marker with one date: 16 May 1966.

There are 9 unidentified graves in this cemetery.

Last Name	Date of Birth	Spouse	Tombstone
Given Name	Date of Death		
(Maiden Name)	Age at Death		

Benjamin Wickliff Kitchen Family
(Update of Kitchen Family on Rd. 622 in Vol. I)

Hall Finished marker on wooden pedestal
　Mildred Ella Kitchen Denton Feb. 1866 (1) John A. Denton
　　　　　　　　　　　　　　　　　　　(2) Alexander S. Hall

　　Other Info: She was the daughter of William Lewis Kitchen and Martha Susan Robertson Kitchen.

Kitchen　　　　　　Jan. 1894　　Finished marker on
　　　　　　　　　　　　　　　　　wooden pedestal
　Benjamin Wickliff Jr. 1934

　　Inscription: Son of Benjamin Wickliff Kitchen Sr. and Betty Susan Denton Kitchen.

Kitchen　　　　　　1 March 1863　Finished marker on
　　　　　　　　　　　　　　　　　wooden pedestal
　Benjamin Wickliff Sr. 9 April 1930 Betty Susan Denton Kitchen

　　Inscription: Husband of Betty Susan Denton; on back-Children of Benjamin Wickliff Kitchen Sr. and Betty Susan Denton Kitchen: Thomas Richard Kitchen, Oct. 1881-27 Jan. 1934, Ruth Inez Kitchen Robertson Flournoy, 10 Sept. 1884-27 Feb. 1934, Charles Yost Kitchen, 13 Sept. 1886-25 Sept. 1970, William Lewis Kitchen (2), Jan. 1889-25 Sept. 1970, John Denton Kitchen Sr, 2 Nov. 1891-6 May 1979 (also Benjamin Wickliff Kitchen Jr., Jan 1894-1934)

Kitchen　　　　　　5 Nov. 1864　　Finished marker on
　　　　　　　　　　　　　　　　　　wooden pedestal
　Betty Susan Denton (12 March)1939 Benjamin Wickliff Kitchen Sr.

　　Inscription: Wife of Benjamin Wickliff Kitchen Sr.; on back-Estelle Kitchen Stephans, 13 April 1897-19 Nov. 1963, Melva Carrie Kitchen Swan, 8 Sep. 1899-6 Feb. 1986, Kruger McKinley Kitchen, 1903-, Ruby Ethel Kitchen(1), 1903-

Last Name Given Name (Maiden Name	Date of Birth Date of Death Age at Death	Spouse	Tombstone
Kitchen Florence Dawn	25 Jan. 1921 Mar. 1923		yes

Other Info: She was the daughter of John D. Kitchen Sr..

Kitchen infant		Finished marker on wooden pedestal	

Other Info: Child of Annie Ragland and Thomas Richard Kitchen.

Kitchen John D. (Denton) (Sr.)	2 Nov. 1891 6 May 1979		yes

Other Info: His parents were Benjamin Wickliff and Betty Susan Denton Kitchen.

Kitchen Martha Susan Robertson	26 May 1836 9 Jan. 1915	Finished marker on wooden pedestal William Lewis Kitchen	

Inscription: Wife of William Lewis Kitchen, Mother of Ann Elizabeth Kitchen, Mildred Ella Kitchen Denton Hall, Benjamin Wickliff Kitchen Sr.

Kitchen Ruby Ethel (2)	1906 1907 18 months	Finished marker on wooden pedestal	

Kitchen Thomas R. (Richard)	1882 (or 1881) 1934	Annie Ragland Kitchen	yes

There are 3 unidentified graves in this cemetery.

LeSueur-Call Family on Rd. 617

Allen John T.			yes

Inscription: Co. A, 19 VA HVARTY, CSA (no dates)

Last Name Given Name (Maiden Name	Date of Birth Date of Death Age at Death	Spouse	Tombstone
Call Charles L.			yes

Inscription: Co. C, 3 VA RES, CSA (no dates)

| Call
    Josephine (Allen) | 13 June 1877
28 Sept. 1966 | | yes |

| Call
    Phillip Joshua | 14 June 1938
52 years, 2 months | | no |

Other Info: Dunkum Funeral Home marker

| Call
    Willie Rolfe | | | no |

Other Info: Known to be buried here.

| Childress
    Robert L. | | | yes |

Inscription: Tr. B, 4 VA CAV, CSA (no dates)

| LeSueur
    Emma Lee | 13 July 1865
28 May 1945 | James Samuel LeSueur | yes |

| LeSueur
    James Samuel | 1859
1942 | Emma Lee LeSueur | no |

Other Info: Dunkum Funeral Home marker

| Raikes
    G. W. | 19 July 1885
15 March 1938 | | yes |

Inscription: Gone but not Forgotten

Other Info: Footstone: GWR

| Wootton
    J. W. | | | etched fieldstone |

There are 21 unidentified graves in this cemetery.

Last Name Given Name (Maiden Name	Date of Birth Date of Death Age at Death	Spouse	Tombstone

Maple Grove Penecostal Church

Branch Beatrice G.	12 Nov. 1895 28 Sept. 1966		yes
Branch Ella Vest	18 Nov. 1890 5 Dec. 1984	 Ortho Edd Branch	yes

Inscription: Earth has no sorrow that heaven cannot heal.

Other Info: Footstone: Mother; Shares a headstone with her husband.

Branch Frank W.	6 Jan. 1926 20 Feb. 2002		yes
Branch James W.	8 April 1945 29 Aug. 1964		yes

Other Info: Joseph W. Bliley Funeral Home marker

Branch John O.	8 March 1924 19 Jan. 1998		yes

Other Info: Joseph W. Bliley Funeral Home

Branch Ortho Edd	6 Oct. 1897 25 March 1959	 Ella Vest Branch	yes

Inscription: Earth has no sorrow that heaven cannot heal

Other Info: Footstone: Father; Shares a headstone with his wife.

Bryant Amy Renee	26 April 1972 28 April 1972		yes
Bryant Calvin C. Sr.	1925 1988		no

Other Info: Whitten Bros. Funeral Home marker

Last Name Given Name (Maiden Name)	Date of Birth Date of Death Age at Death	Spouse	Tombstone
Bryant Charlie E.	31 Aug. 1881 20 Mar. 1972	Polly G. Bryant	yes

Inscription: Each duty done, they rest in peace.

Other Info: Footstone: Father; Shares a headstone with his wife.

Bryant Clyde L.	25 June 1915 12 Jan. 1963		yes

Other Info: Footstone: C.L.B.

Bryant David Banks	4 June 1943 14 Aug. 1966		yes

Inscription: PFC, 572 Engineer Co., Vietnam

Bryant Ezra Russell Sr.	7 Aug. 1922 8 Nov. 1999		yes
Bryant Flora Coates	26 May 1898 20 May 1960		yes

Inscription: Asleep in Jesus

Other Info: Footstone: F.C.B.

Bryant Kaelynn Renee	2003 2003		no

Other Info: Dunkum Funeral Home marker

Bryant M. Pauline Wright	31 Oct. 1920 14 May 1984	Ralph David Bryant	yes

Inscription: Death is only a shadow across the path to heaven.

Bryant Mamie Jamerson	March 1940 Sept 1968		yes

Last Name Given Name (Maiden Name	Date of Birth Date of Death Age at Death	Spouse	Tombstone
Bryant 　Minnie Burks	2 May 1901 10 Sept. 1966	Russell Roy Bryant	yes

Inscription: Into thy hands I commend my spirit.

Other Info: Shares a headstone with her husband; Footstone: Mother

Bryant 　Polly G.	23 Dec. 1884 10 Oct. 1959	Charlie E. Bryant	yes

Inscription: Each duty done, they rest in peace.

Other Info: Footstone: Mother; Shares a headstone with her husband.

Bryant 　Ralph David	25 Dec. 1911 Dec. 1995	M. Pauline Wright Bryant	yes

Inscription: Death is only a shadow across the path to heaven.

Other Info: Shares a headstone with his wife.

Bryant 　Russell Roy	1 Nov. 1901 2 Dec. 1994	Minnie Burks Bryant	yes

Inscription: Into thy hands I commend my spirit.

Other Info: Shares a headstone with his wife; Footstone: Father

Burney 　Elsie May B.	3 Nov. 1915 3 Feb. 1974	James Thomas Burney	yes

Inscription: Precious Lord take my hand.

Other Info: Footstone: Mother; Shares a headstone with her husband.

Burney 　Herman Hacks	29 Oct. 1940 15 May 1986		yes

Inscription: Married: 6 Sept. 1964

Other Info: Footstone: Husband; Dunkum Funeral Home marker

Last Name Given Name (Maiden Name)	Date of Birth Date of Death Age at Death	Spouse	Tombstone
Burney James Thomas	4 Oct. 1909 10 July 1979	Elsie May B. Burney	yes

Inscription: Precious Lord take my hand

Other Info: Shares a headstone with his wife.

Carroll baby			no
Cunningham Samuel P.	27 Dec. 1894 14 Dec. 1966		yes
Griffin Earl H.	11 Jan. 1884 23 Feb. 1981		yes

Inscription: SGT, US Army, World War II

Other Info: Footstone: Father

| Griffin
  Mary T. | 14 Feb. 1907
30 Jan. 1972 | | yes |

Other Info: Footstone: Mother

| Gunter
  Kenneth L. | 23 Sept. 1948
10 Jan. 1957 | | yes |

Other Info: Footstone: Son

| Gunter
  Lacy D. | 25 April 1912
7 Jan. 1976 | Evelyn G. Gunter | yes |

Inscription: Father; I Love You

Other Info: Footstone: Lacy Douglas Gunter, TEC 4, US Army, World War II (same dates as are on the headstone)

| Gunter
  Sammy L. | 1925
2000 | | no |

Other Info: Robinson Funeral Home marker

Last Name Given Name (Maiden Name)	Date of Birth Date of Death Age at Death	Spouse	Tombstone
Gunther Elizabeth C.	18 Sept 1886 29 Feb. 1964	Robert W. Gunther	yes

Inscription: Rest in Peace

Other Info: Footstone: Mother; Shares a headstone with her husband.

Gunther Robert L.	12 July 1907 9 Sept. 1977	Louise R. Gunther	yes

Inscription: In Loving Memory

Other Info: Footstone: Father

Gunther Robert W.	16 Oct. 1881 21 Nov. 1956	Elizabeth C. Gunther	yes

Inscription: Rest in Peace

Other Info: Footstone: Father; Shares a headstone with his wife.

Jamerson Edward W.	11 April 1934 13 Sept. 1995	Beatrice B. Jamerson	yes

Inscription: Our Children: Butch, David, Bruce, Tony, Wanda; In God's Care

Other Info: Footstone: Daddy

Leftwich Alexander H.	16 Feb. 1925 24 Aug. 1993	Cora H. Leftwich	yes

Inscription: Wed-13 April 1946

Other Info: Footstone: Alexander Leftwich Jr., TEC 5, US Army, World War II (gives the same dates as the headstone)

Lester Connie A. "Bumper"	7 Sept. 1944 11 Oct. 1986	Jud Ray Lester	yes
Maxey William Jennings Jr.	18 May 1917 19 Feb. 1985	Lula Bryant Maxey	yes

Last Name Given Name (Maiden Name)	Date of Birth Date of Death Age at Death	Spouse	Tombstone
Ragland Harry			no

Other Info: Known to be buried here; son of Henry Douglas Ragland

| Ragland
Henry Douglas | 15 Oct. 1876
21 April 1961 | | no |

Other Info: Dunkum Funeral Home marker

| Ragland
Otha Morris 1 | 1 April 1904
9 May 1993 | Daisy Beatrice Ragland | yes |

Inscription: (On back of headstone-Ragland Children: Minnie, Melvin, Prentice, Julia, Junior, Gracie, Nancy, Charles, Helen, Earl, Betty, Barbara, Fleta, Carol)

| Rankin
Charles W. | 1956
1988 | | no |

Other Info: Whitten Funeral Home marker

| Stevens
Mary Branch | 21 May 1924
17 Feb. 1959 | | yes |

Inscription: Rest in Peace

Other Info: Footstone: Daughter

| Thompson
Carolyn | | Sherwood Thompson | no |

Other Info: Wooden marker gives the names of Sherwood and Carolyn Thompson.

| Thompson
Sherwood | | Carolyn Thompson | no |

Other Info: Wooden marker gives the names of Sherwood and Carolyn Thompson.

Last Name Given Name (Maiden Name	Date of Birth Date of Death Age at Death	Spouse	Tombstone
Winters Doris B.	1932 1992		no

Other Info: Dunkum Funeral Home marker

George Maxey Family off Rd. 705

Agee Georgie Ellen	27 Sept. 1890		no

Other Info: Known to be buried here. She was the daughter of Nannie Lee Maxey, a sister of George W. Maxey.

Agee James Ballard Maxey	18 Oct. 1863		no

Other Info: Known to be buried here. He was the son of George W. and Mary J. Maxey also buried in this cemetery.

Agee Nettie May	8 April 1889 14 July 1889		no

Other Info: Known to be buried here. She was a daughter of Nannie Lee Maxey who was the sister of George W. Maxey.

Harris Mary Ellen Maxey	21 Oct. 1858 27 Oct. 1885		no

Other Info: Known to be buried here. She was the sister of George William Maxey, buried in this cemetery and Abram Thomas Maxey buried in a cemetery nearby.

Harris Mary Lula	3 Aug. 1876 22 Dec. 1891		no

Other Info: Known to be buried here. She was the daughter of Mary Ellen Maxey Harris, also buried in this cemetery.

Last Name Given Name (Maiden Name)	Date of Birth Date of Death Age at Death	Spouse	Tombstone
Maxey George William	3 Oct. 1827 30 Dec. 1890	Mary Jane Ferguson Maxey	no

Other Info: Known to be buried here. He and his wife were the parents of George Albert Maxey (interred at Sharon Baptist Church) and Abram Thomas Maxey (interred in another family cemetery close by) These two brothers married sisters.

Maxey Mary Jane Ferguson	23 June 1823 19 June 1903	George William Maxey	no

Other Info: Known to be buried here.

Thomas Maxey Family on Rd. 705

Agee Robert A.	1853 1924		yes

Other Info: He was the brother of Ellen Pocahontas Agee Maxey. Another sibling, Laura Alice Agee Maxey is buried elsewhere.

Maxey Abram Thomas	15 Nov. 1856 11 Jan. 1931	Ellen Pocahontas Agee Maxey	yes

Other Info: Shares a headstone with his wife. They were married on 21 Sept. 1881.

Maxey Ellen Pocahontas (Agee)	31 Dec. 1849 20 July 1938	Abram Thomas Maxey	yes

Other Info: Shares a headstone with her husband.

Maxey George Albert	19 June 1931 1931		no

Other Info: Known to be buried here. His parents were Leonard Maxey and Etta Self Maxey.

Last Name Given Name (Maiden Name)	Date of Birth Date of Death Age at Death	Spouse	Tombstone
Maxey infant			no

Other Info: Known to be buried here. Year of birth, death are unknown. Parents were Leonard Maxey and Etta Self Maxey.

Maxey Samuel Thomas	16 July 1923 19 July 1923		no

Other Info: Known to be buried here. His parents were Leonard Maxey and Etta Self Maxey who are interred at Sharon Baptist Church.

There are 4 unidentified graves in this cemetery including those known to be buried here.

McCraw Family at "Elysian Grove"

McCraw Frank			no

Other Info: Reported in a WPA Survey to be buried here.

McCraw R. M. (Richard Miller)	14 Nov. 1841 15 Jan. 1862		yes

Inscription: In Memory of

Other Info: Tombstone has been reported and described by the WPA Survey of 1937 and others. It could not be found in a recent survey. His parents were Cary Harrison and Susanna Hix McCraw. He died in the Civil War.

There are several other unidentified graves in this cemetery.

Miles Family on Rd. 655

Miles Eliza (Liza) Davis	1841 1903	George Overton Miles	no

Other Info: Known to be buried here.

Last Name Given Name (Maiden Name)	Date of Birth Date of Death Age at Death	Spouse	Tombstone
Miles George (Overton)	1838 1889	Eliza (Liza) Davis Miles	yes

Inscription: Co. F, 1 VA INF, CSA

Other Info: His father was Henry Miles who was born in 1798. His brother was Robert M. Miles, who is also buried here.

| Miles
  Robert | 1834 | | yes |

Inscription: Co. D, 56th INF, CSA

Other Info: His father was Henry Miles.

Moore-Proffitt Family on Rd. 627

| Goolsby
  J. Pink | 24 Sept. 1875
27 Feb. 1898 | | yes |
| Moore
  Basil H. | 8 Sept. 1893
11 Jan. 1924 | | yes |

Inscription: In God's Care

| Moore
  Ella Jane | 17 Feb. 1891
21 May 1910 | | yes |

Inscription: Asleep in Jesus

| Moore
  F. Kerfoot | 2 July 1903
3 July 1951 | | yes |

Inscription: In God's Care; B. of L.F. and E.

Other Info: Has a Thacker Bros Funeral Home marker

| Moore
  James Walker | 1 June 1869
27 Jan. 1926 | | yes |

Last Name Given Name (Maiden Name)	Date of Birth Date of Death Age at Death	Spouse	Tombstone
Moore Joseph	Aug. 1836 21 May 1904	Nannie S. Moore	yes

Inscription: Father; Our father has gone to a mansion of rest, to the glorious land by the Deity blest.

Other Info: He shares a stone with his wife and L. Kemper Moore.

Moore L. Kemper	19 Sept. 1873 18 Oct. 1927		yes

Inscription: Brother; Tho' lost to sight, to memory dear

Other Info: Shares a headstone with Nannie S. and Joseph Moore.

Moore Nannie S.	March 1839 17 June 1907	Joseph Moore	yes

Inscription: Mother; We trust our loss will be her gain and that with Christ she's gone to reign.

Other Info: Shares a stone with her husband and L. Kemper Moore.

Moore Philip S.	12 April 1887 53 years		yes
Proffitt J. Ellen	11 April 1847 7 Jan. 1928		yes
Proffitt J. Parker	26 Dec. 1876 9 Feb. 1890		yes
Proffitt James Warmsley	27 July 1824 12 March 1914		yes
Proffitt Oliver G.	11 Dec. 1850 22 Sept 1932		yes

There are 13 unidentified graves in this cemetery.

Last Name	Date of Birth	Spouse	Tombstone
Given Name	Date of Death		
(Maiden Name	Age at Death		

Moore-Pryer Family on Rd. 1003

Moore   1 Feb. 1853   yes
   Allen W.   24 Sept 1910

   Inscription: I know that my Redeemer liveth

   Other Info: Footstone: AWM

Pryor   6 May 1849   yes
   Pattie W.   30 Dec. 1913

   Other Info: Footstone: PWP

There is one unidentified grave in this cemetery.

Moorman Family on Rd. 604

Moorman   31 May 1849   yes
   Catherine E. (Emma) 10 Aug. 1879 Joel Thomas Moorman

   Other Info: Footstone: CEM; Shares a headstone with her son, Leonard H. Moorman.

Moorman   22 Nov. 1870   yes
   Leonard H. (Hildrup) 14 April 1902

   Other Info: Shares a headstone with his mother, Catherine E. Moorman. His father was Joel Thomas Moorman.

There are 2 unidentified graves in this cemetery.

Cleveland J. Morris Family off Rd. 791

Morris   16 March 1858   yes
   Cleveland J.   20 Sept. 1915   Elnora Webb Morris

   Inscription: Husband of Elnora Morris

Last Name Given Name (Maiden Name)	Date of Birth Date of Death Age at Death	Spouse	Tombstone
Morris Elizabeth Peters	25 June 1897 9 Dec. 1911		yes

Inscription: Daughter of C.J. and Elnora Morris; Gone to a better land.

Morris Elnora Webb	7 July 1850 2 Jan. 1940	Cleveland J. Morris	yes

Inscription: Wife of C.J. Morris; At Rest

Morris Rhoda Pearl	22 Nov. 1899 15 March 1912		yes

Inscription: Daughter of C.J. and Elnora Morris; Not lost but gone before.

Morriss Family at "Montevedio"

Horsley Carrie Lee Morriss	1896 1918	Percy Robert Horsley	no

Other Info: Known to be buried here.

Horsley Percy Robert	1887	Carrie Lee Morriss Horsley	no

Other Info: Known to be buried here.

Morriss Ella Ora Davis	1861 1939	Walter Clarence Morriss	no

Other Info: Known to be buried here.

Morriss infant	1892 1892		no

Other Info: Known to be born here. The infant's parents were Walter C. and Ella O.D. Morriss.

Last Name Given Name (Maiden Name	Date of Birth Date of Death Age at Death	Spouse	Tombstone
Morriss Walter Clarence	1858	Ella Ora Davis Morriss	no

    Other Info: Known to be buried here.

Rachel Morriss Family off Rd. 664 — African American

Morriss Rachel	13 May 1950 66 years	Wiley J. Morriss	no

    Other Info: Thacker Bros. Funeral Home marker; Her parents were Robert Cook and Elvira Miller.

Morriss Wiley J.		Rachel Morriss	no

    Other Info: Known to be buried here.

There are 34 unidentified graves in this cemetery.

Moseley-Eldridge Slaves at "Rolfeton"

Eldridge Jennie	1855 died of old age		no

    Other Info: Reported in the Death Records of Buckingham Co. Owner was B.R. Eldridge,

Eldridge Maurice	5 Nov. 1856 6 months		no

    Other Info: Known to be buried here. His parents were Ellen and Maurice. His owner was Rolfe Eldridge

Eldridge (no name)	1858		no

    Other Info: Known to be buried here. Owner was Rolfe Eldridge.

Last Name Given Name (Maiden Name	Date of Birth Date of Death Age at Death	Spouse	Tombstone
Eldridge Timothy	15 April 1856 9 years		no

Other Info: Known to be buried here. His mother was Maria. His owner was Benjamin R. Eldridge.

Eldridge Willis	9 June 1862 23 years		no

Other Info: Reported in the Death Records of Buckingham Co. Owner was B.R. Eldridge.

There are 14 visible graves, but probably many more in this cemetery.

Mourner's Valley Baptist Church — African American

Agee Thomas Edward	21 May 1929 2 Nov. 1985		yes

Inscription: Give thanks unto the Lord for He is Good. For His mercy endureth forever-Psalms 107:1

Allen Albert	1917 1987		yes

Inscription: US Army, World War II

Other Info: Reid's Funeral Home marker gives these dates: 25 Dec. 1917, 31 July 1987; Footstone is a military stone.

Allen Charlene G.	1953 1959		no

Other Info: Unidentified funeral home marker

Last Name Given Name (Maiden Name)	Date of Birth Date of Death Age at Death	Spouse	Tombstone
Allen Charles Allen Sr.	1856 1919	Martha Ann Allen	yes

Other Info: Father of 14 children; Shares a headstone with his wife. He and his wife donated the land for this church building and the cemetery. Some of their children who are buried here are Samuel, Robert, Albert and Isaiah Allen.

| Allen
Charles Jr. |

2-23-66 | (1) Willie Sue Allen
(2) Lurt Allen | no |

Other Info: Unidentified funeral home marker; buried between his 2 wives.

| Allen
Huston |
Oct. 1940 | | yes |

Other Info: Shares a stone with Josephine Allen Taylor.

| Allen
Isaiah | 19 Oct. 1910
8 May 1989 | | yes |

Inscription: PVT, US Army, World War II

Other Info: Footstone is a military stone

| Allen
Katie | 1924
1948 | | no |

Other Info: Reid's Funeral Home marker

| Allen
Lurt | 1896
11 April 1931 | Charles Allen Jr. | yes |

Inscription: Mother of 7 children

Other Info: Footstone: LA; mother of 7 children

Last Name Given Name (Maiden Name)	Date of Birth Date of Death Age at Death	Spouse	Tombstone
Allen Martha Ann	1862 29 Dec. 1930	Charles Allen Sr.	yes

Other Info: Footstone: MA Mother of 14 children; Shares a headstone with her husband.

Allen Robert			Etched fieldstone

Allen Robert	24 April 1919 14 April 1981		yes

Inscription: US Army, World War II

Allen Samuel	20 March 1926 14 April 1964		yes

Inscription: Virginia, PFC, 1204 AREA SVC Unit, World War II

Allen Thomas	1916 1974		no

Other Info: Reid's Funeral Home marker

Allen Willie Sue	1894 8 July 1923	Charles Allen Jr.	yes

Inscription: The mother of six children

Ayers Alexander	27 Feb. 1949 31 Mar. 1976		yes

Inscription: Lord, What Wait I for my Hope is in Thee. Psalms 39:7

Ayers Gertrude	1940 1976		no

Other Info: Reid's Funeral Home marker; Gertrude Ayers and Thomas E. Agee were siblings. Her mother-in-law was Louise Ayres also buried here.

Last Name Given Name (Maiden Name	Date of Birth Date of Death Age at Death	Spouse	Tombstone
Ayers Guy Matthew			no

Other Info: Reid's Funeral Home marker-gives one date: 5-29-1966

| Ayers
    Houston L. | 1915
1995 | | no |

Other Info: Reid's Funeral Home marker

| Ayers
    Ida C. (Chambers) | 23 Oct. 1912
5 Sept. 1997 | | yes |

Other Info: Ida C. Ayers and Jack Junius Chambers were brother and sister.

| Ayers
    Louise Virginia | 25 July 1920
27 Oct. 1984 | | yes |

Inscription: Mother; Jesus He is Sweet I Know

| Ayers
    Lucie V. | 1921
1976 | | no |

Other Info: Reid's Funeral Home marker

| Ayers
    Micheall | | | no |

Other Info: Unidentified funeral home marker with dates missing. Micheall Ayers and Percy Ayres were cousins.

| Ayers
    Paul | 1921
1977 | | no |

Other Info: Reid's Funeral Home marker.

| Ayers
    Paul | | Virginia Ayers | |

Other Info: Known to be buried in this cemetery. He and his wife, Virginia Ayers were the parents of Robert M. Ayers who is buried on private property on Rd. 678.

Last Name Given Name (Maiden Name	Date of Birth Date of Death Age at Death	Spouse	Tombstone
Ayers Robert James	20 Nov. 195_ 10 months		no

Other Info: Reid's Funeral Home marker

Ayers Shirley	1950 1976	Burris Ayers	no

Other Info: Shirley Ayers is buried with an infant son who both died at his birth. She is the daughter of Walter Gough also buried in this cemetery. Her mother-in-law, Louise Ayres is also buried in this cemetery.

Ayers Virginia		Paul Ayers	

Other Info: Known to be buried in this cemetery.

Ayres Charlotte Ann	20 March 1959 57 years		no

Other Info: Thacker Bros. Funeral Home marker

Ayres Jessie J.	1945 1983		no

Other Info: Reid's Funeral Home marker; His mother, Ida C. Ayers is also buried in this cemetery.

Ayres John Lee	31 Dec. 1958 1 yr, 2 mo.		no

Other Info: unidentified funeral home marker

Ayres Percy	20 Dec. 1938 4 Feb. 2002		no

Other Info: This is an above ground vault-Reid's FH

Last Name Given Name (Maiden Name)	Date of Birth Date of Death Age at Death	Spouse	Tombstone
Ayres Willie	1908 1984		no

Other Info: Reid's Funeral Home marker.

| Booker
  Classie L. |
22 June 1958 | | no |

Other Info: Thacker Bros. Funeral Home marker

| Booker
  James | 1924
1985 | | no |

Other Info: Reid's Funeral Home marker.

| Booker
  John | 1893
1976 | | no |

Other Info: Reid's Funeral Home marker

| Carter
  Kyrie A. | 10 Sept 1994
11 Mar 1998 | | yes |

Inscription: Asleep in Jesus

Other Info: Mother of this child is Kim Carter.

| Chambers
  Aaron E. | 22 April 1925
13 Feb. 1993 |
Alice B. Chambers | yes |

Inscription: In Loving Memory

| Chambers
  Cathren J. | June 1885
Nov. 1957 |
George Chambers | yes |

Other Info: Shares a headstone with her husband.

| Chambers
  Charlie | 2 July 1891
6 Feb. 1932 | | yes |

| Chambers
  George | Oct. 1876
Feb. 1946 |
Cathren J. | yes |

Other Info: Shares a headstone with his wife.

Last Name Given Name (Maiden Name	Date of Birth Date of Death Age at Death	Spouse	Tombstone
Chambers Henry L.	1946 1985		no

Other Info: Reid's Funeral Home marker.

Chambers Jack Junius	16 Feb. 1928 5 July 2000		no

Other Info: Above ground vault-Reid's FH

Chambers James H.	7 Mar. 1919 24 Sept 1983		yes

Inscription: MM2 US Navy, World War II

Chambers John H.	4 Apr. 1909 17 Mar. 1975		yes

Inscription: TEC 5, US Army, World War II

Chambers Minnie			no

Other Info: Dunkum Bros. Funeral Home marker with dates missing.

Chambers Pauline	19 June 1925 Nov. 1936		yes

Inscription: In Loving Memory

Chambers Ruth E.	7 July 1942 12 Dec. 2000		yes

Other Info: Also has a Reid's Funeral Home marker.

Chambers Sallie			no

Other Info: This is a Reid's Funeral Home marker with one date on it: 10-17-1966

Last Name Given Name (Maiden Name)	Date of Birth Date of Death Age at Death	Spouse	Tombstone
Chambers Willie M. Jr.	25 July 1933 3 April 1983		yes

Inscription: PFC, US Army, Korea

Coleman Alfred M.	1919 1996 76 years	Mary Ayres Coleman	no

Other Info: Thacker Bros. Funeral Home marker

Coleman Mary Ayres	1924 1989 65 years	Alfred M. Coleman	

Inscription: no

Other Info: Thacker Bros. Funeral Home marker

Edwards Maggie Chambers	9 May 1902 18 April 1966		yes
Forbes Solomon Jr.	24 Nov. 1946 10 Oct. 1999		yes

Inscription: Always in our Hearts

Ford Callie	1901 1974		no

Other Info: Reid's Funeral Home marker

Ford Frank	1919 1975		no

Other Info: Reid's Funeral Home marker

Ford Lucas R.	1978 1980		no

Other Info: Reid's Funeral Home marker.

Last Name Given Name (Maiden Name)	Date of Birth Date of Death Age at Death	Spouse	Tombstone
Ford Nancy	1923 1988		no

Other Info: Reid's Funeral Home marker.

Gough Jennie V.	1896 1971		no

Other Info: Reid's Funeral Home marker.

Gough Timothy Archie	18 Dec. 1956 4 Dec. 1991		yes
Gough Walter	28 Oct. 1923 14 June 1995		yes

Inscription: US Navy, World War II

Jones Brenda M.	22 July 1965 17 July 1982		yes

Other Info: Also has a Reid's Funeral Home marker.

Lawrence Lucinda			no

Other Info: This is an unidentified funeral home marker with one date: 3-4-65.

Lee Annie Chambers	19 May 1920 30 Oct. 1960		yes

Inscription: In Loving Memory

Lee Howard A. Sr.	1921 1992	Arlene G. Lee	yes
Patterson Ruby	1902 1998		no

Other Info: Reid's Funeral Home marker.

Last Name Given Name (Maiden Name)	Date of Birth Date of Death Age at Death	Spouse	Tombstone
Redmond Annie M.	1907 1969	James Redmond	yes

Other Info: Shares a headstone with her husband.

Redmond James	1897 1980	Annie M. Redmond	yes

Other Info: Shares a headstone with his wife.

Rogers Phyllis L.	18 Jan. 1944 21 April 2001		no

Other Info: This is an above ground vault-Reid's FH

Taylor Charles Bernard	1957 1986		yes

Inscription: US Army

Other Info: Also has a Reid's Funeral Home marker.

Taylor Dallas	1930 1998		no

Other Info: Reid's Funeral Home marker.

Taylor Josephine Allen	Oct. 1940		yes

Other Info: Shares a headstone with Huston Allen.

Toney John M.	1941 1999		no

Other Info: Reid's Funeral Home marker.

Turner Cornelius	1883 1988 105 years	Moses Turner	no

Other Info: Thacker Bros. Funeral Home marker; She and her husband are the parents of James Turner.

Last Name Given Name (Maiden Name)	Date of Birth Date of Death Age at Death	Spouse	Tombstone
Turner George W.	 21 Dec. 1977		no

Other Info: Lugo's Funeral Home marker

Turner James D.	1917 1975		no

Other Info: Reid's Funeral Home marker

Turner James Earl	1932 1992		no

Other Info: Thacker Bros. Funeral Home marker.

Turner Moses	1892 1977	 Cornelius Turner	no

Other Info: Reids Funeral Home marker

Turner Robert E.	1919 1988		no

Other Info: Reid's Funeral Home marker.

There are at least 18 graves in this cemetery, without identification or marked with illegible funeral markers.

Mt. Olive Baptist Church — African American

Anderson Earl F.	1957 1980		no

Other Info: Reid's Funeral Home marker

Anderson Maggie Christine	20 Sept. 1957 19 Jan 1998		no

Other Info: This is an above ground vault: Reid's FH

Buckingham Burials

Last Name Given Name (Maiden Name	Date of Birth Date of Death Age at Death	Spouse	Tombstone
Anderson Moses	25 June 1926 6 Jan. 1986		yes

Inscription: US Navy, World War II

Other Info: Has an above ground vault. The birth year on the vault is 1927 rather than 1926: Reid's FH; Moses Anderson was the father of Earl F. Anderson and Maggie Christine Anderson also buried in this cemetery.

Bell Edgar	1 Aug. 1886 8 Nov. 1973		yes

Inscription: Virginia, PVT, US Army, World War II

Other Info: Edger Bell and Rosa B. Harvey were siblings.

Booker Annie Brown	May 1890 3 Nov. 1958		yes
Booker Eddie	1 April 1924 Oct. 1962		yes

Inscription: Virginia, USNR, World War II

Booker Howard J.	20 Sep. 1943 18 Aug. 1980		yes

Inscription: SP 4, US Army, Vietnam

Other Info: Howard J. Booker and Moses J. Booker were brothers.

Booker James	1950 1975		yes

Inscription: Gone but not Forgotten

Booker James Andrew	12 April 1942 28 July 1990		yes

Last Name Given Name (Maiden Name)	Date of Birth Date of Death Age at Death	Spouse	Tombstone
Booker Joseph W.	27 March 1945 10 Dec. 1982		yes

Other Info: Joseph W. Booker was the grandson of Alfred Lee also buried in this cemetery.

Booker Lucy C.	22 April 1918 18 July 2002		no

Other Info: This is an above ground vault-Reid's FH

Booker Moses J.	29 Oct. 1915 25 Jan. 1985		yes

Inscription: PVT, US Army, World War II

Booker Walter J. (Junior) Sr	17 March 1933 18 May 1993		yes

Other Info: Has a Dunkum Funeral Home marker

Braxton Overton	1931 1941		no

Other Info: Dunkum Funeral Home marker

Chambers Egar			no

Other Info: Reid's Funeral Home marker-somewhat illegible, no dates

Chambers Elijah	15 Dec. 1919 25 Feb. 1978		yes

Inscription: PVT, US Army, World War II

Chambers Eugene	1917 2001		no

Other Info: Reid's Funeral Home marker

Last Name Given Name (Maiden Name)	Date of Birth Date of Death Age at Death	Spouse	Tombstone
Chambers James F.	1949 2001		no

Other Info: This is an above ground vault-Reid's FH

Chambers King D.	1912 1977		no

Other Info: Reid's Funeral Home marker

Chambers Onell A.	1955 1991		no

Other Info: Dunkum Funeral Home marker

Chambers Shirley Sr.	1922 2002		no

Other Info: This is an above ground vault-Dunkum FH

Chambers W. Russell	1910 1974		no

Other Info: This is an above ground vault with the added inscription: Rest in Peace, God Loves You.

Chambers Walter Lee	6 Feb. 1947 21 Feb. 1969		yes

Other Info: Walter Lee Chambers and Onell A. Chambers were siblings.

Fogg Audrey G.	20 Dec. 1952 13 Feb. 2000		no

Other Info: This is an above ground vault: Reid's FH

Ford John B.	1918 1982		yes

Inscription: US Army, World War II

Last Name Given Name (Maiden Name)	Date of Birth Date of Death Age at Death	Spouse	Tombstone
Garrett			

    Other Info: The mother of Emmett Lanxton Garrett is known to be buried in this cemetery, in an unmarked grave.

| Garrett
  Emmett Lanxton | 9 Nov. 1921
29 May 1997 | | yes |

    Inscription: US Army, World War II, Korea

    Other Info: Also has an above ground vault.

| Gray
  Mary Lizzie | 1918
1988 | | no |

    Other Info: Reid's Funeral Home marker; Mary Lizzie Gray, Joseph Lee and Chris Alexander Lee were siblings, and are all buried in this cemetery.

| Harvey
  George | 1892
1966 |
Rosa B. Harvey | yes |

    Inscription: Peace, perfect peace

| Harvey
  Rosa B. (Bell) | 1900
1988 |
George Harvey | yes |

    Inscription: Rest in Peace

| Jones
  Earl | 1945
1987 | | no |

    Other Info: Earl Jones was the son of Samuel R. Jones.

| Jones
  Sam (Samuel) R. | 24 May 1924
21 Feb. 1992 | | yes |

    Inscription: PFC, US Army, World War II

    Other Info: Has a Dunkum Funeral Home marker.

Last Name Given Name (Maiden Name	Date of Birth Date of Death Age at Death	Spouse	Tombstone
Kidd Henry O.	15 March 1930 13 Sept. 1993		yes

Inscription: In Loving Memory

Other Info: Has a Dunkum Funeral Home marker

Lee Alfred, Deacon	22 Sept. 1888 28 Aug. 1976		ye

Inscription: Gone but not Forgotten

Lee Annie Elizabeth	8 June 1913 3 Oct. 1998	Tommy Houston Lee Sr.	yes

Other Info: Shares a headstone with her husband; also has an above ground vault: Reids FH

Lee Chris Alexander, Deacon	4 Oct. 1924 19 June 1980		yes

Lee Elton Sr.	4 Sept 1928 24 Jan 2002		no

Other Info: This is an above ground vault-Reid's FH

Lee James E.	11 Jan 1917 20 Dec. 1979		yes

Inscription: US Army, World War II

Lee Joseph	1907 1989		no

Other Info: This is an above ground vault-Reid's FH

Lee Lunell B.	1888 1960	Robert Edward Lee	yes

Inscription: Absent, not Dead

Last Name Given Name (Maiden Name)	Date of Birth Date of Death Age at Death	Spouse	Tombstone
Lee Mary Lou	2 Sept 1907 3 Feb. 1995		no

Other Info: This is an above ground vault-Reid's FH

Lee Moses G.	10 May 1930 28 April 1981		yes

Lee Robert Edward	1895 1975	Lunell B. Lee	yes

Other Info: Robert Edward Lee and Lunell B. Lee were the parents of James E. Lee and Moses G. Lee also buried in this cemetery.

Lee Sam, Rev.	29 Nov. 1905 12 Mar 1995		

Other Info: This is an above ground vault-Reid's FH

Lee Tommy Houston Sr.	1 Jan. 1912 20 Sept 1998	Annie Elizabeth Lee	yes

Other Info: Also has an above ground vault: Reid's FH. Tommy Houston Lee Sr. and Annie Elizabeth Lee are the parents of Houston Lee Jr., the husband of Virginia C. Lee who is buried in this cemetery.

Lee Virginia C.	1941 1999	Houston Lee Jr.	yes

Other Info: Also has an above ground vault with these dates: (born) 23 Dec. 1941, (died) 27 Aug. 1999-Reid's FH. Virginia C. Lee was the niece of Rev. Sam Lee and Mary Lou Lee also buried in this cemetery.

Logan Garfield	16 Feb. 1917 7 May 1976	Nannie B. Logan	yes

Inscription: In My Father's House are Many Mansions

Other Info: Shares a headstone with his wife. Has an above ground vault.

Last Name Given Name (Maiden Name)	Date of Birth Date of Death Age at Death	Spouse	Tombstone
Logan Josephine	1879 1974		no

Other Info: This is an above ground vault.

Logan Nannie B.	29 Mar. 1920 2002	Garfield Logan	yes

Inscription: In My Father's House are Many Mansions

Other Info: Shares a headstone with her husband. Has an above ground vault.

Marshall Dolly Lee	12 Mar 1951 22 Feb 1995		yes

Other Info: The father of Dolly Lee Marshall was Chris Alexander Lee also buried in this cemetery.

Mitchell Agatha Wright	13 March 1887 25 Feb. 2001		no

Other Info: This is an above ground vault.-Reid's FH; Agatha Wright Mitchell was the mother of Annie Elizabeth Lee also buried in this cemetery.

Patterson Garfield	1904 1988		no

Other Info: Reid's Funeral Home marker

Shuler Lovie	1914 1996	Samuel Shuler	yes

Other Info: Shares a headstone with her husband. Has a Bland-Reid Funeral Home marker.

Shuler Samuel	1914 1989	Lovie Shuler	yes

Other Info: Shares a headstone with his wife. Has a Bland-Reid Funeral Home marker.

Last Name Given Name (Maiden Name)	Date of Birth Date of Death Age at Death	Spouse	Tombstone
Taylor Minnie Chambers	1924 2002 77 years		no

Other Info: Thacker Bros. Funeral Home marker. Note: This cemetery has 8 graves without identification or illegible funeral markers.

Nativity Catholic Church

Bates William Joseph	30 March 1921 13 Dec. 1995	Marie B. Bates	yes

Inscription: Col., US Army, WW II, Korea, Vietnam

Clarke Robert Benjamin	13 Jan.1913 17 Feb. 2001		yes

Inscription: Loving Memories Last Forever

Defeo Rose L.	16 April 1916 16 Feb. 1990		yes

Heinlman Constance M.	22 May 1934 20 Aug. 1994		yes

Inscription: A 2C, US Air Force, Korea

Laird Joseph Robert Sr.	12 Oct. 1919 13 Dec. 1994		yes

Lutz George Howard	20 July 1933 5 June 1998	Linda Hannah Lutz	yes

Inscription: Beloved Husband and Father

McKay Mona Crane	1912 1994		no

Other Info: Shorter Funeral Home marker

Last Name Given Name (Maiden Name)	Date of Birth Date of Death Age at Death	Spouse	Tombstone
Minyard H. Rickie	25 June 1949 9 Nov. 1990		yes

Inscription: L. CPL, US Marine Corps, Vietnam

Minyard Raymond H.	7 Aug. 1916 24 April 1994		yes

Inscription: SGT, US Army, World War II

Pelletier Arthur Cleary	28 April 1907 22 Jan. 1989		yes

Inscription: SGT, US Army, World War II

Pelletier Norberta Lutz	26 Sept. 1911 22 Dec. 2003		yes

Inscription: Loving Wife and Mother

Polonski Jonathan R.	12 Feb. 1975 14 June 1998		yes
Sauve Patricia Goetz	14 June 1935 3 April 1997	Dudley Sauve	yes

New Hope Baptist Church — African American

Banks John D.	18 Sept. 1935 17 Nov. 1979		yes
Banks Terry Clay	23 Feb. 1973 24 March 1996		yes

Other Info: Reid's Funeral Home marker gives death date as 1986; His father, John D. Banks, is also buried in this cemetery.

Beard Lina C.	30 March 1904 18 July 1973		yes

Last Name Given Name (Maiden Name)	Date of Birth Date of Death Age at Death	Spouse	Tombstone
Booker Latosma	1986 1986		no

  Other Info: Reid's Funeral Home marker

| Brown
  James C., Rev. | 27 Feb. 1917
2 June 1993 | | yes |
| Brown
  Lucille | | | no |

  Other Info: Thomas Funeral Home marker with one date: 2 Feb. 1978

| Brown
  Nannie Bell | 1896
1947 | | yes |
| Brown
  Reuben | 16 Jan 1956
85 years | | yes |

  Inscription: Rest in Peace

| Brown
  William A. | | | no |

  Other Info: Wooden Cross with name penciled on it.

| Cabbel
  Charlie E. | | | no |

  Other Info: Thomas Funeral Home marker with one date: 1 March 1983

| Cabbell
  Charles H. | May 1867
5 Feb. 1948 | | yes |
| Cabbell
  Fannie | 29 April 1868
6 May 1948 | | yes |

  Other Info: Very old cement stone

Last Name Given Name (Maiden Name	Date of Birth Date of Death Age at Death	Spouse	Tombstone
Cabbell Henry	1857 Nov. 19__		yes

Other Info: Very old cement stone; some of it is illegible

Cabbell John	15 Apr 1862 6 Oct. 1939		yes

Inscription: An honest man, the noblest work of God

Cabbell Josephine T.	16 Feb. 1912 (not inscribed)	William L. Cabbell Sr.	yes

Other Info: Shares a headstone with her husband.

Cabbell Sidney W.	16 Aug. 1918 15 April 1963		yes

Inscription: Virginia, Sgt., US Army, World War II

Cabbell Virginia T.	27 Dec. 1875 5 Feb. 1941		yes
Cabbell William	July 1954		yes

Other Info: Very old and illegible tombstone

Cabbell William	1820 1928		yes
Cabbell William L. Jr.	20 March 1936 28 Feb. 1978		yes
Cabbell William L. Sr.	27 Sept 1906 6 June 1979	Josephine T. Cabbell	yes

Other Info: Shares a headstone with his wife.

Cabble Essie			no

Other Info: Known to be buried here

Last Name Given Name (Maiden Name	Date of Birth Date of Death Age at Death	Spouse	Tombstone
Cabell Overton			no

Other Info: Thomas Funeral Home marker with one date: 16 Feb. 1974

| Carter
Annie Amelia Janes | 28 July 1911
11 Sept 1979 | | yes |

| Carter
Charlie | 1915
1998 | | |

Inscription: no

Other Info: A. L. Gilliam Funeral Home marker

| Carter
Pierce Forest | 30 Oct. 1905
17 Oct. 1985 | | yes |

| Coleman
Emma F. | 4 June 1912
24 May 1989 | | yes |

| Coleman
Ethel J. | 15 Jan. 2001 | | no |

Other Info: Thomas Funeral Home marker

| Coleman
Hiawatha L. | 5 Aug. 1909
15 Apr. 1980 | | yes |

| Coleman
James E. | 2 Nov. 1992 | | no |

Other Info: Thomas Funeral Home marker

| Collins
Jessie Maxey | 1908
1991 | | yes |

Other Info: Jessie Maxey Collins is the mother of Charles Maxey.

| Eldridge
Velma S. | 2 Nov. 1918
30 April 1977 | | yes |

Last Name Given Name (Maiden Name)	Date of Birth Date of Death Age at Death	Spouse	Tombstone
Fleming May Ellen Cox	1859 1840		yes
Fleming William Waverly, Rev.	1877 1956		yes

   Inscription: Pastor: Mount Olivet Baptist Church, Newark, New Jersey, 1915-1955

Gray Nancy	30 June 1950 95 years		yes
Hartwell Lottie E.	1898 1965		yes

   Inscription: At Rest

   Other Info: Has a Reid's Funeral Home marker

Hartwell Queenie	1855 1926		yes

   Inscription: At Rest

Jackson Herman Jr.	22 Sept 1958 15 Dec. 1974		yes

   Inscription: Son

James William H.	1905 1985		yes

   Inscription: PFC, US Army, World War II

Janes Bettie Sears	3 Aug. 1910 16 Aug. 1981		yes
Janes Edward			yes

   Inscription: Virginia, Sgt, US Army, December 5, 1925 (only date)

Last Name Given Name (Maiden Name)	Date of Birth Date of Death Age at Death	Spouse	Tombstone
Janes Fannie			no

Other Info: Thomas Funeral Home marker with one date: 18 Aug. 1995

Janes George E. Sr.	7 July 1903 27 April 1971		yes
Janes Josephine Lee	5 March 1869 27 July 1969		yes

Other Info: Has a Reid's Funeral Home marker

Jeffery Bettie	 infant		Etched fieldstone

Inscription: (no dates)

Johnson Bessie L.	1902 2000		no

Other Info: Reid's Funeral Home marker

Johnson George	2 Feb. 1905 5 Oct. 1987	 Mabel T. Johnson	yes

Inscription: Father

Other Info: Shares a headstone with his wife.

Johnson Mabel T.	13 Dec. 1908 30 May 1977	 George Johnson	yes

Inscription: Mother

Other Info: Shares a headstone with her husband.

Lee Adiline	16 Jan 1811 1863	 W. D. Lee	yes

Last Name Given Name (Maiden Name)	Date of Birth Date of Death Age at Death	Spouse	Tombstone
Lee Bernard T.	1915 1979		no

Other Info: Reid's Funeral Home marker

Lee Beulah	1940 1987		no

Other Info: Reid's Funeral Home marker

Lee Charlie F.	1934 1987		no

Other Info: Reid's Funeral Home marker

Lee Edward T.	2 Oct. 1909 7 Sept 1973		yes

Inscription: Virginia, PVT, US Army, World War II

Lee Eliza G.	3 May 1880 5 Dec. 1964		yes
Lee Harding W.	23 July 1922 13 June 1946		yes
Lee James G.			no

Other Info: Reids Funeral Home marker with one date: 5-1-67

Lee John H.	23 May 19__ 26 May 19__		yes
Lee John T.	24 Jan. 1904 19 June 1957		yes
Lee Mary B.			no

Other Info: Joseph Jenkins Jr. Funeral Home marker with one date: 7-19-01

Last Name Given Name (Maiden Name	Date of Birth Date of Death Age at Death	Spouse	Tombstone
Lee Maude A.	17 Dec. 1895 5 Jan. 1963		yes
Lee Oliver A.	1946 1952		yes
Lee Pauline A.	1915 1988		no

Other Info: Reid's Funeral Home marker

Lee Pearl Virginia	19 Apr. 1900 Dec. 20 2000		no

Other Info: This is an above ground vault.

Lee Robert E.	1892 1968		no

Other Info: Reid's Funeral Home marker

Lee Robert Jr.	21 July 1976		yes

Inscription: POW

Other Info: Lived with C. H. Dowdy Family

Lee Roger H.	25 Dec. 1917 4 June 1982		yes
Lee Samuel	6 June 1915 7 Oct. 1970		yes

Inscription: The Lord is My Shepherd

Other Info: Footstone: Father

Lee Thomas			no

Other Info: Reid's Funeral Home marker with one date: 2-14-1969

Last Name Given Name (Maiden Name)	Date of Birth Date of Death Age at Death	Spouse	Tombstone
Lee Thomas			no

Other Info: Reid's Funeral Home marker with one date: 3-22-68

| Lee
  Walker | 1912
1978 | | no |

Other Info: Reid's Funeral Home marker

| Lee
  Walker | June 1880
10 Nov. 1930 | | yes |

Inscription: Shall we meet beyond the river, where the surges cease to roll, where in all is bright forever, sorrow never shall press the soul. By his devoted wife.

| Lee
  William D. |
66 years | Adiline Lee | yes |

| Lewis
  Mary | | | yes |

Other Info: Dates are illegible.

| Lewis
  Senora | 1886
12 Dec. 1906 | | yes |

Inscription: By Her Daughters

| Lyrel
  Mered | 27 Oct. 192_
Dec. 1942 | | yes |

Other Info: Very old cement tombstone, somewhat illegible

| Matha
  Annie Curtis |
Dec. 1902 | | Etched fieldstone |

| Maxey
  Charles | 23 July 1930
13 April 1987 | | yes |

Inscription: In Loving Memory, Husband and Father

Last Name Given Name (Maiden Name)	Date of Birth Date of Death Age at Death	Spouse	Tombstone
McLarty Alberta	15 May 1882 12 Nov. 1928		yes

Inscription: Sleep on and take thy rest.

Mosle Dock			Etched fieldstone

Inscription: (no dates)

Mosley Nannie	1877 1970		yes
Palmer James D.	1995 1995 infant		yes

Inscription: Son and Brother

Patterson Nec.			Etched fieldstone (illegible)

Other Info: Thomas Funeral Home marker has one date-9 May 1970

Scruggs Howard E.	24 Sept. 1925 29 May, 2001		yes

Inscription: PFC, US Army, World War II

Other Info: Has a Reid's Funeral Home marker.

Sears Mary	1866 1948		yes
Smith Annie	1915 1989		no

Other Info: Unidentified funeral home marker

Smith Emma	9 June 1874 8 Sept 1977	Joseph Smith	yes

Other Info: Shares a headstone with her husband.

Last Name Given Name (Maiden Name)	Date of Birth Date of Death Age at Death	Spouse	Tombstone
Smith James M.	29 Sept. 1948 10 Jan 2000		yes

Inscription: Father

| Smith
Joseph | 15 Jan. 1872
9 Jan. 1936 | Emma Smith | yes |

Other Info: Shares a headstone with his wife.

| Smith
Pamela "Noot" | 15 July 1968
3 Jan. 2000 | | yes |

Inscription: Beloved mother, daughter, sister

| Smith
Rosa | 1923
1973 | | yes |

Inscription: mother

| Smith
Tammy H. | 13 Oct. 1970
9 Dec. 1970 | | yes |

Inscription: Our Daughter

| Smith
W. (William) Sr. | 1914
Doc. 1968 | | yes |

Other Info: Father

| Smith
William Jr., Doc. | 1944
1990 | | no |

Other Info: This is an above ground vault-Reid's FH

| Stanton
Cernata | 1882
1941 | | yes |

| Staten
Edith C. |
24 Sept. 2001 | | no |

Other Info: Thomas Funeral Home marker

Last Name Given Name (Maiden Name	Date of Birth Date of Death Age at Death	Spouse	Tombstone
Thomas Garfield P.	3 Feb. 1946		yes
Thomas Julia B.			yes

   Inscription: 14 Oct. 1932

Thomas William			yes

   Other Info: Tombstone has only one date: 10 Dec. 1965; Has a Reid's
   Funeral Home marker

Thompson Daniel	13 June 1930 21 June 1991		yes

   Inscription: PFC, US Army, Korea

Toney Emma	1880 1957		yes
Toney George	1877 1956		yes
Toney George R.	29 Jan. 1849 6 Apr. 1923		yes
Toney Lucy A.	13 July 1856 1915		yes

   Inscription: Mother, thou has from us flown, to the regions far above.
   We to thee erect this stone, consecrated by our love.

   Other Info: Footstone: LAT

Walker Julia Brown	20 Sept 1888 10 Feb. 1977		no

   Other Info: This is an above ground vault

Last Name Given Name (Maiden Name)	Date of Birth Date of Death Age at Death	Spouse	Tombstone
White Frank E.	3 April 1919 24 March 1964		no

Other Info: Unidentified funeral home marker

White Lana Francis	31 March 1900 18 Oct. 1912		yes

Inscription: Beloved

White Lucy	9 Mar 1877 25 Nov. 1924		yes

Inscription: To the memory of my dear wife.

Williams Margaret Lee	24 Aug. 1939 19 Dec. 1961		yes
Woodson Jeter	1866		yes

Inscription: Somewhat illegible

Woodson Martha	1869		yes

Inscription: Somewhat illegible

Other Info: This cemetery has 56 graves that either have no identification, or have illegible tombstones or illegible funeral markers.

Newton-Moss Family off Rd. 744

Call Nanie	1849 24 April 1911		etched fieldstone

Last Name Given Name (Maiden Name)	Date of Birth Date of Death Age at Death	Spouse	Tombstone
Davis Aubrey H.	12 Feb. 1916 6 Nov. 1954		yes

Inscription: Husband; Darling, we miss thee

Other Info: Footstone: Father

Davis Carris J.	1878 1954	Robert J. Davis	yes

Other Info: Shares a headstone with her husband.

Davis Robert J.	1882 1934	Carrie L. Davis	yes

Other Info: Shares a headstone with his wife.

Davis Sarah Elizabeth	1905 1969		yes

Other Info: Has a Dunkum Funeral Home marker

Godsey Arvertice Taylor	1894 1967	John Renny Godsey	yes

Other Info: Shares a headstone with her husband.

Godsey Cal	7 June 1916		yes
Godsey Chester Irene	died before 1940 Child		no

Other Info: Known to be buried here. Parents Earnest and Louise Taylor Godsey

Godsey Edna Virginia	died about 1940 Child		no

Other Info: Known to be buried here. Parents Earnest and Louise Taylor Godsey

Last Name Given Name (Maiden Name)	Date of Birth Date of Death Age at Death	Spouse	Tombstone
Godsey John Renny	1890 1971	Arvertice Taylor Godsey	yes

Other Info: Shares a headstone with his wife. They were the grandparents of Edna V., Chester Irene, and Shirley Marie Godsey, children buried in this cemetery.

Godey Shirley Marie	died about 1940 Child		no

Other Info: Known to be buried here. Parents Earnest and Louise Taylor Godsey

Moss Annie		William Moss	no

Other Info: Known to be buried here.

Moss Flossie Taylor	1871 1954		yes

Moss Gordon General	1883 1965		yes

Moss William		Annie Moss	no

Other Info: Known to be buried here.

Newton Addie Lue	20 Oct. 1880 18 June 1904		yes

Inscription: In Memory of; Budded on earth to bloom in heaven.

Newton Alfred P.	22 March 1888 24 Feb. 1914		yes

Inscription: They who knew him best will bless his name and keep his memory dear while life shall last.

Other Info: Footstone: APN

Last Name Given Name (Maiden Name)	Date of Birth Date of Death Age at Death	Spouse	Tombstone
Newton Andrew W.	12 Nov. 1885 4 Feb. 1909		yes

Inscription: In Memory of; A precious one from us has gone, a voice we loved is stilled. A place is vacant in our home which never can be filled. God in his wisdom has recalled the boon his love had given; and though the body slumbers here, the soul is safe in heaven.

Other Info: Footstone: AWN

Newton George W.	29 June 1870 7 Feb. 1929		yes

Inscription: Our Father; Charitable Neighbor

Newton James Alfred	20 June 1913 9 July 1970	Mildred Call Newton	yes

Other Info: Shares a headstone with his wife.

Newton John E.	19 Feb. 1878 24 Aug. 1892		yes

Inscription: At Rest

Other Info: Footstone: JEN

Newton Mickey J.	7 Nov. 1874 8 Aug. 1920		yes

Inscription: Our Mother; Asleep in Jesus

Newton Mildred Call	9 July 1909 14 Oct. 1947	James Alfred Newton	yes

Other Info: Shares a headstone with her husband.

Newton T. A. "Tas" Jr.	24 Dec. 1908		etched fieldstone

Last Name Given Name (Maiden Name)	Date of Birth Date of Death Age at Death	Spouse	Tombstone
Newton Wesley	26 Feb. 1845 22 Oct. 1913		yes

    Inscription: In Memory, Father: Laid down the cross to wear a crown.

    Other Info: Footstone: WN

Taylor Noah	__Feb.___ (illegible)		etched fieldstone
Taylor Sallie G.	17 Aug. 1917 10 March 1972		yes

    Inscription: Rest in Peace

There are at least 25 unmarked graves in the 3 sections of this large cemetery. Five have been identified.

Onion Family at Slate River Farm off Rd. 649 — African American

Onion John	1879 1944		no

    Other Info: Dunkum Funeral Home marker

There are 9 unidentified graves in this cemetery.

Pankey Family at Traveler's Rest

Day Mary (Pankey)	18 Oct. 1813 21 Oct. 1860	John Day	yes

    Inscription: In Memory of...Wife of John Day; I Here Remainth a Rest for the People of God.

Last Name Given Name (Maiden Name)	Date of Birth Date of Death Age at Death	Spouse	Tombstone
Glover David W.	27 Sept. 1798 14 Nov. 1862	Sarah Fearn Jones Glover	no

Other Info: Known to be buried in this cemetery. He was the father of Stephan A. Glover who is buried in the nearby Glover Family cemetery.

Glover Sarah Fearn Jones	30 March 1794 24 July 1877	David W. Glover	no

Other Info: Known to be buried in this cemetery.

There are 5 unmarked graves in this cemetery, including 2 which known to be buried here.

Pankey Family off Rd. 607 — African American

Cabell Frances	18 March 1931		no

Other Info: Known to be buried here.

Christian Carline	1934		no

Other Info: Footstone only-inscribed Our Carline Baby, in God we trust. She was the infant daughter of William and Lucille Christian.

Christian Della	3 May 1983 6 Dec. 1952		A plaque

Christian Roberta R.	1876 1955		no

Other Info: Known to be buried here.

Evans Annie	1910 1972		no

Other Info: Unidentified funeral home marker.

Last Name Given Name (Maiden Name)	Date of Birth Date of Death Age at Death	Spouse	Tombstone
Johnson Ernest Junior	22 July 1951 14 Sept. 1968		yes

Inscription: In God's Care

Jones Charlie A.	6 Feb. 1921		no

Other Info: Illegible Appomattox Co. funeral home marker-Known to be buried here.

Jones Esther Pankey	26 Aug. 1890 24 May 1969		no

Other Info: Known to be buried here. She was the mother of Otis Jones, William E. Jones, Annie Evans, Willie R Jones and Maggie J. Morgan also buried in this cemetery.

Jones Otis J.	1933 1997		no

Other Info: Bland-Reid Funeral Home marker

Jones Samuel			no

Other Info: West Funeral Home marker with one date: 1970

Jones Tom	1882 1966		no

Other Info: Unidentified funeral home marker.

Jones William E.	31 May 1927 31 Jan. 1944		yes

Other Info: Dunkum Funeral Home marker: Elma Jones, 1927-1944

Jones Willie R. (Roosevelt)	24 May 1922 10 June 1951		yes

Inscription: Virginia, SGT, 809 Amph Truck Co., World War II

Other Info: Headstone for an above ground vault.

Last Name Given Name (Maiden Name)	Date of Birth Date of Death Age at Death	Spouse	Tombstone
Morgan Maggie J.	1913 1986		no

Other Info: Bruce and Stiff Funeral Home marker

Pankey Charles Allen	(1894) 20 Jan. 1912 18 years		yes

Other Info: Headstone inscribed: CAP with death date and age only.

Pankey James	1866 1935	Margaret Robertson Pankey	yes

Inscription: Thy Kingdom Come

Other Info: Shares a headstone with his wife.

Pankey James Leonard	4 July 1934		no

Other Info: Illegible funeral home marker-known to be buried here.

Pankey Lucy Rose	17 July 1904 30 April 1985	William McKinley Pankey	yes

Inscription: In Loving Memory; Mother

Other Info: Shares a headstone with her husband.

Pankey Maggie (Margaret Robertson)	1872 1961	James Pankey	yes

Inscription: Thy Kingdom Come

Other Info: Shares a headstone with her husband.

Pankey Robert	11 Dec. 1911		no

Other Info: Known to be buried here.

Last Name	Date of Birth	Spouse	Tombstone
Given Name	Date of Death		
(Maiden Name)	Age at Death		

Pankey 17 Sept. 1900 yes
William McKinley 27 Nov. 1984 Lucy Rose Pankey

    Inscription: In Loving Memory

    Other Info: Shares a headstone with his wife.

Robertson no
Caroline 3 Aug. 1925

    Other Info: Known to be buried here.

Robertson no
Delia 1936

    Other Info: Known to be buried here.

Robertson no
T. (Tom) E. 24 Feb. 1944

    Other Info: Known to be buried here.

Patteson-Tucker Family off Rd. 659

Patteson 24 Dec. 1851 yes
A. M. (Antonia M. Tucker) 4 April 1929 Thomas A. Patteson

    Inscription: Mother: In my house are many mansions - (remainder below ground)

    Other Info: Shares a headstone with her husband. They were the parents of Annie F., Mary L. and Ella Henrie Patteson also buried in this cemetery, and Thomas and Lottie Patteson.

Patteson 30 Sept. 1884 yes
Annie F. 9 March 1925

    Inscription: Rest in Peace

Last Name Given Name (Maiden Name)	Date of Birth Date of Death Age at Death	Spouse	Tombstone
Patteson Ella Henrie	 15 years		no

Other Info: Known to be buried here. Her parents, A.M. and T. A. Patteson and her sisters, Annie F. and Mary L. Patteson are also buried here.

Patteson Mary L. ("Lulie")	5 Oct. 1879 31 May 1974		yes
Patteson T. A. (Thomas)	3 March 1825 26 April 1900	Antonia M. Tucker Patterson	yes

Inscription: In my father's house are many---(rest is below ground)

Other Info: Shares a headstone with his wife. He was 53 years old and his wife was 27 years old when they married.

Tucker Eliza M. C.	12 Nov. 1846 10 Sept. 1863 17 years		no

Other Info: Known to be buried here.

Tucker George W.	17 Jan. 1859 3 Aug. 1862		no

Other Info: Known to be buried here.

Tucker Henry	10 Sept. 1797 7 May 1859	Louisa A. Tucker	no

Other Info: Known to be buried here.

Tucker Louisa A. Tucker	about 1820 19 July 1965	Henry Tucker	no

Other Info: Known to be buried here.

Last Name Given Name (Maiden Name	Date of Birth Date of Death Age at Death	Spouse	Tombstone
Tucker Martha A.	14 July 1856 10 July 1862		no

Other Info: Known to be buried here.

| Tucker
  Rebecca W. |
3 Sept. 1866
about 66 years | | no |

Other Info: Known to be buried here. She was the sister of Henry Tucker.

Payne Family on Rd. 750 — African American

There are several graves beside the unoccupied Payne Family home with no identification. The last known person to live in this home is Beatrice Payne (living)

Proffitt Family at James River Park

| Proffitt
  Mary Rosalind Fields Bryant | 9 April 1881
2 Aug. 1922 |
(1) A. J. Bryant
(2) M. T. Proffitt | yes |

Inscription: Wife of AJ Bryant, MT Proffitt

There are at least 6 unidentified graves in this cemetery.

Radford Family off Rd. 793 — African American

| Harris
  Allen | | | no |

Other Info: Known to be buried here.

| Harris
  Sarah |
about 1958/1959 | | no |

Other Info: Known to be buried here.

Last Name Given Name (Maiden Name)	Date of Birth Date of Death Age at Death	Spouse	Tombstone
Harris Walter	in late 1950s		no

Other Info: Known to be buried here.

Harris Washington			no

Other Info: Known to be buried here.

Harris Watson			no

Other Info: Known to be buried here. He was the father of William and Allen Harris also buried in this cemetery.

Harris William	15 Oct. 1891 31 Oct. 1969		yes

Inscription: Virginia, PFC, US Army, World War I

Jackson Hattie	60 years		no

Other Info: Unidentified funeral home marker with one date: 3 March 1936. She was the mother of William and Linwood Radford also buried in this cemetery.

Radford Elizabeth	about 1985	William Radford	no

Other Info: Known to be buried here.

Radford John L	4 July 1948		no

Other Info: Chiles Funeral Home marker

Last Name Given Name (Maiden Name)	Date of Birth Date of Death Age at Death	Spouse	Tombstone
Radford Linwood	early 1960s		

Other Info: Never married.

Radford Morris Neal			no

Other Info: Known to be buried here.

Radford William	13 April 1899 8 May 1971	Elizabeth Radford	yes

Inscription: In memory of my husband

Ragland Family on US 56

Gunter Jesse Frank	29 Aug. 1906 22 March 1972	Ruby Moyer Gunter	yes

Other Info: Shares a headstone with his wife. Footstone: Father

Gunter Ruby Moyer	24 Feb. 1915 5 June 1979	Jesse Frank Gunter	yes

Other Info: Shares a headstone with his wife. Footstone: Mother

Ragland Ann W.	7 April 1856 14 Feb. 1914		yes

Other Info: Footstone: AWR

Ragland Lula Camm	14 July 1908 21 May 1997	Roy Leonard Ragland	yes

Other Info: Footstone: Mother; Has a Dunkum Funeral Home marker.

Ragland Roy Leonard	21 Dec. 1903 18 July 1976	Lula Camm Ragland	yes

Other Info: Footstone: Father; Has a Dunkum Funeral Home marker. He and his wife are the parents of Georgia R. Bryant.

Last Name Given Name (Maiden Name)	Date of Birth Date of Death Age at Death	Spouse	Tombstone
Ragland Roy Tucker	8 July 1925 27 April 1994		yes

Inscription: PFC, US Army World War II

Other Info: Has a Dunkum Funeral Home marker.

Ragland Warden N.	10 Nov. 1857 (not inscribed)		yes
Wade Frank T.	26 Jan. 1919 27 July 1919		yes
Wade Mildred M.	24 Aug. 1891 29 July 1971	Thomas Lee Wade	yes

Other Info: Shares a headstone with her husband.

Wade Thomas Lee	17 May 1888 26 Oct. 1934	Mildred M. Wade	yes

Other Info: Shares a headstone with his wife.

There are 7 unidentified graves in this cemetery.

Reynolds Family off Rd. 607 — African American

Irving Catherine McIvor	17 April 1922 21 Aug. 2001		yes

Other Info: She was the granddaughter of Georgianna Reynolds who is also buried in this cemetery, and the daughter of Marilee Reynolds.

Neilson Leslie L.	1891 1945	Pauline A. Neilson	yes

Other Info: Shares a headstone with his wife.

Last Name Given Name (Maiden Name)	Date of Birth Date of Death Age at Death	Spouse	Tombstone
Neilson Pauline A.	1897 not inscribed	Leslie L. Neilson	yes

Other Info: Shares a headstone with her husband.

| Reynolds
Georgianna | | | no |

Other Info: Known to be buried here. She was the mother of Pauline A. Neilson and Joe Reynolds, grandmother of Catherine McIvor Irving all buried in this cemetery. Her mother's name was Elisa Wright.

| Reynolds
Joe | | | no |

Other Info: Known to be buried here.

| Reynolds
Wendell G. | 28 Sept. 1912
18 Sept. 1968 | | yes |

Inscription: SGT, US Army, World War II

Other Info: Has an unidentified funeral home marker: Wendell George Reynolds, 1912-1968

| Thomas
Bernard |

10 years | | no |

Other Info: Known to be buried here, the grandson of Charlie Wright.

| Wright
Arthur |
about 1940 | | yes |

Other Info: He was the brother of Georgianna Reynolds who is also buried in this cemetery, and Charlie Wright. His mother was Elisa Wright.

Last Name Given Name (Maiden Name)	Date of Birth Date of Death Age at Death	Spouse	Tombstone

Ridgeway Baptist Church on Rd. 652 — African American

Ayres Eliza Agnes	1882 1967		yes
Ayres John N.	11 July 1910 5 Aug. 1972	Lillian Irene Ayres	yes
Ayres Lillian Irene	30 Oct. 1915 21 June 1996 80 years	John N. Ayres	yes

Other Info: Has a Thacker Bros. Funeral Home marker.

Ayres William Daniel	3 Sept 1965 50 years		no

Other Info: Thacker Bros. Funeral Home marker

Banks Edna Earl	7 Aug. 1904 8 July 1968 64 years		yes

Inscription: Beloved Mother

Banks Octavious	1893 1978 84 years		yes

Inscription: PVT, US Army, World War I

Other Info: Has a Thacker Bros. Funeral Home marker.

Bowman Beatrice B.	1903 1973		yes
Bowman John E.	6 Jan. 1895 12 July 1985		yes

Inscription: PVT, US Army, World War I

Buckingham Burials

Last Name Given Name (Maiden Name	Date of Birth Date of Death Age at Death	Spouse	Tombstone
Bowman Mary E.	1881 1957		yes

Inscription: Mother

Brittle Edwin Winfrey	9 July 1959 60 years		

Other Info: Thacker Bros. Funeral Home marker

Brittle James	1892 1966		no

Other Info: Johnson Bros. Funeral Home marker

Brown Charlie M.	1914 1979 64 years		no

Other Info: Thacker Bros. Funeral Home marker

Burton Carrie L.	22 July 1897 13 Oct. 1992	Isaac H. Burton	yes

Other Info: Shares a headstone with her husband.

Burton Delores M.	1937 2003		no

Other Info: Reids Funeral Home marker

Burton Isaac H.	11 Dec. 1892 10 May 1962	Carrie L. Burton	yes

Other Info: Shares a headstone with his wife.

Burton Maggie E.	26 Feb. 1924 19 Apr. 1943		yes

Inscription: At Rest

Last Name Given Name (Maiden Name)	Date of Birth Date of Death Age at Death	Spouse	Tombstone
Flowers James Hopkins	27 April 1932 6 Jan. 1969		yes

Inscription: Virginia, PFC, US Army

Flowers James Preston	1872 1964		yes
Flowers Leonard G.	1900 1988 88 years		no

Other Info: Thacker Bros. Funeral Home marker

Flowers Mary E.	4 July 1891 23 May 1961		yes
Flowers Samuel L.	18 March 1878 19 Feb. 1957		yes
Ford Leeolian V.	23 Jan. 1913 31 Mar. 1994		yes

Inscription: In God's Care

Other Info: Her parents were Emma and Grover Ford who are buried in a family cemetery nearby.

Hamlett Versie L.			yes

Inscription: Rest in Peace (no dates)

Johns Farrel D.	19 June 1933 26 Feb. 1999		yes

Inscription: The Lord is My Shepherd

Jones Allie Marshall	11 May 1914 28 Mar. 1984		yes

Inscription: S1, US Navy, World War II

Last Name Given Name (Maiden Name)	Date of Birth Date of Death Age at Death	Spouse	Tombstone
Jones Frank E.	25 Oct. 1923 5 Nov. 1980		yes

Inscription: SC3, US Navy, World War II

Jones James	25 Mar. 1926 6 May 1987		yes

Inscription: PVT, US Army, World War II

Jones Jerry Lee	1940 1982		no

Other Info: Thacker Bros. Funeral Home marker

Jones John	7 Jan. 1967 68 years		no

Other Info: Unidentified funeral home marker

Jones Nancy			no

Other Info: Thacker Bros. Funeral Home marker-Gives one date-Nov. 1969

Leigh Mattie B.	1891 1966		yes
Manero Minnie Ernestine	1904 1994 89 years		no

Other Info: Thacker Bros. Funeral Home marker

Marshall Ada	27 Nov. 1892 28 Nov. 1953		yes
Mosley John W. Sr.	1 May 1931 16 Sept. 1976		yes

Inscription: Our Loving Father

Last Name Given Name (Maiden Name	Date of Birth Date of Death Age at Death	Spouse	Tombstone

Other Info: Footstone: John Willie Mosley, PFC, US Army, 1931-1976

Parson Mattie E.	28 June 1892 18 Jan. 1971	Willie D. Parson	yes

Other Info: Shares a headstone with her husband.

Parson William E. Jr.	16 Aug. 1977 58 years		no

Other Info: Unidentified funeral home marker

Parson Willie D.	27 July 1893 16 May 1983	Mattie E. Parson	yes

Other Info: Shares a headstone with his wife.

Randolph Alice Lee	1894 1989 95 years		no

Other Info: Thacker Bros. Funeral Home marker

Randolph Doshie Jones	20 June 1906 6 Feb. 1988		yes

Other Info: Has a Thacker Bros. Funeral Home marker.

Randolph Francis W.	1896 1985		yes

Other Info: Also has a Thacker Bros. Funeral Home marker.

Randolph Lovie	8 Aug. 1895 31 Mar. 1995		yes

Other Info: Has a Thacker Bros. Funeral Home marker.

Randolph Luther			no

Other Info: Funeral Marker-illegible-only date is March '53

Last Name Given Name (Maiden Name)	Date of Birth Date of Death Age at Death	Spouse	Tombstone
Randolph Mary			no

Other Info: Unidentified funeral home marker with one date: 1954

Reed Nannie B.	1909 1976		no

Other Info: Johnson Bros. Funeral Home marker

Rorie Walter	25 May 1898 4 June 1962		yes
Sellers Charles	1 Nov. 1954		no

Other Info: J. F. Bell Funeral Home marker

Smith	20 Aug. 1964 50 years		no

Other Info: Thacker Bros. Funeral Home marker with given name missing.

Taylor Ida B.	24 Feb. 1959	Walker E. Taylor	yes

Other Info: Shares a headstone with her husband.

Taylor Walker E.	11 Feb. 1959	Ida B. Taylor	yes

Other Info: Shares a headstone with his wife.

Wingfield Alice Scott	18 Oct. 1956		no

Other Info: Thacker Bros. Funeral Home marker

Last Name Given Name (Maiden Name)	Date of Birth Date of Death Age at Death	Spouse	Tombstone
Wingfield George	1904 1971		no

Other Info: Johnson Bros. Funeral Home marker

| Wingfield
Harry S. | 3 Oct. 1893
27 March 1986 | Mabel Burton Wingfield | yes |

Inscription: PVT, US Army, World War I

| Wingfield
James H. | 23 Nov. 1924
24 Dec. 1991 | | yes |

Inscription: Rest in Peace

Other Info: His parents were Mabel Burton Wingfield and Harry S. Wingfield.

| Wingfield
James H. Jr. | 8 June 1951
22 Aug. 1994 | | yes |

Inscription: Rest in Peace

| Wingfield
Lucy | 23 June 1894
6 Mar. 1976 | | yes |

Inscription: 6th Mt. Zion Male Usher Bd, and Ladies Aux.

| Wingfield
Mabel Burton | 13 May 1900
8 Aug. 1984 | Harry S. Wingfield | yes |

Inscription: Gone but not Forgotten

Other Info: Also has a Thacker Bros. Funeral Home marker.

| Wingfield
Richard P. Sr. | 19 Aug. 1936
12 Dec. 2003 | | no |

Other Info: Bland-Reid Funeral Home marker

| Woodson
Callie | 27 Jan. 1912
11 May 1982 | | yes |

Inscription: Rest in Peace

Last Name Given Name (Maiden Name	Date of Birth Date of Death Age at Death	Spouse	Tombstone
Woodson Rose	1921 1957		no

Other Info: This is an above ground vault.

Robertson Family and Slaves at "Stone House Farm"

O'Conner

Other Info: Husband and wife in unmarked graves, side by side.

Robertson (wife)		W. H. Robertson	no

Other Info: Known to be buried here.

Robertson Clara A.	1874 1957	Willie R. Robertson	yes

Other Info: Shares a headstone with her husband; Footstone: CAR

Robertson David C.			yes

Inscription: Co. B, Wis. Legion, VA Arty, CSA

Robertson W.H.			yes

Inscription: Co. B, 25 BN, Local Defense, CSA

Robertson Willie R.	1867 1908	Clara A. Robertson	yes

Other Info: Shares a headstone with his wife. Footstone: WRR

Last Name Given Name (Maiden Name)	Date of Birth Date of Death Age at Death	Spouse	Tombstone
Robertson Willie R.	6 April 1902 30 March 1970		yes

Inscription: Son

Other Info: There is one unidentified grave in the family cemetery, and 20-25 unidentified graves of slaves and others outside the family cemetery.

Rose Family on Rd. 627 — African American (updated from Vol. I)

Anderson Hudson Mat	9 Aug. 1916 27 July 1970	Margaret Anderson	yes

Inscription: Virginia, SGT, US Army, World War II

Other Info: Has an O.F. Howard Funeral Home marker. He was the son-in-law of Annie Jones Powell.

Burrell Mary Rose	17 May 1890 21 Jan. 1970		yes
Chambers Lucy Jones	15 Sept. 1888 28 March 1976		yes
Jones Robert L.	30 Aug. 1907 2 March 1964		yes

Inscription: In memory

Other Info: His mother, Annie Jones Powell is also buried in this cemetery.

Powell Annie Jones	18 May 1890 13 Sept. 1960		yes

Inscription: In memory of our mother; At Rest

Other Info: Has a Thacker Bros. Funeral Home marker. She was the mother of Robert L. Jones also buried in this cemetery.

Last Name Given Name (Maiden Name)	Date of Birth Date of Death Age at Death	Spouse	Tombstone
Rose John W.	1868 1950	Josephine Rose	yes

   Inscription: Husband

| Rose
   Josephine | 1875
1959 | John W. Rose | yes |

   Inscription: Wife

| Rose
   Martha E. | 1 April 1896
16 July 1961 | | yes |

   Other Info: She was the niece of John W. Rose.

| Rose
   Susan J. | 7 Sept. 1871
1 Nov. 1957 | | yes |

   Inscription: Family

   Other Info: She was the sister of John W. Rose.

There are 17 unidentified graves in this cemetery.

Rush Family on Rd. 691

| Buschmann
   Linda Rush | 2 May 1952
25 Nov. 1994 | | yes |

   Inscription: Mother; In loving memory

   Other Info: Has a Dunkum Funeral Home marker.

| Fitzgerald
   Joseph | 29 Aug. 1817
29 Aug. 1879 | Martha J. Fitzgerald | yes |

   Other Info: Shares a headstone with his wife.

| Fitzgerald
   Martha J. | 26 March 1882
18 Oct. 1907 | Joseph Fitzgerald | yes |

   Other Info: Shares a headstone with her husband.

Buckingham Burials

Last Name Given Name (Maiden Name)	Date of Birth Date of Death Age at Death	Spouse	Tombstone
Rosen Margaret Rush	28 Dec. 1916 22 Oct. 1961		yes
Rush Elsie Lann	26 Jan. 1923 3 Feb. 1999	Thomas Clyde Rush	yes

Other Info: Shares a headstone with her husband.

Rush George T.	27 June 1856 23 March 1927	Mildred F. Rush	yes

Other Info: Shares a headstone with his wife.

Rush Lucy M.	17 March 1898 14 April 1963	P. Floyd Rush	yes

Other Info: Shares a headstone with her husband.

Rush Mildred F.	12 Jan. 1859 26 July 1946	George T. Rush	yes

Other Info: Shares a headstone with her husband.

Rush P. Floyd	7 March 1889 28 Jan. 1976	Lucy M. Rush	yes

Other Info: Shares a headstone with his wife.

Rush Thomas Clyde	30 June 1919 17 Sept. 1992	Elsie Lann Rush	yes

Other Info: Shares a headstone with his wife.

Rush Thomas Clyde Jr.	18 Oct. 1947 6 Sept. 1969		yes

Inscription: Virginia, LCpl, Co. E, 7 Mar., 1 Mar. Div. Vietnam, PH & CS

Last Name	Date of Birth	Spouse	Tombstone
Given Name	Date of Death		
(Maiden Name)	Age at Death		

Saunders Family on Rd. 612 — African American

Clark
   Viola F.
               1908
               1992
                            no

Other Info: E.B. Allen Funeral Home marker

Saunders
   Mazie   Robert Saunders

Other Info: Known to be buried here.

There are 7 unidentified graves in this cemetery.

Self Family on Rd. 701

Howell   yes
   Robert P.

Inscription: Co. C, 25 VA Inf, CSA

Maxey   yes

Other Info: This is an illegible tombstone with one date legible: 1862

Maxey   no
   Nancy H.

Other Info: Known to be buried here.

(not known)   3 July 1898
   Julia   4 Aug. 1899

Other Info: Known to be buried here.

Self   no
   Abram

Other Info: Known to be buried here.

Self   1 Nov. 1897   yes
   Andrew L.   22 Aug. 1986

Last Name Given Name (Maiden Name)	Date of Birth Date of Death Age at Death	Spouse	Tombstone
Self 　Edward Hill	29 July 1890 22 Jan. 1912		Cement slab covering grave

Inscription: In Memory of

Other Info: Footstone: EHS

Self 　Florence Merkey	11 Aug. 1910 14 Aug. 1998		yes
Self 　George R.	18__ 1892		yes

Inscription: Ist VA Inf. CSA

Self	1832		Cement slab covering grave
H. (Frank Hill)	1892		
Self 　Jesse Maxey	15 June 1901 29 May 1976		yes
Self 　John A.	2 June 1859 21 Nov. 1922	Kate Maxey Self	yes

Other Info: Shares a headstone with his wife.

Self 　Kate Maxey	17 Dec. 1865 18 April 1953	John A. Self	yes

Other Info: Shares a headstone with her husband.

Self 　Ollive G.	24 Oct. 1888 29 Oct. 1947		yes, broken
Self 　Violet	8 May 1905 18 Dec. 1906		Cement slab covering grave

Inscription: In memory of

Last Name	Date of Birth	Spouse	Tombstone
Given Name	Date of Death		
(Maiden Name	Age at Death		

Selph   yes
    Bennie   17 March 1957
                    71 years, 1 month, 13 days

    Other Info: Has a Ranson-Smith Funeral Home marker.

Stearrett   yes
    Stephanie Ellen   10 May 1985

    Inscription: Daughter of Glenn and Sandra Stearrett

Winfrey
    Sallie

    Other Info: Known to be buried here.

Self Family on Rd. 722

Self   13 April 1876   yes
    James Holman   11 Feb. 1958   Mildred Baber Self

    Inscription: Daddy, At Rest; Gone but not Forgotten

    Other Info: He and is wife are the parents of L.L. and S.S. Self (living), and several infants who died at birth and are also buried here.

Self   21 Sept. 1887   yes
    Mildred Baber   12 May 1940   James Holman Self

    Inscription: Mother; Prepare to Meet me in Heaven

Shaw Family at "Raleigh"

    Other Info: This cemetery is unmaintained and nearly destroyed. There are no identifiable graves.

Last Name	Date of Birth	Spouse	Tombstone
Given Name	Date of Death		
(Maiden Name)	Age at Death		

Shepherd Family at "Slate River Farm"

Shepherd
Buck   April 1949   Ethel Loving Shepherd   no

Other Info: Known to be buried here.

There are 4 other unidentified graves in this cemetery.

Slate Rive Baptist Church — African American

Anderson   14 Nov. 1919   no
Grandville L. 28 Oct. 1985

Other Info: This is an above ground vault with the inscription: PVT, US Army

Austin   1944   no
Laura C.   1992

Other Info: Reids Funeral Home marker

Ayers   1892   no
Octavia   1960

Other Info: Unidentified funeral home marker

Booker   24 Feb. 1912   yes
James Coleman 4 Oct. 1979

Inscription: PVT, US Army, World War II

Booker   1909   yes
Mary Ella   9-4-69

Inscription: yes

Booker   26 Feb. 1909   yes
Nelson R. Sr. 6 Sept. 1958

Last Name Given Name (Maiden Name	Date of Birth Date of Death Age at Death	Spouse	Tombstone
Booker Robert Henry Jr.	1931 1961		no

Other Info: Unidentified funeral home marker

Booker Robert Henry Sr.	22 May 1901 10 June 1957		yes
Booker Walker A.	1931 1999		no

Other Info: Unidentified funeral home marker

Branch Pauline Virginia, Mrs.	14 Sept. 1943 29 May 1987 44 years		no

Other Info: Mimm's Funeral Home marker

Brandsford David A.	15 Sept. 1887 2 Jan. 1978		yes
Bransford Elizabeth	 4 May 1959		yes
Brown Dorothy J.	12 March 1914 16 Feb. 1966	 James Madison Brown	yes

Other Info: Shares a headstone with her husband.

Brown Edna E. (Edmonds)	1905 1979	 Junius Brown	no
Brown Emma Gertrude Onion	1908 1989		no

Other Info: This is an above ground vault

Brown James M. (Madison)	27 Jan. 1915 12 Sept 2000	 (1) Dorothy J. Brown (2) Jessie F. Brown	yes

Other Info: Shares a headstone with his first wife.

Last Name Given Name (Maiden Name)	Date of Birth Date of Death Age at Death	Spouse	Tombstone
Brown Jessie Forbes	18 April 1928 25 May 2000	James Madison Brown	yes

Inscription: In God's Care

Other Info: This is the 2nd wife of James M. Brown.

| Brown
Junius | | Edna E. Brown | no |

Other Info: Reids Funeral Home marker-no dates

| Brown
Nannie | 4 Aug. 1939
58 or 68 years, 11 mos., 3 days | | no |

Other Info: Dunkum Funeral Home marker

| Brown
Robert N. | 1937
1984 | | no |

Other Info: Reids Funeral Home marker; He is the son of Junius Brown and Edna E. Brown also buried in this cemetery.

| Clayborne
Horace | 4-6-1953
91 years | | no |

Other Info: Unidentified funeral home marker

| Conwell
Terese A. | 19 Oct. 1962
11 Sept. 1994 | | no |

Other Info: This is an above ground vault.

| Cunningham
A. (Andrew) | 30 March 1966 | | no |

Other Info: Unidentified funeral home marker

Last Name Given Name (Maiden Name	Date of Birth Date of Death Age at Death	Spouse	Tombstone
Cunningham Annette			no

Other Info: Unidentified funeral home marker gives one date: 1 Jan. 1970

| Cunningham
Nellie Miller | 1921
1964 | | no |

Other Info: Unidentified funeral home marker

| Cunningham
Robert Henry | | | no |

Other Info: Unidentified funeral home marker-dates are missing

| Dibble
Anna B. | | | no |

Other Info: O. F. Howard Funeral Home marker gives one date: 8 March 1966.

| Edmonds
Alexander M. | 1919
2000 | | no |

Other Info: Reids Funeral Home marker

| Edmonds
Clarence Junious | 30 March 1914
30 Jan. 1968 | | yes |

Inscription: Virginia, PFC, US Army, World War II

| Edmonds
Earl Randolph | 1929
1970 | | no |

Other Info: Unidentified funeral home marker

| Edmonds
Paul A. | 21 Feb. 1911
26 Dec. 1976 | | yes |

Inscription: US Army, World War II

Last Name Given Name (Maiden Name)	Date of Birth Date of Death Age at Death	Spouse	Tombstone
Forbes Charlie M.	1899 1975		yes

    Inscription: Wife and Children

Forbes Classie G.	1939 1979		yes

    Inscription: Husband and Children

Forbes Eugene	1933 1995		no

    Other Info: Reids Funeral Home marker

Forbes Mildred W.	10 May 1893 21 Dec. 1985		yes

    Inscription: In Loving Memory of our Mother

    Other Info: Has a Reids Funeral Home marker

Hamlett Arthur T.		Irene J. Hamlett	yes

    Inscription: Precious Lord Take My Hand

    Other Info: Shares a headstone with his wife.

Hamlett Irene J.		Arthur T. Hamlett	yes

    Inscription: Precious Lord Take My Hand

    Other Info: Shares a headstone with her husband.

Harding May Beth	3 July 1887 16 Oct. 1951		yes
Hill James Franklin	4 May 1895 2 July 1958		yes

    Inscription: Virginia, PVT, US Army, World War II

Last Name Given Name (Maiden Name)	Date of Birth Date of Death Age at Death	Spouse	Tombstone
Johnson Allen Coleman			no

Other Info: Unidentified funeral home marker with no dates.

| Johnson
Doris F. "Leechie" | 19 July 1937
4 June 1999 | | no |

Other Info: This is an above ground vault: Reids FH

| Jones
Annie Park (Gough) | 18 Aug. 1884
23 April 1959 | James Robert Jones | yes |

Other Info: Footstone: Wife

| Jones
Carmen | 1970
1990 | | no |

Other Info: Reids Funeral Home marker

| Jones
Carol Powell | 9 Aug. 1917
2 Mar. 1995 | Willie E. (Ted) Jones | yes |

Other Info: Shares a headstone with her husband.

| Jones
E. W. (Buck) | | | yes |

Other Info: This is a concrete stone with name only on it.

| Jones
Edward E. (Erin) | 16 Mar. 1913
24 Jan. 1996 | | yes |

Other Info: Has an above ground vault: Edward Erin Jones, March 15, 1913; Jan. 24, 1996, Reid's FH.

| Jones
Elsie May (Booker) | 5 Sept. 1909
10 Aug. 1961 | Henry P. Jones | yes |

Inscription: Sleep on Mother

Other Info: Footstone: Wife

Last Name Given Name (Maiden Name	Date of Birth Date of Death Age at Death	Spouse	Tombstone
Jones Henry P.	30 Sept. 1908 20 Aug. 1981	Elsie May Booker Jones	yes

Other Info: Footstone: Father

Jones James C.	1942 1994		no

Other Info: Reids Funeral Home marker

Jones James P.	18 Oct. 1912 17 Sept. 1994		yes

Inscription: PFC, US Army, World War II

Other Info: His parents were James Robert Jones and Annie Park Jones.

Jones James Robert	27 Aug. 1880 14 Oct. 1952	Annie Park Jones	yes

Other Info: Footstone: Husband

Jones Joann	1962 1962		no

Other Info: Unidentified funeral home marker

Jones John Dashwood "Pal"	6 Nov. 1912 21 Feb. 1996		yes

Inscription: Rest in Peace

Other Info: Also has an above ground vault.

Jones Lillian Belle (Gough)	1 July 1887 26 Feb. 1964	Paul Irving Jones	yes

Inscription: Sleep on Mother

Other Info: Footstone: wife

Last Name Given Name (Maiden Name	Date of Birth Date of Death Age at Death	Spouse	Tombstone
Jones Paul Irving	20 Feb. 1877 25 Feb. 1972	Lillian Belle Gough Jones	yes

Inscription: Sleep on Father

Other Info: Footstone: Husband

| Jones
Pauline | 1886
1944 | | no |

Other Info: Unidentified funeral home marker

| Jones
Robert B. | 1909
1982 | | yes |

Inscription: TEC 5, US Army, World War II

| Jones
Virgil | 8 Sept. 1916
1 March 1985 | | yes |

Inscription: CPL, US Army, World War II

| Jones
William H. | 12 Oct. 1873
2 Feb. 1957 | | yes |

Inscription: At Rest

| Jones
William Horace | 30 May 1920
5 Feb. 1998 | | yes |

Inscription: US Navy, World War II

| Jones
Willie E. (Ted) | 18 Feb. 1903
3 Dec. 1972 | Carol Powell Jones | yes |

Other Info: Shares a headstone with his wife.

| King
Ethel F. | 1909
1981 | | no |

Other Info: Reids Funeral Home marker

Last Name Given Name (Maiden Name)	Date of Birth Date of Death Age at Death	Spouse	Tombstone
Kyle Margaret S.	12 March 1904 11 July 1943		yes

Inscription: Asleep in Jesus

Lee Clarence	6 June 1895 1 May 1953		yes

Inscription: Virginia, CPL, CO A, 338 SVC BN QMC, World War I

McDonald Gladys	1938 1982		no

Other Info: Reids Funeral Home marker

Moss Henrietta	1896 1981		no

Other Info: Unidentified funeral home marker

Moss Joseph A.	1946 1974		no

Other Info: Unidentified funeral home marker

Nabors Mabel I.	12 May 1913		no

Other Info: This is an above ground vault with birth only.

Neighbors Edward	21 July 1942 18 Jan. 1986		no

Other Info: This is an above ground vault with the inscription: Master Sgt, US army, Vietnam

Nickolas John	 14 Feb. 1986		no

Other Info: Reids Funeral Home marker

Last Name Given Name (Maiden Name	Date of Birth Date of Death Age at Death	Spouse	Tombstone
Perkins Annie E.	1901 1999	James Henry Perkins	no

Inscription: no

Other Info: Unidentified funeral home marker

Perkins James Henry	1895 1960	Annie E. Perkins	no

Other Info: Unidentified funeral home marker

Perkins Ralph	26 May 1926 30 May 1995		no

Other Info: Reids Funeral Home marker

Perkins Williams			no

Other Info: Unidentified funeral home marker gives one date: 6-20-66

Perkins Willie E.			no

Other Info: Unidentified funeral home marker gives one date: 6-20-66

Shelton Joseph G.	14 Nov. 1906 6 Dec. 1944		yes
Shelton Mary G.	14 Oct. 1908 11 Feb. 1963		yes
Smith Elsie M.	1914 1983		no

Other Info: Reids Funeral Home marker

Staunton Agnes West	11 Apr. 1895 10 Jan. 1964		yes

Other Info: Footstone: AWS

Last Name Given Name (Maiden Name)	Date of Birth Date of Death Age at Death	Spouse	Tombstone
Taylor James			no

Other Info: Unidentified funeral home marker gives one date: 6-20-66.

Thomas Dee A.			no

Other Info: Reid's Funeral Home marker-gives one date: 6-20-66

Tyrone Christian	1972 1972		no

Other Info: Unidentified funeral home marker. This infant was the grandchild of James Madison Brown also buried in this cemetery.

West Alonza	1897 1996		no

Other Info: Reids Funeral Home marker

West Dorothy L.			no

Other Info: Unidentified funeral home marker gives one date: 10 June, 1926

West Jack	1864 1953		yes

Inscription: Blessed are the Dead Which Die in the Lord

West Mary M.	1983 1990	Ernest West	no

Other Info: Mary M. West has her name on the doublestone of her husband's gravesite, which is located in the West Family Cemetery, in the woods, off Rd. 649. She decided sometime after her husband's burial that she did not want to be buried in the woods. An unidentified funeral home marker marks this grave site.

Last Name Given Name (Maiden Name	Date of Birth Date of Death Age at Death	Spouse	Tombstone
West Pauline	1911 1984		no

Other Info: This is an above ground vault: Reids FH

| West
  Solomon | 1907
1954 | | yes |

Inscription: Husband and Father

| West
  (Sister of Dorothy L. West) | | | no |

Other Info: Illegible Funeral Marker

| Woodford
  Donna L. | 1963
1999 | | no |

Other Info: Reids Funeral Home marker.

There are 16 unmarked graves in this cemetery.

Henry Smith Family on Rd. 722 — African American

| Dyer
  John | 1944-1945 | | no |

Other Info: Known to be buried here. He was the brother of Harriet Dyer Smith.

| Smith
  Gracie | 19 Aug. 1938 | | no |

Other Info: Known to be buried here. Her parents were Henry and Harriet D. Smith. Her death date is in the Ebenezer Baptist Church records.

| Smith
  Harriet Dyer "Aunt Harriet" | 16 July 1945 | Henry Smith | no |

Other Info: Known to be buried here. Death date is in the Ebenezer Baptist Church records.

Last Name Given Name (Maiden Name)	Date of Birth Date of Death Age at Death	Spouse	Tombstone
Smith Henry, Deacon	about 1856 3 July 1934	Harriet Dyer Smith	no

Other Info: Known to be buried here. Death date is in the Ebenezer Baptist Church records.

There are 12 unidentified graves in this cemetery, including those known to be buried here.

William Smith Family on Rd. 646

There are 17 unidentified graves in this cemetery.

Snoddy-Bransford Family at "Old Walter Bransford Place"

Bez W. Sr.	9 Feb. 1881 13 March 1959		yes
Bransford Mattie A.	1865 1930	Maurice J. Bransford	yes

Other Info: Shares a headstone with her husband.

Bransford Maurice J.	1858 1933	Mattie A. Bransford	yes

Other Info: He was the son of Ann E. and Robert W. Bransford; shares a headstone with his wife.

Bransford Robert W.		Ann E. Bransford	yes

Inscription: Co. B, 41st VA Infantry, CSA

Other Info: Census records show that he was born about 1842; he and his wife were the parents of Maurice J., Claudius P., Morris J., Edmonia E. and an infant born in 1869.

Last Name Given Name (Maiden Name	Date of Birth Date of Death Age at Death	Spouse	Tombstone
Gentry Alice Flournoy	1925 1925 6 weeks		yes
Lane Emma H.	1895 1967	Frank L. Lane Sr.	yes
Lane Frank L. Sr.	1883 1945	Emma H. Lane	yes
Lane Nannie	7 April 1863 25 May 1932		yes
Lane Romulus B.	27 Sept. 1856 17 April 1935		yes

Other Info: His mother was Cecelia A. Layne.

Snoddy Nora B.	29 June 1887 10 Aug. 1944		yes

Inscription: Mother

Other Info: Footstone: NBS

Snoddy William T.	22 June 1877 25 April 1914		yes

Inscription: Father

Stinson David W.		Mary Lee Stinson	yes

Inscription: Co. D., 56th VA Infantry, CSA

Other Info: Military pension records show that he was born about 1842, died on 11 May 1914; married on 14 Nov. 1901 at age 59 years.

Last Name Given Name (Maiden Name)	Date of Birth Date of Death Age at Death	Spouse	Tombstone

Thomas Snoddy Family on Rd. 677

Auton Frances Nuckols	1885 1963		no

Other Info: Unidentified funeral home marker. Her husband is known to be buried in an unmarked grave next to hers.

Bransford Milton M.	1875 1935	Neva M. Bransford	yes

Other Info: Shares a headstone with his wife.

Bransford Neva M.	1874 1942	Milton M. Bransford	yes

Other Info: Shares a headstone with her husband.

Nuckols Joseph Henry	8 July 1882 29 May 1935		yes

Nuckols Nannie A. Snoddy			no

Other Info: Unidentified funeral home marker (no dates) She was the sister of Thomas Snoddy.

Snoddy James T.	1858 1915	Nannie Waddell Snoddy	yes

Inscription: Father;There is still a blessed sleep from which no one ever wakes to weep.

Other Info: Footstone: JTS Shares a headstone with his wife. His parents were John W. and Lucy J. S. Snoddy.

Snoddy John W.	1 Oct. 1838 21 June 1902	Lucy J. Snoddy Snoddy	yes

Other Info: Footstone: JWS. Shares a headstone with his wife. They were the parents of James T. Snoddy and Lorenzo W. Snoddy also buried here, and Clinton Lee Snoddy buried elsewhere.

Last Name Given Name (Maiden Name	Date of Birth Date of Death Age at Death	Spouse	Tombstone
Snoddy Lorenzo W.	24 Nov. 1879 29 March 1932		yes

Inscription: Our brother; Just sweetly rest.

Other Info: His parents were John W. and Lucy J. S. Snoddy

Snoddy Lucy J. Snoddy	31 May 1844 5 March 1908	John W. Snoddy	yes

Other Info: Footstone: LJS Shares a headstone with her husband.

Snoddy Nannie Waddell	1866 1903	James T. Snoddy	yes

Inscription: Mother; There is still a blessed sleep from which no one ever wakes to weep.

Other Info: Footstone: NWS Shares a headstone with her husband

William Snoddy Family on Rd. 653

Snoddy William H.	17 March 1924 12 Dec. 1993	Betty V. Snoddy	yes

Other Info: Footstone: William H. Snoddy, PFC, US Army, World War II (same dates given as are on headstone).

Spencer Family at "Brierhook"

Spencer R. W.	1842-1923		yes

Inscription: At Rest

Other Info: There is an unmarked grave beside this one.

Watson Spicey Scott		Thomas Gal Watson	no

Other Info: Known to be buried near this cemetery.

Last Name Given Name (Maiden Name)	Date of Birth Date of Death Age at Death	Spouse	Tombstone
Watson Thomas Gal	1795 after 1850	Spicey Scott Watson	no

Other Info: Known to be buried near this cemetery. He was the son of William Watson Sr. and Fannie Wilkinson Watson.

Spencer Family on Rd. 646

Spencer Joseph T.		Mary Susan Spencer	yes

Inscription: Co. B, 25th VA Inf, CSA

Spencer Mary Susan	26 Jan. 1848 4 Aug. 1904	Joseph T. Spencer	yes

Inscription: Wife of Joseph T. Spencer

(Spencer) William Thomas	21 May 1892 6 Oct. 1905		yes

Inscription: Son

Spencer-Moseley Family at "Dixie"

Lancaster Mrs. Frances	1 Oct. 1795 31 Sept. 1846		yes

Inscription: To the memory of

Moseley Capt. Francis	7 or 17 June 1774 6 March 1826		yes

Inscription: In memory of

Last Name Given Name (Maiden Name)	Date of Birth Date of Death Age at Death	Spouse	Tombstone
Moseley Elizabeth H.	11 March 1817 27 Oct. 1833		yes

Inscription: Here Lies-

Other Info: There is at least one unidentified grave in the Moseley section of this cemetery-that of an infant, and many in the pasture between the Spencer and Moseley family sections.

Richardson Lucy Ann Layne	16 July 1813 21 March 1900	Roland McKenney Richardson	no

Other Info: Known to be buried here. Her parents were George Woodson Layne and Sarah F. Gilliam Layne.

Spencer Elmira (or Elmina) Frances Bagby	22 March 1810 11 April 1879	John James Spencer	no

Other Info: Known to be buried here. Her father was Henry "Harry" Bagby

Spencer Eubelia (Buckner) Richardson	6 Nov. 1847 8 May 1942	Samuel Franklin Spencer	yes

Other Info: Shares a headstone with her husband. Her parents were Roland McKenney Richardson and Lucy Ann Layne Richardson.

Spencer James G. (Gray) Sr.	27 Dec. 1877 29 (or 24) May 1964	Mary Wilson Pratt Spencer	yes

Other Info: Shares a headstone with his wife. His parents were Samuel Franklin Spencer and Eubelia Buckner Richardson Spencer.

Last Name Given Name (Maiden Name)	Date of Birth Date of Death Age at Death	Spouse	Tombstone
Spencer John James, Rev.	19 May 1808 1 Nov. 1889	(1) Mary Price Staple or Staton Spencer 2) Elmira (or Elmina) Frances Bagby Spencer (3) Mrs. Lizzie Taylor Spencer	no

Other Info: Known to be buried here. His parents were William and Elizabeth Harris Baker Spencer.

| Spencer
Mary (Wilson) Pratt | 25 July 1890
21 Oct. 1978 | James Gray Spencer Sr. | yes |

Other Info: Shares a headstone with her husband. Her parents were Dr. Whitcomb Eliphalet Pratt and Florence LaSalle Moseley Pratt.

| Spencer
Samuel Franklin | 28 July 1921
16 Nov. 1923 | | yes |

Inscription: Our darling; Budded on earth to bloom in heaven.

Other Info: His parents were James Gray and Mary Wilson Pratt Spencer.

| Spencer
Samuel Franklin | 13 Nov. 1845
19 Nov. 1922 | Eubelia Buckner Richardson Spencer | yes |

Other Info: Shares a headstone with his wife. His parents were John J. Spencer and Elmira (Elmina) Frances Bagby Spencer.

| Spencer
Samuel Franklin | 7 July 1880
1 Aug. 1960 | Lena Marshall Spencer | no |

Other Info: Known to be buried here. His parents were John James and Elmira (Elmina) Frances Bagby Spencer.

| Spencer
William Overton | 9 March 1838
11 June 1888 | | no |

Other Info: Known to be buried here. His parents were John James Spencer and Elmira (Elmina) Frances Bagby Spencer.

There are at least 8 unidentified graves, including 5 known to be buried in the Spencer section of this cemetery.

Last Name	Date of Birth	Spouse	Tombstone
Given Name	Date of Death		
(Maiden Name)	Age at Death		

Samuel Spencer Family off US 24 — African American

Brightful	6 June 1947		no
infant	6 June 1947		

    Other Info: Known to be buried here. His mother is Evelyn Spencer Brightful.

Banks	3 May 1932		yes
Hobert Roy	12 Oct. 1957		

    Inscription: West Virginia, SGT, Co. A, 19 Engineer Bn

    Other Info: Has a Richie and Johnson Funeral Home marker-West Virginia. His parents were Izetta S. and Roy Banks.

Banks	1902		yes
Roy	1966	Izetta Spencer Banks	

    Inscription: Husband-Father

Kyle			no
Addie Walker		Jesse Kyle Sr.	

    Other Info: Known to be buried here. She was an aunt of Minnie W. Spencer and sister of Monroe Walker also buried in this cemetery.

Kyle			no
George			

    Other Info: Known to be buried here. His parents were Addie W. and Jesse Kyle Sr.

Kyle			no
Jesse Sr.		Addie Walker Kyle	

    Other Info: Known to be buried here.

Last Name Given Name (Maiden Name	Date of Birth Date of Death Age at Death	Spouse	Tombstone
Spencer 　Earl	17 April 1923 Sept. 1924 17 months		no

Other Info: Known to be buried here.

Spencer 　Jesse E.	16 June 1915 20 Dec. 1967		yes

Inscription: Virginia, SGT, 810 Base Unit, AAF, World War II

Spencer 　Minnie W. (Walker)	1881 1976	Samuel L. Spencer	yes

Inscription: Mother

Other Info: Shares a headstone with her husband. She and her husband were the parents of Charles D. Walker, Jesse E. Spencer, and Earl Spencer also buried in this cemetery, Armeta S. Jordan, Monroe and Wilber Spencer buried at St. Joy Church cemetery, John P. Spencer buried at Holy Trinity Baptist Church cemetery, Evelyn Spencer Brightful and 7 other children. Her parents were Monroe and Izetta Walker.

Spencer 　Samuel L.	1878 1940	Minnie Walker Spencer	yes

Inscription: Father

Other Info: Shares a headstone with his wife.

Walker 　Charles D. (Spencer)	1901 1971		yes

Other Info: He lived as a youth with his grandparents, Monroe and Izetta Walker and took their surname.

Walker 　Izetta	28 Dec. 1934 79 years	Monroe Walker	no

Other Info: Known to be buried here. She and her husband were the parents of Minnie W. Spencer.

Last Name Given Name (Maiden Name	Date of Birth Date of Death Age at Death	Spouse	Tombstone
Walker Johnny			no

Other Info: Known to be buried here. He was a brother of Minnie W. Spencer.

Walker Joseph			no

Other Info: Known to be buried here. He was a brother of Minnie W. Spencer.

Walker Monroe		Izetta Walker	no

Other Info: Known to be buried here.

Spreading Oak Baptist Church — African American

Agee Annie M.	1951 1994		no

Other Info: This is an above ground vault-Reids FH

Agero Elsie May	18 March 1946 23 Aug. 1948/9		yes

Andrews Jean E. Banks	22 Nov. 1940 5 May 2001		yes

Other Info: Daughter of Robert and Irene Banks, also buried here.

Ayers Artie	1900 1991		yes

Other Info: Has a Reids Funeral Home marker.

Ayers Emmit	3 Sept 1905 5 Nov. 1983		yes

Ayers John R.	25 Sept. 1898 5 Oct. 1965		yes

Last Name Given Name (Maiden Name)	Date of Birth Date of Death Age at Death	Spouse	Tombstone
Bamgbade Carolyn Y. Banks	29 Sept 1951 14 Aug. 2001		yes

Inscription: Daughter of Robert and Irene C. Banks

| Banks Annie | 1902 1981 | | yes |

Inscription: Mom

| Banks Daniel M. | | | yes |

Inscription: (no dates)

Other Info: Has a Colbert Funeral Home marker.

| Banks Elisha | 1929 1991 | | no |

Other Info: Unidentified funeral home marker

| Banks Fletcher E. | | | yes |

Inscription: (no dates)

| Banks Floyd | 1885 1951 | | yes |

Inscription: Well Done Thou Good and Faithful Servant

| Banks Fredrick M. | 29 Nov. 1949 25 March 1966 | | yes |

Other Info: He was the grandson of Hallie Jackson also buried in this cemetery.

Last Name Given Name (Maiden Name)	Date of Birth Date of Death Age at Death	Spouse	Tombstone
Banks Irene Carter	22 June 1918 19 Sept. 1998	Robert Banks	yes

Inscription: An Angel Returns Home; Wife of Robert Banks

Other Info: Also has an above ground vault: Reids FH Her husband and children-Jean Andrews, Carolyn Bamgbade, Melvin L. Banks and her brother, Lucheon Carter are also buried in this cemetery.

| Banks
James Edward | 20 April 1937
1 May 2002 | | yes |

Inscription: Husband and Father; In His will is our Peace-Dante

| Banks
James Henry | 1904
1983 | | yes |

Inscription: Dad

| Banks
Lawrence | Dec. 1909
Nov. 1968 | | yes |

| Banks
Leslie J. | 6 Feb. 1906
15 April 1969 | Marjorie Banks Banks | yes |

Other Info: Footstone: Leslie Banks, Maryland, SGT, US Army, World War II, 6 Feb. 1906, 15 April 1969

| Banks
Melvin L. | 22 June 1942
26 June 1965 | | yes |

Inscription: Virginia, PFC, Co. D, 538 Engr. Cbt. Bn.

| Banks
Robert | 16 Oct. 1911
2 Sept 1974 | Irene C. Banks | yes |

Inscription: Husband of Irene C. Banks

Other Info: Footstone: Robert Banks, 16 Oct. 1911, 2 Sept. 1974

| Banks
Robert Thornton | 1 Feb. 1933
1 July 1993 | | yes |

Inscription: Now Cometh Eternal Rest

Last Name Given Name (Maiden Name	Date of Birth Date of Death Age at Death	Spouse	Tombstone
Bledsoe Vernon Wayne	1964 1964		no

Other Info: Unidentified funeral home marker

Booker Alice R.	19 June 1904 30 Aug. 1991		yes
Booker Charlie R.	15 March 1900 28 Aug. 1989		yes
Booker Ethel Q.	1903 1961		yes
Booker Nannie B.	1927 1974		no

Other Info: Reids Funeral Home marker. She was the sister of Addie J. Green and Jeffery P. Green, also buried in this cemetery.

Brown Mary J.			no

Other Info: This is an unidentified funeral home marker with one date: 22 May 1955. Katie R. Williams was the undertaker.

Brown Rosa Anna (Jackson)	10 May 1933 9 May 1992		yes

Other Info: Footstone: Mother; also has a Thackers Bros. Funeral Home marker. Her parents were Samuel and Lottie C. Jackson

Bryant Lorene M.	3 April 1919 12 July 1969		yes

Inscription: Beloved Wife

Burns Viola C.	9 Aug. 1892 31 Dec. 1968		yes

Inscription: Grandmother

Last Name Given Name (Maiden Name)	Date of Birth Date of Death Age at Death	Spouse	Tombstone
Byrd Eunice	3 March 1903 18 March 2002		yes

Inscription: Gone but not Forgotten

Carter Lucheon Cleveland	25 July 1908 29 May 1998		yes

Inscription: TEC 5, US Army

Chambers Alvin Meredith	19 Sept. 1958 28 Sept. 1977		yes

Other Info: Grandson of Eliza Chambers, also buried here.

Chambers Bennie Lewis Sr.	9 Jan. 1952 26 Dec. 1979		yes

Inscription: Brother

Other Info: His parents were Bennie S. and Gracie V. Chambers.

Chambers Bennie S.	12 Aug. 1918 1 Sept 1995	Gracie V. Chambers	yes

Inscription: US Army, World War II

Other Info: Footstone is a military stone: Bennie S. Chambers, CPL, US Army, World War II, 12 Aug. 1918, 1 Sept. 1995; He was the son of Lewis Eli Chambers and Mary Lee Chambers.

Chambers Calvin D. (Delaware)	2 Feb. 1908 27 Dec. 1993	Essie Ernease J. Chambers	yes

Other Info: Shares a headstone with his wife; Footstone-Calvin Delaware Chambers, S1, US Navy, World War II, Feb. 2 1908, 27 Dec. 1993

Chambers Clarence E.	28 Jan. 1919 7 June 1980		yes

Inscription: Beloved Family

Last Name Given Name (Maiden Name)	Date of Birth Date of Death Age at Death	Spouse	Tombstone
Chambers Eddie Glover	25 June 1918 10 April 1998		no

Other Info: This is an above ground vault-Reid's FH

Chambers Eliza	4 Sept. 1892 30 Sept. 1997		yes

Chambers Essie Ernease J.	18 July 1908 7 July 1994	Calvin D. Chambers	yes

Other Info: Shares a headstone with her husband

Chambers Floyd H.	18 Sept 1959 12 June 1993		yes

Inscription: In Loving Memory

Other Info: Grandson of Eliza Chambers, also buried here.

Chambers Geneva Marie	28 March 1961		no

Other Info: Thacker Bros. Funeral Home marker

Chambers Gracie V.	1 Aug. 1932 11 Nov. 1991	Bennie S. Chambers	yes

Inscription: Mother

Chambers Lewis Eli	14 Dec. 1895 29 March 1964	Mary Lee Stanton Chambers	yes

Inscription: Father

Chambers Lillian Randolph	1881 1975		no

Other Info: Unidentified funeral home marker

Last Name Given Name (Maiden Name)	Date of Birth Date of Death Age at Death	Spouse	Tombstone
Chambers 　Lonnie	1964 1986		no

　　Other Info: Unidentified funeral home marker

Chambers 　Mary Lee (Stanton)	22 Dec. 1899 24 Dec. 1965	Lewis Eli Chambers	yes

　　Inscription: Mother

Chambers 　Sallie	1 Apr. 1891 28 Aug. 1951		yes
Chambers 　Thomas	15 Aug. 1886 9 Sept. 1960		yes
Chambers 　Tommy R.	26 March 1936 5 March 2003		yes
Chambers 　Walter Bernard	20 Feb. 1956 23 March 2000		yes

　　Inscription: His steps were ordered by the Lord.

　　Other Info: He is the father of Walter Bernard Chambers Jr., and the son of Bennie S. Chambers and Gracie V. Chambers who are also buried in this cemetery.

Chambers 　Walter Bernard Jr.	3 Jan. 1981 18 Jan. 2003		yes

　　Inscription: Let not your heart be troubled, for I am with thee; thy name receive me

Chambers 　Wavely	5 May 1882 14 May 1956		yes

　　Inscription: By (the) children

Clark 　Alexand(er)	16 May 1904 8 Dec. 1977		yes

Last Name Given Name (Maiden Name	Date of Birth Date of Death Age at Death	Spouse	Tombstone
Clark Bertha P. (Paige) Jones	6 Sept 1923 2 April 2000		yes

Inscription: Our Loving Mother

Other Info: Community Funeral Home marker gives birth year as 1922.

Eldridge Evelyn J.	23 Nov. 1915 1 June 1998		yes

Inscription: Beloved Mother; Loved and Remembered

Ford Elizabeth B.	1886 1968		yes

Ford Martha	18 July 1959		no

Other Info: L. C. Gray Funeral Home marker

Ford Mary	1865 1959		yes

Goines Caroline C.			yes

Inscription: (no dates)

Goines John Moses			yes

Inscription: (no dates)

Green Addie J.			no

Other Info: Has a Reids Funeral Home marker with one date: 9-6-70.

Green Jeffrey P.	1933 1990		yes

Inscription: US Army, Korea

Last Name Given Name (Maiden Name)	Date of Birth Date of Death Age at Death	Spouse	Tombstone
Holman Clarence "Tuffy"	24 Jan. 1948 17 April 1999		yes

Inscription: Brother

| Holman
  John | 24 March 1907
12 April 1985
78 years | | no |

Other Info: Thacker Bros. Funeral Home marker

| Holman
  Lawrance Sr. | 25 Feb. 1913
27 Nov. 1992 | Mary Virginia Holman | yes |

Inscription: Father

Other Info: Shares a headstone with his wife.

| Holman
  Mary Virginia | 12 May 1916
12 April 1988 | Lawrance Holman Sr. | yes |

Inscription: Mother

Other Info: Shares a headstone with her husband. She was the daughter of Alma Gregory.

| Holman
  Mattie Lee | 1879
1951 | | yes |

Inscription: Gone but not Forgotten

| Holman
  Mildred A. | 15 Nov. 1886
28 Sept. 1988 | | yes |

Inscription: In Loving Memory

Other Info: Has a Reids Funeral Home marker. She is the mother of Hortense M. Jones and the mother-in-law of Jeffrey P. Green also buried in this cemetery.

| Holman
  Samuel | 7 April 1885
28 Jan. 1961 | | yes |

Last Name Given Name (Maiden Name	Date of Birth Date of Death Age at Death	Spouse	Tombstone
Jackson Ada			yes

Inscription: In Memory of (no dates)

Other Info: She was the daughter of Hallie Jackson also buried in this cemetery.

Jackson Alphonza	1 Jan. 1937 28 March 1996		yes

Inscription: Beloved Husband, Father and Grandfather

Jackson Ann Shirley Elizabeth	13 March 1931 3 Jan. 1981		yes

Inscription: In Loving Memory

Other Info: Her parents were Samuel and Lottie C. Jackson also buried in this cemetery.

Jackson Benny R.	1923 1987		yes

Other Info: Has a Reid's Funeral Home marker. Was the son of Hallie Clark Jackson.

Jackson Eddie H.	12 Sept. 1926 30 Oct. 2002		yes

Inscription: Husband and Father

Other Info: Has a Reids Funeral Home marker

Jackson George	15 July 1927 23 July 1971		yes

Other Info: Has a Reid's Funeral Home marker.

Jackson Hallie C. (Clark)	27 Aug. 1900 7 May 1979		yes

Inscription: In Loving Memory of Mother and Grandmother

Last Name Given Name (Maiden Name)	Date of Birth Date of Death Age at Death	Spouse	Tombstone
Jackson 　James	1940 2002		no

　　Other Info: Reids Funeral Home marker

| Jackson
　Jimmy | | | no |

　　Other Info: Reid's Funeral Home marker with the dates missing. His mother was Hallie Clark Jackson also buried in this cemetery.

| Jackson
　John Junius | 1923
1985 | | yes |

　　Inscription: At Rest

| Jackson
　Lottie C. | 1907
1979 | Samuel Jackson | yes |

　　Inscription: Gone but not Forgotten

| Jackson
　Samuel | 1907
1969 | Lottie C. Jackson | yes |

　　Inscription: Father; Gone but not Forgotten

| Jackson
　Susie C. | 1902
1987 | | no |

　　Other Info: This is an above ground vault-Reids FH. She was the sister of Lottie Jackson also buried in this cemetery.

| Jackson
　Virginia | 1939
1979 | | yes |

　　Inscription: In Loving Memory

　　Other Info: Her parents were Samuel and Lottie C. Jackson, also buried in this cemetery.

| Jackson
　Walter | 18 Aug. 1935
16 April 1994 | | no |

　　Other Info: This is an above ground vault-Reids FH

Last Name Given Name (Maiden Name	Date of Birth Date of Death Age at Death	Spouse	Tombstone
Jackson Willie	6 Jan. 1883 10 Dec. 1969		yes

Other Info: Has a Reids Funeral Home marker; He was the brother of Samuel Jackson also buried in this cemetery.

Jackson Willie Raymond	24 Jan. 1942 6 Jan. 2002		yes

Inscription: Let the work I've done speak for me.

Other Info: Has a Reid's Funeral Home marker; He is the brother of Samuel Jackson also buried in this cemetery.

Johnson Gertrude G.	1923 1984	Russell L. Johnson	yes

Other Info: Shares a headstone with her husband.

Johnson Russell L.	1923 1986	Gertrude G. Johnson	yes

Other Info: Shares a headstone with his wife.

Jones Blanche Pearl	20 March 1900 19 Jan. 1955	Richard Jones	yes

Inscription: She is not dead, but sleepth

Other Info: She is the mother of Bertha P. Jones and John R. Jones, and grandmother of Edward L. Jones and Ernest Jones, all buried in this cemetery.

Jones Cora Banks	10 Sept. 1909 10 Oct. 1943		yes

Jones Edward L. Sr. "Les"	24 Sept. 1946 12 Nov. 1995		yes

Inscription: In God's Care

Other Info: Has a Community Funeral Home marker

Last Name Given Name (Maiden Name)	Date of Birth Date of Death Age at Death	Spouse	Tombstone
Jones Efford R.	8 Nov. 1941 6 Nov. 1991		yes

Inscription: Brother

Other Info: Has a Community Funeral Home marker.

Jones Elizabeth C.	31 Mar. 1879 4 Feb. 1951		yes

Inscription: Asleep in Jesus; By the children

Jones Ernest	9 Jan. 1949 17 April 2001		yes

Inscription: US Army, Vietnam

Jones Ernestine			no

Other Info: Reids Funeral Home marker gives one date: 6 May 1965.

Jones Florence B.	27 July 1916 5 March 1972		yes

Inscription: Sister; In God's Care

Jones Gomex Earl	12 Dec. 1941 14 Jan. 2003		yes

Inscription: US Army, Vietnam

Jones Hortense M.	9 Aug. 1909 18 Oct. 1976		yes

Inscription: In Loving memory; God Knows Those that are His.

Other Info: She is the daughter of Mildred a. Holman also buried in this cemetery.

Jones Irene B.	22 June 1944 5 June 1960		yes

Inscription: Sister

Last Name Given Name (Maiden Name	Date of Birth Date of Death Age at Death	Spouse	Tombstone
Jones John L., Rev.	25 Nov. 1877 11 May 1945		yes

Inscription: Asleep in Jesus

Jones John R.	13 April 1919 26 Nov. 1957		yes

Inscription: Father

Jones Junious L.	3 Nov. 1935 5 April 1995		yes

Inscription: US Army

Other Info: Has a Thacker Bros. Funeral Home marker

Jones Marie Jackson	19 Oct. 1937 22 Dec. 1992		no

Other Info: This is an above ground vault-Reid's FH

Jones Tom W.	1921 1942		yes

Inscription: Father Not My Will but Thine be Done

Jones William T.	3 May 1905 28 May 1985		yes
Maxey Curley	25 Aug. 1908 10 March 1965		yes
Maxey Ella V.	15 Dec. 1917 16 July 1985		yes

Inscription: Mother; In Loving Memory

Last Name Given Name (Maiden Name)	Date of Birth Date of Death Age at Death	Spouse	Tombstone
Maxey Fletcher	6 June 1957		yes

Inscription: (no dates)

Other Info: L.C. Gray Funeral Home marker gives death date.

Maxey Nora			yes

Inscription: (no dates)

Maxey Ralph R.	14 Dec. 1912 9 Nov. 1982		yes

Inscription: In Loving Memory

Miller Irene H.	1897 1974		yes

Other Info: Reid's Funeral Home marker

Murray Pokey Banks	4 July 1929 12 May 1990		yes
Payne Cornelias	1864 1966		yes
Perkins Sallie G.	2 March 1901 4 Feb. 1981		yes
Randolph Ada E.	7 May 1901 10 Sept. 1973		yes

Inscription: Mother: In God's Care

Other Info: Her siblings were Irene Miller, Hallie Jackson and Alexander Clark who are all buried in this cemetery.

Randolph Annie Mae	23 Feb. 1935 24 Feb. 1968		yes

Inscription: Mother; In God's Care

Last Name Given Name (Maiden Name)	Date of Birth Date of Death Age at Death	Spouse	Tombstone
Randolph Herman H., Rev.	27 June 1931 3 March 1990		yes

Other Info: Has a Reids Funeral Home marker.

Randolph Loveline			no

Other Info: Unidentified funeral home marker gives one date: 3-22-67.

Raphey Mary Ann	3 Oct. 1903 16 Oct. 1946		yes
Stallion Fannie B. (Booker)	15 June 1914 17 June 1973		yes

Other Info: Has a Reids Funeral Home marker.

Stanton Lorenzo A.	28 Feb. 1966 23 Nov. 1989		yes

Inscription: Always in our Hearts

Other Info: Grandson of Eliza Chambers, also buried here.

Stanton Virginia B.	1923 1992		yes

Other Info: Has a Colberts Funeral Home marker.

Stanton Wayne C.	1960 1998		yes
Stovalle Gerldin A.	20 Aug. 1912 17 April 1981		yes

Inscription: Gone but not Forgotten

Taylor Alma	19 June 1923 10 June 1969		yes

Inscription: Mother

Last Name Given Name (Maiden Name	Date of Birth Date of Death Age at Death	Spouse	Tombstone
Withers Gertrude Laura	18 May 1907 19 May 1997		yes

Inscription: Beloved Mother, Grandmother and Great Grandmother

There are 10 unidentified graves in this cemetery.

Sprouse Family at "Sprouse's Corner"

Moss Zella Pembleton Catlett		(1) Harrison Thomas Catlett (2) ____ Moss	no

Other Info: Known to be buried here.

Scott George			yes

Inscription: Co. A, 22nd VA Inf, CSA

Sprouse E.V.	April, 1880 April, 1880		slate stone

Inscription: EVS, Died 1880

Other Info: This was the stillborn child of Emily Virginia Sprouse, who died in childbirth.

Sprouse E.V. (Emily Virginia)	Sept. 1860 April 1880	John Josiah Sprouse	yes, broken

Inscription: At Rest

Sprouse Frank M. (Marrow)	1884 (14 March) 1942		yes

Other Info: He was the son of Henry Wesley Sprouse.

Last Name	Date of Birth	Spouse	Tombstone
Given Name	Date of Death		
(Maiden Name)	Age at Death		

Sprouse   no
   Henry Wesley

Other Info: Known to be buried here. He was the father of Frank M. Sprouse also buried in this cemetery.

There are 3 unidentified graves in this cemetery, including 2 known to be buried here.

St. Andrew's Baptist Church

Bailey   10 Nov. 1901   yes
   Annie Virginia   20 July 1905

Inscription: Beloved daughter of Richard Ellis and Blanche Roberts Bailey; Asleep in Jeus, blessed thought.

Other Info: Footstone: AVB

Bailey   30 March 1871   yes
   Blanche Roberts   5 June 1935   Richard Ellis Bailey

Inscription: Wife of Richard E. Bailey; She believed and sleeps in Jesus

Other Info: Footstone: BRB

Bailey   12 Oct. 1855   yes
   Richard Ellis   26 Feb. 1931   Blanche Roberts Bailey

Inscription: Son of Wm. W. and Virginia R. Bailey; Blessed are the pure in heart for they shall see God

Other Info: Footstone: REB

Baird   1 March 1900   yes
   Albert Franklin Sr.   20 Nov. 1970

Last Name	Date of Birth	Spouse	Tombstone
Given Name	Date of Death		
(Maiden Name)	Age at Death		

Baird   20 March 1867   yes
   Carrie Virginia (Lewis)   29 June 1937   William Henry Baird

Inscription: In God we Trust

Other Info: Shares a headstone with her husband.

Baird   1 Aug. 1924   yes
   Charlie W.   6 April 2001   Margaret A. Bowers Baird

Inscription: The Lord is my shepherd, I shall not want; Our children: Ann, George, Mary, Linda, Charlie Jr., Harvey, Elizabeth, James. Married May 8, 1946.

Other Info: Shares a headstone with his wife.

Baird   5 Feb. 1927   yes
   Courtney C.   21 July 1928

Inscription: My precious baby at rest

Other Info: Footstone: Daughter.

Baird   1885   yes
   Harvey Lee   1947   Mary Jones Baird

Other Info: He and his wife were the parents of 14 children including: Myrtle Marshall, Pearl V. Davis, James H. Baird, Katherine G. Baird, Courtney C. Baird, all buried in this cemetery, and Elizabeth B. Edwards.

Baird   23 Sept. 1937   yes
   James H.   23 June 1957

Inscription: My darling boy at rest

Other Info: Footstone: Son His parents were Harvey L. and Mary J. Baird also buried in this cemetery.

Last Name Given Name (Maiden Name)	Date of Birth Date of Death Age at Death	Spouse	Tombstone
Baird Katherine G.	31 Dec. 1919 30 Jan. 1930		yes

Inscription: My precious little girl at rest.

Other Info: Footstone: Daughter.

| Baird
Margaret A. (Bowers) | 21 Jan. 1922
12 March 1985 | Charlie W. Baird, Sr. | yes |

Inscription: The Lord is my shepherd, I shall not want.; Our children: Ann, George, Mary, Linda, Charlie Jr., Harvey, Elizabeth, James; Married May 8, 1946

| Baird
Mary Jones | 12 April 1896
14 Aug. 1969 | Harvey Lee Baird | yes |

Other Info: She and her husband were the parents of 14 children.

| Baird
William Henry | 28 July 1858
1 July 1948 | Carrie Virginia Lewis Baird | yes |

Inscription: In God we Trust

Other Info: Shares a headstone with his wife.

| Blanks
Edward L. (Lyle) | 1909
1997 | Nell Baird Blanks | yes |

Inscription: In loving memory

| Bryant
Alexander E. | 5 March 1872
8 March 1955 | Martha Staton Bryant | yes |

| Bryant
Luther E. (Everett) | 5 May 1921
24 Jan. 1947 | | yes |

Inscription: At Rest

Last Name	Date of Birth	Spouse	Tombstone
Given Name	Date of Death		
(Maiden Name	Age at Death		

Bryant 6 Sept. 1874 yes
Martha S. (Staton) 12 Oct. 1963 Alexander E. Bryant

    Other Info: Footstone: Mother ; She and her husband were the parents of Luther E. Bryant also buried in this cemetery.

Caul 17 Oct. 1893 yes
Lucy Spencer 5 Oct. 1974

    Other Info: She was the daughter of George L. and Angie V. Spencer, and the sister of John Paulette Spencer all buried in this cemetery.

Cobb 21 Dec. 1905 yes
Mary E. (Ellis) Bailey 28 May 1933

    Inscription: Beloved daughter of Richard Ellis and Blanche Roberts Bailey; Waiting the Lord's return

    Other Info: Footstone: MEBC; Her sister, Pauline Bailey Ripley, and her parents are also buried in this cemetery.

Davis 1909 yes
John Pitt 1995 Pearl V. Baird Davis

    Other Info: Shares a headstone with his wife.

Davis 1914 yes
Pearl V. (Baird) 1974 John Pitt Davis

    Other Info: Shares a headstone with her husband. Her parents were Harvey L. and Mary J. Baird.

Dunkum 25 July 1980 yes
Brandy Elizabeth 8 May 2001

    Other Info: Her parents are Kim and Elizabeth Dunkum. Her sister, Melissa A. Dunkum is also buried in this cemetery.

Last Name Given Name (Maiden Name	Date of Birth Date of Death Age at Death	Spouse	Tombstone
Dunkum Melissa A. (Ann)	24 Aug. 1985 3 Feb. 1986		yes

Inscription: Our Little Angel

Other Info: Footstone: Melissa Ann Dunkum; She was the daughter of Kim and Elizabeth Dunkum. Her sister, Brandy Dunkum is also buried in this cemetery.

Edwards Walter D.	3 May 1910 21 Sept. 1995	Elizabeth Baird Edwards	yes
Edwards Walter H.	5 March 1939 21 Aug. 1967	Bertha A. Edwards	yes

Inscription: The Word is a light unto my path.

Other Info: He was the son of Walter D. and Elizabeth B. Edwards.

Goff Kenneth James	17 May 1999 21 July 1999		yes
Hanes Elmo	1915 1931		yes

Inscription: At Rest

Other Info: He was the foster son of William H. and Carrie V. Baird.

Hanson Clifton	27 July 1908 20 April 1974		yes
Johnson Albert T.	30 Nov. 1871 18 June 1952/1932		yes

Other Info: He was the brother of Ida M. Johnson, also buried in this cemetery.

Johnson Hallie R. (Reynolds)	1879 1934	Robert N. Johnson	yes

Last Name Given Name (Maiden Name)	Date of Birth Date of Death Age at Death	Spouse	Tombstone
Johnson Ida M.	1856 1935		yes

Other Info: She was the sister of Albert T. Johnson, also buried in this cemetery.

Johnson James Mundy	23 May 1877 4 March 1924	Josie Reynolds Johnson	yes

Other Info: Shares a headstone with his wife.

Johnson Josie Reynolds	3 June 1883 12 June 1967	James Mundy Johnson	yes

Other Info: Shares a headstone with her husband. She is the sister of Hallie Reynolds Johnson also buried in this cemetery.

Johnson Robert N.	22 March 1874 30 Oct. 1951	Hallie Reynolds Johnson	yes

Inscription: Private, 4 VA Infantry, Sp. Am. War

Johnson Thomas W.	1877 1946		yes
Jones Doria Louise "Toni"	23 Dec. 1948 12 April 1984		yes
Leonard Bernard L.	19 May 1917 22 Feb. 1990		yes

Inscription: PFC, US Army, World War II

Leonard Earl D.	20 March 1920 2 Nov. 1970		yes

Other Info: Shares a headstone with his parents, Ernest C. and Willie E. Leonard. His brother, Woodrow W. and sister, Hazel A. Leonard are also buried in this cemetery. Footstone: PVT, US Army, World War II. Note: Birthday on headstone (20 March 1920) and footstone (27 March 1920) differ.

Last Name Given Name (Maiden Name)	Date of Birth Date of Death Age at Death	Spouse	Tombstone
Leonard Ernest C.	12 Aug. 1881 6 April 1951	 Willie E. Reynolds Leonard	yes

Other Info: Shares a headstone with his wife and son, Earl D. Leonard.

Leonard George Carlyle	12 Aug. 1958 24 April 1960		yes
Leonard Gus	1927 2001		no

Other Info: Dunkum Funeral Home marker

Leonard Hazel A.	12 March 1922 19 Nov. 1994		yes

Other Info: Her parents, Ernest C. and Willie E. Leonard, and brothers, Earl D. and Woodrow W. Leonard are also buried in this cemetery.

Leonard Willie E. (Reynolds)	1 April 1891 22 Jan. 1954	 Ernest C. Leonard	yes

Other Info: Shares a headstone with her husband, and son, Earl D. Leonard.

Leonard Woodrow W.	13 April 1914 7 June 1985		yes

Inscription: PFC, US Army, World War II

Marshall Myrtle Baird	24 July 1924 5 May 2000	 Harold V. Marshall	yes
Meeks Barbara P.	5 Feb. 1920 5 Aug. 1999	 Horace W. Meeks	yes

Other Info: Shares a headstone with her husband.

Meeks Horace W.	22 July 1908 10 Jan. 2000	 Barbara P. Meeks	yes

Other Info: Shares a headstone with his wife.

Last Name Given Name (Maiden Name)	Date of Birth Date of Death Age at Death	Spouse	Tombstone
Moore Arthur Hall	28 June 1910 25 June 1980		yes

  Inscription: PFC, US Army, World War II

  Other Info: He was the foster son of P.P. Glove.

| Nicholas
  Dale A. | 27 May 1916
9 June 1979 | Elsie Baird | yes |

  Inscription: Love lives on.

| (non-inscribed)
  Ellis | | | yes |

  Inscription: Resting

| Ragland
  Catherine | | Morris Ragland | no |

  Other Info: Known to be buried here.

| Ragland
  Gracie M. | 15 Nov. 1942
15 Nov. 1942 | | yes |

| Ragland
  John W. | 13 June 1931
1 March 1932 | | yes |

  Inscription: Brother

| Ragland
  Julia L. | 16 Nov. 1939
7 Dec. 1939 | | yes |

| Ragland
  Morris | | Catherine Ragland | no |

  Other Info: Known to be buried here with his wife and several of their children.

| Reynolds
  Samuel Anderson | Nov. 1933 | | yes |

  Inscription: Rest in Peace

Last Name Given Name (Maiden Name	Date of Birth Date of Death Age at Death	Spouse	Tombstone
Reynolds Samuel B.	25 Nov. 1886 9 Aug. 1953	Vadney Wright Reynolds	yes

Other Info: Footstone: Samuel B. Reynolds, Virginia, Private, 9th Company, 155 Depot Brig., World War II (same dates as on tombstone). Shares a headstone with his wife.

Reynolds Vadney W. (Wright)	19 April 1907 28 March 1993	Samuel B. Reynolds	yes

Other Info: Shares a headstone with her husband.

Ripley Pauline Bailey	22 Nov. 1903 22 July 1983		yes

Other Info: Footstone: PBR

Roberts Alice C.	19 Nov. 1873 12 April 1951		yes

Inscription: Sleep until the resurrection morn.

Roberts Fred N.	22 March 1895 9 Feb. 1959	Theresa S. Roberts	yes

Inscription: Virginia, Wagoner, 401 Engr., Pon Park, World War I

Other Info: Shares a headstone with his wife and son, Fred. N. Roberts Jr.. He and his wife were the parents of Marvin S. Roberts, also buried in this cemetery.

Roberts Fred. N. Jr.	22 July 1926 15 Nov. 1986		yes

Other Info: Shares a headstone with his parents.

Roberts Guy Bowles	26 Feb. 1902 25 Nov. 1969		yes

Inscription: The Lord is my shepherd

Other Info: Footstone: Son

Last Name Given Name (Maiden Name	Date of Birth Date of Death Age at Death	Spouse	Tombstone
Roberts Marvin S.	5 June 1897 25 Nov. 1971	Merle Staton Roberts	yes

Other Info: Footstone: MSR; Shares a headstone with his wife. His parents were Fred N. and Theresa S. Roberts also buried in this cemetery.

Roberts Merle S. (Staton)	6 March 1899 9 Dec. 1988	Marvin S. Roberts	yes

Other Info: Footstone: MSR; Shares a headstone with her husband.

Roberts Nathaniel M.	18 March 1864 5 Nov. 1961		yes

Inscription: Rest in Peace

Other Info: Footstone: NMR

Roberts Nellie B.	30 April 1907 30 Aug. 1991		yes
Roberts Theresa S.	3 Feb. 1902 15 March 1970	Fred. N. Roberts	yes

Other Info: Shares a headstone with her husband and son, Fred N. Roberts Jr.

Roberts Thomas Wm.	28 Oct. 1898 31 Jan. 1976		yes

Inscription: PVT, Army Air Force, World War II

Rosser Benjamin W.	1869 1943		yes

Other Info: His daughter, Mary W. Rosser and his brother, Thomas A. Rosser are also buried in this cemetery.

Rosser Lula M.	1900 1988		yes

Other Info: She was the daughter of Thomas A. and Sarah M. Rosser.

Last Name Given Name (Maiden Name)	Date of Birth Date of Death Age at Death	Spouse	Tombstone
Rosser Mary W.	1903 1985		yes

Other Info: She was the daughter of Benjamin W. Rosser also buried in this cemetery.

Rosser Sarah M. (Maxey)	1878 1961	Thomas A. Rosser	yes
Rosser Thomas A.	1867 1946	Sarah Maxey Rosser	yes
Spencer Angie V.	24 Aug. 1867 9 Aug. 1943	George Lou Spencer	yes

Inscription: At Rest

Other Info: Shares a headstone with her husband.

Spencer George L. (Lou)	20 May 1858 13 Dec. 1928	Angie V. Spencer	yes

Inscription: At Rest

Other Info: Shares a headstone with his wife.

Spencer John P. Jr.	24 Nov. 1925 31 March 1926		yes
Spencer John Paulette	5 Nov. 1898 10 May 1978	Lynda Patteson Spencer	yes

Inscription: Rest in Peace

Spencer Lynda P. (Patteson)	8 March 1902 31 Dec. 1991	John Paulette Spencer	yes

Inscription: Rest in Peace

Staton Anna Bryant (nee Johnson)	23 Oct. 1875 4 Dec. 1953		yes

Other Info: Footstone: Mother, She was the mother of Merle Staton Roberts also buried in this cemetery.

Last Name Given Name (Maiden Name	Date of Birth Date of Death Age at Death	Spouse	Tombstone
Stegall Wilbert Ray	23 March 1929 2 April 1960		yes

Inscription: North Carolina, PFC, USMC, World War II

| Stinson
   Mildred F. | 1868
1950 | | yes |

St. Joy Baptist Church — African American

| (Ayers)
   Elizabeth B. (Booker) | 5 Nov. 1896
Bartee 8 Sept. 1980 | | yes |

Inscription: Peaceful Rest

Other Info: E.B. Allen Funeral Home marker: Lizzie B. Ayers

| Ayers
   James Herman | 1907
197__ | | no |

Other Info: E.B. Allen Funeral Home marker

| Bagby
   Lucille W. | 1918
1999 | | no |

Other Info: E.B. Allen Funeral Home marker

| Bartee
   George Jr. | 1930
1990 | | no |

Other Info: Reids Funeral Home marker

| Bartee
   Georgianna T. | 31 Aug. 1932
3 Oct. 2002 | | yes |

Inscription: Rest in Peace

Other Info: Has an E.B. Allen Funeral Home marker.

Last Name Given Name (Maiden Name)	Date of Birth Date of Death Age at Death	Spouse	Tombstone
Bartee James O. "Pooh"	13 Oct. 1975 20 Feb. 1976		yes

Inscription: Precious Memories

Bartee Phyllis Marie	8 March 1967 23 April 1993		yes

Inscription: Rest in Peace

Bartee Roy Lee Sr.	16 March 1937 29 June 1961		yes

Other Info: Has an E.B. Allen Funeral Home marker

Bartee Sam	1933 2002		no

Other Info: E.B. Allen Funeral Home marker

Booker Bethrone	1962 1998		no

Other Info: Bland-Reid Funeral Home marker

Booker Lunell	1919 1986	Phil Booker	no

Other Info: E.B. Allen Funeral Home marker

Booker Phil	1912 1983	Lunell Booker	no

Other Info: E.B. Allen Funeral Home marker. He was the uncle of Sam Bartee and Phyllis Marie Bartee also buried in this cemetery.

Booker Richard	1980 1972		no

Other Info: Reids Funeral Home marker

Last Name Given Name (Maiden Name)	Date of Birth Date of Death Age at Death	Spouse	Tombstone
Booker Samuel	1919 1996		no

Other Info: E.B. Allen Funeral Home marker

Brown John W.	1942 1989		no

Other Info: Reids Funeral Home marker

Brown Richard	 2 Dec. 1967		no

Other Info: Unidentified funeral home marker

Cabell Bettie Gordan, Ms.	 20 Sept. 1936 56 years		no

Other Info: Dunkum Bros. Funeral Home marker

Cabell Rebecca W.	1 May 1861 9 May 1928		yes

Inscription: Gone but not Forgotten

Carson Clara	1896 1983		no

Other Info: Unidentified funeral home marker

Claiborne Mary Catherine	1916 2002	William Mack Claiborne	yes

Inscription: Sleep in Peace

Other Info: Shares a headstone with her husband.

Claiborne William Mack (Deacon)	1910 1986	Mary Catherine Claiborne	yes

Inscription: Sleep in Peace

Other Info: Shares a headstone with his wife.

Last Name Given Name (Maiden Name)	Date of Birth Date of Death Age at Death	Spouse	Tombstone
Clayborne Beatrice A.	1931 2004		yes

Inscription: On a mission for the King

Other Info: Has an E.B. Allen Funeral Home marker.

Clayborne Edith	1939 2005		no

Other Info: Reids Funeral Home marker.

Clayborne James Pilot Pike	1907 1999		no

Other Info: E.B. Allen Funeral Home marker

Clayborne Pearl Ethel	9 Feb. 1906 16 July 1962		yes

Inscription: Mother

Dabney Kenneth N.	1956 1992		no

Other Info: E.B. Allen Funeral Home marker

Davis Willie E.	1881 1962		yes

Inscription: Mother; At Rest

Dyer Nannie	1885 1922	John Dyer	yes

Inscription: Wife of John Dyer; Alive in Jesus

Other Info: Her husband is interred in the Henry Smith Family cemetery.

Last Name Given Name (Maiden Name)	Date of Birth Date of Death Age at Death	Spouse	Tombstone
Gibson Byrd L.	12 Sept. 1889 16 June 1965		yes

Inscription: Loving Father

Gibson Mary M.	22 June 1894 29 Dec. 1984		yes

Inscription: Loving Mother

Glover Earnest T. Sr.	21 Oct. 1945 17 Jan. 2003	Betty C. Glover	yes

Inscription: Gone but not Forgotten

Other Info: Has an E.B. Allen Funeral Home marker.

Hemmings Lottie P.	20 March 1895 9 July 1951		yes
Hemmings Thomas	10 June 1882 23 Nov. 1957		yes

Inscription: In Loving Memory

Horsley Mattie Gordon	1890 1865		yes

Inscription: Sleep in Peace

Horsley Mrs. Martha C.	1878 1969		no

Other Info: Hamlan Curtis Funeral Home marker

Jackson Ella W., Deaconess	18 July 1937 12 Oct. 1998		yes

Inscription: The Lord is my Shepherd

Last Name Given Name (Maiden Name)	Date of Birth Date of Death Age at Death	Spouse	Tombstone
Johnson Jeanette H.	19 Feb. 1921 25 May 1989	Thomas P. Johnson	yes

    Other Info: Shares a headstone with her husband. Has a Dunkum Funeral Home marker

Johnson Thomas P.	27 Sept. 1917 2 Sept. 2002	Jeanette H. Johnson	yes

    Other Info: Shares a headstone with his wife. Has a Dunkum Funeral Home marker.

Jones Amanda	19 Feb. 1926		yes

    Inscription: Mother

Jones Andrew	10 March 1920 10 Jan. 1973		yes

    Inscription: Virginia, PVT, US Army, World War II

Jones Clyde O.	30 Sept. 1939 22 Jan. 2003		yes

    Inscription: Beloved husband

    Other Info: Has an E. B. Allen Funeral Home marker

Jones Doris A.	12 Aug. 1923 18 March 1985		yes

    Inscription: At Rest

Jones Gracie L.	1951 2000		yes

    Other Info: Has a Reids Funeral Home marker

Jones Jennie	1901 1971		yes

    Inscription: Gone but not Forgotten

Last Name Given Name (Maiden Name	Date of Birth Date of Death Age at Death	Spouse	Tombstone
Jones Paige	1912 1986		no

Other Info: E.B. Allen Funeral Home marker

Jones Paul C. Sr.	27 Jan. 1924 7 Oct. 1991		yes

Other Info: Has an E.B. Allen Funeral Home marker

Jones Percy	1893 1980		no

Other Info: This is an above ground vault.

Jones Richard	1849 1942		yes

Inscription: Father

Jones Thomas H. Sr.	1925 1985		no

Other Info: Unidentified funeral home marker

Jones Tommy J.	14 Jan. 1941 27 May 2001		yes

Inscription: A Peaceful Sleep

Jones William	Dec. 1965		no

Other Info: Unidentified funeral home marker

Jones Wyatt N.	15 June 1893 28 Feb. 1963	Nellie M. Jones	yes

Other Info: His wife is interred at Union Hill B.C. Cemetery.

Last Name Given Name (Maiden Name	Date of Birth Date of Death Age at Death	Spouse	Tombstone
Jordan Ameta S. (Spencer)	13 June 1908 19 March 1999		yes

Inscription: We love you Mama-Meta

Other Info: Her parents were Samuel and Minnie W. Spencer buried in the Spencer Family Cemetery off US 24.

| Kidd
   Sadie M. | 1930
2001 | | no |

Other Info: E.B. Allen Funeral Home marker. Her father, Burley Mosley is also buried in this cemetery.

| Kyle
   Frances A. | 1911
2000 | | no |

Other Info: E.B. Allen Funeral Home marker

| Kyle
   George Thomas Jr. | 12 Aug. 1933
30 April 1997 | | yes |

Other Info: Has a Reids Funeral Home marker; He was the son of Frances A. Kyle also buried in this cemetery.

| Kyle
   Gertrude B. | 1906
1993 | Jessie T. Kyle | no |

Other Info: Unidentified funeral home marker

| Kyle
   Jessie T. | 1896
1982 | Gertrude B. Kyle | no |

Other Info: E.B. Allen Funeral Home marker

| Lee
   Mary Etta | 1900
1971 | | no |

Other Info: E.B. Allen Funeral Home marker

Last Name Given Name (Maiden Name	Date of Birth Date of Death Age at Death	Spouse	Tombstone
Monroe Clifford	1960 1994		no

Other Info: E.B. Allen Funeral Home marker. He was the son of Floyd E. Monroe also buried in this cemetery.

| Monroe
Eletha M. | 1937
1999 | Floyd E. Monroe | no |

Other Info: E.B. Allen Funeral Home marker

| Monroe
Ella W. | 1886
1968 | | yes |

Inscription: At Rest

| Monroe
Floyd E. | 1935
1995 | Eletha M. Monroe | no |

Other Info: E.B. Allen Funeral Home marker. His parents were Mattie and General Monroe, and he and his wife were the parents of Clifford Monroe, all buried in this cemetery.

| Monroe
General | 1905
1986 | Mattie W. Monroe | no |

Other Info: E.B. Allen Funeral Home marker; He and his wife were the parents of Floyd E. Monroe, the grandparents of Clifford Monroe, and the great-grandparents of Willie Lamont Monroe all buried in this cemetery.

| Monroe
Mattie W. | 1914
1986 | General Monroe | no |

Other Info: E.B. Allen Funeral Home marker

| Monroe
Willie Lamont | 1974
1993 | | no |

Other Info: E.B. Allen Funeral Home marker

Last Name Given Name (Maiden Name)	Date of Birth Date of Death Age at Death	Spouse	Tombstone
Morgan Gertrude	1917 1988		yes

Other Info: Has an E.B. Allen Funeral Home marker

Morgan Henry W.			no

Other Info: Unidentified funeral home marker with no dates.

Morgan James R.	1956 2003		no

Other Info: E. B. Allen Funeral Home marker

Morgan John Henry	1949 1975		no

Other Info: E.B. Allen Funeral Home marker

Morgan Mary C.	1920 1998		no

Other Info: E.B. Allen Funeral Home marker

Morgan Travis	27 June 1983 18 April 1999		yes

Inscription: Gone but not Forgotten

Mosley Burley	1908 1977		no

Other Info: E.B. Allen Funeral Home marker; He was the father of Sadie M. Kidd and the brother of Robert Mosley also buried in this cemetery.

Mosley Elizabeth	1907 1966		yes
Mosley Robert	1910 1984		no

Other Info: Reids Funeral Home marker

Last Name Given Name (Maiden Name	Date of Birth Date of Death Age at Death	Spouse	Tombstone
Mosley Walter T.	1903 1993		no

Other Info: E.B. Allen Funeral Home marker

Murdock Mary A.	1942 1996		no

Other Info: Reids Funeral Home marker

Nelson Charles Richard	1933 1972		yes

Inscription: Gone but not Forgotten

Perkins Cheryl M. Leftwich	1957 1988		yes

Inscription: Rest in Peace

Roberts Nellie B.	1936 2003		no

Other Info: E. B. Allen Funeral Home marker

Shelton Virginia Kyle	1925 1982		yes

Inscription: Peaceful Slumber

Small Andrew James	8 April 1895 25 March 1972		yes

Inscription: New York, CPL, Co. C, 325 FLD Sig. BN, World War I.

Spencer Corrine	25 May 1910 7 Nov. 1993	Monroe Spencer	yes

Other Info: Shares a headstone with her husband.

Spencer Eva Scott	20 Sept. 1916 30 June 1979	John R. Spencer	yes

Last Name Given Name (Maiden Name	Date of Birth Date of Death Age at Death	Spouse	Tombstone
Spencer Harriet E.	1915 1997		no

Other Info: Reids Funeral Home marker

Spencer infant boy	 3 July 1999		no

Other Info: E.B. Allen Funeral Home marker; His mother is Angela Spencer.

Spencer Joseph A.	1883 1962	 Josephine Spencer	yes

Inscription: At Rest

Spencer Josephine	1883 1981	 Joseph A. Spencer	yes

Inscription: At Rest

Spencer Monroe	17 Oct. 1906 (6 June 1994)	 Corrine Spencer	yes

Other Info: Shares a headstone with his wife; Footstone: Monroe Spencer, US Army, World War II, 17 Oct. 1906-6 June 1994; His brother Wilbur Spencer and sister Ameta S. Jordan are also buried in this cemetery. Their parents were Samuel and Minnie W. Spencer buried in the Spencer Family Cemetery off US 24.

Spencer Wilbur Phillip	4 Oct. 1921 6 Oct. 1998		yes

Inscription: US Army, World War II

Other Info: Also has an above ground vault: Reids FH

Trent Edna	1906 2001		no

Other Info: E.B. Allen Funeral Home marker

Last Name Given Name (Maiden Name)	Date of Birth Date of Death Age at Death	Spouse	Tombstone
Trent Matt Weldon	1914 1976		yes

Inscription: PVT, US Army, World War II

Trent William M.	8 Aug. 1911 6 March 1967		yes

Inscription: Virginia, PVT, 1342 SVC, COMD Unit, World War I

West Charles L.	1932 1959		no

Other Info: Unidentified funeral home marker

West Haywood L.	21 Jan. 1962 13 Nov. 1985		yes

Inscription: US Army

West James M.	1951 1980		no

Other Info: West Funeral Home marker

West Lelia E.	1904 1995		no

Other Info: E.B. Allen Funeral Home marker

West Mary Ann	1935 1959		no

Other Info: Unidentified funeral home marker

West William M.	1900 1972		no

Other Info: E.B. Allen Funeral Home marker

Woolridge Nellie M.	2 Jan. 1892 20 April 1979	Williard Woolridge	yes

Last Name Given Name (Maiden Name)	Date of Birth Date of Death Age at Death	Spouse	Tombstone
Woolridge Williard	12 Aug. 1892 16 Feb. 1962	Nellie M. Woolridge	yes

Inscription: At Rest

| Wright
Edward |
25 Nov. 1998 | | no |

Other Info: Reids Funeral Home marker; His father is Willis Wright. His brother, John Wright is also buried in this cemetery.

| Wright
Harold I | 1932
2002 | | no |

Other Info: E.B. Allen Funeral home marker

| Wright
Hubert | 1906
1975 | | no |

Other Info: Community Funeral Home marker

| Wright
James Nickoles | 29 Oct. 1892
26 Dec. 1962 | | yes |

Inscription: Virginia, PVT, Co. C, 510 ENGR, SVC BN, World War I

Other Info: Unidentified funeral home marker: James Nickolas Wright

| Wright
John Jr. | 28 July 1917
26 Feb. 1981 | | yes |

Inscription: US Army, World War II

| Wright
John Lee | 1874
1949 | Maud Gordon Wright | yes |

Inscription: In Memory of Grandparents of Mattie E. Warren

Other Info: Shares a headstone with his wife.

| Wright
Maria R. | 28 Jan. 1914 | | yes |

Last Name Given Name (Maiden Name)	Date of Birth Date of Death Age at Death	Spouse	Tombstone
Wright Maud Gordon	1890 1958	John Lee Wright	yes

Inscription: In Memory of Grandparents of Mattie E. Warren

Other Info: Shares a headstone with her husband.

Wright Ola H.	1910 1997	Willie Wright	no

Other Info: Unidentified funeral home marker

Wright Willie	 2 Aug. 1965	Ola H. Wright	no

Other Info: Unidentified funeral home marker

Stammer Family on US 15

Stammer Gordon James	16 July 1982 13 Sept. 2000		yes

Inscription: Our Beloved Son, "Jamie"

Other Info: Footstone: In just a moment you touched our hearts forever.

Stanton Family on Rd. 617 — African American

Anderson baby girl	 2 months		no

Other Info: Known to be buried here, the daughter of Lois Anderson.

Anderson Lelia S.	7 Jan. 1877 25 Jan. 1972		yes

Other Info: She was the sister to James Arthur Stanton and Lou G. Johnson also buried in this cemetery.

Last Name Given Name (Maiden Name)	Date of Birth Date of Death Age at Death	Spouse	Tombstone
Booker Carrie J.	14 March 1920 22 Feb. 1992	Charles H. Booker	yes

Other Info: Shares a headstone with her husband.

Booker Charles H.	9 March 1913 18 Sept. 1987	Carrie J. Booker	yes

Other Info: Shares a headstone with his wife.

Booker Howard J.	1922 2003		no

Other Info: Reids Funeral Home marker. He was the father of James J. Booker also buried in this cemetery.

Booker James J.	5 Dec. 1945 3 Dec. 1966		yes

Inscription: In God's Care

Cooper Travone Rayquan	2 July 2000 2 July 2000		yes

Eldridge premature baby			no

Other Info: Known to be buried here.

Eldridge Roger L.	1955 2002		no

Other Info: Reids Funeral Home marker

Johnson David	17 Oct. 1899 29 May 1994	Lou. Gertrude S. Johnson	yes

Other Info: Shares a headstone with his wife. Has an above ground vault: David Johnson, 17 Oct. 1899, 29 May 1994: Reids FH.

Last Name	Date of Birth	Spouse	Tombstone
Given Name	Date of Death		
(Maiden Name)	Age at Death		

Johnson   20 Feb. 1903   yes
    Lou (Gertrude) S.   4 Sept. 2000   David Johnson

    Other Info: Shares a headstone with her husband. Has an above ground vault: Lou Gertrude Johnson, 20 Feb. 1903, 4 Sept. 2000: Reids FH

Johnson   16 Sept. 1926   yes
    Willie K.   28 March 1987

    Inscription: US Army, World War II

    Other Info: Has a Reid's Funeral Home marker. He was the son of David and Lou S. Johnson also buried in this cemetery.

Jones   1917   no
    Annie R.   2000

    Other Info: Reids Funeral Home marker

Lee   no
    baby

    Other Info: Known to be buried here, the premature infant of James and Mattie Lee.

Ross   Aug. 1958   no
    Alvin Sylvester   7 Dec. 1985

    Other Info: Reids Funeral Home marker

Stanton   24 Oct. 1906   yes
    Aaron   16 July 1971   Mary Virginia Stanton

    Other Info: Has a Dunkum Funeral Home marker.

Stanton   14 Oct. 1947   yes
    Andrew Epp   10 March 1997   Carol V. Stanton

    Inscription: Beloved Husband and Devoted Father.

Last Name Given Name (Maiden Name)	Date of Birth Date of Death Age at Death	Spouse	Tombstone
Stanton Cassie Lee	16 June 1914 5 March 1991	George Stanton	yes

Inscription: Rest in Peace

Other Info: Shares a headstone with her husband.

| Stanton
George | Jan. 1909
15 March 1979 | Cassie Lee Stanton | yes |

Inscription: Rest in Peace

Other Info: Shares a headstone with his wife.

| Stanton
James A. (Arthur) | 5 Aug. 1882
16 May 1969 | Margie J. Stanton | yes |

Inscription: In Loving Memory

Other Info: Dunkum Funeral Home marker gives a different birth year 1881; Shares a headstone with his wife.

| Stanton
Junious E. | 26 April 1919
27 April 1993 | | yes |

Inscription: In God's Care

Other Info: Has a Reids Funeral Home marker. He was the father of Andrew Epp Stanton also buried in this cemetery.

| Stanton
Lucille N. | 2 Jan. 1951
24 Mar. 1990 | | yes |

Inscription: Mother

Other Info: She was the grandmother of Lucille Rachelle Stanton and Travone Rayquan Cooper also buried in this cemetery.

| Stanton
Lucille Rachelle | 29 April 1994
3 May 1994 | | yes |

Last Name Given Name (Maiden Name)	Date of Birth Date of Death Age at Death	Spouse	Tombstone
Stanton Margie J.	18 Oct. 1879 4 Feb. 1956	James A. Stanton	yes

Inscription: In Loving Memory

Other Info: Unidentified funeral home marker gives a different birth year 1888; Shares a headstone with her husband.

Stanton Mary Virginia	2 Feb. 1913 28 Jan. 1985	Aaron Stanton	yes

Inscription: At Rest

Other Info: Has a Reid's Funeral Home marker.

Stanton Paul S.	14 Aug. 1921 18 Jan. 1986		yes

Inscription: US Navy, World War II

Other Info: Has a Reid's Funeral Home marker.

Stanton Ralph D.	17 Jan. 1959 31 May 1999		yes

Inscription: Son

Other Info: Has a Reid's Funeral Home marker

Stanton Richard	1 July 1945 12 March 1985		yes

Inscription: Rest in Peace

Turner Annie Booker	23 Oct. 1946 29 Jan. 2002		yes

Other Info: Has a Reid's Funeral Home marker. She was the daughter of Carrie J. and Charles H. Booker also buried in this cemetery.

Last Name Given Name (Maiden Name	Date of Birth Date of Death Age at Death	Spouse	Tombstone

Stevens-Alvis Family off US 60

Alvis John	1778 1828		yes
Alvis Susanah Stevens	1768 1808		yes
Stevens Annie Bocock	1792 1875		yes

Other Info: On the back of this tombstone is an inscription-SAF.

Stevens Elizabeth Taylor	1736 1808		yes
Stevens Thomas	1730 1807		yes

Inscription: Born in England.

Stevens Wm. (Billy)	1771 1845		yes
Strange John	1770 1840		yes

Other Info: Footstone: JFW

Strange Lucy Stevens	1765 1839		yes

Stevens-Alvis Slaves off US 60

Alvis John	18 May 1862 70 years		no

Other Info: From: Record of Buckingham Co. Deaths; Owner was W. W. Alvis.

Last Name Given Name (Maiden Name	Date of Birth Date of Death Age at Death	Spouse	Tombstone
Alvis Margaret	18 July 1861 17 years		

   Other Info: From: Record of Buckingham Co. Deaths; Owner was W. W. Alvis

| Alvis
   Maurice | 15 Oct. 1856
1 year | | no |

   Other Info: From: Record of Buckingham Co. Deaths; Owner was W. W. Alvis

| Alvis
   Peggy | 1 June 1862
70 years | | no |

   Other Info: From: Record of Buckingham Co. Deaths; Owner was W. W. Alvis

| Dunn
   Marcella | 1818
1927 | | yes |

Inscription: This plantation's last slave. Willed in 1845 to W.W. Alvis along with twenty other slaves by Wm. Stevens.

A cement stone in this cemetery reads: Buried here are 54 slaves and 7 ex-slaves.

Alexander Stinson Family off Rd. 754

| Stinson
   Alexander Sr. | | | yes |

   Inscription: In Memory of; Pioneer settler of Buckingham County and American Revolutionary War Patriot who received a land patent from King George the Second of Great Britain, France, and Ireland, in 1743 and lived here until his death, and to his family members who lived here until 1970, many of whom lie buried in the area behind this marker. Erected: 2000 AD by his descendants.

Last Name Given Name (Maiden Name	Date of Birth Date of Death Age at Death	Spouse	Tombstone

Stinson-Carter-Harris Family
(called "The Old Stinson Place" in Vol. I)

Carter Elizabeth A. Stinson (Grandma Carter)	2 Aug. 1819		no early 1900s

Other Info: Thought to be buried here. She was the mother of Susan Jane Carter Harris.

Harris Robert			no

Other Info: Son of Henry Massie Harris (29 July 1868-12 June 1961)

Harris Roland	15 Dec. 1870 7 April 1896		no

Other Info: Known to be buried here. His parents were William Henry and Susan Jane Carter Harris.

Harris Susan Jane Carter	4 Feb. 1838 2 Sept. 1924 86 years	William Henry Harris	no

Other Info: Known to be buried here.

Harris William Henry	23 Jan. 1834 20 July 1876 42 years	Susan Jane Carter Harris	no

Other Info: Known to be buried here. He and his wife were the parents of Willie Sue Harris Stinson who was born after his death.

Stinson Christine Elizabeth	14 May 1918 16 April 1919		no

Other Info: Known to be buried here. She was the daughter of Willie Sue Harris Stinson and William Archie Stinson.

| Last Name | Date of Birth | Spouse | Tombstone |
| Given Name | Date of Death | | |
(Maiden Name	Age at Death		
Stinson	24 Oct. 1905		no
Joseph Morgan	4 July 1906		

Other Info: Known to be buried here. He was the son of Willie Sue Harris Stinson and William Archie Stinson.

| Stinson | 10 Jan. 1907 | | no |
| Tom Henry | 25 Sept. 1907 | | |

Other Info: Known to be buried here. He was the son of Willie Sue Harris Stinson and William Archie Stinson.

Henry Stinson Family off Rd. 607

| Brown | 21 April 1907 | | yes |
| Julia Stinson | 4 March 1995 | | |

Inscription: A loving mother and grandmother; Her children and grandchildren call her blessed.

Other Info: Her parents were William Henry and Ada Stinson also buried in this cemetery.

| Campbell | 30 March 1933 | | yes |
| Kenneth H. | 5 July 1996 | | |

Inscription: He touched so many hearts with his love and kindness for family

Other Info: Has a Robinson Funeral Home marker. Footstone: Kenneth Howard Campbell, CPL, US Marine Corps, Korea (same dates as on headstone).

| Sprouse | 19 June 1917 | | yes |
| Mabel Catherine Stinson | 7 Dec. 1973 | | |

Inscription: Mother

Other Info: Her parents were William Henry and Ada Stinson also buried in this cemetery.

Last Name Given Name (Maiden Name	Date of Birth Date of Death Age at Death	Spouse	Tombstone
Sprouse Truman A (Toby)	6 March 1943 16 July 1998		yes

Inscription: Beloved Husband and Father; For nothing loved is ever lost, and you are loved so much. We love and miss you deeply.

Other Info: He was the son of Mabel Catherine Stinson Sprouse also buried in this cemetery.

Stinson Ada M. (Ada Pear Mason Walker)	19 Jan. 1889 15 Nov. 1973	 William Henry Stinson	yes

Inscription: Mother

Other Info: Footstone: AMS She was the adopted daughter of J.W. Walker also buried in this cemetery.

Stinson Earnest L. (Levi)	24 May 1919 11 June 1992	 Flossie May Stinson	yes

Inscription: Rest in Peace, Gentle Giant

Other Info: Footstone: Earnest Levi Stinson, WT3, US Navy, World War II (same dates as on headstone). His parents were William Henry and Ada Stinson.

Stinson Edward M.	16 July 1927 19 Oct. 1971		yes

Other Info: Footstone: Edward M. Stinson, Virginia, TEC, 53 Signal Co., World War II (same dates as on headstone). Unidentified funeral marker gives as a middle name-Morris. His parents were William Henry and Ada Stinson, also buried in this cemetery.

Stinson Flossie May	24 Dec. 1923 24 Jan. 1995	 Earnest L. Stinson	yes

Inscription: Loving Mom, Granny; A heart of gold

Last Name Given Name (Maiden Name	Date of Birth Date of Death Age at Death	Spouse	Tombstone
Stinson 　Howard	1908 1915		yes

　　Other Info: His parents were William Henry and Ada Stinson also buried in this cemetery.

Stinson 　Irene	1929 1931		yes

　　Other Info: Her parents were William Henry and Ada Stinson also buried in this cemetery.

Stinson 　Linda	25 July 1965 25 July 1965		yes

　　Other Info: Her parents were William Henry and Ada Stinson also buried in this cemetery.

Stinson 　Ressie	1910 1915		yes

　　Other Info: Her parents were William Henry and Ada Stinson also buried in this cemetery.

Stinson 　Roger	6 Sept. 1961 6 Sept. 1961		yes

　　Other Info: His parents were William Henry and Ada Stinson also buried in this cemetery.

Stinson 　William H. (Henry)	9 Jan. 1872 10 Nov. 1946	Ada Pear Mason Walker Stinson	yes

　　Inscription: Father

　　Other Info: Footstone: WHS His parents were Charles Thomas and Catherine Eagle Stinson. This cemetery is called after his name.

Last Name Given Name (Maiden Name)	Date of Birth Date of Death Age at Death	Spouse	Tombstone
Walker J.W.	15 Sept. 1846 1 March 1899		yes

Inscription: Blessed are the dead that die in the Lord; From thence forth, yea saith the Spirit, that their labors and their works do follow them.

Other Info: He was the adopted father of Ada Pear Mason Walker Stinson. His wife is believed to be buried next to him in a grave marked with an etched stone giving again, his name and dates.

Thomas Stinson Family off Rd. 606

Stinson Dillard			no

Other Info: Known to be buried here. He was the son of Thomas Matthew Stinson, buried at the Bryant Family cemetery nearby, and Rosa Bell Stinson who is buried in this cemetery.

Stinson Elizabeth		Thomas Stinson	no

Other Info: Known to be buried here.

Stinson Elizabeth Vest		William Carrington Stinson	no

Other Info: Known to be buried here.

Stinson George (David)		Letitia Via Stinson	yes

Inscription: Co. A, Capt. Lynman's Ambulance Corp. CSA

Other Info: He was the son of Thomas and Susan Stinson. He was paroled at Appomattox at the end of the Civil War.

Last Name Given Name (Maiden Name)	Date of Birth Date of Death Age at Death	Spouse	Tombstone

Stinson Etched Fieldstone
J. W. (John Wesley) 26 Nov. 1913

    Other Info: He was the son of Thomas and Susan Stinson.

Stinson no
James infant

    Other Info: Known to be buried here. He was the son of Lloyd and Mae Stinson, both buried in the nearby Bryant Family Cemetery.

Stinson no
Lester

    Other Info: Known to be buried here. He was a brother to Dillard Stinson also buried here. His parents were Thomas Matthew and Rosa Bell Stinson.

Stinson no
Letitia Via George David Stinson

    Other Info: Known to be buried here.

Stinson 25 Oct. 1829 yes
Martha A. Bryant 19 Sept. 1886 Robert Jackson Stinson

    Inscription: Wife of Robt. J. Stinson; Rest, mother rest, in quiet sleep.

    Other Info: She was the daughter of Powell Bryant and Martha Eagle Bryant buried at the Bryant Family Cemetery nearby.

Stinson no
Mary infant

    Other Info: Known to be buried here, an infant of Lloyd and Mae Stinson, and brother to James Stinson also buried in this cemetery.

Stinson no
Nancy Eagle James W. Stinson

    Other Info: Known to be buried here.

Last Name Given Name (Maiden Name)	Date of Birth Date of Death Age at Death	Spouse	Tombstone
Stinson Nannie S.	1 May 1882		Etched Fieldstone

Inscription: In Memory of

Stinson Robert J. (Jackson)	1 Jan. 1830 20 Sept. 1917	Martha A. Bryant Stinson	yes

Inscription: Kind father of love, thou art gone to thy rest.

Other Info: He was the son of Thomas and Elizabeth Stinson. He also has a military stone: Pvt. Robert J. Stinson, Co. A, Capt. Lynmans Buckingham Ambulance Corp., CSA

Stinson Rosa Bell		Thomas Matthew Stinson	no

Other Info: Known to be buried here.

Stinson Sam			no

Other Info: Known to be buried here, the son of George David and Letitia Stinson.

Stinson Susan		Thomas Stinson	no

Other Info: Known to be buried here.

Stinson Thomas		(1) Susan Stinson (2) Elizabeth Stinson	no

Other Info: Known to be buried here. He was the son of Cary Stinson.

Stinson Tommy	child		no

Other Info: Known to be buried here, the son of William Stinson.

Last Name	Date of Birth	Spouse	Tombstone
Given Name	Date of Death		
(Maiden Name	Age at Death		

Stinson   yes
   Wm (William) C. (Carrington)

   Inscription: 49th VA Inf., Co. H, CSA

   Other Info: He was the son of Thomas and Susan Stinson.

Stout Family on Rd. 628

Stout   9 April 1916   yes
   Ercel Wayne   3 Aug. 1974

   Inscription: PVT, US Army

   Other Info: Has a Dunkum Funeral Home marker

Stuart Brothers on Rd. 607

Stuart   no
   Tom C.   April 1909

   Other Info: Known to be buried here with his brother, William J. Stuart.

Stuart   no
   William J.   April, 1909

   Other Info: Known to be buried here with his brother, Tom C. Stuart. The murder of these two men was written about in "The Ghosts of Virginia" by L.B. Taylor Jr.

Swoope Family on Rd. 648

Glover   1872   yes
   Minnie Swoope   1940   Price Glover

   Other Info: She was the daughter of Dr. Wm. M. and Elizabeth M. Swoope.

Last Name Given Name (Maiden Name)	Date of Birth Date of Death Age at Death	Spouse	Tombstone
Glover Price	1859 1934	Minnie Swoope Glover	yes

   Inscription: Forever with the Lord

| Swoope
    C. Howard | 1875
1897 | | yes |

   Other Info: He was the son of Dr. Wm. M. and Elizabeth M. Swoope.

| Swoope
    Dr. Wm. M. | 1819
1895 | (1)Eliza S. Kyle Swoope
(2)Elizabeth McCraw Swoope | yes |

| Swoope
    E. Mildred | 1847
1865 | | yes |

   Other Info: She was the daughter of Dr. Wm. M. and Eliza S. Swoope.

| Swoope
    Eliza S. (Kyle) | 1822
1864 | Dr. Wm. M. Swoope | yes |

| Swoope
    Elizabeth M. (McCraw) | 1842
1925 | Dr. Wm. M. Swoope | yes |

   Inscription: Mother

| Swoope
    George W. | 29 March 1842
13 Dec. 1862 | | yes |

   Inscription: Co. E, 21 VA INF, CSA

   Other Info: He was the son of Dr. Wm. M. and Eliza S. Swoope.

| Swoope
    Julia T. | 1872
1926 | | yes |

   Other Info: She was the daughter of Dr. Wm. M. and Elizabeth M. Swoope.

Last Name Given Name (Maiden Name)	Date of Birth Date of Death Age at Death	Spouse	Tombstone
Swoope Mabel McDowell	1883 1963		yes

Other Info: She was the daughter of Dr. Wm. M. and Elizabeth M. Swoope also buried in this cemetery.

Swoope Nettie C.	1870 1958		yes

Other Info: She was the daughter of Dr. Wm. M. and Elizabeth M. Swoope.

Swoope Sarah	1880 1906		yes

Other Info: She was the daughter of Dr. Wm. M. and Elizabeth M. Swoope.

Taylor Family off US 15 — African American

Gough Betsy	1825 1902		yes
Hemmings Mary E.	1848 1916	William C. Hemmings	yes
Lee Mattie (Taylor Hemmings)	1876 1944	(1) William C. Hemmings (2) Dots Lee	yes
Sheppard Margaret (Taylor)	1858 1892	George Sheppard	yes

Other Info: She was the daughter of Charlotte and Davy Taylor.

Taylor Mahala	1862 1888		yes

There are 5 unidentified graves in this cemetery.

Last Name Given Name (Maiden Name	Date of Birth Date of Death Age at Death	Spouse	Tombstone

Horace Taylor Family in James River State Park

Taylor Cordelia D.	1889 1948	Horace A. Taylor	yes

Other Info: Shares a headstone with her husband.

Taylor Horace A.	1875 1940	Cordelia D. Taylor	yes

Other Info: Shares a headstone with his wife.

John Taylor Family at James River State Park

Taylor A.C.			yes

Inscription: Co. B, 25th VA INF, CSA (no dates)

Taylor John A	19 Feb. 1909 19 Feb. 1987		yes

Other Info: Footstone: John A. Taylor, 1909-1987 (Robinson Funeral Home)

Taylor John C.			yes

Inscription: Corp., Co. B, 25th VA INF, CSA (no dates)

Taylor L.D.			yes

Inscription: Co. B, 25th VA INF, CSA (no dates)

Taylor Louise E.	30 March 1914 19 March 1989		yes

Other Info: Footstone: Louise Ewers Taylor, 1914-1989 (Robinson Funeral Home)

There are 4 unidentified graves in this cemetery.

Last Name	Date of Birth	Spouse	Tombstone
Given Name	Date of Death		
(Maiden Name)	Age at Death		

Taylor Family on Rd. 631
(also Moss/Meador/Pendleton Family)

Lann   no
   Hattie   child

   Other Info: Known to be buried here. Her parents were Mary Ann
      Elizabeth Shoemaker Lann (Annie) and William A. Lann (Willie.)

Lann   no
   Jimmy   child

   Other Info: Known to be buried here. His parents were Mary Ann
      Elizabeth Shoemaker Lann (Annie) and William A. Lann (Willie).

Moss   11 Aug. 1909   yes
   Lily B.   19 Feb. 1911

Shoemaker   22 Sept. 1884   no
   Nellie Toney   George Pratt Shoemaker "Doc"

   Other Info: Known to be buried here. She was the daughter of George
      M. and Louise Shoemaker Toney. She married George
      Shoemaker on 28 July 1907.

Taylor   no
   Fannie   Jerden Taylor

   Other Info: Known to be buried here.

Taylor   no
   Jerden   Fannie Taylor

   Other Info: Known to be buried here.

Taylor   yes
   Mathew J. Sgt

   Inscription: Co. A, 22 VA INF, CSA (no dates)

Last Name Given Name (Maiden Name	Date of Birth Date of Death Age at Death	Spouse	Tombstone
Taylor Noah	9 Dec. 1940		no

Other Info: Known to be buried here.

Toney George M.	(1 Sept. 1845) (Maryland) (2 Dec. 1915)	(1) Louise Shoemaker Toney (2)Mildred F. Toney	yes

Inscription: Co. E, 21 VA OMG, CSA

Other Info: His parents were Jesse Toney and Eliza Stinson Toney.

Toney Mildred F.	1867 1953	George M. Toney	yes

There are at least 60 unidentified graves in this cemetery, including those known to be buried here, and possibly many more.

Walker Taylor Family on Rd. 690

Taylor Sallie E. Miles	16 Sept. 1868 7 Sept. 1946	Walker Taylor	yes

Taylor Walker	10 March 1867 26 March 1939	Sallie E. Miles Taylor	yes

There are 2 unidentified graves in this cemetery.

Terry Family on Rd. 811

Golden Margaret W. Terry	10 May 1916 11 March 1987		yes

Inscription: A sweet, kind lady, a wonderful friend to all, a person really worth knowing, a helper to all who would call.

Other Info: Unidentified funeral home marker: Margaret Wright Terry Golden; She was the mother of William A. Terry Sr.

Last Name Given Name (Maiden Name)	Date of Birth Date of Death Age at Death	Spouse	Tombstone
Louper Gary			no

Other Info: His ashes rest in an identified grave here.

Louper Raymond			yes, not inscribed

Other Info: Known to be buried here.

Terry Maria Donna Lynn	16 July 1977 27 Sept. 1977		yes

Other Info: She was the great-granddaughter of Margaret Terry Golden, and the granddaughter of William A. Terry Sr.

Terry William A. Sr. "Bill"	12 March 1933 27 Sept. 1996		yes

Inscription: He knew no strangers; His heart and home were open to all. On the back of the headstone: Mary E., Bill A., Cecil T., Robert L., Roy G., Howell G. (Sr.), William R., Amanda A. In loving memory of our Daddy.

Other Info: Footstone: William A. Terry Sr., PVT, US Army, Korea (same dates as on the headstone)

Pleasant Toney Family on Rd. 745

Newton Berry G.	1914 1914		yes

Toney Marion L.	17 July 1937 18 Sept. 1937		yes

Inscription: In Loving Memory

Other Info: He was the brother of Bob Toney.

Toney Susan E.	16 Aug. 1842 10 Aug. 1918	William Pleasant Toney	yes

Last Name Given Name (Maiden Name)	Date of Birth Date of Death Age at Death	Spouse	Tombstone
Toney William P. (Pleasant)	24 Nov. 1843 24 March 1924	Susan E. Toney	yes

Other Info: His parents were Edmond and Mary Toney. There is also a military headstone at the grave site which reads: Private William P. Toney, Co. B., 41st VA Inf. An Iron Cross of Honor has been placed to the left of the military headstone.

Toney Slaves off Rd. 745

Toney Cirus	1 March 1864 6 months		no

Other Info: Reported in the Death Records of Buckingham Co. Owner was Mary and Henry Toney. His mother was Jane.

Toney Harry	27 July 1860 70 years		no

Other Info: Reported in the Death Records of Buckingham Co. Owner was Mary and Henry Toney.

There are 10 unidentified graves in this cemetery including those known to be buried here.

William Toney Family off Rd. 610

Hudgins John H.	1900 1940		yes

Other Info: He was the son-in-law of William and Annie Toney also buried in this cemetery.

Toney Annie H.	3 Aug. 1880 14 Aug. 1951	William S. Toney	yes

Other Info: Shares a headstone with her husband.

Last Name Given Name (Maiden Name)	Date of Birth Date of Death Age at Death	Spouse	Tombstone
Toney Mahlon	22 Feb. 1900 4 April 1918		yes

Inscription: Our Darling

| Toney
   Mary Virginia | 1906
1925 | | yes |

| Toney
   William S. | 10 Apr. 1869
2 Aug. 1944 | Annie H. Toney | yes |

Other Info: Shares a headstone with his wife.

There are 2 tombstones in this cemetery with no inscription on them. One is known to be ___Martin.

Third Liberty Baptist Church — African American

| Austin
   Emma H. | 18 April 1887
21 Aug. 1971 | | yes |

| Austin
   John W. Sr. | 1884
1962 | | yes |

| Austin
   Joseph N. | 1917
1953 | | yes |

| Banks
   Derrick Deware | 1977
1983 | | no |

Other Info: Unidentified funeral home marker

| Banks
   Melton Jr. | 1929
1977 | | yes |

Inscription: PFC, US Army, Korea

| Banks
   Michael | 8 Dec. 1962
3 July 1993 | | yes |

Other Info: Has a Thomas Funeral Home marker.

Last Name Given Name (Maiden Name)	Date of Birth Date of Death Age at Death	Spouse	Tombstone
Banks Sallie P.	20 Oct. 1888 16 Feb. 1968		yes

Other Info: W.A. Hartman Memorials, Charlottesville, VA

Bartlett Freddie L.	1943 2002		no

Other Info: Reids Funeral Home marker

Bartlett Mary Alice	8 Feb. 1961		yes
Bellinger Shirley			no

Other Info: O.F. Howard Funeral Home marker has one date: 15 Feb. 1973

Bolling Baby	1931 1931		yes

Other Info: Shares a headstone with 2 siblings; stillborn birth; parents were George and Victoria Bolling also buried in this cemetery.

Bolling Elmira	6 March 1933 1938		yes

Other Info: Shares a headstone with 2 siblings; parents were George and Victoria Bolling, also buried in this cemetery.

Bolling George W.	8 Sept. 1901 11 Dec. 2001	Queen Victoria Bolling	yes

Other Info: Shares a headstone with his wife.

Bolling George William	1932 1936		yes

Other Info: Shares a headstone with 2 siblings; parents were George and Victoria Bolling also buried in this cemetery.

Last Name Given Name (Maiden Name)	Date of Birth Date of Death Age at Death	Spouse	Tombstone
Bolling Queen Victoria	8 Feb. 1900 1 April 1991	George W. Bolling	yes

Other Info: Shares a headstone with her husband; They were married 72 years; Has a Colbert Funeral Home marker.

Bolling William A.	Nov. 1938 Aug. 1991		yes

Inscription: Father

Other Info: Has a Colbert Funeral Home marker.

Bolling Woodson			yes

Inscription: Our Dolling

Other Info: Tombstone has one date: 1813. This grave is located between the road and the parking area next to the church building. It is not in the cemetery.

Book(e)r Steven	1968 1986		no

Other Info: Reids Funeral Home marker

Booker John E	1 Dec. 1892 7 Aug. 1967		yes

Booker Tarrie	1913 1984		no

Other Info: Unidentified funeral home marker

Bowles Benjamin Jr.	1955 2004		no

Other Info: R. L. Gilliam Funeral Home marker

Bowles Benjamin, "Papa"	28 Feb. 1932 15 Nov. 2003		yes

Inscription: In Loving Memory

Last Name Given Name (Maiden Name	Date of Birth Date of Death Age at Death	Spouse	Tombstone
Bowles Dorothy Mae	6 June 1934 22 April 1962		yes
Other Info: Has a Reid's Funeral Home marker			
Bowles Jimmy Lee	15 Dec. 1958 27 Aug. 1984		yes
Bowles William Kenneth	7 Sept. 1964 17 Dec. 1989		yes
Inscription: Rest in Peace			
Brown Alice	1888 1979		no
Other Info: Unidentified funeral home marker			
Brown David C. V., Mr.	1914 1997		no
Other Info: This is a Thomasson Funeral Home marker.			
Brown Eugene T.	7 Aug. 1932 29 Nov. 1954		yes
Brown James H.	10 Sept. 1923 12 Sept. 1965		yes
Brown Joe Calvin	1950 1998 47 years		no
Other Info: Colbert Funeral Home marker			
Brown John Lewis	1937 1975		no
Other Info: Unidentified funeral home marker			
Cabbell Houston	1876 1973		yes

Last Name Given Name (Maiden Name	Date of Birth Date of Death Age at Death	Spouse	Tombstone
Cabbell Houston A.	2 Aug. 1919 16 Aug. 1999		yes

Inscription: CPL, US Army, World War II

Cabbell Raymond	1926 2004		no

Other Info: Unidentified funeral home marker

Cabbell Ruby	3 Jan.___ 3 Jan.___		yes, somewhat illegible
Cabell Lillian, Mrs.	14 Jan. 1927 8 Feb. 1994		yes

Inscription: In Loving Memory

Carrington Joseph N.	1919 1997		no

Other Info: Colbert Funeral Home marker

Carrington Michael Antwan	23 Jan. 1976 1 May 1993		yes
Carrington Myrtle E.	1947 2002		no

Other Info: Reid's Funeral Home marker

Carter Eugene	15 March 1961 26 June 1988		yes
Davis Fred	1896 1956		yes

Inscription: Virginia, PFC, US Army, World War I

Last Name Given Name (Maiden Name)	Date of Birth Date of Death Age at Death	Spouse	Tombstone
Davis Sallie, Mrs.	11 May 1840 9 Apr. 1928	Rev. W. M. Davis	yes

Other Info: Shares a headstone with her husband; Footstone-SD

Davis W. M., Rev.	15 June 1841 11 April 1926	Sallie Davis	yes

Other Info: Shares a headstone with his wife; Footstone-WMD

Dean Major S.	22 Nov. 1948 22 April 1992		yes

Inscription: Father; Your Loving Family

Dean Maureen Denise	1967 1967		yes

Inscription: In Gods Hands

Eldridge Edna Brown	1938 1980		no

Other Info: Unidentified funeral home marker

Glover Billy Franklin	1942 1991		yes

Inscription: US Army

Glover George E., Mr.	1938 2002		no

Other Info: Thomasson Funeral Home marker

Glover Johnnie Junius	12 Nov. 1912 9 March 1984	Lucille Booker Glover	yes

Other Info: Shares a headstone with his wife.

Glover Johnny J.			yes, with no dates

Last Name Given Name (Maiden Name)	Date of Birth Date of Death Age at Death	Spouse	Tombstone
Glover Lucille Booker	4 May 1917 13 Jan 1979	Johnnie Junius Glover	yes

Other Info: Shares a headstone with her husband.

| Glover
    Maxine (S.) | 9 June 1939
10 Dec. 2002 | Furman W. Glover Sr. | yes |

Other Info: Has a Thomasson Funeral Home marker

| Hartwell
    James B. | 1871
1962 | | no |

Other Info: Ranson and Smith Funeral Home marker

| Hartwell
    Lucy W. | 1897
1971 | | yes |

Inscription: Mother; At Rest

| Hartwell
    Wilson B., Deacon | 1898
1966 | | yes |

Inscription: At Rest

| Henderson
    Emma S. | 1917
2003
85 years | | no |

Other Info: Colbert Funeral Home marker

| James
    Bernard W. Sr. | 28 Oct. 1929
25 May 2000 | | yes |

Inscription: PFC, US Army, Korea

Other Info: Has a Thomasson's Funeral Home marker

| James
    Fountain Curtis | 12 Oct. 1925
24 Dec. 1952 | | yes |

Inscription: Stewards Mate 1st Class, USNR, Enlisted: 8 Dec. 1943, Discharged: 16 April 1946

Last Name Given Name (Maiden Name)	Date of Birth Date of Death Age at Death	Spouse	Tombstone
James Gertrude	1926 1999 Henry Flood James		yes

Other Info: Shares a headstone with her husband

James Henry Flood	1921 1995 Gertrude James		yes

Other Info: Shares a headstone with his wife; Thomas Funeral Home marker gives the death date as 15 Sept. 1995.

James Laura F.	1896 1967 Willard W. James		yes

Inscription: Rock of Ages, Cleft for Me

Other Info: Shares a headstone with her husband.

James Lewis H.	30 July 1899 18 July 1979		yes
James Ronnie LaMarge	13 Sept. 1961 23 Oct. 2001		yes

Other Info: Has a Thomassons's Funeral Home marker.

James Willard W.	1900 1971 Laura F. James		yes

Inscription: Rock of Ages, Cleft for Me

Other Info: Shares a headstone with his wife.

Johnson George G.	2 Sept. 1868 23 May 1950		yes

Inscription: Wife and children

Johnson Nellie V.	8 May 1874 24 Jan. 1960		yes

Inscription: The Children

Last Name Given Name (Maiden Name)	Date of Birth Date of Death Age at Death	Spouse	Tombstone
Johnson Walter	20 Dec. 1920 2 Jan. 1992		yes

Other Info: Footstone: WJ

| Jones
   Annie G. | 9 Oct. 1902
24 June 1992 | | yes |

Inscription: At Rest

| Jones
   Florence B. | 31 Dec. 1898
15 Feb. 1997 | | yes |
| Jones
   George Fox | 12 April 1896
22 Jan 1980 | | yes |

Inscription: PFC, US Army, World War I

| Jones
   Jennie Rollins | 1888
1964 | | no |

Other Info: Ranson and Smith Funeral Home marker

| Jones
   John H. | 20 April 1885
1 July 1979 | | yes |
| Jones
   Lena B. | 1928
2004
76 years | | no |

Other Info: Unidentified funeral home marker

| Jones
   Mary S. | 1924
1945 | | yes |
| Jones
   Maude O. | 6 March 1903
6 Dec. 1978 | Sam Jones | yes |

Inscription: In Loving Memory

Other Info: Shares a headstone with her husband.

Last Name Given Name (Maiden Name)	Date of Birth Date of Death Age at Death	Spouse	Tombstone
Jones Sam	6 Sept. 1901 31 Jan. 1982	Maude O. Jones	yes

Inscription: In Loving Memory

Other Info: Shares a headstone with his wife.

| Jones
Sid Ellis | 27 Sept. 1934
6 March 1996 | | no |

Other Info: This is an above ground vault-Reids FH

| Kinney
Barbara L. | 30 April 1960
24 Sept. 1998 | | yes |

Inscription: Gone but not Forgotten

| Logan
Ida | 1878
1954 | | yes |

Inscription: Mother

| Morgan
Beatrice Richardson | 25 May 1894
4 March 1985 | | yes |

Inscription: Asleep in Jesus

| Opie
Annie L. | 15 Feb. 1912
6 Feb. 1999 | Neal Opie | yes |

Other Info: Shares a headstone with her husband.

| Opie
Jarrell D. | 28 July 1981
10 Feb. 1994 | | yes |

Inscription: In God's Care

| Opie
Neal | 14 Oct. 1910
9 Nov. 1962 | Annie L. Opie | yes |

Other Info: Shares a headstone with his wife; Footstone has the same name and dates on it as the headstone.

Last Name Given Name (Maiden Name)	Date of Birth Date of Death Age at Death	Spouse	Tombstone
Opie 　Thelma	18 Nov. 1936 24 Dec. 1994		yes

　　Inscription: In Loving Memory

　　Other Info: Has a Thomas Funeral Home marker.

| Parker
　Louise P. | 1897
1970 | | yes |

　　Other Info: Smith Funeral Home marker gives the name as Mary L. Parker.

| Perkins
　George W. (Williams) | 4 July 1881
3 Oct. 1968 | | yes |

　　Other Info: Ranson and Smith Funeral Home marker gives birth year as 1870, and name as G. Williams Perkins.

| Perkins
　Virginia | 6 Oct. 1874
28 Feb. 1961 | | yes |

　　Other Info: Ranson and Smith Funeral Home marker gives birth year as 1867, and the name as "Jinnie" Perkins.

| Richardson
　Alfred T. | 15 Oct. 1911
18 Nov. 1936 | | yes |

| Richardson
　Kina | 4 March 1910
16 July 2000 | | yes |

　　Other Info: Has a Thomas Funeral Home marker.

| Richardson
　Maggie | 1883
1939 | John Richardson | yes |

　　Inscription: In Loving Remembrance Of; Wife of John Richardson; At Rest in the Lord

　　Other Info: Footstone: At Rest

Last Name Given Name (Maiden Name	Date of Birth Date of Death Age at Death	Spouse	Tombstone
Richardson Thomas H.	30 May 1886 15 Dec. 1951		yes

Inscription: Asleep in Jesus

Rollins Mary G.	15 Sept. 1915 19 Jan. 1994		yes
Scruggs Albert			no

Other Info: Thomas Funeral Home marker with one date: 8 Feb. 1993.

Scruggs Bernetta R.	15 June 1904 7 Aug. 1976	John L. Scruggs	yes

Other Info: Shares a headstone with her husband.

Scruggs Fannie B.	5 May 1930 7 Dec. 2002	George J. Scruggs	yes

Other Info: Has a Marion Gray Funeral Home marker.

Scruggs John L.	28 Jan. 1903 13 Sept. 1984	Bernetta R. Scruggs	yes

Other Info: Shares a headstone with his wife.

Scruggs Mable E.	1 Nov. 1930 23 June 1994		no

Other Info: This is an above ground vault: Reids FH

Scruggs Maude			no

Other Info: Location of grave unknown.

Scruggs Milvina			no

Other Info: Location of grave unknown.

Last Name Given Name (Maiden Name	Date of Birth Date of Death Age at Death	Spouse	Tombstone
Scruggs Walter	1910 8 Jan. 1984		no

Other Info: Thomas Funeral Home marker.

Staten Joseph Thomas	1932 1965		no

Other Info: Ranson and Smith Funeral Home marker

Staten Lucy B.	3 May 1915 4 Jan. 1988		yes

Inscription: Mother

Staten Robert Willie	1910 1975		no

Other Info: Unidentified funeral home marker

Staten Thomas H.	22 Sept. 1898 19 Jan. 1971		yes

Inscription: Father

Trent John R.	1876 1960	Mary S. Trent	yes

Other Info: Shares a headstone with his wife.

Trent Mary S.	1882 1970	John R. Trent	yes

Other Info: Shares a headstone with her husband.

Watson John B. (Bernard)	1927 1980		yes

Inscription: PFC, US Army, World War II

Watson Queen Elizabeth	14 Jan 1928 20 Sept. 1970		yes

Other Info: Has a Doyne-Burger Funeral Home marker.

Last Name Given Name (Maiden Name	Date of Birth Date of Death Age at Death	Spouse	Tombstone
Watson Robert	22 May 1874 26 April 1923 48 years, 11 months, 4 days		yes
Wheeler Dorothy	1917 1987		no

Other Info: Reids Funeral Home marker

Wheeler
  John Robert Sr.

Other Info: Known to be buried here

Wheeler Leroy Lincoln	24 Dec. 1924 19 Apr. 1987		yes

Inscription: Father; Rest in Peace; (by the) Children

Wheeler Percy J.	1939 2002		no

Other Info: Colbert Funeral Home marker

Wheeler Robert Jr.	1937 1961		no

Other Info: Ranson and Smith Funeral Home marker

White Frank E. Jr.	28 June 1955 24 Nov. 1980		yes
White Susie Clementeen	1 Jan. 1924 16 Dec. 2000		yes
Woodard Johnnie L.	17 Feb. 1901 28 March 1982		yes

Inscription: Father

Last Name Given Name (Maiden Name)	Date of Birth Date of Death Age at Death	Spouse	Tombstone
Woodson Glover T.	8 March 1914 23 Sept. 1977		yes

Inscription: AS, US Navy, World War II

Woodson Joseph E.	1924 1977		no

Other Info: Unidentified funeral home marker

Woodson Joseph L.	15 April 1949 9 Oct. 1973		yes
Woodson Nannie	1944		no

Other Info: Location of grave unknown.

This cemetery has 60 unidentified graves.

Trinity United Methodist Church

Agee Mattie Gilbert	1 Dec. 1892 15 June 1967	Willie Whitcomb Agee	yes

Other Info: Shares a headstone with her husband; Footstone: Mattie

Agee Willie Whitcomb	27 April 1899 5 April 1975	Mattie Gilbert Agee	yes

Other Info: Shares a headstone with his wife; Footstone: Willie

Anderson Mary B. (Branch Gilliam)	4 Apr. 1853 13 Jan. 1921	Reece Moses Anderson	yes

Other Info: Footstone: MBA; Her husband is buried in the Anderson Family Cemetery (Vol. II)

Last Name Given Name (Maiden Name)	Date of Birth Date of Death Age at Death	Spouse	Tombstone
Benway Bob L.	23 Feb. 1933 5 Jan. 1999		yes

Inscription: PVT, US Army, Korea

Boles Charlie C. (Clarence)	1879 1939	Maude E. Steele Boles	yes

Inscription: At Rest

Other Info: Footstone: CCB

Boles James E.	1913 1928		yes

Other Info: Footstone: JEB

Boles Maude E. (Steele)	1888 1856	Charlie Clarence Boles	yes

Other Info: Footstone: MEB; Her parents were Alexander and Sarah Steele.

Boles Wm. R.	1903 1936		yes

Other Info: Footstone: WRB

Clay Charles G.	1862 1937	Mary Henry Clay	yes

Inscription: The Lord is My Shepherd

Other Info: Footstone: CGC

Clay Mary Henry	29 May 1859 19 Dec. 1934	Charles G. Clay	yes

Inscription: The Lord is My Shepherd

Other Info: Footstone: MHC

Last Name Given Name (Maiden Name	Date of Birth Date of Death Age at Death	Spouse	Tombstone
Coates John R. III "Ricky"	1952 1962		yes

Other Info: His Grandparents, Floyd N. and Mamie Guill Ripley are also buried in this cemetery.

Cobb Annie M. Moss	15 July 1876 20 Nov. 1927	John Henry Cobb	yes

Other Info: Shares a headstone with her husband.

Cobb John Henry	9 April 1877 12 Sept. 1929	Annie M. Moss Cobb	yes

Inscription: Father

Other Info: Shares a headstone with his wife.

Cottrell Mrs.			yes

Inscription: (no given name or dates)

Davidson Elsie F. Wisdom	16 June 1907 31 Oct. 1947	(1) Orville E.H. Wisdom (2) _____ Davidson	yes

Dunkum Cora L. (Lee Fitzgerald Coleman)	1879 1974	Edwin M. Dunkum	yes

Inscription: At Rest

Other Info: Shares a headstone with her husband.

Dunkum Edwin M. (Mack)	1878 1948	Cora Lee Fitzgerald Coleman Dunkum	yes

Inscription: At Rest

Other Info: Shares a headstone with his wife. He is the brother of Julian Dunkum.

Last Name Given Name (Maiden Name)	Date of Birth Date of Death Age at Death	Spouse	Tombstone
Duty Ethel Williams	13 Oct. 1897 13 May 1968	L. F. Duty	yes
Duty L.F. (Lemuel Frank)	25 Apr. 1895 17 Aug. 1955	Ethel Williams Duty	yes
Duty W. (Wilburn) Taylor	15 Aug. 1918 Sept. 2000	Edna Agee Duty	yes
Duty Warren K. (Kenneth)	29 May 1932 5 Dec. 1980		yes

   Inscription: US Army, Korea

   Other Info: Footstone: WKD; Moved to Bethlehem Baptist Church Cemetery.

Forbes Bernard Brown	17 Jan. 1893 3 July 1947		yes
Forbes C. J.	8 Dec. 1879 6 Feb. 1945		yes

   Other Info: His sister, Janie Forbes Duty is also buried in this cemetery.

Forbes George T.	13 Oct. 1882 16 June 1971		yes

   Other Info: Shares a headstone with Thomas Parrack Forbes.

Forbes Hattie Evelyn	19 Dec. 1866 19 Mar 1913		yes
Forbes Helen Oliver	30 June 1846 14 May 1917	Peter A. Forbes	yes

   Inscription: Wife of Peter A. Forbes

Forbes Marion Charlotte	9 June 1869 29 July 1936		yes
Forbes Peter Alexander	3 May 1831 5 March 1905	Helen Oliver Forbes	yes

Last Name Given Name (Maiden Name	Date of Birth Date of Death Age at Death	Spouse	Tombstone
Forbes T. (Thomas) Parrack	19 June 1883 1 May 1966		yes

Other Info: Shares a headstone with George T. Forbes.

| Garnett
A. (Alfred) Cooke | 1903
1933 | | yes |

Inscription: His many kind deeds will not be forgotten.

Other Info: Parents were Alfred Cook Garnett and Nellie Noble Garnett also buried in this cemetery.

| Garnett
Alfred Cook | 11 Nov. 1863
30 July 1939 | Nellie Noble Garnett | yes |

Inscription: Father

Other Info: Footstone: ACG; Shares a headstone with his wife.

| Garnett
Frank M. | 1893
1944 | Tina W. Garnett | yes |

Other Info: Shares a headstone with his wife.

| Garnett
Harold | 1932
2003 | | yes |

| Garnett
Nellie Evelyne | 30 June 1898
12 June 1972 | | yes |

| Garnett
Nellie Noble | 3 March 1868
24 Jan. 1939 | Alfred Cook Garnett | yes |

Inscription: Mother

Other Info: Shares a headstone with her husband; Footstone-NG

| Garnett
Tina W. | 1899
1977 | Frank M. Garnett | yes |

Other Info: Shares a headstone with her husband.

Last Name Given Name (Maiden Name)	Date of Birth Date of Death Age at Death	Spouse	Tombstone
Gilliam Hazel Cooper	26 June 1902 21 March 1979	Robert Branch Gilliam	yes
Gilliam John Branch	5 Aug. 1831 2 April 1908		yes

Inscription: At Rest

Other Info: Footstone: JBG

Gilliam John Edwin Jr.	23 Nov. 1902 7 Jan 1974		yes

Other Info: His brother, Samuel E. Shaeffer is also buried in this cemetery.

Gilliam Nannie W.	4 Sept. 1839 4 Aug. 1916		yes

Inscription: Asleep in Jesus

Other Info: Footstone: NWG

Gilliam R. Archie	5 Aug. 1874 4 Sept. 1912		yes
Gilliam Robert Branch	4 June 1892 8 Nov. 1961	Hazel Cooper Gilliam	yes

Other Info: He is the nephew of Hattie Jones and the brother of John Edwin Gilliam Jr., also buried in this cemetery.

Goin A. J.	16 July 1908 13 Jan. 1975		yes
Goin Ada	12 June 1912 7 Dec. 1994		yes
Goin Cleove, Mr.	24 May 1872 27 Oct. 1934		yes
Goin Edie Calvin	25 Nov. 1911 23 March 1985		yes

Last Name Given Name (Maiden Name	Date of Birth Date of Death Age at Death	Spouse	Tombstone
Goin James M.	20 March 1921 3 Apr. 1999	Dorothy S. Goin	yes
Goin John J.			yes

Inscription: Co. B., 46 VA Inf., CSA (no dates)

| Goin
    Luke D. | | | yes |

Inscription: PVT, Virginia, 8 Engr. Training Regt.

Other Info: Tombstone has one date on it: Oct. 6, 1918

| Goin
    Mattie Toney | 25 Aug. 1897
21 March 1977 | | yes |
| Goin
    Peter T. | 23 Oct. 1895
27 Sept. 1959 | | yes |

Inscription: Gone but not Forgotten

Other Info: Footstone: Husband

| Goin
    Richard A. | 1896
1960 | | yes |

Inscription: Virginia, PVT, Co A, 155 Depot Brigade, World War I

Goin Sallie	19 July 1896 29 May 1959		yes
Goin Willie E.	15 March 1920 4 March 1999		yes
Jones Hattie G.	23 March 1885 9 March 1987	Leon W. Jones	yes

Other Info: Shares a headstone with her husband. She and her husband were the parents of Robert Gilliam Jones, also buried in this cemetery.

Last Name Given Name (Maiden Name)	Date of Birth Date of Death Age at Death	Spouse	Tombstone
Jones Leon W.	26 June 1879 20 Aug. 1965	Hattie G. Jones	yes

Other Info: Shares a headstone with his wife.

Jones Robert Gilliam	1914 1978		yes

Inscription: SK1, US Navy, World War II

Morgan Ewell	1862 1927	Maud Kathlene Noble Morgan	yes

Other Info: Shares a headstone with his wife. Footstone: EM; He and his wife were the parents of Jesse A. Morgan and Nellie Gertrude Morgan also buried in this cemetery.

Morgan Jesse A.	10 May 1908 22 Oct. 1982	Myrtle Hardiman Morgan	yes
Morgan Maud K. (Kathlene Noble)	1870 1917	Ewell Morgan	yes

Other Info: Shares a headstone with her husband.

Morgan Nellie Gertrude	7 Sept. 1901 2 April 1984		yes

Other Info: Her brother, Jesse A. Morgan and parents, Ewell and Maud K. Morgan are also buried in this cemetery. Other siblings are: Kathleen Wood and Mary Morgan.

Noble Annie J. (Jones) Garnett	21 June 1842 18 March 1916	James Hugh Noble	yes

Inscription: Wife of J. H. Noble

Other Info: Footstone: AJN She and her husband are the parents of Maud Kathlene Noble Morgan also buried in this cemetery.

Last Name Given Name (Maiden Name)	Date of Birth Date of Death Age at Death	Spouse	Tombstone
Noble James Hugh	1838 1917	Annie J. Garnett Noble	yes

Other Info: Footstone: JHN

Pierce Minnie G.			yes

Other Info: The tombstone has sunken into the ground and the dates are below ground.

Ripley Floyd Nicholas	12 Feb. 1882 2 Aug. 1954	Mamie Guill Ripley	yes

Other Info: Shares a headstone with his wife; Footstone: FNR; He and his wife are the grandparents of John R. Coates III also buried in this cemetery.

Ripley Mamie Guill	26 Oct. 1890 11 Aug. 1966	Floyd Nicholas Ripley	yes

Other Info: Shares a headstone with her husband; Footstone: MGR

Rosen Frank L.	1875 1938	Helen J. Rosen	yes
Rosen Helen J.	1875 1955	Frank L. Rosen	yes

Other Info: Footstone: HJR

Rosen Leslie W.	29 March 1915 (death not inscribed)		yes

Other Info: Has an unidentified funeral home marker with no dates. His parents were Frank L. and Helen J. Rosen.

Shaeffer Lorraine Marie	13 June 1933 29 Dec. 2001	Samuel E. Shaeffer	yes
Shaeffer Samuel E.	15 July 1921 7 May 1995	Lorraine Marie Shaeffer	yes

Inscription: PFC, US Army, World War II

Last Name Given Name (Maiden Name	Date of Birth Date of Death Age at Death	Spouse	Tombstone
Shoemaker John Admund	23 May 1882 6 May 1968	Lillian Sprouse Shoemaker	yes

Other Info: Shares a headstone with his wife.

Shoemaker Lacy M.	12 Dec. 1892 28 Feb. 1929		yes
Shoemaker Lillian Sprouse	11 Sept. 1886 18 March 1960	John Admund Shoemaker	yes

Other Info: Shares a headstone with her husband.

Shumaker Alfred L.	11 Aug. 1905 6 Jan. 1986	Maggie G. (Goin) Shumaker	yes

Other Info: Shares a headstone with his wife.

Shumaker Clarence Daniel	6 Sept. 1924 2 July 1967		yes
Shumaker Eddie Herbert	1 July 1941 5 Nov. 2003		yes
Shumaker Judy Faye	(1960) (1961)		yes

Other Info: Has an unidentified funeral home marker with dates; Footstone: JFS

Shumaker Kimberly Marie	28 March 1967 8 March 1968		yes
Shumaker Maggie G. (Goin)	24 May 1900 4 Feb. 1995	Alfred L. Shumaker	yes

Other Info: Shares a headstone with her husband. Their sons, Clarence Daniel and Sidney A. Shumaker are also buried in this cemetery.

Last Name Given Name (Maiden Name)	Date of Birth Date of Death Age at Death	Spouse	Tombstone
Shumaker Sidney A.	6 Jan. 1935 13 Apr. 1961		yes

Inscription: Virginia, PVT, Co. A, 4th Inf., TNG Regt.

Smith Josie S.	1867 1940		yes

Other Info:

Smith Robert S.	8 Sept. 1847 8 March 1931		yes

Inscription: In God's Care

Other Info: Footstone: RSS

Snoddy Nannie C.	23 Jan. 1880 15 Nov. 1950	Wm. Thornhill Snoddy	yes

Other Info: Shares a headstone with her husband.

Snoddy Wm. Thornhill	13 April 1872 11 Nov. 1926	Nannie C. Snoddy	yes

Other Info: Shares a headstone with his wife.

Spencer Caryl Jackson	9 Jan. 1899 20 Aug. 1958		yes
Spencer Nancy Gilliam	30 July 1897 6 July 1988		yes

Other Info: Her parents were Garland Gilliam and Hattie Rosen.

Steger Clara Walton Wheeler	2 May 1853 22 Feb. 1941		yes

Inscription: Remembered and Loved

Last Name Given Name (Maiden Name)	Date of Birth Date of Death Age at Death	Spouse	Tombstone
Steger Clyde Eugene	29 Sep 1939 23 May 2003		yes

Inscription: US Army

Other Info: Has a Dunkum Funeral Home marker.

Steger Humphrey A.	6 July 1883 4 Aug. 1942		yes
Steger Ruth Hardiman	16 March 1907 26 March 1968		yes
Sudsberry Mary J.	4 Feb. 1906 26 May 1978	William F Sudsberry	yes
Swartz Harold Franklin	30 Sept. 1903 19 Feb. 1991	Louise M. Swartz	yes
Swartz John Franklin	4 Nov. 1973 31 Mar. 1992		yes

Other Info: His grandparents were Harold F. and Louise M. Swartz.

Swartz Louise Morriss	22 Feb. 1914 11 June 2005	Harold F. Swartz	yes
Williams Janie F. (Forbes)	1877 1971	Lewis Williams	yes

Other Info: Shares a headstone with her husband. Her brother, C.J. Forbes is also buried in this cemetery.

Williams Lewis	1868 1950	Janie Forbes Williams	yes

Other Info: Shares a headstone with his wife.

Wisdom Orville E. H.	1912 1938	Elsie F. Wisdom Davidson	yes

Last Name	Date of Birth	Spouse	Tombstone
Given Name	Date of Death		
(Maiden Name)	Age at Death		

Turner Family on US 20 — African American

Ayres   no
    Charlotte Ann

    Other Info: Known to be buried here.

Sanders (or Saunders)   no
    Ray   infant

    Other Info: Known to be buried here.

Taylor   no
    Rosa Ayres   27 May 1921

    Other Info: Known to be buried here. She was the mother of William Howard Taft Turner and Price Turner.

Turner   no
    Price Eldridge

    Other Info: Known to be buried here. He is the brother of William Howard Taft Turner also buried in this cemetery.

Turner   no
    William Howard Taft   7 Sept. 1945

    Other Info: Known to be buried here.

There are 12 unidentified graves in this cemetery, including those known to be buried here

Union Baptist Church

Agee   15 Feb. 1902   yes
    Alice C.   9 April 1992   Thomas H. Agee

    Other Info: Shares a headstone with her husband.

Last Name Given Name (Maiden Name)	Date of Birth Date of Death Age at Death	Spouse	Tombstone
Agee Thomas H.	11 March 1887 14 Feb. 1972	Alice C. Agee	yes

Other Info: Footstone: Thomas Henry Agee, Virginia, PVT, US Army, World War I, 11 March 1887, 14 Feb. 1972; Shares a headstone with his wife.

| Agee
William E. | 26 Nov. 1933
24 Aug. 1981 | Elois W. Agee | yes |

Inscription: Not my will but thine be done.

| Allen
Lou | 1870
1952 | | no |

Other Info: Whitten Bros Funeral Home marker

| Austin
Archibald A. | 13 Feb. 1875
20 March 1955 | Mary Ann Austin | yes |

Other Info: Shares a headstone with his wife.

| Austin
Mary Ann | 4 June 1880
24 May 1946 | Archibald A. Austin | yes |

Other Info: Shares a headstone with her husband.

| Austin
Mattie W. | 24 Feb. 1908
8 Feb. 1995 | R. Gallian Austin | yes |

Other Info: Shares a headstone with her husband.

| Austin
R. Gallian | 4 March 1904
14 Jan. 1988 | Mattie W. Austin | yes |

Other Info: Shares a headstone with his wife.

| Austin
Thomas A. | 8 June 1936
12 July 1998 | | yes |

| Austin
William Thomas | 22 Oct. 1902
26 April 1992 | | yes |

Other Info: Has a Shorter Funeral Home marker.

Last Name	Date of Birth	Spouse	Tombstone
Given Name	Date of Death		
(Maiden Name	Age at Death		

Bagby   25 Nov. 1913   yes
   James Norvil   6 Dec. 1975   Lena Woodson Bagby

   Other Info: Footstone: James Norville Bagby, PFC, Army Air Forces, World War II, 25 Nov. 1913, 6 Dec. 1975; Shares a headstone with his wife.

Bagby   21 June 1910   yes
   Lena Woodson   26 May 1985   James Norvil(le) Bagby

   Other Info: Shares a headstone with her husband.

Brayman   1900   no
   Jack G.   1976

   Other Info: Diuguid Funeral Home marker; Footstone: Jack Bryan Brayman, 7 Dec. 1900, 28 Nov. 1976 (middle initial on the funeral marker and the middle name on the footstone are different)

Brayman   30 Sept. 1864   yes
   Willie Ann   20 Nov. 1956

Bryant   23 Oct. 1902   yes
   Nellie J., Miss   15 July 1976

   Inscription: Loved by all

   Other Info: Footstone: Sister

Bryant   1 April 1893   yes
   Oscar Moses   4 April 1976

   Inscription: Rest in Peace

   Other Info: Footstone: Oscar Moses Bryant, PFC, US Army, World War II, 1 Apr. 1893, 4 Apr. 1976

Bryant   26 Mar. 1904   yes
   Paul W.   16 Aug. 1976

   Inscription: Our Precious Father

   Other Info: Footstone: Father

Last Name Given Name (Maiden Name	Date of Birth Date of Death Age at Death	Spouse	Tombstone
Coleman Alma G.	16 Aug. 1902 28 Feb. 1976	S. Joe Coleman	yes

Other Info: Shares a headstone with her husband.

Coleman Garland E.	31 July 1924 22 Oct. 1989	Susie B. Coleman	yes

Other Info: Footstone: Garland E. Coleman, US Army, World War II, Korea, 31 July 1924, 22 Oct. 1989. Shares a headstone with his wife.

Coleman S. Joe	20 April 1893 2 Feb. 1985	Alma G. Coleman	yes

Other Info: Footstone: Samuel Jones Coleman, Sgt, US Army, World War I, 20 Apr. 1893, 2 Feb. 1985. Shares a headstone with his wife.

Coleman Susie B.	22 Feb. 1902 24 Jan. 1988	Garland E. Coleman	yes

Other Info: Shares a headstone with her husband.

Day Alice B.	10 April 1923 11 April 2000	Burton N. Day	yes

Inscription: Married 13 July 1938; In God We Trust

Day Nannie Bryant	15 July 1890 6 Jan. 1974	Van Buren Day	yes

Inscription: Married 4 Dec. 1910; Just a Closer Walk with Thee

Other Info: Shares a headstone with her husband.

Day Van Buren	2 May 1890 13 Feb. 1980	Nannie Bryant Day	yes

Inscription: Married 4 Dec. 1910; Just a Closer Walk with Thee.

Other Info: Shares a headstone with his wife.

Last Name Given Name (Maiden Name)	Date of Birth Date of Death Age at Death	Spouse	Tombstone
Firmin Betty Day	18 Dec. 1925 9 Oct. 1993	David Mitchell Firmin	yes

Inscription: Married 14 May 1993

Fulcher John Henry Jr.	5 May 1915 11 Feb. 1986	Gladys Seay Fulcher	yes

Inscription: Rest in Peace

Gilliam L. Kyle	1912 1991	Mary C. Gilliam	yes

Gilliam Mary Kyle	1887 1971	John Edwin Gilliam	yes

Inscription: Wife of John Edwin Gilliam

Gilliam William W.	7 April 1914 2 May 1961		yes

Inscription: Virginia, TEC 3, 3514 ORD MAM Co., World War II

Gregory Andrew M.	1904 1940	Margaret C. Gregory	yes

Other Info: Footstone: AMG; Shares a headstone with his wife.

Gregory Margaret C.	1905 1967	Andrew M. Gregory	yes

Other Info: Footstone: MCG; Shares a headstone with her husband.

Gunter Ben Spencer	1899 1971		no

Other Info: Robinson Funeral Home marker

Last Name Given Name (Maiden Name	Date of Birth Date of Death Age at Death	Spouse	Tombstone
Gunter 　Marshall Ren	1874 1955		yes

　　Inscription: Father; In God's Care

　　Other Info: Has a Doyne-Burger Funeral Home marker: Footstone:
　　　　Father

Gunter 　Mattie M.	22 Dec. 1906 24 April 1979	Orville Gunter	yes

　　Inscription: Married 17 May 1943

　　Other Info: Footstone: Mattie M. Gunter, 22 Dec. 1906, 24 April 1979;
　　　　Shares a headstone with her husband.

Gunter 　Orville	19 March 1896 27 March 1968	Mattie M. Gunter	yes

　　Inscription: Married 17 May 1943

　　Other Info: Footstone: Orville Gunter, Virginia, 329 PVT CO D,
　　　　Infantry, World War II, 19 March 1896, 27 March 1968; Shares a
　　　　headstone with his wife.

Hall 　Raymond E.	1911 1988		yes

　　Inscription: Bull of the Woods

Hardiman 　Arthur B.	1909 1944		yes

　　Other Info: Footstone: Arthur B. Hardiman, Virginia, Tech Sgt, 111 FA
　　　　BN 29 DIV, World War II, 2 June 1909, 17 Oct. 1944

Hardiman 　Aubrey J.	1879 1948		yes

　　Other Info: Footstone: AJH

Last Name Given Name (Maiden Name)	Date of Birth Date of Death Age at Death	Spouse	Tombstone
Hardiman Aubrey J. Jr.	15 April 1923 12 May 1982		yes

Other Info: Footstone: Aubrey J. Hardiman Jr., PFC, US Army, World War II, 1923-1982

| Hardiman
Daisy S. | 1888
1964 | | yes |

Other Info: Footstone: DSH

| Hardiman
George W. | 4 Aug. 1913
18 Aug. 1977 | | yes |

Other Info: Footstone: George W. Hardiman, PVT, US Army, World War II, 4 Aug. 1913, 18 Aug. 1977

| Hardiman
Rebecca Clyde | 23 May 1911
18 Dec. 1989 | | yes |

| Harrup
James M. | 1920
1979 | Delsie R. Harrup | yes |

Inscription: Gone but not Forgotten

Other Info: Footstone: James Matthew Harrup, SSGT, US Army, World War II, 26 Jan, 1920, 21 Feb. 1979; Dad

| Heath
Florence D. | 11 Feb. 1921
20 Feb. 1971 | Percy D. Heath | yes |

Inscription: Married 25 Dec. 1938

Other Info: Shares a headstone with her husband.

| Heath
Percy D. | 13 Nov. 1913
4 July 1996 | Florence D. Heath | yes |

Inscription: Married 25 Dec. 1938

Other Info: Shares a headstone with his wife.

Last Name Given Name (Maiden Name)	Date of Birth Date of Death Age at Death	Spouse	Tombstone
McFadden Andrew T.	4 Feb. 1921 15 April 1954		yes

Inscription: Virginia, TEC 5, 334 HARCFT Co. TC, World War II

McFadden Clifford W.	1884 1964		yes

McFadden Jerry	19 Dec. 1852 24 Aug. 1921	Lucy A. Carter McFadden	yes

Inscription: They Died as they lived, a Christian

Other Info: Footstone: JM; Shares a headstone with his wife.

McFadden Lawrence E.	12 Sept. 1925 10 April 2000		yes

McFadden Lucy A. Carter	18 July 1864 24 Sept. 1946	Jerry McFadden	yes

Inscription: His Wife; They died as they lived, a Christian.

Other Info: Footstone: LAM; Shares a headstone with her husband.

McFadden Sarah O.	6 May 1906 21 Aug. 1975		yes

Inscription: Gone, but not forgotten

McFadden Warner W.	28 Sept. 1899 16 Nov. 1993		yes

McFadden William Meridith Jr.	6 Oct. 1914 26 May 1980		yes

Inscription: Now Cometh Eternal Rest

Other Info: Footstone: Father

Last Name Given Name (Maiden Name)	Date of Birth Date of Death Age at Death	Spouse	Tombstone
Ragland Marvin L. Sr.	11 Feb. 1919 18 July 2001	Lucy S. Ragland	yes

Inscription: Married 14 March 1941

Other Info: Footstone: Father

Roberts Ralph Earl	10 Dec. 1910 4 Oct. 1985	Mattie Seay Roberts	yes

Rush Eva Walker	21 April 1884 17 Aug. 1961	Joseph E. Rush	yes

Other Info: Shares a headstone with her husband.

Rush Joseph E.	7 Oct. 1883 1 Apr 1968	Eva Walker Rush	yes

Other Info: Shares a headstone with his wife.

Rush Lacy Walter Jr.	23 April 1907 9 Jan. 1980	Bessie Watson Rush	yes

Inscription: Married 15 June 1942

Other Info: Footstone: Lacy Walter Rush Jr., PVT, US Army, World War II, 23 Apr. 1907, 9 Jan 1980.

Scruggs John William	26 Feb. 1925 20 June 1971		yes

Inscription: God is Love

Scruggs Timothy Lindbergh	31 Aug. 1929 20 June 1981		yes

Other Info: Footstone: Timothy L. Scruggs, CPL, US Army, Korea, 31 Aug. 1929, 20 June 1981

Last Name Given Name (Maiden Name)	Date of Birth Date of Death Age at Death	Spouse	Tombstone
Scruggs William Randall	4 June 1972 4 June 1972		yes

Inscription: Son; Safe in the arms of Jesus

Other Info: W.A. Harman Memorials, Charlottesville VA

Seay Allen W.	13 March 1922 5 Jan. 1972	Virginia G. Seay	yes

Inscription: At final thought, A precious memory

Other Info: Footstone: Father; Shares a headstone with his wife.

Seay Charles Abner	15 Dec. 1918 18 June 1961		yes

Other Info: Footstone: Brother

Seay Ethel Watson	1 May 1892 4 Sep. 1985	William Henning Seay	yes

Other Info: Footstone: Mother; Shares a headstone with her husband.

Seay Virginia G.	5 June 1925 24 March 1982	Allen W. Seay	yes

Inscription: At final thought, A precious memory

Other Info: Footstone: Mother, Shares a headstone with her husband.

Seay William Henning	24 Oct. 1889 4 Jan. 1940	Ethel Watson Seay	yes

Other Info: Footstone: Father; Shares a headstone with his wife.

Serfass Cassie O'Dell Hackett	3 March 1919 24 Sept. 1984		yes

Inscription: Don't wake me, I am just sleeping.

Other Info: Footstone: Sister

Last Name Given Name (Maiden Name	Date of Birth Date of Death Age at Death	Spouse	Tombstone
Spencer Mary E.	4 Feb. 1904 8 April 1991	Robert L. Spencer	yes

Inscription: Nearer my God to thee

Other Info: Shares a headstone with her husband.

Spencer Robert L.	16 June 1903 23 Jan. 1972	Mary E. Spencer	yes

Inscription: Nearer my God to thee

Other Info: Shares a headstone with his wife.

Watson Isabel Day	28 Apr. 1914 30 Dec. 2002	William Irvy Watson	yes

Other Info: Shares a headstone with her husband.

Watson William Irvy	27 Mar. 1910 16 June 1991	Isabel Day Watson	yes

Other Info: Shares a headstone with his wife.

Weekley Arietta S.	15 Mar. 1912 22 May 1984	Arthur T. Weekley	yes

Inscription: Married 3 June 1929

Other Info: Shares a headstone with her husband.

Weekley Arthur T.	19 Aug. 1905 13 Jan. 1998	Arietta S. Weekley	yes

Inscription: Married 3 June 1929

Other Info: Shares a headstone with his wife.

Wooten Charlie R.	11 April 1902 8 May 1976		yes

Inscription: Gone but not forgotten

Other Info: Footstone: Father

Last Name Given Name (Maiden Name	Date of Birth Date of Death Age at Death	Spouse	Tombstone
Wooten Lorene W.	6 Aug. 1913 22 Feb. 1996		yes

Inscription: Practical Nurse; An inspiration to all who knew her.

Other Info: Has a Robinson Funeral Home marker with this name: Lorene G. W. Wooten.

Wright Agnes V.	1920 1990	William J. Wright	yes

Inscription: Together Forever

Other Info: Dunkum Funeral Home marker gives the name: Agnes Virginia Wright.

Wright Annie Laura	1 June 1900 12 Feb. 1993		yes
Wright John Henry	26 Aug. 1917 13 June 1995		yes

Inscription: PFC, US Army, World War II

Other Info: Has a Robinson Funeral Home marker.

Wright Seymore S.	27 Aug. 1872 28 Jan. 1955		yes
Wright Walter L.			yes

Inscription: Virginia, TEC 5, HQ CO, 44 Tank BN, 8 May 1976; Gone but not Forgotten

Union Branch Baptist Church — African American

Etched Fieldstone with given name and one date: 1918
Lara

Last Name Given Name (Maiden Name)	Date of Birth Date of Death Age at Death	Spouse	Tombstone
Agee Charles	1946 1986		no

Other Info: Unidentified funeral home marker

Anderson Carliesa W.	Aug. 1909 Jan 2001 91 years		no

Other Info: Has 2 funeral home markers: Thomasson Funeral Home and Colbert Funeral Home

Anderson Holman	7 May 1919 12 Oct. 1978		yes

Inscription: PFC, US Army, World War II

Anderson Marshall	1927 1966		no

Other Info: Unidentified funeral home marker

Ayers Anna D.	20 Dec. 1919 9 Jan. 1988		yes

Inscription: Always in our hearts

Other Info: Has a Thacker Bros. Funeral Home marker.

Ayers Walter	3 Sept. 1905 25 Oct. 1988		yes

Inscription: Always in our hearts

Other Info: Has a Thacker Bros. Funeral Home marker.

Bank Mary Johnson	1921 1961		no

Other Info: Unidentified funeral home marker

Last Name Given Name (Maiden Name)	Date of Birth Date of Death Age at Death	Spouse	Tombstone
Banks Charlie Octavious	13 Dec. 1923 2 July 1987	Josephine H. Banks	yes

Inscription: TEC 5, US Army, World War II

Banks Fannie M.	1957 2003 46 years		no

Other Info: Unidentified funeral home marker

Banks Josephine H.	13 Sept. 1928 28 Feb. 2001	Charlie Octavious Banks	yes

Inscription: Mother

Banks Junius	1921 1987		no

Other Info: Unidentified funeral home marker

Banks Margie V.	1 Jan. 1949 20 May 1996		yes

Inscription: Beloved mother

Banks Mary E.	1943 1994	Wilbur Banks	yes

Inscription: Mother

Other Info: Shares a headstone with her husband. They are the parents of Wilbur Leonard Banks also buried in this cemetery.

Banks Mrs. Willie Mae	1916 2000		no

Other Info: Thomasson Funeral Home marker

Banks Shirley A.	4 April 1953 20 June 1957		yes

Last Name Given Name (Maiden Name)	Date of Birth Date of Death Age at Death	Spouse	Tombstone
Banks Wilber	1941 2003	Mary E. Banks	yes

Inscription: Father

Other Info: Shares a headstone with his wife.

| Banks
Wilbur Leonard | 11 July 1964
2 May 1996 | | yes |

Inscription: Father; In God's care; Forever in Our Hearts

| Booker
Catherine | 1927
1994 | | no |

Other Info: Reids Funeral Home marker

| Booker
Irene C. | 14 May 1898
21 March 1985 | | yes |

Inscription: Mother; Rest in Peace

| Booker
Kelvin L. | 1963
1999
36 years | | no |

Other Info: Unidentified funeral home marker

| Booker
Mr. W.M. | 30 May 1919 | | yes |

| Booker
Mrs. P. H. | 27 April 1919 | | yes |

| Booker
Robert L. Sr. | 25 Aug. 1897
19 Nov. 1980 | | yes |

Inscription: Father; Rest in Peace

| Booker
Robert Lee Jr. | 4 June 1921
22 Oct. 1983
62 years | | no |

Other Info: Thacker Bros. Funeral Home marker

Last Name Given Name (Maiden Name)	Date of Birth Date of Death Age at Death	Spouse	Tombstone
Bowles George R. Jr.	5 June 1925 27 April 2000 74 years		yes

Inscription: Always in our Hearts

Bowles Helena	1893 1966		yes
Brown Agnes Emmaline (baby)			no

Other Info: Reids Funeral Home marker with one date: 1 April 1969

Burke Horace B.	1908 1983		yes
Chamber Levi	1935 1999		no

Other Info: Reids Funeral Home marker

Chambers Andrew	1964 1988 24 years		no

Other Info: Thacker Bros Funeral Home marker

Chambers Edith Jones	1918 1998 79 years		no

Other Info: Thackers Bros Funeral Home marker

Chambers Willie	8 Sept. 1918 15 Oct. 1965		yes

Inscription: PVT, US Army, 321 QM Truck Co.

Colbert Lula Miller	1901 1964		no

Other Info: Ranson and Smith Funeral Home marker

Last Name Given Name (Maiden Name	Date of Birth Date of Death Age at Death	Spouse	Tombstone
Ford James	8 June 1914 19 Oct. 2001		yes

Inscription: The Lord is my Shepherd, I shall not want.

Ford Martha Johnson	1928 1980		no

Other Info: Unidentified funeral home marker

Geggy	Etched Fieldstone with one name and no dates		

Grimes Donnie	22 Apr. 1939 20 Aug. 2001	Rena M. Grimes	yes

Inscription: Beloved Father; Wed: 31 May 1966; Always in our hearts.

Harris Alice N. (Neil)	20 Feb. 1917 6 April 2001	Cleophas ONeal Harris	yes

Harris Cleophas O.	21 Nov. 1911 24 Dec. 1986 75 years	Alice Neil Harris	yes

Other Info: Thacker Bros. Funeral Home marker: Cleophas ONeal Harris; Footstone: COH; His brother, George Harris and sister, Mary S. Harris are also buried in this cemetery.

Harris Dorothy B.	28 Nov. 1911 11 Sept. 2000		yes

Inscription: Mother; Always in our Hearts

Harris Evelyn E.			yes

Inscription: 1989 (one date)

Harris George	1901 1988		yes

Harris Louise	1917 1983		yes

Last Name Given Name (Maiden Name	Date of Birth Date of Death Age at Death	Spouse	Tombstone
Harris Marie			no

Other Info: Unidentified funeral home marker with no dates

Harris Thornton R.	1 Nov. 1938 22 July 1973		yes
Harris Tom	18 July 1905 27 Jan. 1983		yes
Hutcherson Edward D.	8 Mar. 1952 4 Dec. 1991		yes

Inscription: Son; Rest in Peace

Hutcherson John	1931 1989		no

Other Info: Thacker Bros. Funeral Home marker

Hutcherson Mahald J.	23 April 1981 92 years		no

Other Info: Thacker Bros. Funeral Home marker

Hutcherson Mrs. Augusta Jones	4 July 1932 25 Nov. 1998		yes

Inscription: His eye is on the sparrow

Hutcherson Thomas Wesley	20 Aug. 1923 13 March 1983		yes

Inscription: SC3, US Navy, World War II

Jackson Theodore Lamont	3 April 1973 27 June 1988		yes

Inscription: Always in our Hearts

Last Name Given Name (Maiden Name)	Date of Birth Date of Death Age at Death	Spouse	Tombstone
Johnson Alphonso	1947 1971		yes
Johnson Bertha A.	5 May 1929 5 Nov. 2002		no

Other Info: This is an above ground vault:Reids FH

Johnson Bobby Ann	28 Feb. 1955 1 year, 11 months, 19 days		no

Other Info: Unidentified funeral home marker

Johnson Camel	1942 1971		yes
Johnson Charlie T. "Hike"	23 Oct. 1950 5 June 1993		yes

Other Info: Has a Colbert Funeral Home marker.

Johnson Ella Louise	11 April 1961 19 June 2001		yes

Other Info: Has a Colbert Funeral Home marker.

Johnson Evelyn J. Lee	15 Aug. 1963 20 July 1984		yes

Other Info: Shares a headstone with Hattie J. Johnson; has a Colbert Funeral Home marker

Johnson Fletcher	1955 1977		yes
Johnson Hattie J.	10 July 1926 25 Dec. 1979		yes

Other Info: Shares a headstone with Evelyn J. Lee Johnson

Last Name Given Name (Maiden Name)	Date of Birth Date of Death Age at Death	Spouse	Tombstone
Johnson Henry	1922 1999 76 years		no

Other Info: Colbert Funeral Home marker

Johnson James Henry	23 Aug. 1948 27 May 1986		yes

Inscription: Love is Love Forever More

Other Info: Has a Reids Funeral Home marker.

Johnson Jeremiah Leo	1980 1982		yes
Johnson John W.	18 June 1876 8 May 1930		yes

Other Info: Footstone: JWJ

Johnson Maria	22 July 1882 4 June 1891		yes

Inscription: In Memory of

Johnson Oliver Ollie	13 Feb. 1922 26 Jan. 1968		yes
Johnson Ollie	1896 1970		no

Other Info: Smith Funeral Home marker

Johnson Philmore	1923 1999		no

Other Info: Colbert Funeral Home marker

Johnson Raymond	26 Aug. 1925 15 June 1970		yes

Inscription: Virginia, PVT, World War II

Last Name Given Name (Maiden Name)	Date of Birth Date of Death Age at Death	Spouse	Tombstone
Johnson Sam	1949 1981		yes
Johnson Van Lue	18 May 1895 3 June 1977		yes

Inscription: In Loving Memory; Mother

Johnson Waine			no

Other Info: Reids Funeral Home Marker with one date-1 April 1969

Johnson Walter W.	7 Nov. 1918 28 Nov. 1984		yes

Inscription: PVT, US Army, World War II

Johnson William	1955 1993		no

Other Info: Colbert Funeral Home marker

Johnson Willie	1958 1978		yes
Jones Annie H.	26 Feb. 1877 19 March 1951		yes
Jones Charles G.	14 Oct. 1920 9 Dec. 2003		no

Other Info: This is an above ground vault: Bland and Reid FH

Jones George R.	7 Feb. 1911 22 Aug. 1958	Martha Jones Nicholas	yes

Inscription: A Loving Father

Jones Gertrude B.	1 April 1917 9 Feb. 1986	Henry L. Jones	yes

Other Info: Shares a headstone with her husband

Last Name Given Name (Maiden Name)	Date of Birth Date of Death Age at Death	Spouse	Tombstone
Jones Henry L.	12 March 1912 26 Dec. 1983	Gertrude B. Jones	yes

Other Info: Shares a headstone with his wife; Has a Thacker Bros. Funeral Home marker.

| Jones
Janie | 15 Apr. 1812
15 Apr. 1900 | | yes |

Inscription: A tender mother and a faithful friend

Other Info: Footstone: JJ

| Jones
Louisiana | 16 Nov. 1927 | | yes |

Inscription: Mother; At Rest

Other Info: Footstone: LJ

| Jones
Phillip | 10 June 1908
11 March 1935 | | yes |

Inscription: Age 25 years old and 9 months

Other Info: Footstone: PJ

| Jones
Sidney | | | yes |

Inscription: 1954 (one date)

| Miller
Edgar | 6 Oct. 1903
25 April 1989 | | yes |

Inscription: US Army, World War II

Last Name Given Name (Maiden Name)	Date of Birth Date of Death Age at Death	Spouse	Tombstone
Miller Eugene T. Sr.	14 Sept. 1910 22 Aug. 1979		yes

Inscription: Husband

| Miller
    Fletcher T. | 7 Sept. 1908
27 Oct. 1986 | Ressie G. Miller | yes |

Other Info: Shares a headstone with his wife.

| Miller
    John D. | | | yes |

Inscription: Virginia, 1SGT, US Army, 8 June 1935 (one date only)

| Miller
    John Thomas |
91 years | | no |

Other Info: Unidentified funeral home marker with illegible dates

| Miller
    Joseph | 1875
1964 | | no |

Other Info: Ranson and Smith Funeral Home marker

| Miller
    Kenny | 1920
1961 | | yes |

Other Info: Footstone: Grandfather

| Miller
    Louise B. | 10 Mar. 1919
4 Feb. 1994 | | yes |

Inscription: Wife

| Miller
    Rena | | Etched Fieldstone with name only | |

| Miller
    Ressie G. | 10 Aug. 1909
24 Sept. 1985 | Fletcher T. Miller | yes |

Other Info: Shares a headstone with her husband.

Last Name Given Name (Maiden Name)	Date of Birth Date of Death Age at Death	Spouse	Tombstone
Mills Ella J.	1896 12 Jan. 1973		yes

Inscription: Mother

Miort Johnnie M.			no

Other Info: Colbert Funeral Home marker with dates missing.

Moore Josephine B.	1912 1968		no

Other Info: Johnson Bros. Funeral Home marker

Morgan Mary S. (Harris)	2 Aug. 1907 12 July 1981		yes

Inscription: In Loving Memory

Morton James R.		Etched fieldstone-no dates	

Morton Major T.	4 Dec. 1912 28 Feb. 1914	Etched Fieldstone	

Inscription: At Rest

Morton Susan	6 Feb. 1920		yes

(Name not inscribed)	15March 1905 28 Sept. 1951		yes

Inscription: Our Mother; Sleeping in Jesus.

Nicholas Martha Jones	8 June 1910 12 March 1993	(l) George Jones (2) ___ Nicholas	yes

Inscription: An inspiration to all who knew her

Last Name Given Name (Maiden Name	Date of Birth Date of Death Age at Death	Spouse	Tombstone
Patterson Willis	3 Oct. 1942		yes

Inscription: At Rest

Paul Virginia A.	1894 1940		yes

Inscription: Mother

Powell Florence	22 Nov. 1904 25 Oct. 1981		yes

Other Info: Unidentified funeral home marker: Florence M. Powell

Puryear Eliza			no

Other Info: Unidentified funeral home marker with no dates

Randolph Mrs. Everlean S.	1916 2003		no

Other Info: Thomasson Funeral Home marker

Scott Baby	1985 1985		no

Other Info: Reids Funeral Home marker

Taylor Arthur Jerome	1967 1994 26 years		no

Other Info: Thacker Bros. Funeral Home marker

Taylor J. M.	Etched fieldstone with one date: 1911		

Tutwyler Bernard	14 Feb. 1917 30 June 1963		yes

Other Info: Unidentified funeral home marker: Charles Bernard Tutwyler, 1918-1963 (birth year is different on the tombstone).

Last Name Given Name (Maiden Name)	Date of Birth Date of Death Age at Death	Spouse	Tombstone
Tutwyler Stanley	22 July 1947 20 Dec. 1949		yes

  Inscription: Son

Washington Lou	10 Feb. 1915 11 May 2004		yes
Washington Mrs. Virgie	28 Oct. 1886 21 Oct. 1951		yes
Watkins Mrs. Daisy Anna	26 Nov. 1931 13 Sept. 2000		yes

  Inscription: See you in heaven

| Wilson
  Virginia | 12 Feb. 1906
13 April 1986 | | yes |
| Wingfield
  Ophelia |
2 Feb. 1981
71 years | | no |

  Other Info: Thacker Bros. Funeral Home marker

| Woodson
  Margaret Jane | | | yes |

  Inscription: (name only)

| Woodson
  Obrey James | 7 April 1940
28 Aug. 1998 | | yes |

  Other Info: Has a Colbert Funeral Home marker.

There are 61 unidentified graves in this cemetery.

Last Name Given Name (Maiden Name)	Date of Birth Date of Death Age at Death	Spouse	Tombstone

Union Grove Baptist Church — African American

Agee Bertha Booker	9 Feb. 1906 20 May 1990		yes
Amos Rosa H.	21 Oct. 1910 1 Sept. 1977		yes
Austin Lawrence	1928 2000		no

Other Info: E.B. Allen Funeral Home marker

Booker Henry	2 Feb. 1892 17 Sept. 1944		yes
Booker James Edward	4 July 1895 9 Oct. 1958		yes

Other Info: Has a Harden Funeral Home marker.

Booker Lou	12 Jan. 1861 26 Oct. 1946		yes
Booker Willie E.			yes

Inscription: (no dates)

Cobbs Charlie	5 Oct. 1881 1917		yes
Cobbs Sarah	9 Dec. 1856 10 Feb. 1915 58 years, 2 months, 1 day		yes

Inscription: A Christian woman, a faithful friend

Other Info: Footstone: SC

Last Name Given Name (Maiden Name)	Date of Birth Date of Death Age at Death	Spouse	Tombstone
Cooley Bessie Laury	29 May 1934 2 Dec. 1991		yes

Inscription: Eternal Rest

Other Info: Has an E.B. Allen Funeral Home marker

Corbin	2 May ____		no

Other Info: Illegible funeral marker.

Cunningham Brenda H.	1955 1979		yes

Other Info: Has an E.B. Allen Funeral Home marker

Dean Maggie	29 May 1952	Thomas Dean	yes

Other Info: Her husband is interred at Union Hill Baptist Church cemetery.

Gooden Christine Shelton	30 Jan. 1923 9 March 2001	Allen Gooden	yes

Inscription: Beloved wife, mother, grandmother, teacher, community activist and fun-loving friend

Other Info: Has an E.B. Allen Funeral Home marker; She was the mother of seven children.

Jackson Charlie	17 March 1891 12 March 1952		yes
Jackson Dora B.	17 March 1892 3 March 1982		yes
Jackson Edward			yes

Inscription: (no dates)

Last Name Given Name (Maiden Name)	Date of Birth Date of Death Age at Death	Spouse	Tombstone
Jackson W. (William) F.	1913 1974		yes

  Other Info: Has an E.B. Allen Funeral Home marker

| Lattimer
  Carole Shelton | | | yes |

  Inscription: Carole Shelton Lattimer and Baby

  Other Info: Bland Reid Funeral Home marker gives one date: 7 Sept. 1960.

| Laury
  Abraham | 20 June 1915
19 March 1962 | | yes |

  Inscription: Virginia, TEC 5, 578 Ord. Ammo Co., World War II

| Laury
  Asbury | | | yes |

  Inscription: (no dates)

| Laury
  Charles Washington | 29 May 1922
1 Feb. 1994 | | yes |

  Other Info: Has a Joseph Jenkins Jr. Funeral Home marker.

| Laury
  Isaiah Jr. | 25 March 1913
24 Nov. 1986 | | yes |

  Other Info: Has an E.B. Allen Funeral Home marker

| Laury
  Lue Dora, Mrs. | 22 July 1936
37 years, 6 months, 27 days | | yes |

| Laury
  Lula Elizabeth Austin | 15 May 1930
26 Nov. 1993 | | yes |

  Inscription: Our loving mother, may she rest in peace.

Last Name Given Name (Maiden Name	Date of Birth Date of Death Age at Death	Spouse	Tombstone
Laury Mamie M.	19 Sept. 1904 12 Dec. 1989		yes
Laury Mary E. "Lizzie"	1909 1977		yes

Other Info: Has an E.B. Allen Funeral Home marker.

Laury Rachel, Mrs.	18 Aug. 1941 96 years		yes
Laury Thomas W.	1915 1991		yes
Laury Wilbert	11 Oct. 1903 12 Aug. 1991		yes

Other Info: Has an E.B. Allen Funeral Home marker

Laury William L	22 Feb. 1908 2 April 1979		yes
Pride Abraham	4 Dec. 1965 80 years old		yes

Inscription: Uncle

Pride Hal	(1902) (1942)		yes

Other Info: Dates are from Dunkum Funeral Home marker.

Pride Henry A.			no

Other Info: Unidentified funeral home marker with no dates

Pride Lee L.	14 Aug. 1895 2 Dec. 1949		yes

Inscription: At Rest

Last Name Given Name (Maiden Name)	Date of Birth Date of Death Age at Death	Spouse	Tombstone
Pride Lucy	1913 1972		yes
Pride Martha M.	8 Oct. 1901 19 March 1964		yes

Inscription: At Rest

Pride Samuel	1911 1964		yes

Inscription: Our Father

Pride Tom			yes

Inscription: (no dates)

Pride William Lee	5 Oct. 1920 14 July 1986		yes
Quinn Essie K.	10 Jan. 1919 13 Dec. 2000		yes

Other Info: Has a Joseph Jenkins Jr. Funeral Home marker.

Shelton Annie L.	6 March 1898 17 Nov. 1986		yes

Inscription: At Peace

Other Info: Has an E.B. Allen Funeral Home marker

Shelton Carl Dubois	(1948) (1984)		yes

Other Info: E. B. Allen Funeral Home marker gives the dates.

Shelton Fleming A.	1907 1982		no

Other Info: E.B. Allen Funeral Home marker

Last Name Given Name (Maiden Name	Date of Birth Date of Death Age at Death	Spouse	Tombstone
Shelton Fleming I.	1880 1967		yes

   Inscription: At Rest

   Other Info: Has an E.B. Allen Funeral Home marker.

| Shelton
   Henry Alois | 1921
1992 | | yes |

   Inscription: Eternal Rest

| Shelton
   Mary E. | 23 May 1877
23 Nov. 1947 | | yes |

| Shelton
   William L. | 1906
1974 | | no |

   Other Info: E.B. Allen Funeral Home marker

| Shelton
   William L. | 17 March 1870
4 Sept. 1952 | | yes |

| Shelton
   Willie | 1919
1984 | | yes |

   Inscription: PVT, US Army, World War II

   Other Info: Has a Dunkum Funeral Home marker

| Stinson
   Brown | 5 Oct. 1926 | | yes |

   Inscription: At Rest

| Stinson
   Jennetta | 18 June 1924 | | yes |

   Inscription: Asleep in Jesus

There are 15 unidentified graves in this cemetery

Last Name	Date of Birth	Spouse	Tombstone
Given Name	Date of Death		
(Maiden Name)	Age at Death		

Union Hill Baptist Church — African American

Anderson　　　　　20 May 1913　　　　　　　　yes
William C.　　　　　3 March 1968

　　Inscription: New York, PFC, US Army, World War II

Ayers　　　　　　　　　　　　yes
　Emma Ellis 6 Aug. 1964

　　Other Info: Shares a headstone with Minnie Ellis Hamilton. They were sisters of Celia Ellis Laury also buried in this cemetery.

Bennett　　　　　　　　　　　　　　　　　　no
　Ada

　　Other Info: Unidentified funeral home marker with no dates. Sister of Susin, Fred, Earlie and Morton Bennett.

Bennett　　　　　　　　　　　　　　　　　　no
　Earlie　　　　　　　　　　Mary Bennett

　　Other Info: Unidentified funeral home marker. He was the brother of Fred, Morton, Susin and Ada Bennett.

Bennett　　　　　　　　　　　　　　　　　　no
　Effie

　　Other Info: Unidentified funeral home marker with no dates. Her parents were Earlie and Mary Bennett.

Bennett　　　　　　　　　　　　　　　　　　no
　Fred

　　Other Info: Unidentified funeral home marker. His siblings, Earlie, Morton, Ada, and Susin Bennett are also buried in this cemetery.

Bennett　　　　　　　　　　　　　　　　　　no
　Mary　　　　　　　　　　Earlie Bennett

　　Other Info: Unidentified funeral home marker

Last Name Given Name (Maiden Name	Date of Birth Date of Death Age at Death	Spouse	Tombstone
Bennett Mary M. (Miller)	30 July 1965	Morton W. Bennett	no

Other Info: Unidentified funeral home marker

| Bennett
Morton | | | no |

Other Info: Unidentified funeral home marker. His brothers, Earlie and Fred Bennett are also buried in this cemetery.

| Bennett
Morton W. | 27 June 1908
11 May 1959 | Mary Miller Bennett | yes |

Inscription: Virginia, TEC 5, 3756 QM Truck Co., World War II

Other Info: Has an L.C. Gray Funeral Home marker

| Bennett
Susin | | | no |

Other Info: Unidentified funeral home marker with no dates. She was the sister of Ada, Earlie, Fred, and Morton Bennett all buried in this cemetery.

| Bonderant
Leslie | 1925
1997 | | no |

Other Info: Universal Monument Inc. funeral marker-Wash. D.C.; His mother was Lucy J. Bonderant Patterson.

| Bondurant
Arthur L. | 1927
1988 | | yes |

Inscription: US Army, World War II

Other Info: His mother was Nora Ann Harper Bondurant.

| Bondurant
Nora H. (Harper) | 1905
1961 | Lee Boundurant (Bondurant) | yes |

Inscription: Mother

Other Info: Her parents were Arthur and Lucy Ann Harper.

Last Name Given Name (Maiden Name)	Date of Birth Date of Death Age at Death	Spouse	Tombstone

Boundurant　　　　　　1902　　　　　　　　　　　　　　yes
　Lee　　　　　　　　　　1937　　Nora Harper Bondurant

　　Inscription: In Memory of our Grandfather from the loving
　　　　grandchildren

Braxton　　　　　　　　　　　　　　　　　　　　　　　　　no
　Margaret (Harper)　about 1952

　　Other Info: Unidentified funeral home marker with no dates. Her
　　　parents were Spencer and Mary Ann Hemmings Harper.

Chapman　　　　　　　　1903　　　　　　　　　　　　　　yes
　George W.　　　　　　　1973

　　Inscription: Now Cometh Eternal Rest

　　Other Info: E.B. Allen Funeral Home marker gives the birth year as
　　　1901. His mother was Patsy Chapman.

Claiborne　　　　　　　　25 Dec. 1928　　　　　　　　　　yes
　Evelyn L. (Laury)　　　10 June 1998　Willie Claiborne

　　Inscription: Rest in Peace

　　Other Info: Has an E. B. Allen Funeral Home marker

Cottrell　　　　　　　　　1955　　　　　　　　　　　　　　no
　Dwight D.　　　　　　　2002

　　Other Info: Reids Funeral Home marker. His parents were James D.
　　　and Irene Jones Cottrell.

Cottrell　　　　　　　　　21 July 1924　　　　　　　　　　yes
　James D.　　　　　　　15 Jan. 1987　Irene Jones Cottrell

　　Inscription: PFC, US Army, World War II

　　Other Info: His father was Paul Cottrell.

Last Name Given Name (Maiden Name	Date of Birth Date of Death Age at Death	Spouse	Tombstone
Cottrell Kenja D.	23 Aug. 1983 30 Jan. 1988		yes

Other Info: His parents are Drake and Chiquita Cottrell.

Crawford Joe Lee	23 July 1940 8 July 1998		yes

Other Info: Has a Reids Funeral Home marker.

Dean Thomas		Maggie Dean (buried at Union Grove B.C.)	no

Other Info: Unidentified funeral home marker with no dates.

Eldridge John William ("Buster")	1909 1943		yes

Other Info: His parents were Samuel and Bettie E. Laury Eldridge.

Eldridge Margaret	about 1930		no

Other Info: Unidentified funeral home marker with no dates. She was the sister of Samuel Eldridge.

Eldridge Samuel	about 1940	Bettie E. Laury Eldridge	no

Other Info: Unidentified funeral home marker with no dates.

Elliott Raymond L.	1948 2000	Mary Frances Elliott	no

Other Info: E.B. Allen Funeral Home marker; His father was Curtis Elliott.

Fuller Frank	1900 1987		no

Other Info: E.B. Allen Funeral Home marker

Last Name Given Name (Maiden Name)	Date of Birth Date of Death Age at Death	Spouse	Tombstone
Gordon Annie	1899 1978		no

Other Info: Reids Funeral Home marker; Her parents were Lewis and Adeline Gordon.

| Gordon baby (1) | | | no |

Other Info: Unidentified funeral home marker- no dates. Parents were Joe and Phyllis Gordon.

| Gordon baby (2) | | | no |

Other Info: Unidentified funeral home marker: Parents were Joe and Phyllis Gordon

| Gordon Eliza Rebecca (Mosley) | 4 Dec. 1913 19 April 2003 | Rev. James D. Gordon | yes |

Inscription: In God's Care

Other Info: Has an EB Allen Funeral Home marker

| Gordon James D. Rev. | 25 Aug. 1907 4 March 1980 | Eliza Rebecca Mosley Gordon | yes |

Inscription: Now Cometh Eternal Rest

| Gordon Joe Smith | 22 April 1909 24 Oct. 1972 | Phyllis Gordon | yes |

Inscription: US Navy, World War II

Other Info: His parents were Lewis and Adeline Gordon.

Last Name Given Name (Maiden Name)	Date of Birth Date of Death Age at Death	Spouse	Tombstone
Gordon Lewis		Adeline Gordon	no

Other Info: Unidentified funeral home marker with no dates. He and his wife were the parents of Rev. James D. Gordon, Joe Smith Gordon, Mary Lou Gordon Perkins, Annie Gordon, and Gertrude Gordon Vaughn all buried in this cemetery.

| Gordon
Samuel | | | no |

Other Info: Unidentified funeral home marker with no dates

| Hamilton
Minnie Ellis | 14 Feb. 1964 | | yes |

Other Info: Shares a headstone with Emma Ellis Ayers. They were sisters of Celia Ellis Laury also buried in this cemetery.

| Harper
Amanda E. (Perkins) | 19 Dec. 1924
12 Nov. 1998 | Taylor Harper Sr. | yes |

Inscription: Loving Mother and Wife, Now Cometh Eternal Rest

Other Info: Has an E.B. Allen Funeral Home marker. Her parents were Phillip and Mary Lou Perkins.

| Harper
Anthony Lee | 1954
1982 | | yes |

Inscription: Son

Other Info: His parents were George and Estelle Harper.

| Harper
Arthur | 6 Nov. 1876
1 Jan. 1949 | Lucy Ann Pride Harper | yes |

Inscription: Father

| Harper
Baby | | | no |

Other Info: Fieldstones and an unidentified funeral home marker; Parents were Taylor and Amanda Perkins Harper.

Last Name Given Name (Maiden Name	Date of Birth Date of Death Age at Death	Spouse	Tombstone

Harper
   Don William

1955
1988

Florence Turner Harper

yes

Inscription: Sleep in Peace

Other Info: Has an E.B. Allen Funeral Home marker. His parents were George and Estelle Cunningham Harper.

Harper
   Esau

no

Other Info: Unidentified funeral home marker with no dates; He was the brother of Sam Harper also buried in this cemetery.

Harper
   Essie L.

1903
1983

yes

Other Info: Her parents were Arthur and Lucy Ann Harper.

Harper
   Florence O. (Oliver)

1951
1997

Luther Harper

no

Other Info: Reids Funeral Home marker

Harper
   George W.

10 Feb. 1910
23 March 1986

Estelle Cummingham Harper

yes

Inscription: Sleep in Peace

Other Info: His parents were Arthur and Lucy Ann Harper.

Harper
   Herman A.

1892
1971

yes

Inscription: Uncle

Other Info: He was the brother of Lillie B. Harper Perkins.

Last Name Given Name (Maiden Name)	Date of Birth Date of Death Age at Death	Spouse	Tombstone
Harper James	1907 1925		yes

Inscription: Brother

Other Info: His parents were Arthur and Lucy Ann Harper.

Harper Lizzie	about 1948-1949		no

Other Info: Unidentified funeral home marker with no dates. She was a niece of Spencer Harper.

Harper Lucy Ann (Pride)	1 Sept. 1878 19 May 1962	Arthur Harper	yes

Inscription: Mother

Harper Sam H.	24 March 1889 18 May 1936		yes

Inscription: In Memory of

Other Info: His is the father of Mary H. Couchman, Lacy Harper and Henry Harper.

Harper Samuel H. (Henry)	21 March 1914 3 Jan. 1946	Sarah Jefferson Harper	yes

Other Info: Shares a headstone with his wife. His father was Samuel Harper Sr. also buried in this cemetery.

Harper Sarah J. (Jefferson)	18 Aug. 1906 8 Nov. 2002	Samuel Henry Harper	yes

Other Info: Shares a headstone with her husband. Her mother was Lucy Jefferson also buried in this cemetery.

Last Name Given Name (Maiden Name)	Date of Birth Date of Death Age at Death	Spouse	Tombstone
Harper Taylor (Sr.)	24 Mar. 1919 12 July 2000	Amanda Perkins Harper	yes

Inscription: TEC 5, US Army, World War II

Other Info: Has an E.B. Allen Funeral Home marker. His parents were Arthur and Lucy Ann Harper.

| Harper
   Taylor |
baby | | Etched Fieldstone |

Other Info: His parents were Taylor and Amanda Perkins Harper

| Harper
   Valarie | 1964
1964 | | no |

Other Info: Reids Funeral Home marker

| Harper
   William E. | | | no |

Other Info: Unidentified funeral home marker with no dates.

| Haskins
   Viola Estelle (Bennett) | 1912
1999 |
Thomas Haskins | no |

Other Info: Unidentified funeral home marker.

| Hocker
   Frances | | | no |

Other Info: Unidentified funeral home marker with no dates.

| Hughes
   Nannie C. | 21 July 1901
29 March 1985 |
Jessie Hughes
(buried elsewhere) | yes |

| Jackson
   Andrew | 1897
1972 | | yes |

Inscription: PVT, US Army

Last Name Given Name (Maiden Name	Date of Birth Date of Death Age at Death	Spouse	Tombstone
Jackson Lacy H.	27 July 1962 22 March 1994		no

Other Info: This is an above ground vault: Reids FH. His father was Andrew Jackson.

| Jefferson
Betsy | | | no |

Other Info: Unidentified funeral home marker with no dates. Her daughter was Lucy Jefferson and her granddaughter was Sarah J. Harper.

| Jefferson
John | | | no |

Other Info: Known to be buried here.

| Jefferson
John William | | | no |

Other Info: Known to be buried here.

| Jefferson
Lucy | | | no |

Other Info: Known to be buried here.

| Jones
Nellie M. | 13 Oct. 1894
19 May 1993 | Wyatt N. Jones | yes |

Inscription: Mother; Rest in Peace

Other Info: Has an E.B. Allen Funeral Home marker. Her mother was Laura J. Scott. Her husband is buried at St. Joy B. C. Cemetery.

| Jones
Reginald G. | 1933
1988 | | no |

Other Info: E.B. Allen Funeral Home marker; His parents are Wyatt and Nellie M. Jones.

Last Name Given Name (Maiden Name	Date of Birth Date of Death Age at Death	Spouse	Tombstone
Judge Lucy Jane (Harper)	1915 1961		yes

Inscription: Sister

Other Info: Her parents were Arthur and Lucy Ann Harper.

| Kyle
James D. | 10 June 1891
11 Oct. 1973 | | yes |

Inscription: US Army

Other Info: His father was Rev. Henry Kyle.

| Kyle
Vennie | | | no |

Other Info: Unidentified funeral home marker with no dates.

| Kyle
William A. | | | no |

Other Info: Unidentified funeral home marker with no dates.

| Laury
Bettie (Harper Eldridge) | | (1) Samuel Eldridge
(2) Watson Laury | no |

Other Info: Unidentified funeral home marker with no dates.

| Laury
Celia Ellis | 8 Feb. 1964 | | yes |

Inscription: Grandma

| Laury
John H. (Harold) | 1903
1960 | Manola P. Laury | yes |

Other Info: His mother was Celia Ellis Laury.

Last Name Given Name (Maiden Name	Date of Birth Date of Death Age at Death	Spouse	Tombstone
Laury Manola P.	1906 1988	John Harold Laury	yes

Inscription: Peaceful Rest

Other Info: Has an E.B. Allen Funeral Home marker.

| Laury
   Marvin | 28 Nov. 1946
21 Jan. 1968 | | yes |

Inscription: Virginia, SP 4, US Army

Other Info: His mother was Lilia Laury Mathews.

| Laury
   Monsell B. "Jimmie Cake" | 1947
1994 | | yes |

Inscription: At Rest

Other Info: Has an E.B. Allen Funeral Home marker. His mother was Evelyn L. Claiborne, also buried in this cemetery.

| Laury
   Watson | 1885
1970 | Bettie Harper Eldridge Laury | no |

Other Info: E. B. Allen Funeral Home marker. His mother was Rachel Laury.

| Massie
   Arthur W. | 1919
1983 | Leah Laury Massie | yes |

Inscription: At Rest

Other Info: Has an E.B. Allen Funeral Home marker.

| Mays
   Freddie I. | 1900
1977 | Corrine Mays | yes |

Inscription: Gone but not Forgotten

Other Info: Footstone: FIM; His mother was Laura J. Scott also buried in this cemetery.

Last Name Given Name (Maiden Name	Date of Birth Date of Death Age at Death	Spouse	Tombstone
Miller George			no

Other Info: Unidentified funeral home marker with no dates. He was the brother of Joshua Perkins.

| Miller Robert | before 1935 | | yes |

Other Info: Headstone has no inscribed dates.

| Mosley Charles | | Martha | no |

Other Info: Known to be buried here.

| Patterson George W. | 15 July 1898 25 Dec. 1986 | Lucy J. Bonderant Patterson | yes |

Other Info: Has a Reids Funeral Home marker.

| Patterson Lucy J. (Bonderant) | 1909 1977 | (1) _____ Bonderant (2) George W. Patterson | yes |

Other Info: Has a Reids Funeral Home marker that gives the birth year as 1908.

| Perkins Bettie Lee | 1929 1929 2 days | | no |

Other Info: Known to be buried here, the infant of Joshua and Lillie B. Perkins, also buried in this cemetery.

| Perkins Clarence Jr. | 1952 1997 | Diane Haskins Perkins | no |

Other Info: E.B. Allen Funeral Home marker. His parents were Clarence N. and Dorothy Austin Perkins.

Last Name Given Name (Maiden Name	Date of Birth Date of Death Age at Death	Spouse	Tombstone
Perkins Clarence N.	8 April 1916 1 June 2000	Dorothy Austin Perkins	yes

Inscription: PFC, US Army, World War II

Other Info: His parents were Joshua and Lillie B. Perkins.

Perkins Franklin L.	1954 1993		no

Other Info: E.B. Allen Funeral Home marker; His parents are Leo and Addie Mosley Perkins.

Perkins Joshua	1882 1945	Lillie Bud Harper Perkins	yes

Inscription: Father

Perkins Lillie B. (Bud) (Harper)	1888 1970	Joshua Perkins	yes

Inscription: Mother

Perkins Louise Nash	5 Aug. 1949 28 March 1998	Samuel Perkins	yes

Inscription: Always in our hearts

Perkins Mary Lou (Gordon)	30 Sept. 1894 11 Sept. 1956	Phillip Perkins	yes

Inscription: I will praise thee, O Lord with my whole heart-Psalm 9:1; Loving Grandmother.

Other Info: Has a C. G. Buckingham Gray Funeral Home marker. Her parents were Lewis and Adeline Gordon.

Perkins Phillip	6 Oct. 1896 13 Nov. 1968	Mary Lou Gordon Perkins	yes

Inscription: Maryland, PVT, US Army, World War I

Last Name Given Name (Maiden Name	Date of Birth Date of Death Age at Death	Spouse	Tombstone

Perkins
Richard   no

Other Info: Community Funeral Home marker with one date: 14 Sept. 1972. His parents were Phillip and Mary Lou Perkins.

Perkins   1924   yes
Samuel E. (Edward, Sr.) 1981   Cora Perkins Perkins

Inscription: Blessed in Eternity

Other Info: E.B. Allen Funeral Home marker; His parents were Joshua and Lillie B. Perkins.

Perkins   no
Spencer   (1) Minnie Mallory
                                 (2) Thelma Gray

Other Info: Known to be buried here. His parents were Joshua and Lillie B. Perkins.

Perkins   1930   no
William H. (Henry)   1996

Other Info: Reids Funeral Home marker; His parents were Phillip and Mary Lou Perkins.

Powell   1877   yes
Hettie W. (White)   1955   M. James Powell

Other Info: Footstone: HWP

Powell   1882   yes
M. James   1946   Hettie W. Powell

Other Info: Footstone: MJP. He and his wife are the parents of Carol P. Jones and Penelope P. Forbes.

Reid   27 Sept. 1926   no
Adeline   12 March 2001

Other Info: This is an above ground vault: Reids FH. Her parents were Phillip and Mary Lou Perkins.

Last Name Given Name (Maiden Name)	Date of Birth Date of Death Age at Death	Spouse	Tombstone
Scott John A.	1903 1967	Susie Scott	no

Other Info: Community Funeral Home marker

Scott Laura J.	1876 1939	William Scott	yes

Scott Milton			no

Other Info: Unidentified funeral home marker with no dates. His parents were John A. and Susie Scott.

Scott Susie, Mrs.	1896 1981	John A. Scott	no

Other Info: E.B. Allen Funeral Home marker

Scott William	30 May 1961	Laura J. Scott	no

Other Info: L.C. Gray Funeral Home marker

Smith Dorian	1988 2000		no

Other Info: E.B. Allen Funeral Home marker; His grandparents are Wyatt and Nellie M. Jones.

Thompson Mary			no

Other Info: Unidentified funeral home marker with no dates

Vaughn Gertrude G. (Gordon)	1903 1980		no

Other Info: Reids Funeral Home marker; Her parents were Phillip and Mary Lou Perkins.

Last Name Given Name (Maiden Name	Date of Birth Date of Death Age at Death	Spouse	Tombstone
Vaughters Henry Jr.	1950 1997		yes

Inscription: Peaceful Rest

Other Info: Has an EB Allen Funeral Home marker.

Vaughters Robert Henry	16 May 1918 21 April 1982		yes

Inscription: PFC, US Army

White Rebecca	26 May 1879 20 Oct. 1970		yes

Inscription: Aunt

Other Info: She was the sister of Hettie White Powell, also buried in this cemetery.

Williams Emily (Harper)	1913 1987	Robert Williams	yes

Other Info: Her parents, Arthur and Lucy Ann Harper and her brothers, James, George and Taylor Harper are also buried in this cemetery.

Williams Robert	10 April 1913 19 March 1989	Emily Harper Williams	yes

Inscription: Father

Other Info: Has an E.B. Allen Funeral Home marker.

Wood Gladys L. (Jackson)	1950 1992	Harold Wood	yes

Inscription: Daughter; (by) Loving Mother and Father

Other Info: Has an E.B. Allen Funeral Home marker. Her father was Willie Jackson.

Last Name Given Name (Maiden Name)	Date of Birth Date of Death Age at Death	Spouse	Tombstone
Wright Irene (Bennett)	1904 1933		yes

Other Info: Her parents were Earlie and Mary Bennett.

Unknown Family at "Old Pollard Place" — African American

This cemetery is located on the George Shumaker property off Rd. 752, in the woods. There are many unidentified graves in this cemetery.

Vest Family off Rd. 662

Vest Samuel	29 May 1894 8 Sept. 1953		yes

Inscription: Virginia, PVT, Co. G, 9 Infantry, 2 Div., World War I

Vest Thomas W.	5 May 1888 20 Jan. 1955		yes

Inscription: Virginia, PVT, Co. A, 167 Infantry, World War I

There are 10 unidentified graves in this cemetery.

Matthew Via Family off Rd. 606

Via John James Jr.			no

Other Info: Known to be buried here, the son of John James Via Sr.

Via John James Sr.			no

Other Info: Known to be buried here. His parents were Matthew and Sarah Carter Via.

Last Name Given Name (Maiden Name	Date of Birth Date of Death Age at Death	Spouse	Tombstone

Via
   Matthew   Sarah Carter Via   no

    Other Info: Known to be buried here. He and his wife were the parents of John James Via Sr. also buried in this cemetery, and Mary Frances, Lucy A., Martha J., Catherine R (Becky), Emeline (Emily), Sarah F, William M., and Leticia (Tish) Via.

Via   no
   Sally

    Other Info: Known to be buried here. She was the daughter of John James Via, Jr., and the last known to be buried in this cemetery.

Via   no
   Sarah Carter   Matthew Via

    Other Info: Known to be buried here.

Wade Family off US 15, at Alpha

Apperson   yes
   Thomas J.

    Inscription: Co. C, 3 VA RES, CSA (no dates)

Beck   1 March 1862   yes
   Lelia Irvin   6 Oct. 1939

    Inscription: Blessed are the pure in heart for they shall see God

Guthrie   7 Sept. 1829   yes
   James A.   10 July 1862

    Inscription: Co. F., 20 VA INF, CSA

Harris   25 March 1891   yes
   John Edgar   17 Sept 1941

    Inscription: Husband; There shall be no night here.

Last Name Given Name (Maiden Name	Date of Birth Date of Death Age at Death	Spouse	Tombstone
Wade Alfred Byron	9 Oct. 1861 12 Sept. 1895		yes

Inscription: In loving remembrance of; He is not dead, just sleepeth

| Wade
Afred J. | 16 Feb. 1832
31 May 1866 | yes
Sarah Apperson Wade | |

Inscription: Co. F, 20 VA INF, CSA

| Wade
Dan F. | 5 March 1893
6 Jan. 1935 | | yes |

Inscription: Husband; May the resurrection find thee on the bosom of thy God

| Wade
Samuel Alfred | 17 Oct 1918
21 March 1920 | | yes |

Inscription: Son of Sapah Elizabeth and D.F. Wade; From Mother's Arms to the Arm's of Jesus

In 2003, the Elliott Grays UDC Chapter #1877 erected and dedicated a monument in this cemetery: "Based upon community and family oral history, this cemetery holds the remains of 35 North Carolina confederate soldiers. After release from Pt. Lookout in the summer of 1865 they traveled as far as Alpha, the home of their comrade Alfred Wade. A hospital was set up at the general store and post office, but it was too late for these emaciated soldiers. "

Wade-McFadden Family off Rd. 636

| Carter
Nena E. | 11 Sept. 1891
5 Dec. 1918 | | yes |

Inscription: Gone but not Forgotten

| McFadden
M.J. | | | Brass Marker |

| McFadden
Nannie | | | Brass Marker |

Last Name Given Name (Maiden Name)	Date of Birth Date of Death Age at Death	Spouse	Tombstone
McFadden W. T.			Brass Marker
McFadden Wiley			Brass Marker
McFadden William			Brass Marker
Wade Nannie McFadden	1863 1962		Brass Marker

Other Info: Has a Virginia Funeral Chapel marker.

Wade Patrick			Brass Marker

Walker Taylor Family on Rd. 690

Taylor Sallie E. Miles	16 Sept. 1868 7 Sept. 1946	Walker Taylor	yes
Taylor Walker	10 March 1867 26 March 1939	Sallie E. Miles Taylor	yes

There are 2 unidentified graves in this cemetery.

Watson-Perrow Family

Bagby Elizabeth (Conner)	10 June 1803 1 Dec. 1882	Josiah Bagby	yes

Inscription: In memory of our mother; No mournful woes can reach this peaceful sleeper here, while angels watch the soft repose.

Other Info: Etched footstone: EB She was the mother of Nancy Jane Bagby Perrow, also buried in this cemetery.

Last Name Given Name (Maiden Name	Date of Birth Date of Death Age at Death	Spouse	Tombstone
Bagby 　Josiah	3 Oct. 1796 2 March 1863	Elizabeth Conner Bagby	yes

Inscription: In memory of our father; God my Redeemer lives, and ever from the skies, looks down and watches all my dust, "til He shall bid it rise. Footstone: JB

Other Info: He and his wife are the parents of Nancy Jane Bagby Perrow also buried in this cemetery.

Bagby 　Nannie Sue Perrow	3 April 1872 25 May 1906	William Ryland Bagby	Multi-family Stone

Other Info: Footstone: NSPB Has a temporary marker giving name and dates. Her parents were Daniel W. Perrow and Nancy Ligon Patterson Perrow, also buried in this cemetery.

Bagby 　William G.	5 Jan. 1822 about 1845		no

Other Info: The identity of this grave is uncertain. There is an etched fieldstone: MCB or WCB or WGB. William G. Bagby was the son of Josiah Bagby and Elizabeth Conner Bagby buried in this cemetery.

Gilbert 　Ada Mallie Mertis Perrow	20 May 1874 20 Jan. 1894	Robert Thomas Gilbert	Multi-family Stone

Other Info: Has a temporary marker. Her parents were Daniel W. Perrow and Nancy Ligon Patterson Perrow also buried in this cemetery.

Last Name	Date of Birth	Spouse	Tombstone
Given Name	Date of Death		
(Maiden Name)	Age at Death		

Gregory 27 Sept. 1857 Multi-family Stone
   Allice Lillian Laura Spencer Perrow 25 June 1900
                                                 Millard Gregory

   Other Info: Has a temporary marker. She was the daughter of Daniel W. Perrow and Nancy Jane Bagby Perrow, also buried in this cemetery.

Gregory   Multi-family Stone
   Kathleen   about 1890

   Other Info: Has a temporary marker. She was the daughter of Allice L.L.S. Perrow Gregory and Millard Gregory. Her mother is also buried in this cemetery.

Mann   about 1838   Multi-family Stone
   Meekie Sue Watson 13 April 1857   Richard H. Mann

   Inscription: Etched fieldstone: MWM

   Other Info: Has a temporary marker. Her parents were Daniel P. Watson and Lucy S. Watson also buried in this cemetery.

Patteson   20 April 1818   Multi-family Stone
   Elizabeth G. Perrow "Betsy" 14 May 1902   William Everett
                                                Patteson

   Inscription: Etched fieldstone: EP, May 14, 1902

   Other Info: Has a temporary marker. She was the daughter of Guerrant Perrow and Nancy Watson Perrow.

Perrow   1817   Mulit-family Stone
   Charles   about 1825

   Other Info: Thought to be buried here. Son of Guerrant Perrow and Nancy Watson Perrow.

Last Name Given Name (Maiden Name)	Date of Birth Date of Death Age at Death	Spouse	Tombstone
Perrow Charles	1728 1797		no

Inscription: Etched fieldstone: WCP or WCB-1797

Other Info: The identity of this grave is uncertain. Charles Perrow was the son of Daniel Perrow and Marie Forsee Perrow and the grandfather of Guerrant Perrow, who is buried in this cemetery.

Perrow Daniel W.	(28 May 1828) (28 July 1906)	(l) Nancy Jane Bagby Perrow (2) Nancy Ligon Patterson Perrow	yes

Inscription: Co. K, 4th VA CAV, CSA

Other Info: He was the son of Guerrant Perrow and Nancy William Watson Perrow also buried in this cemetery.

Perrow Daniel Watson Jr.	20 Feb. 1880 21 April 1892		Multi-family Stone

Other Info: Has a temporary marker. His parents were Daniel W. Perrow and Nancy Ligon Patterson Perrow also buried in this cemetery.

Perrow Guerrant	1777 3 Jan. 1843	Nancy William Watson Perrow	Multi-family Stone and Military Stone

Inscription: PVT, 5 VA MIL, War of 1812, 1777-1843

Other Info: He was the son of Daniel Perrow (1749/1750-15 June 1801) and his first wife.

Last Name Given Name (Maiden Name)	Date of Birth Date of Death Age at Death	Spouse	Tombstone
Perrow John Guerrant	21 May 1866 17 Aug. 1886		Multi-family Stone

Inscription: Etched fieldstone: JGP

Other Info: Has a temporary marker. His parents were Daniel W. Perrow and Nancy Ligon Patterson Perrow, also buried in this cemetery.

Perrow Mildred Dorinda	19 Jan. 1834 about 1920		Multi-family Stone

Other Info: Has a temporary marker. She was the daughter of Guerrant Perrow and Nancy Watson Perrow also buried in this cemetery.

Perrow Nancey Elenor	20 May 1826 1901		Multi-family Stone

Inscription: Etched fieldstone: NEP, 1901

Other Info: Has a temporary marker: She was the daughter of Guerrant Perrow and Nancy Watson Perrow also buried in this cemetery.

Perrow Nancy Jane Bagby	18 May 1830 14 Jan. 1860	Daniel W. Perrow	Multi-family Stone

Other Info: Has a temporary marker. She is the daughter of Josiah Bagby and Elizabeth Conner Bagby also buried in this cemetery.

Perrow Nancy Ligon Patterson	22 Nov. 1841 14 Sept. 1925	Daniel Watson Perrow	Multi-family Stone

Other Info: Footstone: NLPP Has a termporary marker giving name and dates. Her parents were John Patterson and Susan Robertson Patterson.

Last Name Given Name (Maiden Name)	Date of Birth Date of Death Age at Death	Spouse	Tombstone
Perrow Nancy William Watson	21 Jan. 1793 26 Aug. 1871	Guerrant Perrow	Multi-family Stone

Inscription: Etched fieldstone: NEP, 26 Aug. 1871

Other Info: Has a temporary marker. She was the daughter of William Watson Sr. and Fanny Wilkinson Watson also buried in this cemetery.

Perrow Salome P.	28 Dec. 1830 16 Jan. 1909		Multi-family Stone

Inscription: Etched fieldstone: SPP, 16 Jan. 1909

Other Info: Has a temporary marker. She was the daughter of Guerrant Perrow and Nancy Watson Perrow also buried in this cemetery.

Robertson Lucy Ann Frances Perrow	15 Sept. 1813 1 Oct. 1889	William I. Robertson	Multi-family Stone

Inscription: Etched fieldstone: LPR

Other Info: Has a temporary marker. She was the daughter of Guerrant Perrow and Nancy Watson Perrow, also buried in this cemetery.

Robertson William I	1812 7 March 1882	Lucy Ann Frances Perrow Robertson	Multi-family Stone

Inscription: Etched fieldstone: WIR, Mar. 1882

Other Info: Has a temporary marker.

Spencer Carolline Watson	27 Oct. 1799 1870/1880	William Spencer	Multi-family Stone

Other Info: There is a somewhat illegible etched fieldstone at this grave which likely reads: CSP, D. 3 Nov. 1873, It may be the grave of Carolline Watson Spencer. She was the daughter of William Watson Sr. and Fanny Wilkinson Watson also buried in this cemetery.

Last Name Given Name (Maiden Name)	Date of Birth Date of Death Age at Death	Spouse	Tombstone
Spencer William	prior to 1850	Carolline Watson Spencer	Multi-family Stone

Other Info: Known to be buried here.

Watson Daniel Perrow	about 1810 14 Aug. 1879	Lucy Stevens Watson	Multi-family Stone

Inscription: Etched fieldstone: DPW

Other Info: Has a temporary marker. He was the son of William Watson Jr. and Meekie/Makey Perrow Watson also buried in this cemetery.

Watson Fanny Wilkinson	about 1769 about 1840	William Watson Sr.	Multi-family Stone

Other Info: Has a temporary marker.

Watson George E.	28 March 1789 11 Nov. 1871	(1) Mary Spencer Watson (2) Mary A. Foster Watson	yes; also on Multi-family Stone

Inscription: PVT, VA MIL, War of 1812

Other Info: He was the son of William Watson Sr. and Fanny Wilkinson Watson, also buried in this cemetery.

Watson James	9 April 1780 about 1813-1817		Multi-family Stone

Inscription: Etched fieldstone: JW A-6

Other Info: Has a temporary marker. He was the son of William Watson Sr. and Fanny Wilkinson Watson also buried in this cemetery.

Last Name Given Name (Maiden Name	Date of Birth Date of Death Age at Death	Spouse	Tombstone
Watson Lucy Stevens	about 1815 11 June 1887	Multi-family Stone Daniel Perrow Watson	

Inscription: Etched fieldstone: LW

Other Info: Has a temporary marker.

Watson Makey/Meekie Perrow	about 1776 about 1850/1860	Multi-family Stone William Watson Jr.	

Other Info: Probably buried here. She was the daughter of Daniel Perrow and his first wife, and the sister of Guerrant Perrow who is also buried in this cemetery.

Watson Mary Ann Foster	about 1818 9 Aug. 1889	Multi-family Stone George E. Watson	

Inscription: Etched fieldstone: MAW

Other Info: Has a temporary marker. She was the daughter of William and Mary Foster.

Watson Mary Spencer	about 1775 about 1853	Multi-family Stone George E. Watson	

Other Info: She is believed to be buried here. Has a temporary marker.

Watson William Joseph	6 Nov. 1859 5 June 1928	Multi-family Stone Nannie Elizabeth Pattie Walker Lucado Watson	

Other Info: Has a temporary marker. Original headstone moved to Pleasant Grove Baptist Church in the 1990s. His parents were George E. Watson and Mary Foster Watson also buried in this cemetery.

Watson William Jr.	1786 1812/1820	Multi-family Stone Makey/Meekie Perrow Watson	

Other Info: Known to be buried here. Son of William Watson Sr. and Fanny Wilkinson Watson also buried in this cemetery.

Last Name Given Name (Maiden Name)	Date of Birth Date of Death Age at Death	Spouse	Tombstone
Watson William Sr.	1775 1844 (or 1846)	yes; also Multi-family Stone Fannie Wilkinson Watson	

Inscription: VA Militia, Rev. War.

Other Info: He and his wife were the parents of James Watson, William Watson Jr., George E. Watson, Nancy William Watson Perrow, and Carolline Watson Spencer all buried in this cemetery, and Wilkinson Watson (1782-about. 1870), Thomas Gal Watson (1795-about 1859) and Powhatan Watson (1797-after 1850). DAR medallion placed in 2002 by Idalyn Stinson, wife of a descendant.

| Webb
Elizabeth | | | no |

Inscription: Etched fieldstone: Elizabeth Webb, Feb. 1864

| Webb
Mary Ana Perrow | 20 May 1823
about 1908 | Multi-family Stone
Robert P. Webb | |

Inscription: Etched fieldstone: MPW

Other Info: Has a temporary marker. She is the daughter of Guerrant Perrow and Nancy Watson Perrow, also buried in this cemetery.

There are 43 unidentified graves in this cemetery, including "those possibly buried here."

Roberta Watson Grave on Rd. 640

| Watson
Roberta | 19 Aug. 1922
23 Aug. 1922 | | yes |

Inscription: Daughter of W.L. and E.H. Watson

Last Name Given Name (Maiden Name)	Date of Birth Date of Death Age at Death	Spouse	Tombstone

West Family off Rd. 649 — African American

Bradshaw Sarah W.	 7 Oct. 1957		no

Other Info: L.C. Gray Funeral Home marker

West Ernest	1891 1947	 Mary M. West	yes

Inscription: Father; Rest in Peace

Other Info: Note: Mary M. West has a tombstone with birth date inscribed (1893), but she is buried at Slate River Baptist Church cemetery.

West W.S., (Solomon) Rev.	28 Sept. 1860 7 March 1933		yes

Inscription: Gone but not Forgotten

Other Info: Footstone: WSW

There are 2 unidentified graves in this cemetery.

J. Y. Wheeler Grave on Rd. 652

Wheeler J. Y.	29 May 1833 20 Dec. 1920		yes

Whitlow-Hardiman Familly off Rd. 1008

Hardiman Hattie Louise	19 Nov. 1938 19 Oct. 1939		yes

Other Info: She was the granddaughter of William Johnson Whitlow and Annie Richards Whitlow.

Whitlow Annie Richards	7 Jan. 1876 9 May 1963	 William Johnson Whitlow	yes

Last Name	Date of Birth	Spouse	Tombstone
Given Name	Date of Death		
(Maiden Name)	Age at Death		

Whitlow Nannie P.	14 Dec. 1846 3 Dec. 1929		no

Other Info: Known to be buried here.

Whitlow Thomas Percy	22 June 1903 11 April 1949		no

Other Info: Known to be buried here.

Whitlow William Johnson	6 Aug. 1872 11 Aug. 1948	Annie Richards Whitlow	yes

There are 12 unidentified graves in this cemetery including those known to be buried here.

James Whorley Family on Rd. 749

Hellard babies	 3 Dec. 1929		yes

Other Info: There are triplets buried here. These were children of Mable and Fred Hellard.

Hellard Fred. W. Sr.	6 Oct. 1886 26 Feb. 1951	Mable A. Whorley Hellard	yes

Inscription: In God's Care

Other Info: Shares a headstone with his wife. Footstone: Father

Hellard Mable A. (Whorley)	30 Sept. 1896 5 Dec. 1929	Fred W. Hellard Sr.	yes

Inscription: In God's Care

Other Info: Shares a headstone with her husband. Footstone: Mother; She was the daughter of James L. and Jennie W. Whorley.

Last Name Given Name (Maiden Name	Date of Birth Date of Death Age at Death	Spouse	Tombstone
Hellard young child	17 Jan. 1924		yes

Other Info: This was the child of Mabel and Fred Hellard.

| Whorley
James L. (Shoemaker) | 4 Jan. 1875
1 March 1967 | (1) Jennie (or Emily) Whorley Whorley
(2) Lillian Lovings Whorley | yes |

Inscription: Our Father; In God's Care

Other Info: Footstone: Father   He was born James L. Shumaker. According to family tradition, by his wife's request, at their marriage, he took her name rather than she take his.

| Whorley
Jennie (Emily) W. (Whorley) | 1877
1911 | James L. (Shoemaker) Whorley | yes |

Inscription: In Memory of Mother; Resting till the resurrection

Other Info: Footstone: JWW

| Whorley
Jennie Rebecca | 29 July 1972
7 Aug. 1972 | | yes |

Inscription: I pray the Lord my soul to keep.

Other Info: She was the daughter of Darlene Whorley and the great-granddaughter of James. L. Whorley.

| Whorley
John B. | 6 Dec. 1908
4 Feb. 1986 | | yes |

Inscription: Father

Other Info: He was the son of James L. and Jennie W. Whorley.

Last Name	Date of Birth	Spouse	Tombstone
Given Name	Date of Death		
(Maiden Name	Age at Death		

Whorley   13 Sept. 1900   yes
  William W. (Whitcomb) Sr.   1 Feb. 1963

  Inscription: Gone, but not Forgotten

  Other Info: Footstone: Father   He was the son of James L. and Jennie
    W. Whorley.

: LOA) DP LO RII 5 G. 607 ² $ I LFDQ $ P HLFDQ

Allen   no
  Abraham   Olivia Allen

  Other Info: Ashes known to be buried here.

Allen   no
  Olivia   Abraham Allen

  Other Info: Ashes known to be buried here.

Jones   16 Oct. 1916   yes
  James Robert   12 May 1998

  Inscription: US Army, World War II

  Other Info: Has a Reids Funeral Home marker.

Wiley   1904   no
  Lillie Wright   1994   Paul Wiley

  Other Info: This is an above ground vault: West FH

Wiley   1881   no
  Paul   1973   Lillie Wright Wiley

  Other Info: West Funeral Home marker

Last Name Given Name (Maiden Name	Date of Birth Date of Death Age at Death	Spouse	Tombstone

Wilkinson Family off Rd. 610

| Wilkinson
Susan Toney | about 1745
after 1844 | William Wilkinson | no |

Other Info: Known to be buried here.

| Wilkinson
William | 1745
1823 | Susan Toney Wilkinson | yes |

Inscription: PVt 6, VA Regt., Rev. War

There at least 18 unidentified graves in this cemetery.

Wise Family on "Dixie Hill Road"

| Wise
Mary Bryant | 5 April 1871
27 March 1923 | | yes |

Inscription: Gone but not forgotten; By: Husband and Children

| Wise
Missouria | 7 Aug. 1906
12 Feb. 1925 | | yes |

Inscription: By The Family

Wood-Golladay Family on Rd. 605

| Cobb
Sidney Ross Jr. | 19 March 1921
24 Aug. 1924 | | yes |

Inscription: Our darling; Our loved one

| Galladay
Emma (L.) Payne | 5 April 1861
22 Dec. 1928 | Josiah F. Galladay | yes |

Inscription: At Rest, Mother: She was a kind and affectionate wife and a fond mother and a friend to all.

Other Info: Footstone: EPG

Last Name Given Name (Maiden Name)	Date of Birth Date of Death Age at Death	Spouse	Tombstone
Galladay Isaac M.	15 Jan. 1846 17 Jan. 1914		yes

Other Info: Footstone: IMG

Galloday Josiah F.	19 May 1852 27 April 1925	yes Emma L. Payne Galloday	

Inscription: At Rest, Husband and Father; Married to Emma L. Payne, March 24, 1886

Other Info: Footstone: JFG

Golladay Mamie C.	26 Nov. 1893 29 March 1922		yes

Inscription: At Rest; Loved by all who knew her

Golladay Mattie Burks	14 May 1858 6 Oct. 1953		yes

Inscription: She was the sunshine of our home.

Other Info: Footstone: MBG She was the mother of Lillian Golladay Wood also buried in this cemetery.

Golladay Samuel M.	1 Nov. 1900 19 March 1954		yes

Inscription: Virginia, PFC, Co. F, 118 Engineers, World War I; PH & OLC

Hughes Archie C.	2 Feb. 1902 12 Feb. 1984	yes Nell G. Hughes	

Inscription: In God's Care

Other Info: Shares a headstone with his wife. He has a Robinson Funeral Home marker.

Last Name Given Name (Maiden Name)	Date of Birth Date of Death Age at Death	Spouse	Tombstone
Hughes Nell G.	30 March 1897 10 May 1990	Archie C. Hughes	yes

Inscription: In God's Care

Other Info: She shares a headstone with her husband.

Jackson Joseph "Joe"	26 March 1912 2 Feb. 1982		yes
Miller Lessie Gertrude	22 Jan. 1918 19 Nov. 1922		yes

Inscription: How hard we tried to save her. Our prayers were all in vain. Happy angels came and took her, from this world of pain.

Other Info: Footstone: LGM

Wood Lillian Golladay	28 July 1886 27 Nov. 1975	W.A. (Pomp) Wood	yes
Wood W. A. (Pomp)	2 Aug. 1889 8 Apr. 1980	Lillian Golladay Wood	yes

Woodland Methodist Church

Adcock Berdie Ragland	8 June 1875 29 March 1956	Willie Henry Adcock	yes

Other Info: Shares a headstone with her husband.

Adcock Lula Dolan	7 Feb. 1909 (not inscribed)	Thomas Gilmore Adcock	yes

Inscription: Gone but not Forgotten

Adcock Thomas Gilmore	1904 1974	Lula Dolan Adcock	yes

Inscription: Gone but not Forgotten

Last Name Given Name (Maiden Name)	Date of Birth Date of Death Age at Death	Spouse	Tombstone
Adcock 　Willie Henry	14 Feb. 1873 17 Sept. 1964	Berdie Ragland Adcock	yes

Other Info: Shares a headstone with his wife.

Bailey 　John		Grace Florence Gunter Bailey	yes

Inscription: (no dates)

Beasley 　Leonard Julian	3 Jan. 1915 13 Aug. 1938		yes

Inscription: Gone but not Forgotten

Beasley 　Nannie G.	1 June 1892 15 Nov. 1980	Royal Oscar Beasley	yes

Inscription: Mother; Gone but not Forgotten

Other Info: She and her husband are the parents of Percy O. Beasley with whom they share a headstone.

Beasley 　Percy O.	7 Aug. 1907 6 Oct. 1972		yes

Inscription: Son; Gone but not Forgotten

Other Info: His parents were Royal Oscar and Nannie G. Beasley with whom he shares a headstone.

Beasley 　Royal Oscar	1 Jan. 1876 4 Oct. 1947	Nannie G. Beasley	yes

Inscription: Father; Gone but not Forgotten

Other Info: He and his wife are the parents of Percy O. Beasley with whom they share a headstone.

Berbey 　Charles Curtis	9 June 1946 8 Dec. 1984		yes

Inscription: US Navy, Vietnam

Last Name Given Name (Maiden Name	Date of Birth Date of Death Age at Death	Spouse	Tombstone
Branch Alice E. (Estelle)	12 Feb. 1912 9 Dec. 1992	William Franklin Branch	yes

Inscription: God is Love

Other Info: Shares a headstone with her husband.

Branch Annie B. (Branch)	29 June 1914 30 Jan. 1991	Richard Emery Branch	yes

Other Info: Footstone: Mother; Shares a headstone with her husband.

Branch (baby)			yes

Inscription: Branch Baby

Branch Chastity Ann	1990 1990		yes

Other Info: Parents are Jo Ann and Kevin Branch.

Branch Clarence F. (Franklin)	4 Sept 1911 11 March 1964		yes

Other Info: Shares a headstone with his parents.

Branch Cornel Buford	11 April 1905 5 Feb. 1974	Eliza Kate Beasley Branch	yes

Inscription: Precious Lord Take my Hand; Married 19 Sept. 1934

Other Info: Shares a headstone with his wife.

Branch Eliza (Kate) Beasley	3 Jan. 1917 3 Aug. 2000	Cornel Buford Branch	yes

Inscription: Precious Lord Take my Hand; Married 19 Sept 1934

Other Info: Shares a headstone with her husband.

Last Name Given Name (Maiden Name)	Date of Birth Date of Death Age at Death	Spouse	Tombstone
Branch Eliza Wilkerson	20 Sept. 1935 23 June 1963	Willie Branch Jr.	yes

Inscription: Gone but not Forgotten

Other Info: Footstone: Mother. Her children are Roger, Elaine and Barry Branch.

Branch Essie	21 Aug. 1901 6 April 1988		yes

Inscription: Beyond the sunset

Other Info: Her parents were John Alley Branch and Laura M. Ragland

Branch Fitz D. (Douglas)	21 May 1897 10 Dec. 1969	Mary Bessie Ragland Taylor Branch	yes

Other Info: Shares a headstone with his wife.

Branch Florence Lee (Taylor)	21 Sept. 1898 14 June 1977	George Freddy Branch	yes

Inscription: Gone but not Forgotten

Other Info: Shares a headstone with her husband. Her parents were James Thomas and Minnie M. Taylor also buried in this cemetery.

Branch Franklin O.	21 May 1938 5 June 1959		yes

Other Info: His parents were Wm. F and Alice E. Branch also buried in this cemetery.

Branch George F. (Freddy)	23 June 1903 22 Oct. 1980	Florence Lee Taylor Branch	yes

Inscription: Gone but not Forgotten

Other Info: Shares a headstone with his wife.

Last Name Given Name (Maiden Name	Date of Birth Date of Death Age at Death	Spouse	Tombstone
Branch Kate Louise	3 Feb. 1916 9 Sept 1983		yes
Branch Mary B. (Bessie Ragland)	4 June 1887 22 July 1970	 (1) James Allen Taylor (2) Fitz Douglas Branch	yes

Other Info: Shares a headstone with her second husband.

Branch Mildred A.	17 June 1905 9 July 1970	 William A. Branch	yes
Branch Moses P. (Perkins)	12 March 1881 16 Feb. 1957	 Ora Lee Wilkerson Branch	yes

Other Info: Shares a headstone with his wife and son.

Branch Nathaniel Alverton	1 April 1909 15 March 1993		no

Other Info: Has a Wells-Sheffield Funeral Home marker.

Branch Ora L. (Lee Wilkerson)	12 Oct. 1892 3 Dec. 1935	 Moses Perkins Branch	yes

Other Info: Shares a headstone with her husband and son.

Branch Pauline T. (Taylor)	28 March 1913 23 May 1945		yes

Inscription: Gone but not Forgotten

Branch Richard Douglas	25 May 1941 21 Sept. 1984		yes
Branch Richard E. (Emery)	7 July 1920 20 July 1988	 Annie Branch Branch	yes

Other Info: Footstone: Father; Shares a headstone with his wife.

Branch William A.	10 Jan. 1871 2 April 1959	 Mildred A. Branch	yes

Last Name Given Name (Maiden Name)	Date of Birth Date of Death Age at Death	Spouse	Tombstone

Branch 13 April 1907 yes
   William F. (Franklin) 9 Aug. 1988   Alice Estelle Branch

   Inscription: God is Love

   Other Info: Shares a headstone with his wife.

Bryant 1914 yes
   Birdie B. (Branch) 1965   George Dewey Bryant

   Inscription: Resting in Peace

   Other Info: Shares a headstone with her husband.

Bryant 1899 yes
   George D. (Dewey) 1965   Birdie Branch Bryant

   Inscription: Resting in Peace

   Other Info: Shares a headstone with his wife.

Bryant 1940 yes
   George D. (Dewey) Jr. 1965

Clark 1911 yes
   Virginia Lee 1932

Crews 11 Dec. 1860 yes
   J. P. 1 Oct. 1931

   Inscription: Gone but not Forgotten

Cunningham 15 Oct. 1867 yes
   George W. 7 Jan. 1955   Laura Moore
                                           Cunningham

   Inscription: His memory is blessed; Erected by Daughter Carrie M.
      Hughes. Shares a headstone with his wife and son.

   Other Info: Footstone: Father; Shares a headstone with his wife, and
      his son, Kemper Cunningham.

Last Name Given Name (Maiden Name)	Date of Birth Date of Death Age at Death	Spouse	Tombstone
Cunningham Infant Daughter	18 Nov. 1942 1942		yes

Inscription: Infant Daughter of Joseph and Nannie Cunningham

Cunningham Jack Walker	8 May 1905 18 Jan. 1929		yes

Cunningham Kemper M.	16 Apr. 1918 3 Jan. 1986		yes

Other Info: Shares a headstone with his parents, George and Laura Cunningham.

Cunningham Laura Moore	4 Sept 1876 26 Jan. 1947	George W. Cunningham	yes

Inscription: A devoted wife and mother; Erected by Daughter Carrie M. Hughes. Shares a headstone with her husband and son.

Other Info: Footstone: Mother; She and her husband share a headstone with their son, Kemper Cunningham. They are also the parents of Martha C. Watts who is buried in this cemetery.

Cunningham Minnie Laura	12 March 1909 17 June 1929		yes

Other Info: Footstone: MLC

Cunningham Reese G.	17 Feb. 1903 8 July 1986		yes

Inscription: PVT, US Army, World War II

Davis Noah Louis "Dave"	12 July 1932 16 Dec. 2004		no

Other Info: Wells-Sheffield Funeral home marker

Last Name Given Name (Maiden Name)	Date of Birth Date of Death Age at Death	Spouse	Tombstone
Davis Wyomma Ragland	18 Aug. 1946 10 Aug. 2003	Charles L. Davis	yes

    Other Info: Wyomma Ragland and Charles L. Davis were married 14 June 1969. Her parents, Rolfe and Louise Ragland, sister, Louise Marie and brother, Norman Loving Ragland are also buried in this cemetery.

Dolan Cabell Odell	7 April 1914 15 June 1984		yes
Dolan Edna Smith	16 April 1908 24 Sept. 1980		yes
Dolan Lula Mildred	1874 1958	William Oswell Dolan	yes

    Inscription: Beloved, how we miss you.

Dolan Melvin Douglas	28 Aug. 1931 28 Aug. 1931		yes
Dolan Percy P.	11 Dec. 1894 27 Feb. 1970		yes
Dolan William Oswell	1864 1962	Lula Mildred Dolan	yes

    Inscription: Beloved, how we miss you.

    Other Info: He and his wife were the parents of Lula Dolan Adcock and Cabell Odell Dolan, also buried in this cemetery.

Eaves Barbara B. (Beasley)	10 July 1922 21 March 1981		yes

    Inscription: Gone but not Forgotten
    Other Info: Sister to Eliza Branch (living)

Gunter Britney E.	27 Aug. 2001 27 Aug. 2001		yes

    Inscription: David and Courtney's Little Angel

Last Name Given Name (Maiden Name)	Date of Birth Date of Death Age at Death	Spouse	Tombstone
Gunter Charles L (Lightfoot)	16 Aug. 1894 23 Sept. 1963		yes

Inscription: Virginia, Wagoner Sup. Co., 317 Infantry, World War I

Other Info: He is the son of Charles R. and Eliza Webb Gunter, and the brother of Walter C. Gunter who are all buried in this cemetery.

Gunter Charles R.	19 Nov. 1857 27 May 1941	Eliza Webb Gunter	yes

Other Info: He and his wife are the parents of Charles L. Gunter, and Walter C. Gunter also buried in this cemetery. Shares a headstone with his wife.

Gunter Charles W.	9 Jan. 1905 9 Aug. 1979	Lula T. Gunter	yes

Inscription: Not my will but thine be done.

Other Info: Shares a headstone with his wife.

Gunter Clarence Albert	29 Nov. 1892 1 March 1954	Lillian Wilkerson Gunter	yes

Other Info: Footstone: Husband

Gunter Eliza Webb	14 Nov. 1859 16 Aug. 1959	Charles R. Gunter	yes

Other Info: Shares a headstone with her husband.

Gunter Jesse E.	18 March 1882 24 Dec. 1955	Lula Jane Webb Gunter	yes

Inscription: In Memory of Our Father

Other Info: Footstone: Father

Gunter John E.	1832 1870		yes

Inscription: In Memory of; PVT, Co. D, 56th VA Inf. CSA

Last Name Given Name (Maiden Name)	Date of Birth Date of Death Age at Death	Spouse	Tombstone
Gunter Lillian Wilkerson		Clarence Albert Gunter	no

Other Info: Known to be buried here.

Gunter Louise D. (Dooley)	24 June 1909 29 April 1971	Walter C. Gunter	yes

Other Info: Whitten Funeral Home marker; Shares a headstone with her husband.

Gunter Lula Jane (Webb)	10 Nov. 1890 24 Oct. 1937	Jesse E. Gunter	yes

Inscription: In Memory of Our Mother; At Rest

Other Info: Footstone: Mother

Gunter Lula T.	7 June 1902 9 Dec. 1981	Charles W. Gunter	yes

Inscription: Not my will but thine be done.

Other Info: Shares a headstone with her husband.

Gunter Richard B.	1837 1891		yes

Inscription: In Memory of; PVT, Co. D, 56th VA. Inf., Buckingham Yancey Guard, CSA

Other Info: Brother to Thomas J. and John E. Gunter also buried in the cemetery.

Gunter Robert Floyed	31 Dec. 1889 28 March 1949		yes

Inscription: Virginia, F1, US Navy, World War I

Gunter Thomas J.	1835 1910		yes

Inscription: In Memory of; PVT., Co. D, 56 VA Inf, CSA

Last Name Given Name (Maiden Name)	Date of Birth Date of Death Age at Death	Spouse	Tombstone
Gunter Walter C.	6 Jan. 1900 16 Feb. 1988	Louise Dooley Gunter	yes

Other Info: Whitten Funeral Home marker; His brother, Charles Gunter and parents Charles R. and Eliza Webb Gunter are also buried in this cemetery. He shares a headstone with his wife.

Horsley Eugene Hamilton	13 Feb. 1917 19 Dec. 1974		yes
Horsley Percy Clarence	23 May 1913 1 June 1956		yes

Other Info: His brother, Eugene Horsley is also buried in this cemetery.

Jordan Helen Wilkerson	1928 1948		yes
Londeree Charles Ira	25 Oct. 1893 24 June 1946	Mattie Ragland Londeree Wilkerson	no

Other Info: He and his wife were married 3 Aug. 1921. His grave is marked by a fieldstone only.

McCulloch			no

Other Info: Fieldstone etched MR. Known to be buried here: Mr. or Mrs. McCulloch

McCulloch			no

Other Info: Fieldstone: Known to be buried here-Mrs. or Mr. McCulloch

McFadden Airl C.	14 June 1937 4 Jan. 1985	Jeanette M. McFadden	yes
McFadden Christopher Scott	2 Dec. 1973 29 July 2004		no

Other Info: Wells-Sheffield Funeral Home marker

Last Name Given Name (Maiden Name)	Date of Birth Date of Death Age at Death	Spouse	Tombstone
McFadden Eddie Lewis	15 March 1906 22 April 1993	Lillie Burnley McFadden	yes

Inscription: The World's Best Parnets

Other Info: Shares a headstone with his wife.

McFadden Joseph Lewis	24 March 1934 22 Feb. 1998	Betty Brown McFadden	yes

McFadden Lillie Burnley	20 Feb. 1908 15 May 1989	Eddie Lewis McFadden	yes

Inscription: The World's Best Parnets.

Other Info: Shares a headstone with her husband.

Meadow Sarah J.	20 May 1886 24 May 1961	William M. Meadow	yes

Inscription: Peacefully at Rest

Other Info: She and her husband share a headstone. Footstone: SJM

Meadow William M.	25 Dec. 1888 (not inscribed).	Sarah J. Meadow	yes

Inscription: Peacefully at Rest

Other Info: He and his wife share a headstone

Oakley Thomas "Bear"	1913 1990 76 years		yes

Other Info: Thacker Bros. Funeral Home marker

Ragland Albert C.	1874 1962	Sarah A. Ragland	yes

Other Info: Shares a headstone with his wife.

Last Name Given Name (Maiden Name)	Date of Birth Date of Death Age at Death	Spouse	Tombstone
Ragland Albert Lee (Bud)	22 Sept. 1904 7 Oct. 1988	Clara Bell Ragland Ragland	yes

Inscription: Father

Other Info: Shares a headstone with his wife.

| Ragland
Alfred W. | 22 Nov. 1880
6 Feb. 1960 | | yes |

Inscription: Father; Sweetly Sleeping

| Ragland
C. (Clarence) Elwood | 3 July 1913
20 Jan. 1976 | Myrtle Branch Ragland | yes |

Inscription: Nearer My God to Thee

Other Info: Shares a headstone with his wife. They had one son- Waverly Ragland.

| Ragland
Casey W. | 24 Aug. 1910
24 Feb. 1960 | | yes |

Inscription: Virginia, PFC, Co. C, 23rd Armd. Inf. Bn., World War II

Other Info: He received the Bronze Star medal

| Ragland
Clara Bell (Ragland) | 28 May 1908
17 Dec. 1991 | Albert Lee Ragland | yes |

Inscription: Mother

Other Info: Shares a headstone with her husband. Their only child was Robert Lee Ragland. Her parents were Emma and Eddie Ragland.

| Ragland
David W. (Washington) | 7 Aug. 1878
3 Oct. 1964 | Mary Gunter Ragland | yes |

Inscription: Father

Other Info: Footstone: Father; Shares a headstone with his wife and son.

Last Name Given Name (Maiden Name	Date of Birth Date of Death Age at Death	Spouse	Tombstone
Ragland Gertie			no

    Other Info: Known to be buried here.

| Ragland
   James Thomas | 17 April 1896
12 June 1946 |
Elsie Ragland Ragland | yes |

    Other Info: His wife is buried in a cemetery at Scottsville.

| Ragland
   John Rolfe | 6 Oct. 1932
4 July 1992 | | yes |

    Inscription: Silently Sleeping

    Other Info: Footstone: Brother

| Ragland
   Joseph Nicholas | 14 Jan. 1884
17 Dec. 1952 |
Susan Demarius Gunter
Ragland | yes |

    Other Info: Shares a headstone with his wife.

| Ragland
   Lee Gould | 12 March 1917
4 June 1938 | | yes |

    Inscription: Son

    Other Info: Footstone: Son, Shares a headstone with his parents.

| Ragland
   Louise B. | 9 Sept. 1912
31 May 1981 |
Rolfe L. Ragland | yes |

    Inscription: Married 23 Dec. 1930

    Other Info: Footstone: Mother

| Ragland
   Louise Marie | 28 Aug. 1938
30 Aug. 1944 | | yes |

    Inscription: Daughter of Rolfe and Louise Ragland; Asleep with Jesus

    Other Info: Footstone: Daughter

Last Name Given Name (Maiden Name)	Date of Birth Date of Death Age at Death	Spouse	Tombstone
Ragland Maggie May	1899 1955		yes
Ragland Margaret Gay	13 Nov. 1935 27 Nov. 1990		yes

Inscription: Sweetly Sleeping

Other Info: Footstone: Sister

Ragland Mary G. (Gunter)	23 Dec. 1885 30 June 1969	David Washington Ragland	yes

Inscription: Mother

Other Info: Footstone: Mother; Shares a headstone with her husband and son.

Ragland Mildred R.	20 Nov. 1874 3 April 1960	William N. Ragland	yes

Other Info: Shares a headstone with her husband.

Ragland Myrtle B. (Branch)	16 March 1916 18 July 1981	Clarence Elwood Ragland	yes

Inscription: Nearer My God to Thee

Other Info: Shares a headstone with her husband. Her parents were Moses and Ora Wilkerson Branch also buried in this cemetery.

Ragland Nora Ellen	11 Feb. 1866 21 Dec. 1955		yes
Ragland Norman Loving	2 Dec. 1933 15 Nov. 2002		yes

Inscription: Peacefully Sleeping

Other Info: His parents were Rolfe and Louise Ragland. His sisters, Louise Marie Ragland and Wyomma R. Davis are also buried in this cemetery.

Last Name Given Name (Maiden Name	Date of Birth Date of Death Age at Death	Spouse	Tombstone
Ragland Rolfe L.	26 May 1906 9 April 1982	Louise B. Ragland	yes

Inscription: Married 23 Dec. 1930

Other Info: Footstone: Father

Ragland Russell N.	18 Oct. 1901 6 Nov. 1926		yes

Inscription: B.R.T No. 389

Ragland Sarah A.	1877 1956	Albert C. Ragland	yes

Other Info: Shares a headstone with her husband.

Ragland Susan (Demarius) Gunter	25 April 1888 26 July 1975	Joseph Nicholas Ragland	yes

Other Info: Shares a headstone with her husband.

Ragland William N.	25 Dec. 1871 8 July 1848	Mildred R. Ragland	yes

Other Info: Shares a headstone with his wife.

Ragland Wm. Lacy	10 Oct. 1910 14 July 1953	Florence Heath Ragland	yes

Other Info: Footstone: Father

Ripley John E.	24 Jan. 1928 12 Jan. 1929		yes

Other Info: Footstone: JER; His parents were Grover and Ola Ripley. His sister was Helen Ripley Simmons.

Ripley Parris R. (Butch)	5 June 1930 17 Nov. 1996		yes

Inscription: CPL, US Army, Korea

Last Name Given Name (Maiden Name)	Date of Birth Date of Death Age at Death	Spouse	Tombstone
Ripley Virgie Branch	19 Sept. 1905 21 June 1959	Willie Thomas Ripley	yes

Inscription: Of Such is the Kingdom of Heaven

Other Info: She and her husband share a headstone. Footstone: Mother

Ripley Willie Thomas	18 June 1903 13 April 1971	Virgie Branch Ripley	yes

Inscription: Of Such is the Kingdom of Heaven

Other Info: Shares a headstone with his wife.

Simmons Thomas Bolton	14 June 1908 28 Nov. 1937	Helen Ripley Simmons	yes

Inscription: In Loving Memory

Other Info: Footstone: TBS; He and his wife were the parents of Thomas M. Simmons, also buried in this cemetery.

Simmons Thomas M.	29 Feb. 1936 22 Nov. 1936		yes

Other Info: Footstone: TMS

Smith Gladys Totty	14 Sept. 1912 20 March 1984		yes

Inscription: Mother; At Peace

Smith Jane Finley	24 April 1872 17 Feb. 1929	John Emitt Smith	yes
Smith John Emitt	13 Nov. 1875 14 Oct. 1932	Jane Finley Smith	yes
Smith Russell P.	27 June 1945 17 Sept. 1948		yes

Inscription: Son of John and Jane (Smith)

Last Name Given Name (Maiden Name)	Date of Birth Date of Death Age at Death	Spouse	Tombstone
Spears Carrie T. (Taylor)	28 April 1904 20 June 1998	Frank E. Spears	yes

Inscription: Not my will but thine be done.

Other Info: Shares a headstone with her husband. Her sister was Florence Lee Taylor Branch also buried in this cemetery.

Spears Frank E.	15 Sept. 1900 6 April 1978	Carrie Taylor Spears	yes

Inscription: Not my will but thine be done.

Other Info: Shares a headstone with his wife.

Sutton Diane Yvonne Haynes	Oct. 1953 Mar. 2000		no

Sutton Otho M (Mills)	24 April 1901 31 May 1983	Ressie Ragland Sutton	no

Inscription: Married 21 April 1921

Other Info: Footstone: Husband; Shares a headstone with his wife. They are the parents of Winifred Mills Sutton also buried in this cemetery.

Sutton Ressie R. (Ragland)	1 April 1902 11 Dec. 1994	Otho Mills Sutton	yes

Inscription: Married 21 April 1921

Other Info: Footstone: Wife; Shares a headstone with her husband. Her parents David W. and Mary G. Ragland, are also buried in this cemetery.

Sutton Winifred Mills	6 Sept. 1928 17 Sept. 1928		yes

Inscription: Asleep in Jesus

Other Info: Her parents were Otho and Ressie Sutton also buried in this cemetery.

Last Name Given Name (Maiden Name)	Date of Birth Date of Death Age at Death	Spouse	Tombstone
Swan Gracie T.	28 April 1922 21 March 1994	William E. Swan	yes

Inscription: Mother

Taylor Bessie Wilkerson	23 Dec. 1900 26 Aug. 1967		yes

Taylor Charlie Lee	14 Feb. 1881 8 Jan. 1942	Minnie Branch Taylor	yes

Other Info: Shares a headstone with his wife.

Taylor Christopher T.	15 Sept. 1914 6 April 1995	Ruby Davis Taylor	yes

Inscription: Gone but not Forgotten

Other Info: Has a Thacker Bros. Funeral Home marker. Shares a headstone with his wife.

Taylor Christopher T. Jr.	26 Dec. 1936 1 July 1953		yes

Inscription: In God's Care

Taylor Earl Lee	17 July 1908 28 July 1967	Lila Tyree Taylor	yes

Inscription: Together Forever

Other Info: His parents were Mary Bessie Taylor Branch and James Allen Taylor. His brother is Lynn Taylor. He shares a headstone with his wife.

Taylor James Allen	9 Aug. 1883 20 March 1954		yes

Inscription: Gone but not Forgotten

Other Info: Footstone: Father

Last Name Given Name (Maiden Name)	Date of Birth Date of Death Age at Death	Spouse	Tombstone
Taylor James Thomas	8 Feb. 1875 5 June 1946	Minnie M. Taylor	yes

Inscription: Gone but not Forgotten

| Taylor
Leslie Wilson | 2 Jan. 1927
20 June 1970 | | yes |

Other Info: His mother was Bessie Wilkerson Taylor also buried in this cemetery.

| Taylor
Lila Tyree | 14 Aug. 1918
9 April 2001 | Earl Lee Taylor | yes |

Inscription: Together Forever

Other Info: Shares a headstone with her husband.

| Taylor
Minnie Branch | 17 Sept. 1887
10 March 1974 | Charlie Lee Taylor | yes |

Other Info: Shares a headstone with her husband.

| Taylor
Minnie M. | 28 Dec. 1877
22 Feb. 1974 | James Thomas Taylor | yes |

Inscription: Gone but not Forgotten

| Taylor
Nannie Cora | 3 Sept. 1969
84 years | | no |

Other Info: Known to be buried here.

| Taylor
Ruby D. (Davis) | 22 June 1919
31 July 2002 | Christopher T. Taylor | yes |

Inscription: Gone but not Forgotten

Other Info: Shares a headstone with her husband.

| Taylor
Wiley Haskins | 26 March 1886
27 March 1948 | | yes |

Last Name Given Name (Maiden Name)	Date of Birth Date of Death Age at Death	Spouse	Tombstone
Walker William S.	20 May 1926 5 March 1985	Unice Adcock Walker	yes

Inscription: SM2, US Navy, World War II

Watts Martha Coreene	13 Nov. 1915 27 Dec. 1993	Robert Edwin Watts	yes

Inscription: Gone but not Forgotten

Other Info: Has a Hill Funeral Home marker

Watts Robert Edwin	12 April 1914 31 Dec. 1951	Martha Coreene Watts	yes

Inscription: Gone but not Forgotten

Whorley George Thomas	5 Dec. 1920 25 Nov. 1983	Kate Taylor Whorley	yes
Wilkerson Alma R.	8 Oct. 1908 4 Dec. 2000	Jessee Herman Wilkerson	yes
Wilkerson Annie Taylor	1885 1970		yes
Wilkerson Camm	2 Jan. 1906 20 Feb. 1970	Lottie Ragland Wilkerson	yes

Other Info: Shares a headstone with his wife. They were the parents of Shirley Lee and William Joel Wilkerson, all buried in this cemetery.

Wilkerson Clearnce (Clarence) O.	8 Sept. 1912 27 June 1954	Mattie Ragland Wilkerson	yes (handcarved)
Wilkerson Devin James "Chunkmunk"	27 March 2000 2 March 2001		yes

Other Info: Grandson of James John Wilkerson also buried in this cemetery.

Last Name Given Name (Maiden Name)	Date of Birth Date of Death Age at Death	Spouse	Tombstone
Wilkerson Edward Camm	22 Feb. 1925 31 Jan. 1965		yes

Inscription: Gone but not Forgotten

Other Info: Footstone: Son

Wilkerson James John	16 May 1923 31 May 1991		yes

Inscription: US Army, World War II, Gone but not Forgotten

Wilkerson Jessee Herman	1904 1964	Alma R. Wilkerson	yes
Wilkerson Lottie Ragland	11 Sept. 1908 14 March 1989	Camm Wilkerson	yes

Other Info: Shares a headstone with her husband.

Wilkerson Mattie R. (Ragland)	1900 1958	(l) Charles Ira Londeree (2) Clarence O. Wilkerson	

Other Info: McHill Funeral Home marker

Wilkerson Samuel Cole	1896 1953		yes
Wilkerson Shirley Lee	19 June 1938 20 July 1980		yes

Inscription: Gone but not Forgotten

Wilkerson Wallace Herman	1940 1965		yes
Wilkerson William Joel	1 Jan. 1932 11 Sept. 1983		yes

Inscription: PVT, US Army, Korea

Last Name Given Name (Maiden Name)	Date of Birth Date of Death Age at Death	Spouse	Tombstone
Wood 　Minnie Lee	10 June 1929 30 April 1986		yes

　　Other Info: Has a Woody's Funeral Home marker

Woody 　Carl Gene	1959 1959		no

　　Other Info: McHill Funeral Home marker; His mother is Lois L. Woody and his grandparents were Mattie R and Charles Londeree also buried in this cemetery.

Woody 　Lois L.	11 Sept. 1929 5 July 1971	Otha E. Woody	yes

　　Inscription: Mother

Woody 　Otha Edward	29 Dec. 1918 8 Jan. 1993	Lois L. Woody	yes

　　Inscription: US Army, World War II

Wooten 　Albert Hayes	23 May 1950 24 July 1993		yes

　　Inscription: Beyond the Sunset

Wooten 　Wayne Lee	25 March 1946 29 Sept. 1985		yes

　　Inscription: Our Loved One

　　Other Info: His father is Herman Sizer Wooten.

Wootten 　George W. (Washington)	4 April 1906 16 May 1979	Lila Ragland Wootten	yes

　　Other Info: Footstone: Father

There are 21 unidentified graves in this cemetery.

Last Name	Date of Birth	Spouse	Tombstone
Given Name	Date of Death		
(Maiden Name)	Age at Death		

Cubie Woodson Family on US 20 — African American

Taylor   3 Jan. 1906   yes
   James H.   3 May 1956

   Inscription: Rest in Peace

   Other Info: Footstone: Husband

Woodson   yes
   Adline   11 Aug. 1929
                      58 years

   Inscription: Gone but not Forgotten

   Other Info: Footstone: AW

There are 13 unidentified graves in this cemetery.

Wooldridge Family off Rd. 662

Wooldridge   5 Nov. 1858   yes
   (Ann Elizabeth Jones) 13 Oct. 1936 James Wooldridge

   Inscription: Mother

   Other Info: Shares a headstone with her husband. She was the daughter of Rebecca Ann Kitchen Jones Slocum. She was the mother of Mary Roberta Wooldridge Kyle who is buried at the Alvis/Coleman/Booker Cemetery.

Wooldridge   6 July 1858   yes
   (James)   16 Aug. 1944 Ann Elizabeth Jones
                                           Wooldridge

   Inscription: Father

   Other Info: Shares a headstone with his wife.

Last Name Given Name (Maiden Name	Date of Birth Date of Death Age at Death	Spouse	Tombstone
Wooldridge James Henry			yes

Inscription: (no dates)

| Wooldridge
John G. | 31 July 1861
11 Dec. 1961 | | yes |

Other Info: Unidentified funeral home marker: John Granderson Wooldridge

| Wooldridge
William Louis | | | yes |

Inscription: (no dates)

Wright-Allen Family on Rd. 604 — African American

| Allen
Billie | | | no |

Other Info: Known to be buried here. He was a half-brother of Sallie Allen Wright.

| Allen
Jimmy | | | no |

Other Info: Known to be buried here. He was the brother of Sallie Allen Wright.

| Allen
Wesley | | | no |

Other Info: Known to be buried here. He was the brother of Sallie Allen Wright.

| Davis
Bob | | | no |

Other Info: Known to be buried here. He was not related to the Wright-Allen family, but his family owned the land on which the cemetery is located at the time of the burials.

Last Name Given Name (Maiden Name	Date of Birth Date of Death Age at Death	Spouse	Tombstone
McCoy Nannie Allen			no

    Other Info: Known to be buried here. She was the sister of Sallie Allen Wright.

Robertson Docia Allen			no

    Other Info: Known to be buried here. She was the sister of Sallie Allen Wright.

Wright Ben		Sallie Allen Wright	no

    Other Info: Known to be buried here.

Wright Sallie Allen	about 1937	Ben Wright	no

    Other Info: Known to be buried here.

There are 15 unidentified graves (8 known to be buried here) in this cemetery.

Charlie Wright Family on Rd. 604 – African American

McAllister Daisy Wright	30 June 1908 13 June 1985		yes

    Other Info: Has a West Funeral Home marker. She was a daughter of Charlie Wright.

McAllister Lawrence E.	18 March 1906 25 March 1956		yes

    Inscription: New York, STM 3, World War II

Last Name Given Name (Maiden Name	Date of Birth Date of Death Age at Death	Spouse	Tombstone
McDaniel Estelle (Wright)	1937 1999		yes

Other Info: She was a daughter of Charlie Wright.

Thomas Marion (Wright)	7 Dec. 1913 11 April 1950	Robert Thomas	yes

Other Info: Footstone: MT, 1913-1950 She was a daughter of Charlie Wright.

Thomas Robert	31 Dec. 1902 6 Aug. 1965	Marion Wright Thomas	yes
Thompson Ada Wright	15 Sept. 1909 2 June 1983		yes

Inscription: Mother

Other Info: She was a daughter of Charlie Wright.

Wright Charlie	14 Oct. 1883 30 Jan. 1960		yes

Other Info: Footstone: Father.

Wright Estelle N.	2 Feb. 1891 18 Nov. 1960		yes

Other Info: Footstone: Mother

Wright Harry B.	9 June 1918 28 Feb. 1984		yes

Inscription: PVT, US Army, World War II

Other Info: Has a West Funeral Home marker. He was a son of Charlie Wright.

Last Name	Date of Birth	Spouse	Tombstone
Given Name	Date of Death		
(Maiden Name)	Age at Death		

| Wright | 2 Jan. 1946 | | yes |
| Harry Jr. | 8 July 1994 | | |

Inscription: US Navy, Vietnam

Other Info: He was the son of Harry B. Wright also buried in this cemetery.

| Wright | 18 March 1919 | | yes |
| Irene L. | 6 April 2001 | Lawton V. Wright| |

Other Info: Shares a headstone with her husband.

| Wright | 15 June 1911 | | yes |
| James S. (Shirley) | 7 Sept. 2001 | | |

Inscription: TEC 5, US Army, World War II

Other Info: Has a Reids Funeral Home marker. He was a son of Charlie Wright.

| Wright | 24 Jan. 1916 | | yes |
| Lawton V. | 16 July 1991 | Irene L. Wright | |

Other Info: Shares a headstone with his wife. He was a son of Charlie Wright.

Young-Moseley Family on Rd. 678 — African American

| Baldwin | 25 Oct. 1927 | | yes |
| Katherine Young | 8 Dec. 2000 | | |

Other Info: Has a Reids Funeral Home marker. Her aunt, Florence A. Young is also buried in this cemetery.

Moseley			no
Florence	infant		
	2 months		

Other Info: Known to be buried here. She was the daughter of Charlie and Maria Moseley and the granddaughter of Florence A. Young.

Last Name Given Name (Maiden Name)	Date of Birth Date of Death Age at Death	Spouse	Tombstone
Young Florence	18 June 1891 10 June 1988	(1) Willie Patterson (2) Jordon Young.	yes

Inscription: In Loving Memory

Other Info: Also has a Thacker Bros. Funeral Home marker: Florence A. Young, age 96 years. Her brother, George Young and her niece, Katherine Young Baldwin are also buried in this cemetery.

| Young
George | 1893
1974 | Isabel M. Young | yes |

Other Info: Shares a headstone with his wife. Also has a Reids Funeral Home marker. He was the brother of Florence A. Young.

| Young
Isabel M. | 1907
1999 | George Young | yes |

Other Info: Shares a headstone with her husband.

There are 21 unidentified graves (including one known to be buried here) in this cemetery.

Zions Baptist Church — African American

Ayers John Stephen	1882 1962		yes
Ayers John William	1909 1936		yes
Ayers Lucy H.	12 Aug 1885 14 Jan 1983		yes

Inscription: Mother

| Ayers
William Billy | 1913
1992 | | no |

Other Info: This is an above ground vault: Reids FH

Last Name Given Name (Maiden Name	Date of Birth Date of Death Age at Death	Spouse	Tombstone
Ayres Amanda	1852 1945		yes

Inscription: In Loving Memory; Mother

Ayres Jessie	1872 13 Feb. 1917		yes
Baker Agnes Pearl	23 Jan. 1902 9 June 1996		no

Other Info: This is an above ground vault: Reids FH

Baker Frank R.	1901 1989		no

Other Info: This is an above ground vault-Reids FH

Baker Irene Florence	24 May 1923 1 March 1997		no

Other Info: Has an above ground vault: Reids FH

Baker James Erwin	6 June 1916 7 May 1984		yes

Inscription: CPL, US Army, World War II

Baker Johnnie	24 Nov. 1928 8 Aug. 1992		yes

Inscription: In Loving Memory

Baker Leonard	21 Sept. 1925 17 Aug. 1999		yes

Inscription: PFC, US Army, World War II

Other Info: Also has an above ground vault: Reids FH. His brother, Milton Baker is also buried in this cemetery.

Last Name Given Name (Maiden Name)	Date of Birth Date of Death Age at Death	Spouse	Tombstone
Baker Lucy E.	14 Nov. 1919 8 May 1988		yes

Inscription: Mother

Other Info: Reids Funeral Home marker gives her name as Lucy W. Baker.

Baker Milton	18 April 1923 22 May 1982		yes

Inscription: TEC 4, US Army, World War II

Other Info: Brother of Leonard Baker also buried in this cemetery.

Baker Richard Sr.	15 Feb. 1910 23 Dec. 1975		yes

Other Info: Has an Allen Funeral Home marker.

Baker Sully D.	1940 2003		no

Other Info: Bland-Reid Funeral Home marker

Baker Thomas W.	14 Nov. 1922 20 March 1973		yes

Inscription: Virginia, PVT, World War II

Baker William E.	1958 2003		no

Other Info: Reids Funeral Home marker.

Barnes Cornelius	1922 1999		no

Other Info: Reids Funeral Home marker

Last Name Given Name (Maiden Name)	Date of Birth Date of Death Age at Death	Spouse	Tombstone
Bartee (David Woodrow) Wilson	19 Oct. 1919 23 Sept 1998	Sis (Inez M.) Bartee	yes

Other Info: Has a Reids Funeral Home marker.

| Bartee
Eleanora B. | 1 Jan. 1900
26 Sept. 1999 | | yes |

Inscription: We Love You Mom

Other Info: Also has an above ground vault: Reids FH

| Bartee
Harvey | 1894
1988 | | yes |

Inscription: US Army, World War I

Other Info: Also has an above ground vault: Reids FH

| Bartee
James | 18 Nov. 1941
27 June 1980 | | yes |

| Bartee
Nathaniel | 1920
1995 | | no |

Other Info: Unidentified funeral home marker

| Bartee
Sis (Inez M.) | 15 Sept. 1921
4 Dec. 1986 | David Woodrow Wilson
Bartee | yes |

Other Info: Has a Reids Funeral Home marker which gives 1985 as the death year.

| Beard
Juston Dashawne | 3 Sept. 1985
23 July 1986 | | no |

Other Info: This is an above ground vault: William M. Bland and Son FH

Last Name Given Name (Maiden Name	Date of Birth Date of Death Age at Death	Spouse	Tombstone
Birch Eric	24 April 1933 22 May 1997		no

Other Info: This is an above gorund vault: Reids FH

Birch Sidney W.	1900 1982		no

Other Info: This is an above ground vault: Reids FH

Boatwright Lewis Cornelius "Neal"	29 Dec. 1968 7 March 2002		no

Other Info: This is an above ground vault: Reids FH

Bolden Bessie Lee	16 Oct. 1891 3 Oct. 1988	Edward Palmer Bolden	yes

Inscription: 2 Timothy 4:7-8

Other Info: Has a Reid's Funeral Home marker.

Bolden Beverly	1939 1976		no

Other Info: Reids Funeral Home marker

Bolden Charlotte E.	4 June 1930 25 Feb. 1987		yes

Inscription: Beloved Mother

Bolden Dora L.	14 Nov. 1882 24 Nov. 1992		no

Other Info: This is an above ground vault: Reids FH

Bolden Earnest E. Sr.	2 April 1938 19 Dec. 2000		yes

Other Info: Has a Reids Funeral Home marker.

Last Name Given Name (Maiden Name)	Date of Birth Date of Death Age at Death	Spouse	Tombstone
Bolden Edward J.	24 Jan. 1915 6 June 1982		yes

Other Info: Has an unidentified funeral home marker which gives the birth year as 1914. His parents, Bessie Lee Bolden and Edward Palmer Bolden, and his brother, John W. Bolden are also buried in this cemetery.

Bolden Edward Palmer	Dec. 1887 20 May 1962	Bessie Lee Bolden	yes

Other Info: He and his wife were the parents of Edward J. and John W. Bolden. James W. Bolden, Phillip L. Bolden, Mary Bolden Giles also buried in this cemetery, were his siblings.

Bolden Franklin Ernest	31 Oct. 1915 7 Oct. 1982		yes

Inscription: PVT, US Army, World War II

Bolden Garfield	1950 1990		no

Other Info: Reids Funeral Home marker

Bolden (James) Randolph	1922 1989		no

Other Info: Reids Funeral Home Marker

Bolden James W.	18 Dec. 1896 11 March 1966		yes

Inscription: Our Beloved Father, In God's Care

Other Info: Also has an above ground vault. He was the brother of Phillip L. Bolden, Edward Palmer Bolden, Mary Bolden Giles all buried in this cemetery, and Alex and John D. Bolden. He was the father of James Randolph, Royal Benjamin, Earnest E. Bolden, Evelyn C. Bolden Carter all buried in this cemetery.

Last Name Given Name (Maiden Name)	Date of Birth Date of Death Age at Death	Spouse	Tombstone
Bolden John Pearson	24 Jan. 1920 24 Feb. 1979		yes

Inscription: STM 1, US Navy, World War II

Bolden John W.	9 Nov. 1913 4 Nov. 1982		yes
Bolden Joseph M.	1915 1977		yes

Other Info: Has a Reids Funeral Home marker.

Bolden Melvin Jerome	27 June 1973 18 Nov. 1995		yes

Inscription: Our darling son

Other Info: Has a Reids Funeral Home marker.

Bolden Phillip L.	30 Jan. 1970 30 Jan. 2000		yes

Other Info: Reid's Funeral Home marker gives birth year as 1968.

Bolden Robert V.	1921 1989		yes

Inscription: US Army, World War II

Other Info: Also has an above ground vault: Reids FH

Bolden Royal B. (Benjamin)	10 March 1927 27 Jan. 2002		yes

Inscription: US Army, Korea

Bolden Saint Luke	27 Apr. 1918 11 Feb. 1983		yes

Other Info: Has a Reids Funeral Home marker

Last Name Given Name (Maiden Name)	Date of Birth Date of Death Age at Death	Spouse	Tombstone
Booker Agnes Beatrice	10 June 1914 15 March 1997		no

Other Info: This is an above ground vault: Reid's FH

Booker Jerry	1902 1986		no

Other Info: This is a Reids Funeral Home marker

Booker Mary E.	1932 2003		no

Other Info: Reids Funeral Home marker

Brown A. C.	4 Jan. 1848 15 April 1930		yes

Inscription: At Rest

Brown Anthony Jesper	15 Sept. 1892 27 July 1942		yes

Inscription: Virginia, PVT, 811 Pioneer Inf., World War I

Brown Arron	1886 1974		yes

Brown Bolden	5 May 1892 21 Dec. 1964		yes

Inscription: New York, PVT, US Army, World War I

Brown Elcy	1860 16 April 1917		yes

Inscription: Faith(ful) in her trust even unto death

Brown Emma W.	1 June 1902 13 June 1965		yes

Inscription: Mother; At Rest

Last Name Given Name (Maiden Name	Date of Birth Date of Death Age at Death	Spouse	Tombstone
Brown Essie B.	2 March 1902 14 Aug. 1976		yes
Brown Garland			no

Other Info: This is an above ground vault with no identification: known to be buried here

Brown George J.	2 Feb. 1865 21 Nov. 1933	Mary V. Brown	yes

Other Info: Shares a headstone with his wife.

Brown George Jordan	18 Oct. 1937 20 Dec. 2003		yes

Inscription: US Army

Other Info: Has also, an above ground vault: Bland-Reid FH

Brown Hattie	1916 1965		yes
Brown James			yes

Inscription: PVT, 1 Cl, 152 Depot Brig., 19 Feb. 1923

Brown James Bolden	16 July 1950 2 June 2001		yes

Inscription: A1C, US Air Force

Other Info: Also has an above ground vault: Reids FH

Brown Julia	1904 1981		no

Other Info: This is an above ground vault.

Last Name Given Name (Maiden Name	Date of Birth Date of Death Age at Death	Spouse	Tombstone
Brown Louis			no

Other Info: This is an above ground vault with no identification: known to be buried here.

| Brown
Martha | | | no |

Other Info: This is an above ground vault with no identification: known to be buried here.

| Brown
Mary V. | 26 May 1870
June 1933 | George J. Brown | yes |

Inscription: Wife; At Rest

Other Info: Shares a headstone with her husband.

| Brown
Minnie P. | 27 Jan. 1947
20 Oct. 1978 | | no |

Other Info: This is an above ground vault: Reids FH; also has a Reids Funeral Home marker which gives her name as Minnie S. Brown

| Brown
Patsy | 8 Sept. 1845
14 July 1927 | | yes |

Inscription: Faithful to her trust even unto death.

| Brown
Randolph | 1909
1971 | | yes |

Inscription: In Memory of; Our Beloved Father, Rest in Peace

Other Info: Has a Reids Funeral Home marker: R. Randolph Brown

| Brown
Ray | | | no |

Other Info: Reids Funeral Home marker with no dates

Last Name Given Name (Maiden Name)	Date of Birth Date of Death Age at Death	Spouse	Tombstone
Brown Royal A.	13 April 1888 18 Oct. 1966		yes

Inscription: Virginia, PFC, US Army, World War I

| Brown
Ruby J. | 10 Sept. 1927
19 Jan. 1994 | | no |

Other Info: This is an above ground vault: Bland-Reid FH.

| Brown
Sandy | | | no |

Other Info: This is an unidentified funeral home marker with one date: 28 Jan. 1970

| Brown
Stephan O. | | | yes |

Inscription: PVT, 90 Aviation Sq, AC; 21 September, 1942

| Brown
Susen | 1885
6 Jan 1919 | | yes |

Inscription: Thy Memory shall be a guiding star in heaven.

| Brown
Thomas | 1901
1975 | | no |

Other Info: Reids Funeral Home marker

| Brown
Thomas H. Jr. | 11 June 1937
5 Aug. 1993 | | yes |

Inscription: Our Heavenly Father

| Brown
Virginia F. | 1915
1987 | | no |

Other Info: This is an above ground vault: Reids FH

Last Name Given Name (Maiden Name)	Date of Birth Date of Death Age at Death	Spouse	Tombstone
Brown William			no

Other Info: This is an above ground vault with no identification: known to be buried here.

Brown William L.	1918 1989		no

Other Info: This is an above ground vault: Reids FH

Brown Wilson	1921 1973		

Other Info: This is an above ground vault.

Cain Alease Allen	2 Mar. 1928 23 Oct. 1998	Maynard E. Cain	yes

Inscription: Beloved Mother; Rest in Peace

Cain Alice			no

Other Info: Known to be buried in this cemetery; Sister of Robert J. Cain also buried in this cemetery; She never married.

Cain Margaret L. (Dean)	1894 1952	Robert J. Cain	yes

Inscription: Rest in Peace

Other Info: Shares a headstone with her husband.

Cain Marguerite F., Deaconess	22 Feb. 1921 11 Dec. 2000	Deacon Alonzo Cain	yes

Inscription: Married 12 Feb. 1943; Given by the children: Alonzo Jr., Odis, and William

Other Info: Has a Reids Funeral Home marker.

Last Name Given Name (Maiden Name	Date of Birth Date of Death Age at Death	Spouse	Tombstone
Cain Mary Alma	31 July 1927 15 March 1929		yes

Inscription: Our Sister

Cain Maynard E.	8 Apr. 1932 15 Nov. 1968	Alease A. Cain	yes

Inscription: Brother

Other Info: His parents were Robert J. and Margaret L. Dean Cain.

Cain Robert	26 June 1937 13 Jan. 1994		no

Other Info: This is an above ground vault: Reids FH

Cain Robert J.	1891 1977	Margaret L. (Dean) Cain	yes

Inscription: Rest in Peace

Other Info: Shares a headstone with his wife. They are the parents of Maynard Cain who is also buried in this cemetery, and Alonzo, Willy, Warren and James.

Carr Cynthia B.	10 June 1961 8 Nov. 1990		yes

Carter Arnold O.	1954 1973		no

Other Info: Reids Funeral Home marker; also has an above ground vault. His mother was Evelyn C. Bolden Carter.

Carter Evelyn C. Bolden	1926 1987		no

Other Info: Known to be buried in this cemetery.

Last Name Given Name (Maiden Name)	Date of Birth Date of Death Age at Death	Spouse	Tombstone
Carter Gertrude E.	1953 2003		no

Other Info: Reids Funeral Home marker. Her mother was Evelyn Bolden Carter.

Carter James	27 Oct. 1947 7 May 1993		yes

Inscription: We Love You

Other Info: His mother was Evelyn C. Bolden Carter also buried in this cemetery.

Carter Jean T.	1971 1971		no

Other Info: Reids Funeral Home marker

Cox Anna		Arren Cox	no

Other Info: Visible grave; known to be buried here. She was the grandmother of Arthur and Ollie Cox.

Cox Arren		Anna Cox	

Other Info: Reids Funeral Home marker with no dates. He was the brother of Washington Cox and Franklin Cox also buried in this cemetery, and the grandfather of Arthur and Ollie Cox.

Cox Eva J.	18 Oct. 1923 11 Feb. 1993	Arthur Cox	yes

Inscription: In Loving Memory

Other Info: Also has an above ground vault: Reids FH

Cox Franklin			no

Other Info: Known to be buried here

Last Name Given Name (Maiden Name)	Date of Birth Date of Death Age at Death	Spouse	Tombstone
Cox Mattie C.	16 Aug. 1891 3 Jan. 1981	Thomas J. Cox	yes

Inscription: Rest in Peace

Cox Mrs. Willie (Wade)	1912 19_5	Franklin Cox	no

Other Info: This is an above ground vault: Reids FH

Cox Thomas J.	19 July 1889 26 Nov. 1959	Mattie C. Cox	yes

Inscription: Rest in Peace

Other Info: He and his wife are the parents of Ollie and Arthur Cox.

Cox Warren H.			no

Other Info: Reids Funeral Home marker with one date: (August) 1923.

Cox Washington			no

Other Info: Reids Funeral Home marker

Cue Frances	1825 4 April 1926		yes

Cue Gilbert	23 Dec. 1922		yes

Inscription: At Rest

Fisher Selena B. (Brown)	1900 1985		no

Other Info: This is an above ground vault: Bland-Reid FH

Gibson Bolden A.	1864 1931	Eliza W. Gibson	yes

Other Info: Shares a headstone with his wife.

Last Name Given Name (Maiden Name)	Date of Birth Date of Death Age at Death	Spouse	Tombstone
Gibson Clarence Oscar	1947 1982		yes

Inscription: PVT, US Army

Gibson Eliza W.	1866 1946	Bolden A. Gibson	yes

Other Info: Shares a headstone with her husband.

Gibson F.D.	6 Nov. 1822 18 Sept. 1927		yes

Inscription: Holy Bible; Rest soldier rest, Thy war is o'er.

Gibson Giles E.	1905 1978		no

Other Info: This is an above ground vault.

Gibson Maurice Lee	27 March 1984 8 April 1984		yes

Inscription: Infant son of Moses and Martha Gibson

Other Info: Has a Marion Gray Thomas Funeral Home marker

Gibson Nioy	1829 4 May 1903		yes

Inscription: Faith(ful) unto her last, even unto death

Giles Cleveland	23 Apr. 1977	Mary Bolden Giles	yes

Other Info: Shares a headstone with his wife.

Giles Mary B (Bolden)	6 April 1977	Cleveland Giles	yes

Other Info: Shares a headstone with her husband. Has an M.G. Thomas Funeral Home marker.

Last Name Given Name (Maiden Name)	Date of Birth Date of Death Age at Death	Spouse	Tombstone
Grant Sallie L.	1913 1975		yes
Green Allen	25 March 1919 27 Dec. 1984	Edith M. Green	yes

Inscription: Wed 4 July 1939; We loved them a lot, But God loves them more.

Other Info: Also has an above ground vault: Reids FH. Shares a headstone with his wife.

| Green
Allen, Jr. | 1 Aug. 1942
24 Aug. 2003 | | no |

Other Info: This is an above ground vault: Reids FH

| Green
Edith M. (Gray) | 14 May 1922
17 Aug. 2000 | Allen Green (Sr.) | yes |

Inscription: Wed 4 July 1939; We loved them a lot, but God loves them more.

Other Info: Also has an above ground vault: Reids FH; Shares a headstone with her husband.

| Harris
John | | | no |

Other Info: Unidentified funeral home marker with one date: 9 Jan. 1980

| Harris
John J. | 1913
1989 | | no |

Other Info: This is an above ground vault: Reids FH. His mother, Sarah Harris and sister, Susie Harris are also buried in this cemetery.

| Harris
Joseph | 1896
9 April 1918 | | yes |

Inscription: Weep not, he is at rest.

Last Name Given Name (Maiden Name)	Date of Birth Date of Death Age at Death	Spouse	Tombstone
Harris Lillian	2 Dec. 1913 4 Dec. 1913		yes

Inscription: In heaven there is one angel.

| Harris
Margary N. | 22 March 1899
6 Sept. 1982 | | yes |

Inscription: Mother

| Harris
Sarah | 12 June 1891
6 March 1956
65 years | | yes |

Inscription: Wife

Other Info: Mother of John J. Harris and Susie Harris also buried in this cemetery.

| Harris
Susie | | | no |

Other Info: Known to be buried here.

| Johnson
Edward W. | 1931
1988 | | no |

Other Info: This is an above ground vault: Reids FH

| Johnson
Frank | 1917
1988 | | no |

Other Info: This is an above ground vault: Reids FH

| Johnson
Hubert N. | 10 Feb. 1919
6 Aug. 1985 | | yes |

Inscription: US Army, World War II

Other Info: Also has an above ground vault: Hubert Johnson, 1919-1986 (death year different from headstone): Reids FH

Last Name Given Name (Maiden Name	Date of Birth Date of Death Age at Death	Spouse	Tombstone
Johnson Lynn	5 March 1898 21 Oct. 1964		yes

Inscription: Father

Other Info: Has a Reids Funeral Home marker.

Johnson Mildred J.	27 July 1931 20 Aug. 2002		no

Other Info: This is an above ground vault: Reids FH

Johnson Nathaniel C.	1983 1986		yes

Inscription: Love you always

Johnson Susie B.	1894 1987		no

Other Info: This is an above ground vault: Reids FH

Landrine Martha B.	3 Nov. 1907 16 Feb. 1987		yes

Inscription: Our Beloved Mother

Lee George	1900 1979	Mary Lee	yes

Inscription: Rest in Peace

Other Info: Shares a headstone with his wife.

Lee James			no

Other Info: Known to be buried in this cemetery.

Lee John	16 Aug 1866 June 1945	Lucy Lee	no

Other Info: Known to be buried in this cemetery. His parents are William and Patience Lee.

Last Name Given Name (Maiden Name	Date of Birth Date of Death Age at Death	Spouse	Tombstone
Lee Lucille			no

Other Info: Known to be buried in this cemetery. Her mother is Nanny Ennels Lee.

| Lee
   Lucy | | John Lee | no |

Other Info: Known to be buried in this cemetery.

| Lee
   Mary | 1904
1969 | George Lee | yes |

Inscription: Rest in Peace

Other Info: Shares a headstone with her husband.

| Lee
   Nanny Ennels | | | no |

Other Info: Known to be buried in this cemetery. She is the mother of Lucille Lee.

| Lee
   Patience | | William Lee | no |

Other Info: Known to be buried in this cemetery.

| Lee
   Sallie E. | 1901
2003 | | no |

Other Info: Reids Funeral Home marker

| Lee
   Samuel | | | no |

Other Info: Known to be buried in this cemetery.

| Lee
   Viola Swan | 28 Jan 1911
22 Aug. 1982 | Jerry Lee | yes |

Last Name Given Name (Maiden Name)	Date of Birth Date of Death Age at Death	Spouse	Tombstone
Lee William	16 Aug 1836	Patience Lee	no

Other Info: Known to be buried here in this cemetery. He and his wife are the parents of John Lee.

| Monroe
Delores | 1956
1990 | | no |

Other Info: Known to be buried in this cemetery.

| Moore
John Archer | 2 July 1924
26 Apr. 1999 | | yes |

Inscription: PFC, US Army, World War II

Other Info: Has a Reids Funeral Home marker.

| Morris
Royal F. | 29 June 1907
1 Feb. 1924 | | yes |

Inscription: At Rest

| Patterson
Annie B. | 1905
2000 | | no |

Other Info: Reids Funeral Home marker

| Patterson
Pauline L. | 1885
1982 | | yes |

Other Info: Has a Reids Funeral Home marker.

| Payne
Archie | 1953 | | yes |

| Reed
Mamie J. | | | no |

Other Info: Unidentified funeral home marker

Last Name Given Name (Maiden Name)	Date of Birth Date of Death Age at Death	Spouse	Tombstone
Romby Mary A. (Alice)	1911 2000		yes

Other Info: Has a Reids Funeral Home marker.

| Rose
  Blanche | 1 May 1927
29 June 1971 | | yes |

Inscription: Mother and Grandmother

Other Info: Has a Reids Funeral Home marker.

| Rose
  Evelyn | 9 Jan. 1915
12 Feb. 1973 | | yes |

Other Info: Has a Reids Funeral Home marker.

| Scruggs
  Jamar V. "Outlawz" | 19 Dec. 1981
22 Feb. 2002 | | yes |

Other Info: Has a Reids Funeral Home marker.

| Scruggs
  Marvin A. | 1968
1987 | | no |

Other Info: This is an above ground vault: Reids FH

| Sear
  Calvin Roger | 16 Dec. 1958
9 July 1990 | | yes |

Inscription: Loving Memories, Wife, Parents and Family

| Sharp
  Polly | | | no |

Other Info: Known to be buried here in this cemetery.

| Sharpe
  Carrie L. | 1922
2001 | | yes |

Other Info: Has a Reids Funeral Home marker.

Last Name Given Name (Maiden Name)	Date of Birth Date of Death Age at Death	Spouse	Tombstone
Swan Walter M.	1913 1990		yes

Inscription: US Army, World War II

Swann Annie Leah	1934 1998	Ely David Swann	yes

Other Info: Shares a headstone with her husband.

Swann Edward C.	1903 1973		no

Other Info: Reids Funeral Home marker

Swann Ely David	1927 1996	Annie Leah Swann	yes

Other Info: Shares a headstone with his wife.

Swann Gertrude B.			yes

Inscription: In Memory of (no dates)

Other Info: Has a Reids Funeral Home marker.

Swann Mack	29 May 1944 17 Sept. 1993		no

Other Info: Bland-Reid Funeral Home marker

Swann Mark	1893 1942		no

Other Info: Unidentified funeral home marker

Swann Pearline W.	1912 1998		no

Other Info: Reids Funeral Home marker

Last Name Given Name (Maiden Name	Date of Birth Date of Death Age at Death	Spouse	Tombstone
Swann Stanley			no

Other Info: Bland-Reid Funeral Home marker (no dates)

| Swann
  Victoria | 19 Jan. 1950
2 Nov. 2001 | | no |

Other Info: This is an above ground vault: Reids FH

| Taylor
  Edwood | 1881
1918 | | yes |

| Trent
  Buster | 1917
1988 | | no |

Other Info: Unidentified funeral home marker

| Trent
  Jerry | 1898
1982 | | no |

Other Info: Unidentified funeral home marker

| Trent
  Mary W. | 1915
1988 | | no |

Other Info: Reids Funeral Home marker

| Tyree
  Deborah Colmore | 19 May 1961
28 Dec. 1992 | Curtis O"Neal Tyree Sr. | yes |

Inscription: Together Forever-He maketh no mistakes

Other Info: Has a Community Funeral Home marker

| Tyree
  Edna Estelle | 27 July 1934
1 Sept. 1998 | | no |

Other Info: This is an above ground vault: Reids FH

Last Name Given Name (Maiden Name	Date of Birth Date of Death Age at Death	Spouse	Tombstone
Tyree John Randoph	13 March 1927 21 July 1997		no

Other Info: This is an above ground vault: Reid's FH; inscribed: In Loving Memory

| Tyree
   Leroy | 28 May 1958
11 March 1984 | | yes |

Inscription: Husband

Other Info: Has a Reids Funeral Home marker

| Wade
   Alice | 16 April 1937 | | no |

Other Info: Known to be buried in this cemetery.

| Wade
   Dan Henderson | 1918
1989 | | yes |

Inscription: US Army, World War II

| Wade
   Mary E. | 1875
1956 | | yes |

Inscription: Our Mother

Other Info: Mother of Nannie Wade who is also buried in this cemetery.

| Wade
   Nancy | 1843
May 1918 | | yes |

Inscription: Our Mother; A tender mother and faithful friend

| Wade
   Nannie E. | 1915
1929 | | yes |

Other Info: Her mother was Mary E. Wade, also buried in this cemetery.

Last Name Given Name (Maiden Name)	Date of Birth Date of Death Age at Death	Spouse	Tombstone
Wann Watt			no

Other Info: This is an unidentified funeral home marker with one date: 27 Dec. 1981

| Watkins
Bennie | 26 Nov. 1921
24 June 1951 | | yes |

Inscription: Virginia, TEC 5, 91 Eng GS Regt, World War II

| Watkins
Charles L. | 1917
1990 | | yes |

Inscription: US Army, World War II

Other Info: Also has an above ground vault:Reids FH

| Watkins
Henry | 2 Nov. 1929
10 Jan. 2001 | | yes |

Inscription: CPL, US Army

Other Info: Has a Reids Funeral Home marker.

| Watkins
Leatha B. | 11 Sept .1913
20 Nov. 1982 | | yes |

| Watkins
Lillian W. | 1907
1977 | | no |

Other Info: This is an above ground vault.

| Watkins
Moses | 1907
1988 | | no |

Other Info: This is an above ground vault: Reid's FH

| Watkins
Nannie B. | 1890
1977 | | yes |

Inscription: Mother

Other Info: Has a Reids Funeral Home marker.

Last Name Given Name (Maiden Name	Date of Birth Date of Death Age at Death	Spouse	Tombstone
Watkins Robert J.	1927 1974		yes
Wheeler Alice B.	1877 1975		no

Other Info: This is an above ground vault.

Woodson Connie			no

Other Info: Unidentified funeral home marker with one date: 12 - 8 - 67

Woodson Howard	20 July 1907 Dec. 2003	Mary Frances Woodson	yes

Other Info: Shares a headstone with his wife.

Woodson James Edward	17 July 1948 24 Mar. 2001		yes

Inscription: PVT, US Army, Vietnam

Other Info: Has a Reids Funeral Home marker.

Woodson John Edward	8 Sept. 1891 25 Oct. 1977		yes

Inscription: US Army, World War I

Woodson Mary Frances	25 Oct. 1908 24 March 1990	Howard Woodson	yes

Other Info: Shares a headstone with her husband.

Woodson Robert Frank	26 Aug. 1916 16 Nov. 1965		yes

Inscription: Virginia, PFC, US Army, World War II

Last Name Given Name (Maiden Name	Date of Birth Date of Death Age at Death	Spouse	Tombstone
Woodson Walker Solomon	16 June 1927 6 Dec. 1971		yes

   Inscription: Virginia, TN, US Navy, World War II

   Other Info: His brothers, Howard, Robert F., and Wiley G. Woodson are all buried in this cemetery.

| Woodson
   Wiley G. | 1911
2003 | | no |

   Other Info: Reids Funeral Home marker; His brothers, Walker S. and Howard Woodson are also buried in this cemetery.

| Young
   Willie | 1915
1977 | | no |

   Other Info: This is an above ground vault.

There are 28 unidentified graves in this cemetery.

Zions Grove Baptist Church — African American

Allen Alice L.	23 Jan. 1887 10 July 1982		yes
Allen Ballard	 31 Aug. 1954		yes
Allen Booker			yes, but illegible

   Other Info: L.C. Gray Funeral Home marker: Booker Allen, Dec. 26, 1955

| Allen
   Charlie V. | 25 Dec. 1907
9 Aug. 1952 | | yes |
| Allen
   James M. | 1911
1971 | | yes |

   Inscription: Gone but not Forgotten

Last Name Given Name (Maiden Name	Date of Birth Date of Death Age at Death	Spouse	Tombstone
Allen Thomas B.	1918 1980		no

Other Info: Reids Funeral Home marker

Allen William	March 1905 (Humphrey) 30 Oct. 1978		yes

Baker Glover L.			no

Other Info: Reids Funeral Home marker with no dates

Baker Mary Virginia	1927 1985		no

Other Info: Colbert Funeral Home marker

Baker Thomas E.	1953 1973		no

Other Info: Unidentified funeral home marker

Banks (no given name)	1969		no

Other Info: Smith Funeral Home marker with one date

Banks Major	16 April 1895 12 May 1965		yes

Banks Major M. Jr.	21 Apr. 1920 30 June 1942		yes

Inscription: PVT, 97 Engrs., World War II

Banks Marie	21 March ___ illegible 59 years		no

Other Info: Reids Funeral Home marker

Last Name Given Name (Maiden Name)	Date of Birth Date of Death Age at Death	Spouse	Tombstone
Banks Susie J. (James)	1913 1991	Lewis Banks	yes
Banks Virginia (P.)	22 Feb. 1896 23 Nov. 1985		yes
Barnett Lucien	1940		yes
Barnes Freeman Jr.	1908 1980		no

Other Info: Unidentified funeral home marker

| Barnes
Virginia J. | 1915
1985 | | no |

Other Info: Colbert Funeral Home marker

| Bland
Samuel Henry | 1 April 1922
8 July 2000 | | no |

Other Info: Thomas Funeral Home marker

| Brown
Charles Robert | 1916
1982 | | yes |

Inscription: SGT, US Army, World War II

| Carter
Charlie Lewis | 1925
1982 | | yes |

Inscription: MMC, US Navy, World War II, Korea, Vietnam

| Carter
R. (Richard) D. | | | Etched fieldstone |

Inscription: At Rest (no dates)

| Cason
Jeannette S. | 4 Jan. 1931
3 March 1990 | | yes |

Inscription: Rest

Last Name Given Name (Maiden Name	Date of Birth Date of Death Age at Death	Spouse	Tombstone
Chambers Essie Lee	25 Aug. 1882 14 May 1955		yes

Inscription: PVT, Co A, 542 SVC BN, Engr Corps, World War I

Clayton Joan M. (Pollard)	24 Mar. 1940 3 June 1975		yes

Coleman Marcus S.			yes

Inscription: Virginia, PVT, 29 Depot Sery Co., ASC, 2 Nov.1936

Davis John H. (Henry)	22 Jan. 1897 11 May 1980	Mary H. Davis	yes

Other Info: Shares a headstone with his wife.

Davis Mary H.	8 April 1899 21 Oct. 1984	John H. (Henry) Davis	yes

Other Info: Shares a headstone with her husband; has a Marion Gray Thomas Funeral Home marker.

Duncan Baby	4 April 1958		Etched Fieldstone

Duncan George O.	28 Sept. 1913 26 April 1985		yes

Inscription: TEC 4, US Army, World War II

Other Info: Has a Chiles Funeral Home marker

Duncan James C., Deacon	13 Nov. 1919 23 Feb. 1991		yes

Inscription: Always in our hearts

Duncan Lena L. (Perkins)	7 April 1921 27 Oct. 1996		yes

Inscription: Always in our hearts

Last Name Given Name (Maiden Name	Date of Birth Date of Death Age at Death	Spouse	Tombstone
Duncan Louise Agnes (Turnstall)	3 Dec. 1919 28 Dec. 1996		yes

Inscription: Loving Mother and Grandmother

Duncan Mary Louise	26 Oct. 1926 16 Mar. 1996		yes
Duncan Sallie B.	26 Aug. 1889 5 May 1958		yes
Duncan Thomas E.	1951 1995		no

Other Info: Reids Funeral Home marker

Gregory Allen Ray	1950 1981		yes
Gregory Floyd Alvin	29 Jan. 1948 19 Dec. 1984		yes
Gregory Pearl Daisy	28 Sept. 1912 2 Dec. 1992		yes
Harris Bessie A.	1911 1982		no

Other Info: Unidentified funeral home marker

Harris Joe W.	1927 1986		no

Other Info: Unidentified funeral home marker

Harris William	1905 1985		no

Other Info: Unidentified funeral home marker

Hartman William A.	11 March 1909 6 Feb. 1928		yes

Inscription: 515 Class-Armstrong Night School

Last Name Given Name (Maiden Name	Date of Birth Date of Death Age at Death	Spouse	Tombstone
Holman Carrie	1 April 1889 1 May 1962		yes

Inscription: Beloved wife and mother

| Holman
  Hattie | 18 Aug. 1911
1 Feb. 1944 | | yes |

Inscription: In Memory of

Other Info: Footstone: HH

| Holman
  Jessee | 1881
1970 | | yes |

Inscription: Father

| Hughes
  W.M. | 4 July 1872
29 Nov. 1922 | | yes |

Inscription: My trust is in God

| Jackson
  Roxanne D. | 20 June 1960
28 Dec. 2001
41 years | | no |

Other Info: Colbert Funeral Home marker

| James
  Edith W. (Woodson) | 9 Dec. 1933
20 Dec. 1987 | | yes |

Inscription: Mother

| Johnson
  Beulah W. (Woodson) | 18 Nov. 1914
5 Aug. 1993 | | yes |

| Johnson
  Booker | Aug. 1899
18 April 1975 | Thelma J. Johnson | yes |

Inscription: In God's Care

Last Name Given Name (Maiden Name	Date of Birth Date of Death Age at Death	Spouse	Tombstone
Johnson Clyde E.	1903 1960		no

Other Info: Ranson and Smith Funeral Home marker

Johnson Emma	1872 1967		yes

Inscription: Mother; Rest in Peace

Other Info: Shares a headstone with her son, William Johnson.

Johnson Lettie	25 Dec. 1890 26 Oct. 1969		yes

Johnson Mamie Woodson	15 April 1885 31 Oct. 1986		yes

Inscription: Mother; She is just away.

Johnson T.	1870 1959		no

Other Info: Ritchie Johnson Funeral Home marker

Johnson William	1901 1967		yes

Inscription: Son

Other Info: Shares a headstone with his mother, Emma Johnson.

Jones Cora Carter	1857 21 Sept. 1920 63 years		yes

Inscription: In Memory of Mother

Other Info: Footstone: CCJ

Last Name Given Name (Maiden Name)	Date of Birth Date of Death Age at Death	Spouse	Tombstone
Jones Edgar	3 Dec. 1906 11 Oct. 1927		yes

Inscription: At Rest

Other Info: Footstone: EJ

Jones Edith M. (Duncan)	21 Sept. 1921 1 Nov. 1981		yes

Other Info: Has an above ground vault inscribed: Mother: Reids FH

Jones Eliza J.	9 Feb. 1945	Joseph Jones	yes

Inscription: Mother; The wife of Rev. Joseph Jones; At Rest

Other Info: Footstone: EJJ

Jones Ernie	1919 1991 71 years		yes

Other Info: Has a Colbert Funeral Home marker.

Jones Florence	12 April 1894 18 June 1968		yes
Jones John Henry	1941 1999 58 years		no

Other Info: Unidentified funeral home marker

Jones John Robert Sr.	17 April 1918 10 Dec. 1964		yes
Jones Joseph, Rev.	1859 11 June 1933	Eliza J. Jones	yes

Inscription: Be Ye therefore followers of God as dear children-Eph. 5:1

Other Info: Footstone: JJ

Last Name Given Name (Maiden Name)	Date of Birth Date of Death Age at Death	Spouse	Tombstone
Jones Katie	May, 1890 Sept. 1981		yes

    Other Info: Has a Reids Funeral Home marker

Jones Lucy A. (Allen)	14 June 1920 28 Aug. 1986		yes

    Inscription: Until we meet again

    Other Info: She has a Reids Funeral Home marker.

Jones Thelma Young	17 Aug. 1917 28 July 2000		no

    Other Info: This is an above ground vault: Thomasson FH

Jones Thomas J. (Junious)	2 Jan. 2002		no

    Other Info: Joseph Jenkins Jr. Funeral Home marker

Jones Virginus M.	14 Feb. 1881 17 Dec. 1964		yes
Jones William	1926 1967		yes

    Inscription: Courtesy of Greenwood Memorial

Kirby Pattie Pollard	1912 1953		yes

    Inscription: Buckingham Co. School Teacher for 17 years-Donated by the teachers and pupils of Zions Grove School

    Other Info: Footstone: Pattie P. Kirby

Logan Baron Montell	5 Sept. 1961 24 Mar. 1990		yes

    Inscription: Peace, Quiet, Forever in our hearts

Last Name Given Name (Maiden Name)	Date of Birth Date of Death Age at Death	Spouse	Tombstone
Logan Helen W. (Bell)	1929 2000 70 years		no

Other Info: Colbert Funeral Home marker

Logan John Nelson	13 March 1926 14 April 1995		yes

Inscription: PFC, US Army, World War II

Logan Willie J.	1917 1990		yes

Inscription: Loving Husband and Father

Mallory Hubert	1912 1989		no

Other Info: This is an above ground vault: Reids FH

Mallory Nettie P. (Allen)	18 April 1916 15 Nov. 1999		no

Other Info: This is an above ground vault: Reids FH

McKellan Maylan Redwood	12 Dec. 1923 20 Sept___		yes
Miller Mabel (Jones)	10 March 1910 19 July 1998		yes

Other Info: Has a Reids Funeral Home marker.

Miller Thelma P. (Pollard)	17 April 1922 26 June 1945		yes

Inscription: At Rest

Other Info: Footstone: Thelma P. Miller, 17 April 1922, 26 June 1945

Last Name Given Name (Maiden Name)	Date of Birth Date of Death Age at Death	Spouse	Tombstone
Moore Odell Young	1915 1990		no

Other Info: This is an above ground vault: Reids FH

Nedrick Sister Quinnie T. (Woodson)	1898 1980		yes

Other Info: Has a Johnson Jenkins Funeral Home (Wash. DC) marker.

Newton Dorothy B.	24 Dec. 1942 7 Dec. 2001		yes

Inscription: Beloved Mother; Always in our hearts

Other Info: Has a Thomasson's Funeral Home marker: Dorothy B.T. Newton, 1943-2001 (birth year is different from that on the tombstone).

Perkins James	 1995		no

Other Info: Colbert Funeral Home marker

Perkins Levitt Earl	22 Nov. 1900 13 Oct. 1976	 Mary Elnora Perkins	yes

Inscription: Asleep in Jesus

Pittman Dorothy White	14 Sept. 1914 9 July 1965		yes
Pollard Jennie	1880 1955		yes
Pollard John D.	20 June 1884 3 April 1966	 Martha F. Pollard	yes

Inscription: Prepare to meet thy God

Pollard Joyce L.	29 July 1949 5 May 1950		yes

Other Info: Shares a headstone with William K. Pollard

Last Name Given Name (Maiden Name	Date of Birth Date of Death Age at Death	Spouse	Tombstone
Pollard Martha F.	15 May 1891 27 Feb. 1984	John D. Pollard	yes

Inscription: Prepare to meet thy God

| Pollard
William K. (Kenneth) | 27 March 1924
23 Aug. 1990 | | yes |

Inscription: US Army

| Pollard
William | 1887
1955 | | yes |

| Pollard
William K | 17 March 1948
6 May 1967 | | yes |

Other Info: Shares a headstone with Joyce L. Pollard

| Randolph
(Deacon) Clarence | 15 Sept. 1905
14 Sept. 1988 | Virgie H. Randolph | yes |

Inscription: Precious Lord take my hand

Other Info: Shares a headstone with his wife.

| Randolph
Virgie H. | 10 Oct. 1910
23 March 1971 | Deacon Clarence
Randolph | yes |

Inscription: Precious Lord take my hand

Other Info: Shares a headstone with her husband.

| Redwood
Elenora (Eleanor) | 1898
1984 | Watson J. Redwood | yes |

Other Info: Shares a headstone with her husband.

| Redwood
James T. | 23 March 1915
11 Jan. 1946 | | yes |

Last Name Given Name (Maiden Name	Date of Birth Date of Death Age at Death	Spouse	Tombstone
Redwood Watson J.	1891 1967	Elenora (Eleanor) Redwood	yes

Other Info: Shares a headstone with his wife.

Scruggs Beulah	1875 1955		yes

Scruggs Mrs. Emma			yes

Inscription: (gives only March 20)

Tindall Charlie			yes

Inscription: Courtesy of Greenwood Memorial Gardens (no dates)

Tindall Mary	1890 1974		no

Other Info: Thomassons Funeral Home marker

Tindall William			yes

Inscription: Coutesy of Greenwood Memorial Gardens (no dates)

White Abe	15 Sept. 1881 14 March 1968		yes

White Lawrence Blackwell	1890 1975		yes

Inscription: PVT, US Army, World War I

White Lillie Woodson	24 April 1888 18 May 1962		yes

White Mandy	1860 1925		yes

White Rufus J. (Jr.)	21 Sept. 1916 15 Jan. 1938		yes

Last Name Given Name (Maiden Name	Date of Birth Date of Death Age at Death	Spouse	Tombstone
White Rufus (Sr.)	5 June 1887 12 Dec. 1969		yes
White Willie Sue	27 June 1952		yes
Williams Alexander	30 March 1938 31 March 1986		yes
Williams Anita L.	30 May 1965 30 Dec. 1979		yes

Inscription: Until we meet again

Other Info: She is buried next to 2 sisters, Chandra and Cynthia and a brother, Kevin, all of whom lost their lives in a house fire.

Williams Chandra R.	24 March 1970 30 Dec. 1979		yes

Inscription: Until we meet again

Williams Cynthia D.	13 Jan. 1968 30 Dec. 1979		yes

Inscription: Until we meet again

Williams Kevin E.	8 June 1973 30 Dec. 1979		yes

Inscription: Until we meet again

Williams Mary Elizabeth	23 Nov. 1918 25 Oct. 1972		yes

Inscription: Gone but not Forgotten

Williams Mary Jane	8 May 1947 24 Aug. 1998		yes

Inscription: Gone but not Forgotten; If tears could build a stairway, and memories a lane, I's walk right up to Heaven and bring you home again.

Last Name Given Name (Maiden Name)	Date of Birth Date of Death Age at Death	Spouse	Tombstone
Wood(son) (Jose)phine	Oct. 187_ 1944		yes, broken
Woodson Florence	1892 1924		yes

Inscription: Rest in Peace

Woodson Nancy Jean	1952 1968		yes

Other Info: Has a Ransons Funeral Home marker

Woodson Pattie	1897 1978		no

Other Info: Unidentified funeral home marker

Woodson Ralph	1935 1986		yes
Woodson Rufus	8 Sept. 1903 29 Sept. 1963		yes

Inscription: West Virginia, PVT, US Army, World War II

Woodson Tarlton	6 Jan. 1891 27 Jan. 1974		yes

Inscription: US Army, World War II

Young Ernest	1915 1992		yes

Inscription: CPL, US Army, World War II

Other Info: Has an above ground vault: Ernest L. Young, 1914-1992 (shows a birth year that is different from the birth year on the tombstone): Reid's FH

Last Name Given Name (Maiden Name	Date of Birth Date of Death Age at Death	Spouse	Tombstone
Young Humphrey P.	1893 1966		no

Other Info: This is an above ground vault.

Young Nannie (F.)	1893 1976		no

Other Info: This is an above ground vault.

There are 64 unidentified graves in this cemetery.

Last Name Given Name (Maiden Name	Date of Birth Date of Death Age at Death	Spouse	Tombstone

INDEX

(AYERS), Elizabeth B. (Booker) Bartee 430
(BENTLEY), Froney Stanton 9
(NON-INSCRIBED), Ellis 426
(Not Known) Julia 378
(SPENCER), William Thomas 397
ABRIL, Lucy F. G. 212
ADAMS, Annie 190 Eugene 1 Jennie 1 Mary A. 1 Milton Sr. 1 Richard R. 1
ADCOCK, Albert Thomas 237 Berdie Ragland 559-560 Betty B. (Ballowe) 237 Buford S. 237 Daniel M. 237 239 Delores Baker 238 Dorothy 252 Dorothy Taylor 237 George 238 James Willis Sr. 238-239 John 2 Lillie L. 247 Lindsey 238 Lula Dolan 559-560 Minnie 238 Morton B. 238 Pearl 239 245 Ray Murphy 237-238 Sarah 2 Sarah A. (Adcock) 238-239 Thomas Gilmore 559 Tucker R. Sr. 237-238 Walker 238 Willie Henry 560 Willis L. 238-239
AGEE, Alice C. 492-493 Amanda (Allen) 214 Annie M. 402 Bertha Booker 518 Bettie Wood 3 Caesar Alexander 215 Charles 504 Charles E. 37 Charlie 215 Earl 5-6 Ellen Pocahontas 314 Elois W. 493 Floyd Arthur 215 Georgie Ellen 313 Helen Juanita 5 Howard W. 3 James Ballard Maxey 313 Jessie E. Allen 37 John W. (Willie) 3 Larry Kirk 5 Lelia 215 Lizzie (Elizabeth) 4 Louise B. 33 Lucille 226-227 Lucy A. 37 Margie 5 Mattie Gilbert 480 Nettie May 313 Norman Daniel 215 Randolph 215 Robert A. 314 Samuel P. 3 Tabler 3 Thelma M. 121 Thomas Edward 321 323 Thomas H. 492-493

AGEE, (continued) Vincent Harry 5-6 Vincent Sr. 5-6 William E. 493 Willie Whitcomb 480
AGERO, Elsie May 402
AGGE, Virginia 5-6
ALLEN, Billie 583 Abraham 556 Agnes 190 Albert 321-322 Alice L. 614 Amanda 214 America E. 209 Archer 37 Ballard 614 Barbara 8 Booker 614 Charlene G. 321 Charles Allen Sr. 322-323 Charles Jr. 322 Charles Sr. 190 Charlie V. 614 Curtis Preston 38 Edith Webb 151 Esther 8 Helen B. 215 Henry B. 7 Huston 322 Isaiah 322 Jack W. 151 James M. 614 Jane Lou 9 Jimmy 583 John T. 305 Josephine 306 Katie 322 Leonard Barnes Jr. 7 Lou 493 Lucy 622 Lurt 322 Margaret 7 Martha Ann 190 322-323 Mary 38 Mary B. 38 Mary Ellen Lydia 152 Nettie P. 623 Olivia 556 Preston R. 38 Rachel Austin 23 Robert 23 322-323 Ruth Virginia 7 Samuel 322-323 Sanford Philip 152 Sweden Cyrus 152 Thomas 323 Thomas B. 615 Viola E. 38 Wesley 583 William (Humphrey) 615 William Evan 38 Willie Sue 190 322-323 Zack Sr. 215
ALVIS, Caroline Lewis 15 Elisa Susan 15 John 449 Lucy Ann 14 Margaret 450 Maurice 450 Peggy 450 Prudence Branch Moseley 11 Susanah Stevens 449 William M. 11 William W. 11 449-450
AMOS, Annie Rachel 17 Arthur Reuben 16 Christine K. 16 David W. 19 Etta 16 Henry 16 James 16 Katie 16

AMOS, (continued)
L.W. (Lindsey Walker) 19
Lovette Evelyn Mrs 17 Malcolm
Alloyd 17 Nina Belle (Stratton)
20 Rosa H. 518 Terry Daniel 17
Thomas Lee 87
ANDERSON, Alvin Early 38 Annie
21 39 Annie F. Eldridge 39
Annie Virginia 23 Baby Girl 444
C.B. 39 Carl E. 23 Carliesa W.
504 Carrie Burke 22 Charles F.
39 Charles T. 136 Earl F. 331-
332 Edna B. 39 Fannie 21
Florence G. 39 George Sam 39
Glenn W. 39 Grandville L. 381
Hobhouse 303 Holman 504
Hudson Mat 375 James David
20 James Deacon 137 James
Lewis 20 Joshua 274 Joshua Jr.
275 King 303 Lelia S. 444 Lucy
21 Maggie Christine 331-332
Marshall 504 Martha 20 Mary 21
Mary B. (Branch Gilliam) 480
Moses 332 Myrtie Gardner Seal
20 Nelson T. 40 Sarah 21 Sarah
Agnes Flood 20 Sarah H. 21
Ulyssses W. 275 Wilbur Grant
275 William 40 William C. 524
William F. 21
ANDREWS, Jean 404 Jean E.
Banks 402
ANTHONY, Margaret C. 115
ANTRIM, R. E. (Eldridge) 112 114
APPERSON, Calvin Talmage 22
Harrison 22 P.L. 23 S.G. 23
Sallie F. (England) 23 Thomas
J. 542 Tom 23 William J. 22
ARMISTEAD, Annie 191
AUSIN, Lawrence 518
AUSTIN, Abraham 24 Addie M. 24
Archibald A. 493 Emma H. 466
James 24 Jimmy 191 John
Daniel 24 John S. 24 John W.
Sr. 466 Joseph N. 466 Kate 24
Laura 191 Laura C. 381
Laurence 24 Lula Elizabeth 520
Mary Ann 493 Mattie W. 493

AUSTIN, (continued)
Nettie Mundy 285 Ordell 24
Pearl 26 R. Gallian 493 Rachel
23 Sallie 24 Sherry 25 Thomas
A. 493 Thomas E. 285 Thornhill
25 Thornhill Bones 25 Virginia
25 Virginia L. 175 William 25
William Rufus 25 William
Thomas 493 Willie Lewis 285
AUTON, Frances Nuckols 395
AYERS, Alexander 323 Anna D.
504 Artie 402 Beulah 25 Burris
324 David E. 137 Emma Ellis
524 529 Emmit 402 Gertrude
323 Guy Matthew 324 Houston
L. 324 Ida C. (Chambers) 324
James Herman 430 John R. 402
John Stephen 587 John William
587 Layman 137 Louise Virginia
323-325 Lucie V. 324 Lucy H.
587 Mark S. 191 Micheall 324
Minnie 144 Nathan 191 Noner
191 Octavia 381 Paul 32 324
324-325 Robert 191 Robert
James 325 Robert M. 324
Robert M. (McKinley) 32 324
Rosa 137 Ruby M. 40 Sarah
191 Shirley 324 Tempy 191
Virginia 32 324-325 Walter 504
Wesley 192 William Billy 587
William H. (Howard) 25
AYRERS, Lorenzo 137
AYRES, Amanda 588 Bettie
(Dunkum) 31 Betty M. 28
Catherine A. 40 Charlotte Ann
325 492 Eliza Agnes 367
Emanuel 26 George Mckenna
29 Gracie V. 137 Hannah L. 29
Infant 31 James C. Jr. 137
James E. 29 James Edmond 29
Jessie 588 Jessie J. 325 John
31 John Lee 325 John N. 367
Laura E. 29 Lillian Irene 367
Lizzie May 29 Luther 137 M.C.
(Melissa Duncan) 31 Mayo G.
29 Percy 324-325 Ray 137
Rosa 492 Sallie H. 29

AYRES, (continued)
Sarah F. 29 Walker 137 William
Daniel 367 Willie 326 Willie H.
30
BABER, George 33 Ida M. 32-33
Joseph W. 32-33 Louise B.
Agee 33 Martha 33 Mildred 380
Wyatt Somers 268
BAGBY, 2 Infants 235 Elizabeth
(Conner) 544-545 548 Elmira
(or Elmina) Frances 398-399
James Norvil 494 Josiah 544-
545 548 Josiah J. Bagby 235
Lena Woodson 494 Lucille W.
430 Nannie Sue Perrow 235
545 Virginia E. 209 William G.
545 William Riley 235 William
Ryland 545
BAILEY, Annie Virginia 419
Blanche Roberts 419 422 Grace
Florence Gunter 560 Infant 148
John 560 Mary E. 422 Patricia
Coleman 148 Richard Ellis 419
422 Virginia 419 Wm. W. 419
BAIRD, Albert Franklin Sr. 419 Ann
420 Carrie Virginia (Lewis) 420-
421 423 Charlie Jr. 420 Charlie
W. 420-421 Courtney C. 420
Elizabeth 420-421 George 420
Harvey 420 Harvey Lee 420-
421 James 420 James H. 420
Katherine G. 420 Linda 420
Margaret A. (Bowers) 420-421
Mary 420 Mary Jones 420-421
Myrtle 420 425 Pearl V. 420
William Henry 420-421 423
BAKER, Agnes Pearl 588 Eliza Y.
208 Frank R. 588 Glover L. 615
Irene Florence 588 James Erwin
588 Johnnie 588 Leonard 588
Lucy E. 589 Mary Virginia 615
Milton 588-589 Richard Sr. 589
Sully D. 589 Thomas E. 615
Thomas W. 589 William E. 589
BALDWIN, Infant Daughter 152
Katherine Young 586-587
Rebecca B. 152 Samuel L. 152

BALLOWE, Beatrice C. 152
Benjamin F. 152 Betty 237
Charles E. 239 Elsie I. 246
Margie 239 Norman E. 239
Rosa B. 243 250 Ruby Duncan
239
BAMGBADE, Carolyn Y. Banks
403-404
BANK, Mary Johnson 504
BANKS, Annie 403 Arvis L. 121
Carolyn Y. 403 Charlie 121
Charlie Octavious 505 Charlie
R. 40 Daniel M. 403 David 121
Derrick Deware 466 Edna Earl
367 Elisha 403 Fannie M. 505
Fletcher E. 403 Floyd 403
Fredrick M. 403 George Franklin
34 Haywood D. 26 Hobert Roy
400 Ida 34 Irene Carter 403-404
Izetta Spencer 400 J. Archie
122 James Edward 404 James
Henry 404 Jean E. 402 John D.
340 Josephine H. 505 Junius
505 Lawrence 404 Leslie J. 404
Lewis 616 Major 615 Major M.
Jr. 615 Margie V. 505 Marie 615
Mark Antonio 34 Mary E. 505
Melton Jr. 466 Melvin L. 404
Michael 466 Mrs. Willie Mae
505-506 Octavious 367 Pearline
R. 275 Pokey 416 Richard 122
Robert 403-404 Robert
Thornton 404 Rosa Lee (Ayers)
137 Roy 400 Sallie P. 467
Shirley A. 505 Susie J. (James)
616 Swan 122 Terry Clay 340
Virginia (P.) 616 Wilber 505-506
Wilbur Leonard 505-506
_____ 615
BANTON, Barnard 35 Belle
(Godsey Newton) 231 Bessie
Caul 35 Charles (Lafayette) 231
Christina Rebecca Garrett 232
Cleveland A. 34 Docia 35-36
Emmett Elwood 231 Florence
34 Infant (1) 34 Infant (2) 35
Isabelle Garrett 231

BANTON, (continued)
  James H. 35 John R. 232 Lattie
  A. 232 Marvin Lee 32 Mary Lou
  232 Mary Marie Garrett 232
  Mattie 35 232 Powell 35 Susie
  R. 232 Virginia 37 Walker E.
  232 William J. (James) 4
BARMETT, Lucien 616
BARNES, Cornelius 589 Freeman
  Jr. 616 Virginia J. 616
BARR, Rutha 152 William C. 152
BARTEE, (David Woodrow) Wilson
  590 Bruce 216 Eleanora B. 590
  George Jr. 430 Georgianna T.
  430 Harvey 590 James 590
  James O. (pooh) 431 Laureen
  G. 216 Lola L. J. 68 Nathaniel
  590 Phyllis Marie 431 Robert
  James 40 Robert L 68 Roy Lee
  Sr. 431 Ruth Sears 40 Sam 431
  Sis (Inez M.) 590
BARTLETT, Freddie L. 467 Mary
  Alice 467
BATES, Carl Edward 87 96 99
  William Joseph 339
BEARD, Juston Dashawne 590
  Lina C. 340
BEASLEY, Barbara 566 Bertha
  Ragland 239 Calwell W. 239
  Carl C. 152 Eliza (Kate) 561
  Eliza Webb 153 Ella (Ragland)
  239-240 Ellen I. 153 Emmett W.
  239 Etta May 240 Frank E. 153
  John Webb 153 Julian Henry
  153 Kemper M. 153 L. Earl 153
  Lena Mae 153 Leonard Julian
  560 Linda Dianne 153 Melvin
  Carl 240 Nannie G. 560 Percy
  O. 560 Priscilla Ann 153 Robert
  Gene 240 Robert L. 239-240
  Royal Oscar 560 Ruby M. 240
  Ruth Dunkum 153-154
  Sylvester V. 153 Thomas 240
  W. H. 153-154 William Houston
  153-154
BECK, Lelia Irvin 542
BELL, Edgar 332 Helen W. 623

BELLINGER, Shirley 467
BELLS, Ned 192
BENDERS, Elendra P. 40
BENNETT, Ada 524-525 Earlie
  524-525 541 Effie 524 Fred
  524-525 George W. 68 Irene
  541 James Edward 68 Mary 525
  541 Mary M. (Miller) 525 Morton
  524-525 Morton W. 525 Susin
  524-525 Viola Estelle 532
BENTLEY, Robert 9 Sarah Stanton
  40
BENWAY, Bob L. 481
BERBEY, Charles Curtis 560
BERKELEY, Cora Lee 72 Edwaard
  Elias 72 Thomas Alfred 72
BERSCH, Gladys 159 Jacob C.
  154 Peter O. 154
BETHEL, Earl E. 216
BEZ, W. Sr. 393
BIRCH, Eric 591 Sidney W. 591
BLAKE, Ella 41
BLAND, Samuel Henry 616
BLANKS, Edward L. (Lyle) 421 Nell
  Baird 421
BLEDSOE, Vernon Wayne 405
BOATWRIGHT, E. L. 74-75 Lewis
  Cornelius (Neal) 591 Mary Alice
  74-75 Mary V. 75 Thomas 74-75
  Walter Leake 74-75 William
  Thomas 75
BOCOCK, Annie 449 Nicholas
  Flood 76 Octavia Rose Gantt 76
BOLDEN, (James) Randolph 592
  Alex 592 Alsenda M. 77 Bessie
  Lee 591-592 Beverly 591
  Charlotte E. 591 Charlotte M. 78
  Dora L. 591 Earnest E. Sr. 591-
  592 Edward J. 592 Edward
  Palmer 592 Emily J. 78 Ethel B.
  78 Evelyn 592 Franklin Ernest
  592 Garfield 592 James 78
  James W. 592 John D. 592
  John Pearson 593 John W. 592-
  593 Joseph M. 593 Mary 592
  602 Melvin Jerome 593 Nannie
  Louise 78 Phillip L. 592-593

BOLDEN, (continued)
  Robert V. 593 Royal B.
  (Benjamin) 592-593 Saint Luke
  593
BOLES, Charlie C. (Clarence) 481
  James E. 481 Maude E.
  (Steele) 481 Wm. R. 480
BOLLING, Baby 467 Elmira 467
  George W. 467 George William
  467 Janie Mae 41 Queen
  Victoria 468 Thomas 216
  William A. 468 Woodson 468
BONDERANT, Leslie 525 Lucy J.
  525 536
BONDURANT, Arthur L. 525 Nora
  H. (Harper) 525-526
BONSELL, Martha E. 209
BOOK(E)R, Steven 468
BOOKER, Agnes Beatrice 594
  Alice R. 405 Amanda E. 192
  Annie 448 Annie Brown 332
  Bethrone 431 Billy W. 138
  Bobby 138 C. 77 Carrie J. 445
  448 Cary A. 78 Catherine 506
  Celia F. 41 Charles 138 192
  Charles H. 445 448 Charlie J.
  122 Charlie R. 405 Classie L.
  326 Eddie 332 Edwin Marshall
  11 Elizabeth 430 Elsie May 386-
  387 Ernest O. 138 Ethel Q. 405
  Fannie 417 Florence T. 275
  Henry 122 518 Hobert 138
  Howard J. 332 445 Ida Branch
  11 Irene C. 506 James 138 326
  332 James Andrew 332 James
  Coleman 381 James Edward
  518 James J. 445 Jerry 594
  Jewell Howard 12-13 John 326
  John E. 468 John R. (Richard)
  12-13 John Richard III 12 John
  Richard Jr. 12 John W. 78
  Joseph W. 333 Kate 138 Kelvin
  L. 506 Latosma 341 Lillian Mae
  Roeblad 12 Lou 216 518 Lucille
  471 Lucy C. 333 Lunell 431
  Lynwood J. 138 Maggie R. 78
  Malcolm A. (Alvis) 12

BOOKER, (continued)
  Martha Bertha Coleman 12-13
  Martha C. 41 Mary E. 594 Mary
  Ella 381 Mary Ford 26 Mary
  Frances 138 Mildred 122 Minnie
  Lee 139 Moses J. 332-333 Mr.
  W.M. 506 Mrs. P. H. 506 Nannie
  B. 405 Nelson R. Sr. 381 Olivia
  14 Pearl L. (Lee) 139 Phil 431
  Richard 431 Robert Coleman
  12-13 Robert Henry Jr. 382
  Robert Henry Sr. 382 Robert L.
  Sr. 506 Robert Lee Jr. 506
  Robert M. 12 Roger Jr. 26
  Rosella Elizabeth 79 Ruby J.
  122 Samuel 432 Shirley
  (Swann) 139 Susanna Taylor 12
  Tarrie 468 Walker A. 382 Walter
  J. (Junior) Sr. 333 Whitley 139
  Willie E. 518
BOOTH, Irene Bryant 98 Richard T.
  (Tamaridge) 87
BOUNDURANT, Lee 525-526
BOURNE, Annie Rachel Amos 17
BOWERS, Margaret A. 420-421
BOWLES, Benjamin (Papa) 468
  Benjamin Jr. 468 Dorothy Mae
  469 George R. Jr. 507 Helena
  507 Jimmy Lee 469 William
  Kenneth 469
BOWLING, Frank Thomas 122
  Jennie M. 123
BOWMAN, Beatrice B. 367 John E.
  367 Mary E. 368
BRACEY, Betty Hix 154 Lucille Cox
  154 M. Virginia 154 Mary Cox
  154 Thomas Hix 154
BRADBY, Nannie (Brown) Davis
  216
BRADLEY, 216 A.P. 216 James
  123 Mary V. 126 Ogden M. 123
  William 123
BRADSHAW, Sarah W. 553
BRAGG, Clara 248 Edwin D. 240 J.
  Russell 240-241 Jennie R. 240-
  241 Mary E. (Ragland) 240

BRANCH, Alice E. (Estelle) 561-562 564 Annie B. (Branch) 561 563 Baby 561 Barry 562 Beatrice G. 307 Charles Henry 216 Chastity Ann 561 Clara 217 Clarence F. (Franklin) 561 Cornel Buford 561 Elaine 562 Eliza (Kate) Beasley 561 Eliza Wilkerson 562 Ella Vest 307 Essie 562 Fitz D. (Douglas) 562-563 Florence Lee (Taylor) 562 Frank W. 307 Franklin O. 562 George F. (Freddy) 562 Henry 41 Horace 41 Ida 12 James W. 307 Jo Ann 561 John Alley 562 John O. 307 Kate Louise 563 Kevin 561 Laura M. Ragland 562 Mary 14 480 Mary B. (Bessie Ragland) 562-563 577 Mildred 225 Mildred A. 563 Miss Virgie 41 Moses P. (Perkins) 563 573 Myrtle 571 573 Nathaniel Alverton 563 Ora L. (Lee Wilkerson) 563 573 Ortho Edd 307 Pauline T. (Taylor) 563 Pauline Virginia Mrs. 382 Richard Douglas 563 Richard E. (Emery) 561 563 Roger 562 Steven Douglas 77 William A. 563 William F. (Franklin) 561-562 564 Willie Jr. 562
BRANDSFORD, David A. 382
BRANSFORD, Abraham Moseley 290-292 Ann Ee. 393 Claudius P. 392 Edmonia E. 392 Elizabeth 382 Janie Lonkard 290-292 Mattie A. 393 Maurice J. 392-393 Milton M. 395 Morris J. 392 Neva M. 395 Robert W. 393 Wm. S. (William Samuel) 290
BRANT, Arlene Shelor 108
BRAXTON, Margaret (Harper) 526 Overton 333 _____ 177
BRAYMAN, Jack G. 494 Willie Ann 494

BRIDDLE, Maude 192
BRIDGES, Dorothy Ann 41
BRIGHTFUL, Infant 400
BRITTLE, Edwin Winfrey 368 James 368 Virginia Agee 5-6
BROOKS, Katherine Gartree 274 Lucy 274 Peter 274
BROWN, George J. 595-596 Robert D. Sr. 84 A. C. 594 Agnes Emmaline (baby) 507 Albert 41 Alice 469 Alma A. 241 Alma W. 285 Annie E. (Elizabeth) (Ragland) 241 Anthony Jesper 594 Arron 594 Baby 42 Bee 83 Bessie G. 217 Beulah P. (Peaks) 42 Bolden 594 Calvin Coolage 192 Capt. L. 208 Charles Robert 616 Charles V. 192 Charlie M. 368 David 217 David C.v. 469 David D. 83 Dorothy J. 382 Edna 471 Edna E. (Edmonds) 382-383 Edna Johnson 83 Elcy 594 Eli 42 Elliott S. 241 Emma 139 Emma Gertrude Onion 382 Emma Lee Johnson 292 Emma W. 594 Essie B. 595 Eugene T. 469 Florence Winn 42 Frances Zenith Penn 83 Garland 595 George 241 George Jordan 595 Hattie 595 Hester F. 83 J.G. 42 James 595 James Bolden 595 James C. Rev. 341 James H. 469 James M. (Madison) 382-383 Jennie Sears 42 Jessie Forbes 382-383 Jinnie 42 Joe Calvin 469 Joe L. 84 John Lewis 469 John W. 432 Jonah 139 Julia 595 Julia Stinson 452 Junious 43 Junius 382-383 Kenneth Maurice 217 Lewis 192 Lillian Elizabeth 139 Lonnie P. 155 Lorraine 43 Louis 596 Lucille 341 Lucy (Jones) 217 Martha 84 596 Mary J. 405 Mary V. 595-596 Minnie P. 596 Mollie 84 Nannie 216 383

BROWN, (continued)
Nannie Barker 155 Nannie Bell 341 Norman 84 Ollie 139 Patsy 596 Payton 84 Payton Jerome 84 Payton Jr. 84 Perch 140 Phillip Matthew 217 Randolph 596 Ray 596 Reuben 341 Richard 432 Robert N. 383 Robert T. Milton 84 Rosa Anna (Jackson) 405 Royal A. 597 Ruby J. 597 Sandy 597 Selena 601 Stephan O. 597 Susen 597 Tearle Preston 155 Thomas 597 Thomas H. Jr. 597 Tommy 85 Virginia F. 597 William 217 598 William A. 217 341 William Ernest 85 William L. 598 William Russell 85 Willie L. 140 Wilson 598

BRYANT, A.J. 362 Alexander E. 421-422 Allen Hoover 88 92 Amy Renee 307 Ann Gunter 91 95 Annie E. 105 108-109 Annie Elizabeth (Tyree) 88 90 94 B. (Benjamin) Franklin 88 Baby Girl 88-89 Bessie Bryant 88 92 Bettie R. 88 Birdie B. (Branch) 564 Calvin C. Sr. 307 Calvin David 88 92 Carrington C. 89 Catherine Elizabeth Bryant 89-92 94 97 102 Charlie E. 308-309 Clifford Bryant 88 Clifford Earl 241 Clyde L. 308 Crawford D. 108-109 Curtis 88 Curtis Elliott 89 Dale 89 Damarcus L. (Mark) 89 David Banks 308 David C. 109 David M. 88-89 92 94 102 Edmonia Mrs. 105 Edna Mae Storm 93 104 Edna Rose 109 Elizabeth Stinson 89 93-94 Ella Jane 89 91 Ellen Dian(e) 90 93 Elsie 111 Emma Londeree 241-242 244 Emory Houston 90 Evelyn N. 90 Ezra Russell Sr. 308 Flora Coates 308 Floyd W. 90 93 Frances C. 290-292 G. (George) Clemon 90 92

BRYANT, (continued)
George D. (Dewey) 564 George D. (Dewey) Jr. 564 George Thomas 109 Georgia R. 364 Gilbert A. 109 Grace Farrish 241-242 Harry 241-242 Harry Willard 241-242 244 Harry William 90 92 Herbert Carroll 105 Hiawatha 106 Howard Elliott 88-91 93 96 Hubbard M. (Matthew) 91-92 Irene 87 Irving Leslie 91 James 89 91 93-95 James Camden 109 James Ralph (Jimmie) 242 Joe W. 106 John Everett 106 John H. 106 John R. 106 John Tilden 90-91 Joseph Tavern 91 Judy 242 Kaelynn Renee 308 Lafayette 91 Lillie Bryant 90-91 Lillie Byrd 241 Lillie S. (Stinson) 91-92 Lizzie R. 106 Lorene M. 405 Lorine Stinson 93 Louise 94 Lucy A. 92 94 109 Lucy Via 89 92 94 102 Luther E. (Everett) 421-422 Luther Harry 88 92 M. Pauline Wright 308-309 Maggie Bell 106 Mamie Jamerson 308 Martha Eagle 93 456 Martha S. (Staton) 421-422 Martin Harrison 87 Mary 110 Mary Francis 94 Mary Ida (Bryant) 89 92-93 95 Mary Stanley 107 Mary Susan 105 Mary Via 92-93 Maude Ellis Burks 88-91 93-94 96 Maude Isabell 93 Minnie Burks 94 309 Minnie Frances 90 93 Nannie 87 Nannie Vest 93 Nellie Duree 107 Nellie J. Miss 494 Oscar Moses 494 Otis Reid 93 104 P. Alexander 111 Paul W. 494 Percy Hilbert 110 Peter A. 107 Polly G. 309 Powell 87 93 456 Powhatan 92-94 Ralph David 308-309 Ralph Eldridge 242 Raymond M. 92-93 Richard T. 98 Robert Lee 107 Roy Edward 94 Roy Lee 90 94

BRYANT, (continued)
Ruby 94 Russell 94 Russell Roy 309 Sallie (Ragland) 242 Sam 94 Sam C. 107 Samuel (infant) 94 Susie Dunning 110 Thomas C. 92 94 Viola 89 102 William 105 William Cullen 94 William David 89 91-92 94 97 102 William David (2) 88 90 94 William Martin 87 William N. 107 William R. 105 William Wilson (Tete) 89 92-93 95 Willie 98 100
BURCHER, Earl B. 242
BURKE, Carrie 22 Horace B. 507
BURKS, (wife Of John A.) 111 Al Gould 111 Albert Crews 111 Clifford 93 Elsie Bryant 111 John A. 111 Martha 93 Mattie 558 Maude Ellis 88-91 93-94 96 Minnie 94
BURNEY, Elsie May B. 309-310 Herman Hacks 309 James Thomas 309-310
BURNLEY, Nettie 258
BURNS, Viola C. 405
BURRELL, Mary Rose 375
BURTON, Carrie L. 368 Delores M. 368 Isaac H. 368 Mabel 373 Maggie E. 368 Nannie B. 17
BUSCHMANN, Linda Rush 376
BYRD, Eunice 406 Evelyn Carter 115
B_____, John Harris 17 Mhw 30
CABBEL, Charlie E. 341
CABBELL, Charles H. 341 Fannie 341 Henry 342 Houston 469 Houston A. 470 John 342 Josephine T. 342 Raymond 470 Ruby 470 Sidney W. 342 Virginia T. 342 William 321 342 William L. Jr. 342 William L. Sr. 342
CABBLE, Essie 342
CABELL, Arthur Preston 112 Bettie Gordan Ms. 432 Clifford 115 Clifford (Jr) 115

CABELL, (continued)
Elizabeth Thorton Mrs. 112 Evalee (Wright) 112 Frances 357 Hammett Lawton 112 John S. (Sam) 112 Josie 113 Lillian Mrs. 470 Lucy Galt 115 Marcia J. 113 Margaret C. (Couch Anthony) 155 Margaret L. 113 Marion Winston 113 Marion Winston (Grandson) 113 Nannie C. 113 Overton 343 Rebecca W. 432 Thomas E. 113 Virginia L. 113 William M. 114 Winston 112-113
CAIN, Alease Allen 598 Alice 140 598 Alonzo Dea. 598-599 Alonzo Jr. 598 David 140 Isiah 140 James 599 Margaret L. (Dean) 598-599 Marguerite F. Deaconess 598 Mary Alma 599 Maynard E. 599 Odis 598 Robert 599 Robert J. 598-600 Warren 140 599 William 598 Willie 599 Wirt 140
CALL, Charles L. 306 Josephine (Allen) 306 Mildred 355 Nanie 352 Phillip Joshua 306 Willie Rolfe 306
CALLAGHAN, Alice Celeste 85
CAMDEN, Rebecca A. Miller 243 Walter T. 243
CAMPBELL, Kenneth H. 452
CAREY, Antoinette M. 218 Betty E. 68 Calvin Joe 218 Edna E. Mrs. 218 John H. Sr. 218 Martha D. 218 Robert 218 Ruby 230 Tom 218 William 218 William E. 219
CARR, Alma F. 155-156 Cynthia B. 599 Deanna J. 155 Infant Baby 155 Mark Anthony 155 Robert P. 155-156 Ronnie P. 155
CARRINGTON, Joseph N. 470 Michael Antwan 470 Myrtle E. 470
CARROLL, Baby 310
CARSON, Clara 432 Samuel R. 123

CARTER, Annie Amelia Janes 343
Arnold O. 599 Bill 95 Charles
Jesse 115-116 Charlie 343
Charlie Lewis 616 Cora 620
Elizabeth A. Stinson (Grandma
Carter) 451 Eugene 470 Evelyn
C. Bolden 592 599-600 G.L. 116
George P. 116 Gertrude E. 600
Irene 403-404 James 600
James Eddie 116 Jean T. 600
John Deacon 192 Kate
Moorman 116 Kim 326 Kyrie A.
326 Lucheon Cleveland 404
406 Lucy A. 499 Martha A. 116
Mary 95 Maude 115-116 Minnie
116-117 Moorman Harry 116
Nena E. 543 Patrick B. 116
Pierce Forest 343 R. (Richard)
D. 616 Rachel 193 Susan Jane
451 Susie 193
CASON, Jeannette S. 616
CATLETT, Harrison Thomas 418
CATTRELL, James Rev. 193
CAUL, Charlie 35 Lucy Spencer
422 Mattie B. (Banton) 35
CHAMBER, Levi 507
CHAMBERS, Aaron E. 326 Agnes
Moseley 120 Alice B. 326 Alvin
Meredith 406 Andrew 507 Anis
17 Bennie Lewis Sr. 406 Bennie
S. 406-408 Bettie 123 Calvin D.
(Delaware) 406-407 Cathren J.
326 Charlie 326 Clarence E.
406 Darrell Foster 117 David E.
118 David Ervin 118 Dorothy K.
118 Eddie Glover 407 Edith
Jones 507 Egar 333 Elijah 333
Eliza 406-407 Elizabeth M. 117
Ella W. 219 Emma H. 193
Emma L. 213 Essie Ernease J.
406-407 Essie Lee 617 Eugene
333 Fannie M. 118 Floyd H. 407
Geneva Marie 407 George 119-
120 326 George Lewis 120
George W. 219 Gilbert Deacon
193 Gracie V. 406-408 Henry L.
326 Ida 324

CHAMBERS, (continued)
Jack Junius 324 327 James
Ceasar 118 James F. 333
James G. 219 James H. 327
Joe Nathan 118-119 Joe Rev.
119 John 117 John H. 327
Joseph 193 Josh 219 Katie 119
King D. 333 Lewis Eli 407-408
Lillian Irene 26 Lillian Randolph
407 Lonnie 408 Lucy Jones 375
Maggie 328 Martha 117 193
Martha C. 219 Mary Lee
(Stanton) 407-408 Matilde 120
Minnie 193 327 Monroe 219
Nathan 118 Onell A. 333
Pauline 327 Peggie 194 Peter
194 Reuben 123 Robert Burton
285 Ruth E. 327 Sallie 327 408
Sarah E. 43 Shirley Sr. 333
Susan E. 117 Thomas 408
Tommy R. 408 Unnamed
Female Infant 120 Vinton
Marcell (Bennie) 118-119 Virga
(or Virgie) (Spencer) 119-120
W. Russell 333 Walter Bernard
408 Walter Bernard Jr. 408
Walter Lee 333 Wavely 408
Wilber 120 Willie 507 Willie M.
Jr. 328 Willie Moses Sr. 119
CHAPMAN, George W. 526 Hezzie
156 Morris R. 156 Patsy 526
Sarah Ann 156 William H. 156
William McKinley 156
CHARLTON, Sarah Anderson 21
CHASTAIN, Rene 121
CHATMAN, Cornelia (Chambers)
123 Glover Jr. 219
CHENNAULT, Margaret F. 43
CHIDESTER, Duke A. 107 Mamie
B. 107
CHILDRESS, Emmett L. 232
Fannie B. 232 Jackson 232
Joseph 232-233 Robert L. 306
Virginia A. 233
CHRISTIAN, Carline 357 Della 357
Frances Ann 156 Mary Susan
Booker 13 Roberta R. 357

CLABO, Pinkney L. 156 Viola H. 156
CLAIBORNE, Evelyn L. (Laury) 526 535 Garnett 146 Laura Garnett 147 Martha E. Scruggs 146-147 Mary Catherine 432 Temple I. (Irving) 146-147 Thomas O. 147 William Mack (Deacon) 432
CLAIRBORNE, Dolly Price 189 Lossin C. 189
CLARK, Alexand(er) 408 416 Bertha P. (Paige) Jones 409 Rosby D. 85 Vernell B. 85 Viola F. 378 Virginia Lee 564
CLARKE, Alice C. 114 Robert Benjamin 339
CLAY, Charles G. 481 Mary Henry 481
CLAYBORNE, Beatrice A. 433 Edith 433 Horace 383 James Pilot Pike 433 Pearl Ethel 433
CLAYTON, Joan M. (Pollard) 617
CLIBORNE, John 148 Leonard C. 95 Leonard T. 95 Lucy Jones 95 97
COATES, Flora 308 John R. III (Ricky) 482 488
COBB, Annie M. Moss 482 John Henry 482 Mary E. (Ellis) Bailey 422 Sidney Ross Jr. 557
COBBS, Charlie 518 Malinda 194 Sarah 518
COLBERT, Lula Miller 507
COLEMAM, Thomas Edwin 13-14
COLEMAN, Alfred M. 328 Alma G. 495 Ami Lynn 157 Annie 14 Annie A. (Amanda Gregory) 149 Benjamin Bryan 157 Clayton M. 149 Cyril Moseley 148-149 Dollie Woodall 157 Earnest 194 Eliza Moseley 149-150 Elizabeth Duryee 148-149 Emma F. 343 Ethel J. 343 Frank R. 149-150 Frank W. (Walker) 149 Garland E. 495 Gladys Coleman 149 Hazel Garris 13 Hiawatha L. 343

COLEMAN, (continued) Ida Megginson 13 Irene Walker 150 James E. 343 Marcus S. 617 Marian V. 149-150 Marshall 150 Martha Bertha 13 Mary Ayres 328 Minnie Profitt 13-14 Robert Ingersol 13 S. Joe 495 Susie B. 495 Thomas Braxton 150-151 Tom Fitzgerald 149 William Henry 149-150
COLES, Hazel Jones 302 Mary 213 Robert A. 301
COLLIER, Renee 79 Sam 271
COLLINS, Hattie 123 Jessie Maxey 343
COLMORE, Deborah 610
CONNER, Elizabeth 544-545 548
CONWELL, Terese A. 383
CONYERS, Alma L. 43
COOK, Elizabeth 175 Floyd W. 175 Ida B. 176 Ida W. 176 Robert 320
COOLEY, Bessie Laury 519
COOPER, Naomi E. 124 Travone Rayquan 445 447 Wilbur 43
CORBIN, Letcher Wade 79 _____ 519
COSBY, Laura E. 287 Mary 287 Mary M. 285 William 287 William C. 285
COTTRELL, Chiquita 527 Drake 527 Dwight D. 526 Edward 177 George Melvin 177 Irene Jones 526 Isaiah 177 James 177 James D. 526 Kenja D. 527 Major 177 Martha 178 Mrs. 482 Paul 526 Paul B. 178 Paul Burley 178 Paul D. 178
COUCHMAN, Mary H. 531
COX, Anna 600 Arren 600 Arthur 600 Clara 43 Eva J. 600 Franklin 600-601 Guy W. 43 Matthew Joel 179 Mattie C. 601 Mrs. Willie (Wade) 601 Thomas J. 601 Warren H. 601 Washington 601
CRAWFORD, Joe Lee 527

CREWS, (2 Infants-twins) 179 J. P. 564
CRUMP, Carl T. 157 Carrie B. 157 James G. 157 Lewis B. 157 Luther H. 157-158 Mamie Woodall 158 Martha M. 158 Vera T. 157-158 Viva S. 157 W. Harvey 158 William Calvin 158 William David 158
CUE, Frances 601 Gilbert 601
CUNNINGHAM, A. (Andrew) 383 Andrew 220 Annette 384 Brenda H. 519 George W. 564 Gertrude L. 28 Infant Daughter 565 Jack Walker 565 Joseph 565 Kemper M. 564 Laura Moore 564 Minnie Laura 565 Nannie 565 Nellie Miller 384 Reese G. 565 Robert Henry 384 Samuel P. 310
CUTTINO, George Jr. 220
DABNEY, Alex 179 Decker 180 Helen 180 Kenneth N. 433 William E. 180
DADE, Clarence F. 85-86 Minnie E. 85-86
DAMERON, Clementine B. 181 Miss Sallie 181 Robert B. 181
DANIEL, Gladys Wright 299 Jennetta White 44 Myrtle Miller 243 Robert 299 Thomas Dabney 243
DANIELS, Shorty 96
DAVIDSON, Elsie F. Wisdom 482 491 Mary F. 3
DAVIS, A.B. 181 Ashby Grigg 158 Aubrey H. 353 Aubrey Mitchell 184 Benzie 184 Bernard L. 181 Bessie 220 Bob 583 Caroline (Wood) 183 Carrie E. 181 Carris J. 353 Charles L. 566 Doris Robertson 185 Duane T. 220 Eliza (Liza) 315-316 Etta Mae 158 Eugene 183-184 Fred 470 Gertrude Price 184-185 Gordon Langhorn 184 Gordon Langhorn Jr. 184 Herman Foster 184

DAVIS, (continued)
Isiah 220 J. H. (John H.) (Jack) 183 Jefferson 183 Jimmy 184 John H. (Henry) 617 John Pitt 422 Joshua 182 Joshua Lee 182 Julian Rein 184 Lillie 220-221 Lucille Mitchell 185 Mamie A. 182 Margaret 184 Mary E. 182 Mary H. 617 Nannie Brown 216 Noah Louis (Dave) 565 Pearl V. (Baird) 420 422 Robert Earland 185 Robert J. 353 Robert N. 182 Rosa Anderson Gray 21 Rosa E. 182 Sallie Mrs. 471 Sarah Elizabeth 353 Thomas Jeff Jr. 184-185 Thomas Jefferson 184-185 Travis H. 182 Virginia Coleman 150 Virginia G. 220 Virginia Mary 221 W. M. Rev. 471 Walter 220-221 William 185 Willie E. 433 Wyomma Ragland 566 573
DAVISON, John W. 3
DAY, Alice B. 495 Isabel 502 John 356 Mary (Pankey) 356 Mary F. (Johnson) 221 Nannie Bryant 495 Van Buren 495 Willie Ann 107
DEAN, Fannie 194 James Rev. 194 Maggie 519 527 Major S. 471 Margaret L. 598 Maureen Denise 471 Thomas 519 527 William R. 2
DEDMOND, Grace D. 158-159 John E. 158-159 John E. Jr. 159 Roger Dale 159
DEEDEE, Davis Uwinski 185
DEFEO, Rose L. 339
DENTON, Betty Susan 304 John A. 304 Mildred Ella Kitchen 304
DIBBLE, Anna B. 384
DICKINSON, Ronald L. 159
DIGGS, Emma 194
DIXON, Alice L. 185 Amanda C. 186 Geneva 187 John Henry 186 John Madison 186-187

DIXON, (continued)
  John Tery 187 Lloyd Allen 186
  Madison P. 186 Mary A. 187-
  188 Mary Atkins 186 Montague
  Uriah 186 Ruth A. Ewers 186-
  187 W.N. 187-188
DOLAN, Cabell Odell 566 Edna
  Smith 566 Lula Mildred 566
  Melvin Douglas 566 Percy P.
  566 William Oswell 566
DOOLEY, Louise 568
DOUGLAS, Mariah 194
DOZIER, Hamlet M. 275
DRAKE, George Howard 188 Ida
  Virginia Garrett 188
DRYER, Rebecca C. 221
DUDLEY, Gladys L. 159 Mattie
  Mosley 68 Rosa 276
DUNCAN, Baby 617 Bernice
  Esther 269 Edith M. 621 George
  O. 617 Infant Son 270 James C.
  Deacon 617 Lena L. (Perkins)
  617 Louise Agnes (Turnstall)
  618 M.R. 269-270 Mary Louise
  618 Mattias (Mathias) 31-32
  Melissa 31-32 Percy A. 270
  Rosa B. (Ballowe) 243 Sallie B.
  618 Thomas E. 618 Tyler M.
  243 250 W.A. 269-270
DUNKUM, Bettie 31 Brandy
  Elizabeth 422-423 Cora L. (Lee
  Fitzgerald Coleman) 482 Edwin
  M. (Mack) 482 Elizabeth 422-
  423 Gladys Bersch 159 Julian
  482 Kim 422-423 Melissa A.
  (Ann) 422-423
DUNN, Kathleen Stiles 159
  Marcella 450 Mary Moseley 14
  Nim Bennie 159 Ridley B. Alvis
  14 William 14
DUNNEVANT, Ann Ranson 189
  Irene 189 Johnny 189
DUNNOVANT, Samuel A. 189
DUTY, Ethel Williams 483 Janie
  Forbes 483 L.F. (Lemuel Frank)
  483 W. (Wilburn) Taylor 483
  Warren K. (Kenneth) 483

DYER, Arzie 197 Chris Deacon
  194 John 392 433 Manervia 195
  Nannie 433 Vence 195
EAGLE, Martha 93 Rhonda Kay
  95-96
EANES, Edward 243 Edward L.
  243-244 Fred T. 243-244 Helen
  243 Lynn 243 Oliver W. 243-244
  Pearl M. 243-244 Ruby 243
  Sylvia Ann (Miller) 244
EAVES, Barbara B. (Beasley) 566
EDMONDS, Alexander M. 384
  Clarence Junious 384 Earl
  Randolph 384 Edna 382 Joseph
  R. 141 Mattie Ruth 141 Paul A.
  384 Virginia L. 44
EDWARDS, Bertha A. 423
  Elizabeth Baird 420 423 Maggie
  Chambers 328 Walter D. 423
  Walter H. 423
EICHORN, Ruth 211
ELDRIDGE, (No Name) 320 Annie
  F. 39 Annie Florence 195
  Benjamin H. 44 Bernice 276
  Bettie 44 Bettie E. Laury 527
  Carrie Jones 276 Clara Herbert
  44 Cora B. 44 Cora L. 46 Curtis
  B. Sr. 44 Dimple 44 Edna Brown
  471 Edward G. 45 Edward K 45
  Eleanor N. 45 Elisah 45 Elmore
  Jr. 45 Evelyn D. 45 Evelyn J.
  409 Fanny D. 45 George 45
  Harold Ivan 46 Harold W. 46
  James Granville 46 James M.
  46 Jennie 320 Jessie Dorothy
  Elizabeth Greenwood 204-205
  John 205 John Jr. 204-205 John
  William (Buster) 527 Katie 46
  Lillian 205 Linwood Taylor 46
  Margaret 527 Marshall 46 Mary
  Anna 46 Maurice 320 Morton H.
  46 Oretha M. 47 Premature
  Baby 445 Preston 47 Preston
  Simon 47 Robert 47 Robert
  Cortley 47 Robert Stanley 47
  Roger L. 445 Rolfe E. Dea. 276
  Samuel 47 527 534

ELDRIDGE, (continued)
　Thomas B. 45 Thomas E. 47
　Timothy 321 Velma S. 343
　William Elmore 47 William H. 47
　Willis 321 Wm. Rolfe 205
ELLIOTT, Mary Frances 527
　Raymond L. 527
ELLIS, Celia 524 529 534 Emma 524
ENNELS, Nanny 606
EPPS, Natalie 141
EUBANK, Lucy Ann Alvis 14 Mary Branch 14
EUBANKS, Phyllise Hutcherson 206 Terry M. 206
EVANS, Annie 358 James 209 Martha 208 Mary Mrs. 208 Thomas H. 208 William 209 William M. 209
EWING, Malcolm 14 Olivia Booker 14
FALLS, Laythan M. 159 Ruby D. 159
FARRISH, Joyce (Bryant) 244 Shirley D. 244
FENDER, Robbie P. 160 Walter S. 160
FERGUSON, Mary Jane 313-314
FIELDS, Augustine E. 224 Mary Rosalind 362
FIRMIN, Betty Day 496 David Mitchell 496
FISHER, Selena B. (Brown) 601
FITZGERALD, Cora L. 482 F. 221 Joseph 376 Mar 221 Martha J. 376 Mary Anderson Lewis 21
FLEMING, May Ellen Cox 344 William Waverly Rev. 344
FLOOD, Ann E. 259-260 Sarah Agnes 20
FLOURNOY, Alice 394 Ruth Inez Kitchen Robertson 304
FLOWERS, James Hopkins 369 James Preston 369 Leonard G. 369 Mary E. 369 Samuel L. 369
FLOYD, Vincent Daniel 96
FOGG, Audrey G. 333

FORBES, Janie 483 Alfred 212 Alfred J. 221 Bernard Brown 483 Bertha M. 212 C. J. 483 Charlie M. 385 Classie G. 385 Eugene 385 George T. 483-484 Hattie Evelyn 483 Helen Oliver 483 Hester K. 26 Janie 491 Jessie 382-383 Kate 195 Marion Charlotte 483 Mildred W. 385 Oscar Reed 212 Penelope L. 221 Penelope P. 538 Peter Alexander 483 Sallie 212 Solomon Jr. 328 Susanna B. 212 Susie O. 212 T. (Thomas) Parrack 483-484
FORD, Anna E. 48 Callie 328 Charlie C. 48 Diamond 213 Dorothy 48 Elizabeth B. 409 Elizabeth Miss 213 Emma L. Mrs. (Chambers) 213 369 Frank 328 George Huston 48 Grover H. 214 Grover Harrison 213 369 James 507 John B. 333 Johnnie 213 L.L. Rev. 214 Leeolian V. 369 Lucas R. 328 M. Eva 214 Maria 214 Martha 409 Martha Johnson 508 Mary 26 409 Nancy 329 Pearl Austin 26 Phillip 214 R. Blanche 48 Rosa Wright 214 Roslyn 214 Thelma Stinson 96 101 William (Will) 214 William Henry 27
FORREST, W. M. Rev. 195
FOSTER, C. D. 264 Ewell J. 264 Laura 264 Mary 551 Mary A. 264 Mary Ann 550-551 William 551
FOUNTAIN, Sidney 231 W.H. (or C.) 124
FRANCISCO, Male Child 231
FULCHER, Gladys Seay 496 J. Rosser 160 John Henry Jr. 496 Mary Jamerson 160
FULLER, Daisy (Davis) 222 Frank 527
GALLADAY, Emma (I.) Payne 557-558 Isaac M. 558

GALLODAY, Josiah F. 557-558
GANNAWAY, Catharine S. 209
  John 209 Martha H. 209
GANTT, Octavia Rose 76
GARLAND, Lula Ragland 241
GARNETT, A. (Alfred) Cooke 484
  Alfred Cook 484 Annie 487-488
  Frank M. 484 Harold 484 Nellie
  Evelyne 484 Nellie Noble 484
  Tina W. 484
GARRETT, (mother Of Emmett
  Lanxton) 335 Anderson Wert
  222 Annie L. 234 Arthur W. 222
  Aubrey Rolf 233 Barbara Ann
  222 Christina Rebecca 232 Ella
  O'bryant 233 Emmett Lanxton
  335 Geo. Washington 233-234
  George Rolf 233 John Ed 222
  John Wesley 222 Landon Levi
  Sr. 233 Larry Melvin 233 Louisa
  W. Gormus 233-234 Lucille 235
  Mary E. 222 Rickey L. 180
  Robert A. Sr. 222 Roy Garland
  234 Sarah E. 223
GARRISON, George W. 270
GAYLE, Emmet Patterson 35
GEGGY, (Union Br. Ch) 508
GENTRY, Alice Flournoy 394
GIBSON, Bolden A. 601-602 Byrd
  L. 434 Clarence Oscar 602 Eliza
  W. 601-602 F.D. 602 Giles E.
  48 602 Martha 602 Mary M. 434
  Maurice Lee 602 Moses 602
  Naomi Lou 160 Nioy 602 Percell
  48
GILBERT, Ada Mallie Mertis
  Perrow 545 Humphrey 235
  Joseph C. 235 Judith Albina
  (Elbinah) 235 Leanna F. 236
  Mattie 480 Paulina 235 Robert
  Thomas 545 Sophia Jane 236
  William P. 235 William Riley 235
GILES, Cleveland 602 Mary B
  (Bolden) 592 Mary Bolden 602
GILLIAM, Sidney Branch 237 Alice
  E. 160 Ann Steger 236-237
  Arnold C. 160 C. 49

GILLIAM, (continued)
  Garland 490 Hazel Cooper 485
  John Branch 485 John Edwin
  496 John Edwin Jr. 485 John
  Henry 160 L. Kyle 496 Mary C.
  496 Mary Kyle 496 Nancy 490
  Nannie Duncan 161 Nannie W.
  485 R. Archie 485 Robert
  Branch 485 Robert Hendricks
  (Big Bob) 236-237 Robert Isham
  (Little Bob) 236 Sidney 236
  Susan Ellen 237 William W. 496
GILLISPIE, Emma C. 223 Melvin
  212
GILLS, Earl Irving 161 Ella Wilson
  161 Harriet W. 161 Henry W.
  161 Hugh Andrews 161 Ida M.
  161 Irene Leona 161 John H.
  161 John W. 161 Leona D. 162
  Lillie Roxie 162
GLOVER, Stephan A. (Anthony)
  259-260 Ann E. (Elizabeth)
  (Flood) 259-260 Anthony Dibrell
  259 Bessie N. 223 Billy Franklin
  471 Charles Benjamin 259
  David W. 357 Earnest T. Sr. 434
  Edward Lee 260 Frank Eugene
  223 George A. 223 George E.
  Mr. 471 Hallie Spencer 259
  Howard Jr. 223 Howard Sr. 223
  James David 259 John 223
  Johnnie Junius 471 Johnny J.
  471 Joseph Walter Spriggs 259
  261 Louis Thomas 260 Lucille
  Booker 472 Mary J. 209 Mary J.
  Flood 260 Maxine (S.) 472
  Minnie Swoope 458-459 Price
  458-459 Rebeccca Susan
  Anderson 259-260 Richard A.
  (Asbury) 259-260 Richard
  Monroe 260 Sarah Elizabeth
  260 Sarah Fearn Jones 357
  Twins 261
GODSEY, Arvertice Taylor 353-354
  Cal 353 Chester Irene 353-354
  Earnest 353

GODSEY, (continued)
Edna Virginia 353-354 John
Renny 353-354 Louise 353
Shirley Marie 354
GOFF, Kenneth James 423
GOIN, A. J. 485 Ada 485 Cleove
Mr. 485 Dorothy S. 486 Edie
Calvin 485 James M. 486 John
J. 486 Luke D. 486 Maggie 489
Mattie Toney 486 Peter T. 486
Richard A. 486 Sallie 486 Willie
E. 486
GOINES, Caroline C. 409 John
Moses 409
GOLDEN, Margaret W. Terry 463-464
GOLLADAY, Mamie C. 558 Mattie
Burks 558 Samuel M. 558
GOODE, Berta 261-262 Claude Jr.
262 Claude Sr. 261 Effie Rip
262 Frances Scruggs 49 Infant
Male 262 James 261-262
Thomas B. 262
GOODEN, Allen 519 Christine
Shelton 519
GOODWIN, Emily 276
GOOLSBY, Alice 195 J. Pink 316
GORDAN, Bettie 432
GORDON, Adeline 528-529 537
Annie 528 Baby(1) 528 Bay (2)
528 Eliza Rebecca (Mosley) 528
Gertrude 539 James D. Rev.
528 Joe Smith 528 Lantz 185
Lewis 528-529 537 Mary Lou
529 537 Maud 443-444 Phyllis
528 Rosemay Davis 185
Samuel 529 Stuart 185 Stuart
D. 185
GORMAS, Augustus 234 Rebecca
Whitlo 234
GORMOURS, Georgia 263-264
Pattie 263 Sarah J. 263 William
G. 263
GORMOUS, William Sr. 263
GORMUS, Judy Walden 188
Louisa W. 233-234 Wesley 188

GOSS, Alease R. Harvey 49
Donald Harvey 49
GOUGH, Andrew 27 Annie Park
386-387 Annie V. (Virginia) 195
Betsy 460 Frances 195 Herbert
S. 196 Jennie V. 329 Lillian
Belle 387-388 Lloyd D. 196
Timothy Archie 329 Walter 325
329 Warren Harden 196 Wilson
E. 196
GOVERNOR, Augustine E. (Fields)
224 Onizene A. 224
GRANT, Sallie L. 603
GRAY, Annie E. 79 Baby 286
Charlie 276 Edna 49 Eligah 276
Elise (Logan) Shelton 286-288
James Wesley 141 Lucius Cary
286 Mary Lizzie 335 Nancy 344
Rosa Anderson 21 Rose 276
Sallie B. 276 Sue 141
GREEN, Addie J. 409 Allen 603
Allen Jr. 603 Edith M. (Gray)
603 James R. 224 Jeffrey P.
409-410
GREENE, Ruth M. 5
GREENWOOD, Jessie Dorothy
Elizabeth 204-205
GREGORY, Alexander 141 Alfred
Randolph 49 Allen Ray 618
Allice Lillian Laura Spencer
Perrow 546 Alma 410 Andrew
M. 496 Annie 141 Christopher
C. 49 Clarence 141 Clinton H.
244 Cora L. 244 Curtis 49
Deacon Emmett 140 142
Dorothy Lee 49 Edkie 142
Elizabeth 140 142 Eugene 49
Fannie D. 79 Floyd Alvin 618
George W. 79 George Wesley
Jr. 80 Hilton 50 Irene E. 50
James 50 James Franklin 50
James T 50 Jennie Mae 50
Junious 50 Kate B. 51 Kathleen
546 Kevin D. 80 Laura Foster
264 Leroy 51 Leslie 51 Lucy
142 Lucy W. 51 Margaret C.
496 Marion 255 Marsha 51

GREGORY, (continued)
Mary B. 51 Millard 546 Moses
51 142 Nat. Lancaster 264-265
Nathaniel Marshall 264 Orville
Bell 265 Pearl Daisy 618 Polly
51 Randolph 51 Ruby 52 Sarah
Jane 142 Stephen 52 Tillman
Arthur 265 Virginia Marshall
Saunders 264-265 Wanda
Melissa 52 William L. 52 Willie
142
GRIFFIN, Earl H. 310 Harry Lee 68
James W. 68 Kiah D. 69 Mary
T. 310
GRIFFITH, Archie Ray 162 Erma
E. Deal 162 Grace E. 162 John
Leroy 162 Noah C 162
GRIGG, Edward 209-210 Edward
Marshall 150-151 Harriet H.
209-210 Julian 150-151 Julian
A. 150-151 Nellie Coleman 150-
151 Peter S. 210 Philip N. 210
Rodney Duane 151
GRIMES, Donnie 508 Rena M. 508
GUILL, Mamie 488
GUNTER, Ben Spencer 496
Britney E. 566 Bruce 96 Charles
L (Lightfoot) 567 569 Charles R.
567 569 Charles W. 567-568
Clarence Albert 567-568 Eliza
Webb 567 569 Evelyn G. 310
Jesse E. 567-568 Jesse Frank
364 John E. 567-568 Kenneth
L. 310 Lacy D. 310 Lillian
Wilkerson 567-568 Louise D.
(Dooley) 568-569 Louise R. 311
Lula Jane (Webb) 567-568 Lula
T. 567-568 Mamie Burks 77
Marshall Ren 497 Mary 571 573
Mattie M. 497 Orville 497
Richard B. 568 Robert Floyed
568 Ruby Moyer 364 Sammy L.
310 Susan Demarius 572 574
Thomas J. 568 Thomas W. 77
Walter C. 567-569
GUNTHER, Elizabeth C. 311 Janie
S. 261 John W. 261

GUNTHER, (continued)
R. W. (Buster) 261 Robert L.
311 Robert W. 311
GUTHRIE, Bettie 266 Elizabeth
Coleman 265 J. J. (John James)
265 James A. 542 William Jr.
(Buck) 265
GUTHRIE, Martha Goodman 265
HACKETT, Andrew L. 96 Ann 267
Annie Blade 267 Barbara (A.) R.
(Ragland) 245 253 Bessie W.
(Wade) 266-268 Bessie Wade
245 Calvin E. 266 Cassie O'Dell
501 Dennis M. 245 Edmund W.
(Word) 245 Elizabeth M. Tate
Pool 267 Henry 245 James J.
96 John Preston 267 Mary E.
Raker 96 Mary Elizabeth Word
267-268 Otis Lee 245 Pearl
Adcock 239 245 Princey 267
Princey A. 267 Sarah Elizabeth
(Eliza) (Dolan Or Stark) 267
Shirley Astroth 245 Thomas 267
Thomas E. 245 Thomas E.
(Edmund) 266-268 Willis J. 268
Willis Walker 267-268
HADNESS, Clementine F. 32
HAISLIP, Foster S. 265
HALL, Alexander S. 304 Boots 1-2
Mildred Ella Kitchen Denton
304-305 Raymond E. 497 Susie
Adams 1-2
HAMILTON, Minnie Ellis 524 529
HAMLETT, Arthur T. 385 Irene J.
385 Versie L. 369
HAMLIN, Clara 277
HAMNER, Amanda 269 Annie
Putney 268 Ila H. Jones 268
Manoah S. 268 Sarah Morris
269 Walter Leland 269 William
Edward 269 Wyatt Leland 269
HANES, Eliza 22 Elmo 423
HANLEY, Beatrice 124
HANSON, Clifton 423
HARDIMAN, Arthur B. 497 Aubrey
J. 497 Aubrey J. Jr. 498

HARDIMAN, (continued)
 Daisy S. 498 George W. 498
 Hattie Louise 553 Rebecca
 Clyde 498
HARDING, Mae Beth 385
HARPER, Amanda E. (Perkins)
 529 532 Anthony Lee 529
 Arthur 529-532 534 540 Baby
 529 Bettie 534 Don William 530
 Esau 530 Essie L. 530 Estelle
 Cunningham 530 Florence O.
 (Oliver) 530 Florence Turner
 530 George W. 530 540
 Herman A. 530 James 531 540
 Lacy 531 Lillie B. 530 536-537
 Lizzie 531 Lucy Ann (Pride)
 529-532 534 Nora H. 525 Sam
 H. (Henry) (Sr.) 530-531
 Samuel H. (Jr.) 531 Sarah J.
 (Jefferson) 531 533 Spencer
 531 Taylor (baby) 532 Taylor
 (Sr.) 529 532 540 Valarie 532
 William E. 532
HARPR, Margaret 526
HARRIS, Thornton R. 509
 (husband Of Georgia Gormours)
 263-264 A. B. (Alexander
 Benjamin) 270-271 Alice N.
 (Neil) 508 Allen 362-363
 Americus B. 286 Annie L. 196
 Baby 52 Bennie B. (Benjamin
 Beadle) 270-271 Bertha 7
 Bertha E. 289 Bessie A. 618
 Carrington 6 Christine 80
 Cleophas O. 508 Clifton P. 142
 David H. 271 Dorothy B. 508
 Edith Miller 245 Edwin A. 271
 Evelyn E. 508 Francis Tilden
 245 Garland 124 George 508
 Georgia Gormours 263-264
 Gertrude E. 52 Infant 271 Isiah
 271 Jack 272 James W. 272
 Joe 80 Joe W. 618 John 603
 John Edgar 542 John J. 603-
 604 Joseph 80 603 Katie C.
 (Marion Catherine Collier) 272
 Kenneth Ayres 272 Leon N. 142

HARRIS, (continued)
 Lillian 604 Louise 508 Maggie
 196 Marcia J. 286 Margary N.
 604 Marie 509 Marion Catherine
 Collier (Katie C.) 270 Marshall 6
 Mary Ellen Maxey 313 Mary J.
 270 Mary J. (Mollie) 272 Mary
 Lula 313 Mary S. 508 515
 Minnie Carter 116-117 Mr.
 William 52 Queen B. 17 Robert
 451 Robert W. 271 Roland 451
 Russell Harrison 6 Sarah 362
 603-604 Susan Jane Carter 451
 Susie 603-604 Tom 509 Walter
 363 Walter Howard 18
 Washington 363 Watson 363
 William 2 363 618 William Henry
 451 Willie A. 270-271 Willie
 Cleveland 272 Winston 7
HARRUP, Delsie R. 498 James M.
 498
HARTMAN, William A. 618
HARTWELL, James B. 472 Lottie
 E. 344 Lucy W. 472 Queenie
 344 Wilson B. Deacon 472
HARVEY, Alice Lowe 162 Charlie
 52 Clarence Lee 277 George
 335 Mary A. 162 Mary Alice 162
 Mrs. Lottie B. 53 Richard Eddie
 163 Robert Len 53 Rosa B.
 (Bell) 332 335 Roy William 164
HASKINS, Robert 292 Thomas 532
 Viola Estelle (Bennett) 532
 Virginia Johnson 292
HAYES, James Colbert 163 Mack
 163 Martha A. 163
HAYNES, Diane Yvonne 576
HEATH, Florence D. 498 Percy D.
 498
HEDGEMAN, Amanda 207 Bennie
 206-207 Calvin 206 Charlie
 Bennie 206 Fannie R. 206-207
 John E. 206-207 Polly 206-207
 William Macarthur 207
HEINLMAN, Constance M. 339

HELLARD, Babies 554 Fred. W. Sr. 554 Mable A. (Whorley) 554 Young Child 555
HEMLEY, Willie A. 124
HEMMINGS, Lottie P. 434 Mary E. 460 Thomas 434 Willa Jones 286
HENDERSON, Emma S. 472
HENDRICK, Edith Irene 210 Elijah H. 210
HENLEY, Rannie 124
HENSON, Irene 117 J Walter 117 Pattie 117
HESS, Martha Baber 33
HICKS, Annie Coleman 14 Patrick Henry 14-15
HIGGENBOTHAM, Mrs. Nelson T. (Mary Nelson Trent) 303
HIGGENBOTHAN, Sidney E. 303
HILL, George Ellis 196 James Franklin 385 Judie 196 Kindora 266 Myrtle Chapman 163 Rosa L. 196
HIX, Bessie Susan 163 Hilda Baldwin 163 Susie Garnett 163 Thomas Bocock 163 Thomas Cook 163
HOBSON, Elizabeth E. 209
HOCKER, Frances 532 George Walker 273
HODNETT, Anne Eyres 274 John 274 John (Sr.) 274 Lucy (Lucia) Brooks 274 Philip 274
HOLEMAN, James 197 Mollie 197
HOLLAWAY, Elsie J. 293 William O. 293
HOLLIND, Frank 277 Mattie 277
HOLMAN, Carrie 619 Clarence (Tuffy) 410 Hartwell J. (James) 301 Hattie 619 Jessee 619 John 410 Judith Spencer 301 Lawrance Sr. 410 Mary Virginia 410 Mattie Lee 410 Mildred A. 410 Samuel 410 Sarah Y 31 Sarah Y. 31 Tandy 301
HOLMES, Herbert A. 274
HOME, Mary Ann (Jones) 124

HOOPER, Benjamin A. 163 Mary H. 163
HOPKINS, Fannie Lowe 164 Jake C. 164
HORNER, J. (John) T. 280
HORSLEY, Alvin 281 Carrie Lee Morriss 319 Daniel 281 Eugene Hamilton 569 Mattie 281 Mattie Gordon 434 Mrs. Martha C. 434 Percy Clarence 569 Percy Robert 319
HOWARD, Jewell 12-13
HOWELL, Ester 103 Robert P. 378
HUDDLESTON, Roberta Jamerson 281-282 Rosa L. (Jamerson) 281-282
HUDGINS, James Edward 224 John H. 465 Sallie Ann 224
HUDSON, Sarah Wade 80
HUGHES, Angie 124 Archie C. 558-559 Bernice 125 Carey J. 125 Carrie M. 564 Ethel 125 James Hasten Sr. 125 Jessie 532 Lucy 125 Nannie C. 532 Nell G. 558-559 Pattie M. J. 125 Sallie 130 W.M. 619
HUTCHERSON, Edward D. 509 John 509 Mahald J. 509 Mrs. Augusta Jones 509 Phyllise 206 Thomas Wesley 509
HUTCHINGS, Carl E. Bates 96 99
IRVING, Catherine Mcivor 365
JACKSON, Ada 411 Alphonza 411 Amos M. 69 Andrew 532-533 Ann Shirley Elizabeth 411 Benny R. 411 Caryl 490 Charlie 519 Dora B. 519 Dorothy T. 27 Eddie H. 411 Edward 519 Ella Mae 180 Ella W. Deaconess 434 Essie Corrine 53 George 411 Gladys L. 540 Hallie C. (Clark) 403 411-412 416 Hattie 363 Herman Jr. 344 James 412 Jimmy 412 John Junius 412 Joseph (Joe) 559 Lacy H. 533 Lottie C. 405 411-412 Minnie B. 86 Rosa Anna 405

JACKSON, (continued)
Roxanne D. 619 Samuel 405
411-413 Susie C. 412 Theodore
Lamont 509 Tonita V. 53
Virginia 412 W. (William) F. 520
Walter 412 Willie 413 540 Willie
Raymond 413
JACOBS, Ephraim E. 125
JAMERSON, Beatrice B. 311
Bossieux Jackson 282 Calvin
Marshall (Boo) 281-282 Charles
H. 164 Daniel Wallace 281-282
Edward W. 311 Evie 282 Evie J.
(Jame) 282 Florence E. 164
Frances 272 Harry 282 Jennie
(Virginia Sharp) 283 John D.
273 Maggie G. 261 P. S.
(Poindexter) 282 Pocahontas
Fariss (Pokey) 282 Robert
Samuel 282 Roberta H. (Harris)
273 Thomas Edgar 282 Thomas
Jackson (Tommy) 282 William
Oscar 261 Willie Early 282
JAMES, Bernard W. Sr. 472 Edith
W. (Woodson) 619 Fountain
Curtis 472 Gertrude 473 Henry
Flood 473 Laura F. 473 Lewis
H. 473 Ronnie Lamarge 473
Susie 616 Willard W. 473
William H. 344
JAMISON, Margaret 283 Richard
B. (Beverly) 283 Thomas P. 284
William J. 2
JANES, Bettie Sears 344 Edward
344 Fannie 345 George E. Sr.
345 Josephine Lee 345
JEFFERSON, Betsy 533 John 533
John William 533 Lucy 531 533
JEFFERY, Bettie 345
JEN, Barbra 53
JENNISON, Rev. Watson W. 53
JOHNS, Farrel D. 369
JOHNSON, Lettie 620 Abbey
Elizabeth 293 298 Abbington
293-294 Abraham Jr. 224 Albert
293 296 Albert T. 423-424 Alice
W. (Walker) 290

JOHNSON, (continued)
Allen Coleman 386 Allie (Alley)
293-295 297-298 Alphonso 510
Amsia 293 296 Angelina 293
Anna 429 Arzie D. (Dyer) 197
Beatrice 294 Bertha A. 510
Bessie L. 345 Beulah W.
(Woodson) 619 Bobby Ann 510
Booker 619 Camel 510 Charlie
294 Charlie T. (Hike) 510
Charlotte T. 294-295 Chatman
294 296 Clarence 294 Clarence
E. 197 Clyde E. 620 Clyde T.
164 David 445-446 Doris F.
(Leechie) 386 Ed 294 Edgar M.
Jr. 164 Edmond Hubbard 290
Edna 83 125 Edward W. 604
Ella Louise 510 Ellen W. 277
Emily 294 Emma 620 Ernest
Junior 358 Evelyn J. Lee 510
Fletcher 510 Frances 293-294
Frances C. (Bryant) 290-292
Frank 604 George 345 George
G. 473 George H. 291
Georgiana Daniel 295 Gertrude
G. 413 Hallie R. (Reynolds)
423-424 Hattie J. 510 Henry
511 Hubert N. 604 Hubert O. 53
Ida M. 423-424 James Alex 125
James Henry 511 James Mundy
424 James R. 246 Jane 298
Jaquin C. 197 Jeanette H. 435
Jeff 126 Jeremiah Leo 511 John
294-295 John H. (Jack) 293-295
297-298 John W. 511 Josie
Reynolds 424 Judith E. 293 295
297 Judith Frances (Fannie)
291 Kyle 197 Lacy Irene 295
Lou (Gertrude) S. 444 446
Lucille 224 Lynn 605 Mabel T.
345 Mamie Woodson 620
Mandie 294 Maria 511 Maria
(md to Napoleon) 295-296
Maria (md to Royal) 295-296
Mary F. 221 Mary S. 224
Mildred J. 605 Nancy 296

JOHNSON, (continued)
Nannie Hill (Bransford) 290-291
Napoleon 295-296 Nathaniel C.
605 Nellie V. 473 Nellie V.
(Ross) 246 Oliver Ollie 511 Ollie
511 Ollie Stuart 296 Philmore
511 Prince 296 Raymond 511
Robert N. 423-424 Rosa Florine
53 Royal 295-296 Russell L.
413 Sadie 296 Sallie C. 54 Sam
512 Sammy David 9 Sarah 294
296 Sasha 296 Susie 126 Susie
B. 605 T. 620 Thelma J. 619
Thomas 290-292 Thomas L.
225 Thomas P. 435 Thomas W.
424 Van Lue 512 Virginia 292
Waine 512 Walter 474 Walter
W. 512 Washington 293 295
297 William 126 512 620
William A. 54 297 William Abner
297 William James 297 William
Jr. 297 William T. (Thomas)
290-291 Willie 512 Willie C. 126
Willie K. 446 Willis 293 298
JONES, (male Child) 302 Allice 54
Allie Marshall 369 Amanda 435
Andrew 435 Ann Elizabeth 582
Annie G. 474 Annie H. 512
Annie K. 126 Annie Park
(Gough) 386 Annie R. 446
Augusta 509 Bernice J. 286
Bertha P. 409 413 Bessie Ann
197 Bettie 126 Bill 97 Blanche
Pearl 413 Brenda 329 Carl Ray
286 Carmen 386 Carol P. 538
Carol Powell 386 Carrie 227
Charles (Chuck) 225 Charles G.
512 Charlie 277 Charlie A. 358
Charlie Samuel 301-302
Christine M. 302 Clara 225
Claudia V. 301-302 Clifford 299
Clyde O. 435 Cora Banks 413
Cora Carter 620 Cora Lee 299
Doria Louise (Toni) 424 Doris A.
435 E. W. (Buck) 386 Earl 335
Eddie Nathaniel 225 Edgar 621
Edith 507

JONES, (continued)
Edith M. (Duncan) 621 Edna
Tucker 299-300 Edward E.
(Erin) 386 Edward L. Sr. (Les)
413 Efford R. 414 Elbert Jr. 299
Elbert Sr. 299 Eliza J. 621
Elizabeth 54 Elizabeth C. 414
Ella 126 Elsie May (Booker)
386-387 Emma Perkins 197
Ernest 413-414 Ernestine 414
Ernie 621 Estelle 302 Esther
Pankey 358 Ethel L. 278 Fannie
L. 197 Fanny 97 Florence 621
Florence B. 414 474 Frank E.
370 Frank Sr. 126 Geneva Ella
96-97 George 302 George Fox
474 George R. 512 515
Gertrude B. 512-513 Gomex
Earl 414 Gracie L. 435 Hal
Coolidge 97 Hattie 198 Hattie G.
485-487 Henry L. 512-513
Henry P. 386-387 Hortense M.
410 414 Ila H. 268 Irene B. 414
James 198 370 James C. 387
James Christian 299-300 James
Elmo 96-97 James P. 387
James Robert 386-387 556
Janie 513 Jennie 435 Jennie
Rollins 474 Jerry Lee 370 Jewel
126 Joann 387 John 370 John
C. Jr. 286 John C. Sr. 286-287
John Dashwood (Pal) 387 John
H. 474 John Henry 621 John L
(Letch) 97 John L. Rev. 415
John R. 413 415 John Robert
Sr. 621 Johnnie W. 54 Joseph
Rev. 621 Junious L. 415 Katie
622 Lawrence 198 Lawrence P.
E. 225 Lelia B. 225 Lena B. 474
Leo . L 97 Leon W. 486-487
Leon Winston Jr. 300 Lillian
Belle (Gough) 387-388 Lillian L.
80 Lilyan D. 300 Lottie P. 286-
287 Louise 257 Louisiana 513
Lucy A. 54 Lucy A. (Allen) 622
Lucy Anderson 21 Lucy B.
(Blanche Bryant) 97

JONES, (continued)
M. A. 303 Mabel 623 Mansfield Onell 54 Margaret Elizabeth (Peg) 300 Marie Jackson 415 Martha 512 Martha Ann 302 Martha Lee 96-97 Mary 420-421 Mary Ann 124 300 Mary Brachett 54 Mary E. 250 Mary S. 474 Mary Shelton 287 Mary V. (Bradley) 126 Matthew Sr. Deacon 127 Maude O. 474 Mildred (Branch) 225 Minnie J. (Stinson) 246 Nancy 370 Nellie 127 Nellie M. 533 539 Nora J. (Steger) 246 Otis J. 358 Paige 436 Paul C. Sr. 436 Paul Irving 387-388 Pauline 388 Percy 435 Peter F. 80 Phillip 513 Pocahantas 198 Reginald G. 533 Richard 413 436 Richard Donald 55 Robert B. 388 Robert Gilliam 486-487 Robert L. 375 Rolf Leon Sr. 287 Rosa Ann 302 Sam 475 Sam (Samuel) R. 335 Samuel 55 358 Sarah 225 277 Sid Ellis 475 Sidney 513 Sopha 198 Taswell 301 Thelma Young 622 Thomas E. Jr. 300 Thomas H. Sr. 436 Thomas J. (Junious) 622 Tom 112 358 Tom W. 415 Tommy J. 436 Virgil 388 Virginus M. 622 Walter 55 Wiley 301 Willa 286 William 436 622 William A. 246 William Claude 97-98 William E. 358 William H. 388 William Horace 388 William T. 415 William W. 127 Willie E. (Ted) 386 388 Willie R. (Roosevelt) 358 Wilmare Deacon 198 Winston 277 Wyatt N. 436 533 539

JORDAN, Ameta S. (Spencer) 437 441 Helen Wilkerson 569

JORDEN, Maria 55

JUDGE, Lucy Jane (Harper) 534

KASSIM, Ida Cook 176

KEAR, Brandon S. 98

KELSEY, Elizabeth A. 164 Frank E. 164 Grace C. 164

KENNY, Lily Mae Turner 178

KERR, William J. Rev. 287

KIDD, Alice Via 99 Cathleen 98 Corine S. 72 Henry O. 336 Ida C. 143 Joe 143 Sadie M. 437 439 Tom L. 143 Troy Lee 98 Virginia Stanton 55 Virginius 99 Wilson 98

KIM, Lee Koon 15

KING, Ethel F. 388 James I. Sr. 127 Macy R. 127 Rebecca (Lee) 127

KINNEY, Barbara L. 475

KIRBY, Fred 164 Maggie Moss 164 Odell J. 165 Pattie Pollard 622 Robert Woodford 165

KITCHEN, Alma Ethelle Swan 72 Ann Elizabeth 305 Annie Ragland 305 Benjamin Wickliff Jr 304 Benjamin Wickliff Sr. 304-305 Betty Susan Denton 304-305 Charles Yost 304 Florence Dawn 305 Infant 305 John Denton Sr. 304-305 Johnnie Denton 72 Kruger Mckinley 304 Martha Susan Robertson 304-305 Ruby Ethel (1) 304 Ruby Ethel (2) 305 Thomas Richard 304-305 William Lewis 304-305

KYLE, Addie Walker 400 Eliza S. 459 Frances A. 437 George 400 George Thomas Jr. 437 Gertrude B. 437 Henry Rev. 534 Ida H. 15 James C. 300 James D. 534 Jesse Sr. 400 Jessie T. 437 John Edward Jr. 69 Margaret S. 389 Mary 496 Mary Wooldridge 15 582 Robert Thomas 15 Tonia Renee 69 Vennie 534 Virginia 440 William A. 534

LAIRD, Joseph Robert Sr. 339

LANCASTER, Mrs. Frances 397

LAND, Elsie 377

LANDRINE, Martha B. 605
LANE, Emma H. 394 Frank L. Sr. 394 Nannie 394 Romulus B. 394
LANN, Hattie 462 Jimmy 462 Mary Ann Elizabeth Shoemaker (Annie) 462 William A. (Willie) 462
LARA, (Union Br. Ch.) 503
LATTIMER, Carole Shelton 520
LAURY, Abraham 520 Asbury 520 Bettie (Harper Eldridge) 534-535 Celia Ellis 524 529 534 Charles Washington 520 Evelyn 526 Isaiah Jr. 520 John H. (Harold) 534-535 Lue Dora Mrs. 520 Lula Elizabeth Austin 520 Mamie M. 521 Manola P. 534-535 Marvin 535 Mary E. (Lizzie) 521 Monsell B. (Jimmie Cake) 535 Rachel 535 Rachel Mrs. 521 Thomas W. 521 Watson 534-535 Wilbert 521 William L 521
LAW, Kenneth Jr. 262
LAWRENCE, Lucinda 329
LAYNE, George F. 75 James E. (Jim) 268 Lucy Ann 398 Mary V. Boatwright 75 Nannie C. Hackett 268
LEE, Adiline 345 Alfred Deacon 333 336 Annie Chambers 329 Annie Elizabeth 336-338 Arlene G. 329 Baby 446 Bernard T. 346 Beulah 346 Charlie F. 346 Chris Alexander Deacon 335-336 338 Clarence 389 Curtis J. 55 Donald 176 Edward T. 346 Eliza G. 346 Ella 198 Elton Sr. 336 Evelyn J. 510 G. M. Rev 201 George 605 George Thomas 55 Glenn A. 55 Harding W. 346 Houston Jr 337-338 Howard A. Sr. 329 James 446 605 James E. 336-337 James G. 346 Jaylah Fleming 55 Jerry 606 John 605 607 John H. 346

LEE, (continued)
John T. 346 Joseph 335-336 Kate 198 Laura E. (Cosby) 287 Lenora 127 Lucille 606 Lucy 605 Lunell B. 336-337 Mary 605 Mary B. 346 Mary Etta 437 Mary Lou 337 Mattie 446 Mattie (Taylor Hemmings) 460 Maude A. 347 Moses G. 337 Myrest A. 143 Nanny Ennels 606 Oliver A. 347 Patience 605-607 Pattie W. 27 Pauline A. 347 Pearl 139 Pearl Virginia 347 Pollie 198 Rebecca 127 Robert 27 Robert C. 27 Robert E. 347 Robert Edward 336-337 Robert Jr. 347 Roger H. 347 Sallie E. 606 Sam Rev. 337 Samuel 347 606 Thomas 340 347-348 Tommy Houston Sr. 336-337 Viola Swan 606 Virginia C. 337 Walker 348 William 605-607 William D. 345 348 William E. Rev 201 ___ Virginia 27
LEEBRICK, Elsie I. Ballowe 246 William Henry 246
LEFTWICH, Alexander H. 311 Cheryl M. 440 Cora 311
LEIGH, Mattie B. 370
LEONARD, Bernard L. 424 Earl D. 424-425 Earl Duval 424 Ernest C. 424-425 George Carlyle 425 Gus 425 Hazel A. 424-425 Willie E. (Reynolds) 425 Woodrow W. 425
LESTER, Connie A. (Bumper) 311 Jud Ray 311
LESUEUR, Emma Lee 306 James Samuel 306 Margaret Ann 183 Mary N. (Nowlin) 273
LEWIS, Alene A. 226 Annie Anderson 21 Betty F. 56 Carrie Alice 56 Carrie Virginia 420-421 423 Charles 56 Darlus Jermaine 5-6 Donna Brittle 6 Edward 56 Emmitt L. 226 Fannie Anderson 21 Hilda J. 226 Irvin 56

LEWIS, (continued)
 John O. 226 Lawrence 56 Mary
 348 Mary Anderson 21 S.
 Francis 56 Senora 348
LINDSEY, Joseph 56 Nannie 57
LOEBER, Mary Louis 8
LOGAN, Archer 57 Baron Montell
 622 Carrington J. 287 Charles
 Stuart Rev. 57 E.H. 57 Elise
 286-288 Estelle L. 143 Garfield
 337-338 George William 287-
 288 Helen W. (Bell) 623 Henry
 57 Herbert Hoover 57 Ida 475
 James Francis 57 Jessie P. 57
 John E. 287 John Nelson 623
 John Wesley 57 Josephine 338
 Mack A. (Alfred) 143 Mary
 Austin 287 Mary M. 58 N.
 Christine 287 Nannie B. 337
 Nathaniel D. 58 Nellie F. 58
 Rosa Nellie 287-288 Willie J.
 623
LONDEREE, Charles Ira 569 580-
 581 Charles L. 241 247 Connie
 B. (Ragland) 241 247 Emma
 241 Evelyn Vernell 252 Lillie L.
 (Adcock) 247 Luther E. 247
 Massie C. (Cabell) 247 Mattie
 Ragland 569 581 Paul A.
 (Arthur) 178 Rosa L. 178
LOUIS, Mary 8
LOUPER, Gary 464 Raymond 464
LOVE, Fulton R. 165 Orin Michael
 Sr. 76
LOWE, Josephine B. 165 Mary S.
 165 Robert Lee 165 W.M.H. 165
LUTZ, George Howard 339 Linda
 Hannah 339
LYLE, Pattie 226
LYREL, Mered 348
MACAGAY, Alejandro (Alec) 98
MACOGAY, Ressie C. (Stinson) 98
MALLORY, Hubert 623 Nettie P.
 (Allen) 623 V. Florence White
 58
MALORY, Robert 127
MANERO, Minnie Ernestine 370

MANIS, Aubry Lee 165 David A.
 165
MANN, Lucy 284 Meekie Sue
 Watson 546 Richard H. 546
MARCH, Edward 247
MARKS, Addie G. 166 Alfred M.
 166 Alice O. 166 George W.
 166 Jesse V. 166 Mary C. 166
MARSHALL, Ada 370 Bessie L.
 199 Charlie 199 Dolly Lee 338
 Harold V. 425 Maude 143 Myrtle
 Baird 420 425
MARTEN, Frances 199
MARTIN, _____ 466
MASON, Betty A. 128 Clarence
 128
MASSIE, Arthur W. 535 Bessie A.
 18 Leah Laury 535
MATHA, Annie Curtis 348
MATHEWS, Lilia Laury 535
MATNEY, Esther Allen 8
MATTHEWS, Leonard W. 128
 Virginia W. 128
MAXEY, 378 Abram Thomas 313-
 314 Charles 35 343 348 Curley
 415 Docia B. (Banton) 35-36
 Ella V. 415 Ellen Pocahontas
 (Agee) 314 Etta Self 314-315
 Fletcher 416 George (Georgia)
 Ann 36 George Albert 314
 George William 313-314 Infant
 315 James (baby) 36 James A.
 35-36 James Glover 36 Jessie
 343 Kate 378 Laura Alice Agee
 314 Leonard 314-315 Lula
 Bryant 311 Mabel (baby) 36
 Mary E. 22 Mary Ellen 313 Mary
 Jane Ferguson 313-314 Mary P.
 247 Nancy H. 378 Nannie Lee
 313 Nora 416 Philip Brooks 128
 Ralph R. 416 Samuel Thomas
 315 Sarah 428-429 William
 Jennings 247 William Jennings
 Jr. 311
MAXIE, Lester J. 27 Nellie 128
 Reuben 128 Ruben 128
MAYO, Mattie V. 58

MAYS, Bland W. 98 Corrine 535 Elisha 226 Freddie I. 535 Lucille (Agee) 226-227 Milicent C. 226 Nannie Tyree 98 104 Riley 226 W. I. E. 226 Walter 227 Willie A. 226-227
MCALLISTER, Daisy Wright 584 Lawrence E. 584
MCCARY, Amanda Hamner 269 Graven Payton 269
MCCOY, Nannie Allen 584
MCCRAW, Cary Harrison 315 Elizabeth M. 458-460 Frank 315 R. M. (Richard Miller) 315 Susanna Hix 315
MCCULLOCH, (Mr.) 569 (Mrs.) 569
MCDANIEL, Estelle (Wright) 585
MCDONALD, Gladys 389
MCDOWELL, Edna 58 Mabel 460
MCFADDEN, Airl C. 569 Alfred McKinley 99 Andrew T. 499 Betty Brown 570 Christopher Scott 569 Clifford W. 499 Eddie Lewis 570 Jane Kidd 99 Jeanette M. 569 Jerry 499 Joseph Lewis 570 Lawrence E. 499 Lillie Burnley 570 Lucy A. Carter 499 M.J. 543 Nannie 543-544 Sarah O. 499 W. T. 544 Warner W. 499 Wiley 544 William 544 William Meridith Jr. 499
MCKAY, Mona Crane 339
MCKELLAN, Maylan Redwood 623
MCLARTY, Alberta 349
MCLAUGHLIN, Louise Gills 166
MCPHERSON, Bertha Anne (Bert) 8
MEADOW, Sarah J. 570 William M. 570
MEEKS, Barbara P. 425 Horace W. 425
MEGGINSON, Elisa Susan Alvis 15
MERKEY, Florence 378
MEYER, Ward Alker 166
MICHELLE, Davis Taylor 185

MILES, Clara Bragg 248 Edward Jackson Jr. 248 Eliza (Liza) Davis 315-316 George (Overton) 315-316 Grerrial 69 Henry 316 James Cook 248 Kenneth Wayne 248 255 Louise Stanley 248 Lucy D. 248 Mabel Ragland 248 255 Robert 316 Thomas J. 248
MILLER, Agnes W. (Williams) 248-250 Anna H. 128 Edgar 513 Elvira 320 Eugene T. Sr. 514 Fletcher T. 514 Flossie Self 249 Frank W. 249 George 536 Irene H. 416 Jake R. 249 John D. 514 John Dan 211 John G. 249 John Thomas 514 Joseph 514 Joseph D. (Jack) 249 Kenny 514 Lessie Gertrude 559 Louise B. 514 Mabel (Jones) 623 Maggie H. 129 Marie 211 Mary 525 Mary E. Jones 250 Mary Lucy 249 Monroe 211 Nellie 384 Percy Ross 249 Rebecca A. 243 Rena 514 Ressie G. 514 Robert 536 Ruth Eichorn 211 Susannah Walker 249 Sylvia Ann 244 Thelma P. (Pollard) 623 Theoplus 129 Thomas 129 Thomas E. 250 Vernon V. Sr. 129 Virginia W. 227 William S. 250 William T. 248-250
MILLS, Ella J. 515
MINYARD, H. Rickie 340 Raymond H. 340
MIORT, Johnnie M. 515
MITCHELL, Agatha Wright 338 Jean 143
MONROE, Alberta J. 129 Clifford 438 Delores 607 Eletha M. 438 Ella W. 438 Floyd E. 438 General 438 Mattie W. 438 Raymond K. 227 Willie Lamont 438
MOODY, Elizabeth Simms 81
MOON, Fitch 250 Virginia 250

MOORE, Allen W. 318 Arthur Hall 426 Basil H. 316 Ella Jane 316 F. Kerfoot 316 James Walker 316 John Archer 607 Joseph 317 Josephine B. 515 L. Kemper 317 Nannie S. 317 Odell Young 624 Philip S. 317
MOORMAN, Antoinette Wise Spencer (Nettie) 205 Catherine E. (Emma) 318 Henry H. 205 Leonard H. (Hildrup) 318
MORGAN, Beatrice Richardson 475 Emmett 69 Ewell 487 Gertrude 439 Henry W. 439 Howard D. 166-167 James R. 439 Jesse A. 487 John Henry 439 Maggie J. 358-359 Mary 487 Mary C. 439 Mary S. (Harris) 515 Maud K. (Kathlene Noble) 487 Myrtle Dixie J. 166-167 Myrtle Hardiman 487 Nellie Gertrude 487 Travis 439
MORRIS, Cleveland J. 318-319 Elizabeth Peters 319 Elnora Webb 318-319 Gladys E. 288 Harry Morris 288 Marvin A. 69 Rhoda Pearl 319 Royal F. 607 Sarah 269
MORRISS, Ella O. D. 319-320 Ella Ora Davis 319 Infant 319 Louise 491 Rachel 320 Walter C. 319-320 Walter Clarence 319 Wiley J. 320
MORTON, James R. 515 Major T. 515 Susan 515
MOSELEY, Agnes 120 Capt. Francis 397 Charles 151 Charlie 586 Daniel 69 Elizabeth H. 398 Florence 586 Jane Walker 151 Maria 586 Minnie (Ayers) 144
MOSLE, Dock 349
MOSLEY, Beatchria 58 Burley 437 439 Charity Perkins 70 Charles 536 Christopher O'Neal 70 Clarance 70 Daniel P. 70 Eliza Rebecca 528 Elizabeth 439
MOSLEY, (continued)
Grace B. 70 Harry 70 John E. Jr. 70 John Ed. 70 John W. Sr. 370 Margaret 71 Martha 536 Mildred Lee 71 Mormon 71 Nannie 349 Richard 129 Richard A. 71 Robert 439 Rosa 71 Ruben Sr. 71 Rulan Jr. 71 Rulan Sr. 71 Sandra G. 71 Stephen 72 Stephen J. 72 Sylvester Ross 72 Thomas Ed. 72 Walter T. 440
MOSS, Annie L. (Lillian) (Garrett) 234 Eddie 129 Emma M. 298 Endia 256 Fabe Henderson 298 Fitzhugh Lee 234 Flossie Taylor 354 Gordon General 354 Henrietta 389 Joseph A. 389 Lily B. 462 William 354 William Reeves 234 Zella Pembleton Catlett 418
MOTTLEY, Alexander S. 167
MURDOCK, Mary A. 440
MURPHY, Lizzie (Elizabeth) Agee 4
MURRAY, Hallie G. 277 Pokey Banks 416
NABORS, Mabel I. 389
NASH, Beatrice 129 Elizabeth H. 250 H.A. 250 Henry 130 Lizzie 130 Sallie (Hughes) 130
NEDRICK, Sister Quinnie T. (Woodson) 624
NEIGHBORS, Edward 389
NEIL, Alice 508
NEILSON, Leslie L. 365-366 Pauline A. 365-366
NELSON, Charles Richard 440
NEWTON, Addie Lue 354 Alfred P. 354 Andrew W. 355 Belle Godsey 231 Berry G. 464 Dorothy B. 624 Ella D. 283 George R. 234 George W. 355 James Alfred 231 355 John E. 283 355 Lillian R. 283 Matilda J. (Jamerson) 282-283 Mickey J. 355 Mildred Call 355

NEWTON, (continued)
T. A. (Tas) Jr. 355 Wesley 356
Willie M. (Jack In The Box) 235
NICHOLAS, Alice B. 86 Dale A.
426 Martha Jones 512 Ossie B.
86 Wash 86 William Earnest 86
NICKOLAS, John 389
NOBLE, Annie J. (Jones) Garnett
487-488 James Hugh 487-488
Maud Kathlene 487
NORMAN, C.P. 58
NORVELL, Bernard 291 Bessie
Bransford 290-291
NUCKOLS, Joseph Henry 395
Nannie A. Snoddy 395
O'BRYANT, Ella 233
O'CONNER, 374
OAKLEY, Thomas (Bear) 570
OLIVER, Carrie (Jones) 227-228
Chapman 227 Chatman J. Sr.
227 Helen 483 Henry R. 227
Herbert 228 Hugh 227-228 John
Thomas 228 Lawrence Calvin
228 Mary A. 228 Minnie S. 228
Nannie 228 Thelma T. 228
ONION, Emma Gertrude 382 John
356
OPIE, Annie L. 475 Jarrell D. 475
Neal 475 Thelma 476
ORANGE, Frank B. 167 Lawrence
H. 167 Lula C. 167 Octavis 167
Robert A. 167 Ruth L. 167 Susie
F. 167 Vola B. 167
PALMER, James D. 349 Rev. G. 7
PALMORE, Betty 250 Ernest D.
243 250-251 J.D. 250 Kelsey
Ann 250 Ollie 199 Sadie R.
(Ragland) 251
PANKEY, Alice 298 Andrew 298
Charles Allen 359 Esther 358
James 359 James Leonard 359
Jane Johnson 298 Lucy Rose
359-360 Maggie (Margaret
Robertson) 359 Mary 356
Robert 359 Robert S. 298
William Mckinley 359-360

PARKER, Annie Shelton 288 Bahi
R. M. Mrs. 81 Louise P. 476
PARNELL, Betty Earland Davis
185
PAROTT, Lawrence G. 167 Patsy
Ann 167
PARSON, Mattie E. 371 William E.
Jr. 371 Willie D. 371
PATTERSON, Annie B. 607
Dorothy V. 168 Fern C. 168
Garfield 338 George W. 536
Joseph Watson 251 Lucy J.
(Bonderant) 525 536 Mary 199
Mary Jane 199 Nec. 349
Pauline L. 607 Ruby 329 Sam
Deacon 199 Willie 587 Willis
516
PATTESON, A. M. (Antonia M.
Tucker) 360-361 Annie F. 360
Elizabeth G. Perrow (Betsy) 546
Ella Henrie 360-361 G. W. 251
John 548 Lynda 429 Marcia B.
251 Mary L. (Lulie) 360-361
Susan Robertson 548 T. A.
(Thomas) 360-361 William
Everett 546PAUL, Virginia A.
516PAYNE, Archie 607 Beatrice
362 Cornelias 416 Emma L.
557-558
PEAKS, Arthur J. 58 Arthur P. 58
Beulah 42 Effie Mrs. 228 Ernest
L. 59 John 59 229 Milton 59
Senobia V. 59 Willie P. 59
PELLETIER, Arthur Cleary 340
Norberta Lutz 340
PENICK, W. Price 168
PENN, Frances Zenith 83
PENNINGTON, Margaret Allen 8
William A. 8
PERKINS, Alice V. 199 Amanda E.
529 532 Annie 229 Annie E.
390 Bettie Lee 536 Catherine
(Daniel) 229 Charity 70
Charlotte Louise 201 Cheryl M.
Leftwich 440 Clarence Jr. 536
Clarence N. 536-537 Cora
Perkins 538 Diane Haskins 536

PERKINS (continued)
Dorothy Austin 536-537 Emma
197 Franklin L. 537 George W.
199-200 George W. (Williams)
476 Jack 200 James 624 James
F. 200 James Henry 390
Joshua 536-538 Kittie 200 Lena
L. 617 Levitt Earl 624 Lillie B.
(Bud) (Harper) 530 536-538
Louise Nash 537 Louise V. 200
Mary C. 197 200 Mary Lou
(Gordon) 529 537-538 Mattie B.
200 Minnie Mallory 538 Mollie
200 Phillip 529 537-538 Ralph
390 Richard 538 Robert Toney
119 Sallie G. 416 Samuel E.
(Edward Sr.) 537 Spencer 538
Thelma Gray 538 Toliver 197
200 Virginia 476 William H.
(Henry) 538 Williams 390 Willie
E. 390
PERROW, (infant) 4 Ada Mallie
Mertis 545 Allice Lillian Laura
Spencer 546 Charles (1728-
1797) 547 Charles (1817-1825)
546 Daniel W. (Watson) 547-
548 551 Daniel Watson Jr. 545
547-548 Guerrant 546-549 551-
552 John Guerrant 548 Mary
Forsee 547 Mildred Dorinda 548
Nancey Elenor 548 Nancy Jane
Bagby 544-545 547-548 Nancy
Ligon Patterson 545 547-548
Nancy William Watson 546-549
552 Nannie Sue 545 Salome P.
549
PERRY, Lizzie B. 86
PETERSON, Lilly Perkins 197 200
PIERCE, Mildred 130 Minnie G.
488
PITTMAN, Dorothy White 624
POLLARD, Jennie 624 Joan M.
617 John D. 624-625 Joyce L.
624 Martha F. 624-625 Pattie
622 Thelma 623 Willarm K.
(Kenneth) 625 William 625
William K 625

POLONSKI, Jonathan R. 340
PORTER, Garry A. 144 Lawton
Charles 229
POWELL, Annie Jones 375 Carol
386 Florence 516 Hettie W.
(White) 538 540 M. James 538
PRATT, Florence Lasalle Moseley
399 Mary Wilson 398-399
Whitcomb Eliphalet Dr. 399
PRICE, Cal 190 Julia 202 Sarah E.
190
PRIDE, Abraham 521 Hal 521
Henry A. 521 Lee L. 521 Lucy
522 Lucy Ann 529-532 540
Martha M. 522 Samuel 522 Tom
522 William Lee 522
PROFFITT, J. Ellen 317 J. Parker
317 James Warmsley 317 M. T.
362 Mary Rosalind Fields
Bryant 362 Oliver G. 317
Vernard C. 168
PRYOR, Pattie W. 318
PURYEAR, Eliza 516
PUTNEY, Lucie J. 75 W. R. MD 76
William Robert 76
QUINN, Essie K. 522
RADFORD, Elizabeth 363-364
John L 363 Linwood 363-364
Morris Neal 364 William 363-
364
RAFFERTY, Asa Menville 168
Floyd Everett 168 Henry T. 169
Nellie Wooten 168 Riley F 168
Tom 169
RAGAND, Waverly 571
RAGLAND, Albert C. 570 574
Albert Lee (Bud) 571 Albert
Thomas 251 Alfred W. 571 Alice
251 Alice V. 241 251 254 Ann
W. 364 Annie E. 241 Annie S.
251 253 Barbara A. 245 253
Berdie 559-560 Bertha 239
Betty S. 110 C. (Clarence)
Elwood 571 573 C. Walker 251
254 Casey W. 571 Catherine
426 Charles L. 252-253
Christine B. 252

RAGLAND (continued)
Clara Bell (Ragland) 571 David W. (Washington) 571 573 576 Dorothy Adcock 252 Eddie 571 Ella 239-240 Elsie Ragland 572 Emma 571 Emma Mildred 252 254 Estelle B. 108 Evelyn Vernell (Londeree) 247 252 Florence Heath 574 Francis Jackson Jr. 252 Frank H. 252 Garland 245 252-254 Gertie 572 Gracie M. 426 Gwyndline Hope 252 Harry 312 Henry Douglas 312 Henryetta 253 Infant Son Of Louise And Garland Ragland 253 James H. 251 253 James Thomas 572 James Thomas Clyde 108 John Rolfe 572 John W. 426 John Willard 253 Joseph 239 253 Joseph Nicholas 572 574 Judy Staton 253-254 Julia L. 426 Lee Gould 572 Lelia P. 252-253 Lewis D. 108 Louise 245 252-253 Louise B. 108 566 572-574 Louise Marie 566 572-573 Lucy S. 500 Lula (Ragland) 252 254 Lula Camm 364 Mabel 248 Maggie May 573 Margaret Gay 573 Marvin L. Sr. 500 Mary E. 240 254 Mary G. (Gunter) 571 573 576 Mary Pearson Rosen 254 Mildred R. 573-574 Morris 426 Myrtle Branch 571 573 Nora E. 251 254 Nora Ellen 573 Norman Loving 566 573 Otha Morris 312 Ressie 576 Robert Lee 571 Rolfe L. 566 572-574 Roy Leonard 364 Roy Tucker 365 Russell N. 574 Sallie 242 Sam 253-254 Sam Jr. 254 Sarah A. 570 574 Susan (Demarius) Gunter 572 574 Thomas Edward (Eddie) 252 254 Thomas H. 241 251 254 Thomas Jr. 254 Tucker 252 Warden N. 365

RAGLAND, (continued)
William N. 573-574 Wm. Lacy 574 Wyomma 566 573
RAIKES, G. W. 306
RAKES, Billy 99
RAMEY, John Edward 169
RANDEL, Craig Davis 185
RANDOLPH, (Deacon) Clarence 625 Ada E. 416 Alice Lee 371 Annie Mae 416 Barbara Allen 8 Doshie Jones 371 Francis W. 371 Herman H. Rev. 417 Jannie 201 Lillian 407 Loveline 417 Lovie 371 Lucy 178 Luther 371 Mary 372 Mrs. Everlean S. 516 Virgie H. 625
RANKIN, Charles W. 312
RAPHEY, Mary Ann 417
REDMOND, Annie M. 330 James 330
REDWOOD, Elenora (Eleanor) 625-626 Frances 130 James T. 130 625 Lucian W. 130-131 Mary E. 130-131 Matilda 131 Watson J. 625-626
REED, Mamie J. 607 Nannie B. 372
REID, Adeline 538
REYNOLDS, Georgianna 365-366 Hallie 423 Joe 366 Josie 424 Linwood A. 169 Marilee 365 Samuel Anderson 426 Samuel B. 427 Vadney W. (Wright) 427 Wendell G. 366 Willie E. 425
RICHARDSON, Alfred T. 476 Beatrice 475 Eubelia 398 Fannie Anderson Lewis 21 Kina 476 Lucy Ann Layne 398 Maggie 476 Roland Mckenney 398 Thomas H. 477
RIPLEY, Floyd Nicholas 488 Grover 574 John E. 574 Mamie Guill 488 Ola 574 Parris R. (Butch) 574 Pauline Bailey 422 427 Virgie Branch 575 Willie Thomas 575
ROBERT, Mary Miles 255

ROBERTS, Alice C. 427 Fred N. 427 Fred. N. Jr. 427-428 Guy Bowles 427 Marvin S. 427-428 Merle S. (Staton) 428-429 Nathaniel M. 428 Nellie B. 428 440 Ralph Earl 500 Theresa S. 427-428 Thomas Wm. 428
ROBERTSON, (wife Of W.H. Robertson) 374 Caroline 360 Clara A. 374 David C. 374 Delia 360 Docia Allen 584 John Boatwright 255-256 John Wayne 255 Kathryn (Schroders) 255 Kenneth L. 255 Louise A. 255 Lucy Ann Frances Perrow 549 Marion Gregory 255 Meta Staton 255-256 T. (Tom) E. 360 Thomas J. 255 Tubal Cain 255-256 W.H. 374 William I 549 William Lewis 256 Willie R. 374 Willie R. (Jr.) 375
ROEBLAD, Lillian Mae 12
ROGERS, Phyllis L. 330
ROLLINS, Jennie 474 Mary G. 477
ROMBY, Mary A. (Alice) 608
RORIE, Walter 372
ROSE, Blanche 608 Evelyn 608 John W. 376 Josephine 376 Martha E. 376 Susan J. 376
ROSEN, Frank L. 488 Hattie 490 Helen J. 488 Leslie W. 488 Louis Tate 256 Margaret Rush 377 Mary Pearson 254
ROSS, Alvin Sylvester 446 Elsie Bryant 99 Nellie V. 246
ROSSER, Benjamin W. 428-429 Ella Staton 256 Julia 256 Lula M. 428 Mary W. 429 Roy 256 Samuel Fletcher 256 Sarah M. (Maxey) 428-429 Thomas A. 428-429
ROUSE, Virginia S. 18
RUNION, Margaret Barbara Jean 169
RUPP, Jessie Bransford 290 292 William 292

RUSH, Annie L. (Jones) 302 Elsie Lann 377 Eva Walker 500 George T. 377 Joseph E. 500 Lacy Walter Jr. 500 Lucy M. 377 Margaret 377 Mildred F. 377 P. Floyd 377 Thomas Clyde 377 Thomas Clyde Jr. 377
RUTLEDGE, Sue Gilliam 169
SANDERS, (or Saunders) Ray 492
SARGENT, Endia (Moss) 256 Fannie S. 256 George Archer 257
SAUNDER, Emily 201
SAUNDERS, Lelia 201 Lillian W. 230 Lucy 201 Mazie 378 Ophelia Anderson 59 Robert 378
SAUVE, Patricia Goetz 340
SAVAGE, Iris Davis 185 Kim 185 Terry 185 Ulysses S. Jr. 185
SCOTT, Baby 516 Bettie 131 Coleman Lee 18 Donald Alan 131 Eva 440 George 418 J. Estelle Gills 169 John A. 539 Judie 131 Laura J. 533 535 539 Louise E. 131 Milton 539 Noel 131 Ralph Edward 131 Rebecca C. 132 Robert H. 132 Robert Lee 132 Susie Mrs. 539 William 539 William Howard Taft 132
SCRUGGS, Albert 477 Alex 60 Ann Mariah 59 Annie E. 59 Bernetta R. 477 Beulah 626 Deacon Nelson S. 59 Deaconess Elizabeth R. 59 Dolores Ann 60 Fannie B. 477 G. Willard 60 Howard E. 349 Jamar V. (Outlawz) 608 John A. 60 John L. 477 John William 500 Mable E. 477 Marvin A. 608 Milvina 477 Mrs. Emma 626 Nancy A. 60 Sarah S. 60 Timothy Lindbergh 500
SCRUGGS,(continued) Virginia 60 Walter 478 William Randall 501

SEAL, James J. 20 Myrtie Gardner 20 Pattie W. Taylor 20
SEAR, Calvin Roger 608
SEARS, Eddie Winn 60 Emmett 60 James W. 60 James Wesley 60 Joseph 61 Lottie 61 Lucy Ann 61 Maggie Walker 61 Mary 349 Robert M. 61 William Fredrick 61
SEAY, Allen W. 501 Bernard 229 Charles Abner 501 Ethel Watson 501 Linwood 229 Virginia G. 501 William Henning 501
SELF, Abram 378 Andrew L. 378 Edward Hill 378 Florence Merkey 378 Flossie 249 George R. 378 H. (Frank Hill) 378 James Holman 380 Jesse Maxey 378 John A. 378 Kate Maxey 378 L.L. 380 Mildred Baber 380 Ollive G. 378 S.S. 380 Violet 378
SELLERS, Charles 372
SELPH, Bennie 379
SENGER, Rickey Dexter 169 Ronald W. 169
SERFASS, Cassie O'Dell Hackett 501
SHAEFFER, Lorraine Marie 489 Samuel E. 489
SHANNON, Joseph E. 73 Violet K. 73
SHARP, George F. 284 John Berry 284 Mary Ann Mann 284 Polly 608 Thomas H. (Old Man Tom Sharp) 284 Thomas Russell 284
SHARPE, Carrie L. 608
SHELTON, Allen 288-289 Allen Harvey 286 288 Annie 288 Annie L. 522 Carl Dubois 522 Carole 520 Christine 519 Desmonia 288-289 Edward 288 Edward L. 288-289 Evelyn E. 288-289 Fleming A. 522 Fleming I. 523 Henry Alois 523 James E. 289

SHELTON, (continued) John Jasper Jr. 289 Joseph G. 390 King 288-289 Mack L. 288-289 Mary E. 523 Mary G. 390 Matilda Coleman 288-289 Tanya Astin 289 Virginia Kyle 440 William L. (Sr.) 523 William L.(Jr.) 522 Willie 523 Willie M. 288-289
SHEPHERD, Buck 381 Ethel Loving 381
SHEPPARD, Margaret (Taylor) 460
SHETLER, James 211 Rachel 211 Uriah 211
SHOEMAKER, George 462 John Admund 489 Lacy M. 489 Lillian Sprouse 489 Nellie Toney 462
SHULER, Lovie 338 Samuel 338
SHUMAKER, Alfred L. 489 Clarence Daniel 489 Eddie Herbert 489 Judy Faye 489 Kimberly Marie 489 Maggie G. (Goin) 489 Sidney A. 489-490
SILBY, D. Branch 170 Martha B. 170
SIMMONS, (child) 263 Betty Harris 263-264 Helen Ripley 574-575 Thomas Bolton 575 Thomas M. 575
SIMMS, Elder James 81 Laura 229 Lillian B. 81
SIMPSON, Elizabeth 170 Patricia Ann 170 Robert Lee 170 W. I. 170
SKINNER, Lorraine V. 170 Milton L. 170
SLAGLE, Caroline Lewis Alvis 15
SLOCUM, Rebecca Ann Kitchen Jones 582
SMALL, Andrew James 440
SMITH, 372 Allen 18 Annie 349-350 Arbie E. H. 170 Clifford 18 Courtney 201 Daniel 132 Dorian 539 Dorothy 18 Edward D. 170 Elsie M. 390 Emma 349-350 George E. 289 Gladys Totty 575 Gracie 392

SMITH (continued)
Harriet Dyer (Aunt Harriet) 392
Helen W. 86 Henry Deacon 392
James M. 350 Jane Finley 575
John Emitt 575 John Henry Sr.
18 Joseph 349 Josie S. 490
Kyle Dwayne 19 Louisa 132
Mckayla Marsha 19 Pamela
(Noot) 350 Robert S. 490 Rosa
19 350 Russell P. 575 Tammy
H. 350 W. (William) Sr. Doc.
350 William Jr. Doc. 350
SNODDY, James T. 395-396 John
W. 395-396 Lorenzo W. 395-
396 Lucy J. 395-396 Lucy J.
Snoddy 395-396 Nannie A. 395
Nannie C. 490 Nannie Waddell
395-396 Nora B. 394 Robert
Harold 257 William H. 396
William T. 394 Wm. Thornhill
490
SOLOMON, Charlotte Louise
Perkins 201
SORRELLS, Harry A. 96 99 Jesse
James 99 Lonie B. (Bryant) 90
99
SORRENTINO, William Etta
(Stinson) 100
SPEARS, Carrie T. (Taylor) 576
Frank E. 576
SPENCER, Angela 441 Angie V.
429 Antoinette Wise 205 Bennie
L. 257 Bettie G. (Shepherd
Guthrie-Kish) 266 Carolline
Watson 549-550 552 Caryl
Jackson 490 Corrine 440-441
Earl 401 Elizabeth Harris Baker
399 Elmira (or Elmina) Frances
Bagby 398 Eubelia (Buckner)
Richardson 398 Eugene T. 278
Eva Scott 440 George L. (Lou)
429 Hallie 259 Harriet E. 441
Infant Boy 441 James G. (Gray)
Sr. 398-399 Jesse E. 401 John
James 266 John James Rev.
398-399 John P. Jr. 429 John
Paulette 429

SPENCER, (continued)
John R. 440 Joseph A. 441
Joseph T. 397 Josephine 441
Lizzie Taylor 399 Louise (Jones)
257 Lucy 422 Lynda P.
(Patteson) 429 Mary (Wilson)
Pratt 398-399 Mary E. 502 Mary
Price Staple Or Staton 399 Mary
Susan 397 Minnie W. 278
Minnie W. (Walker) 400-402 437
441 Monroe 440-441 Nancy
Gilliam 490 Pocahontas 278 R.
W. 396 Robert L. 502 Sallie 31
Samuel 278 Samuel Franklin
398-399 Samuel Franklin Jr 399
Samuel L. 401 437 441 Wilbur
Phillip 441 William 399 549-550
William Overton 399
SPROUSE, E.V. 418 E.V. (Emily
Virginia) 418 Frank M. (Marrow)
418 Henry Wesley 418-419
John Josiah 418 Lillian 489
Mabel Catherine Stinson 452-
453 Truman A (Toby) 453
STALLION, Fannie B. (Booker) 417
STAMMER, Gordon James 444
STANLEY, Louise 248
STANTON, Aaron 446 448 Alice 9
Alvin V. 61 Andrew Epp 446-
447 Blanche C. 61 Carol V. 446
Cassie Lee 447 Cernata 350
Clarence Lee 9 Eddie Mack 61
Emma 9 Evelyn A. 62 Garfield
28 George 447 Godfrey P. 62
Houston J. 9 James A 10 James
A. (Arthur) 444 447-448 James
E. 62 Jennie Mae 10 Jennion
132 John D. 10 John E.
(Edward) 10 Joseph E. 10
Junious E. 447 Lacy Ann 62
Leslie 132 Lorenzo A. 417
Lucille N. 447 Lucille Rachelle
447 Lucy J. 26 28 Margie J.
447-448 Mary Lee 407-408
Mary Virginia 446 448 Mattie A.
10 Nona Allen 62 Norvell 62
Ollie L. 62 Paul S. 448

STANTON, (continued)
    Pearl C. 10 Ralph D. 448
    Ressie 62 Richard 448 Russell
    10 Sarah 40 Vaicous 10 Virginia
    B. 417 W. 62 Walter 11 Wayne
    C. 417
STATEN, Edith C. 350 Joseph
    Thomas 478 Lucy B. 478 Robert
    Willie 478 Thomas H. 478
STATON, Anna Bryant (nee
    Johnson) 429 Ben 257 Catmbay
    257 Drusilla 257 Ella 256 Irving
    F. 257 Judy 253-254 Martha S.
    421 Merle 428 Meta 255-256
    Ruth B. 257 Walter 258
STAUNT, Agnes West 390
STEARRTT, Stephanie Ellen 380
STEELE, Earl A. 170 Maude E.
    481
STEGALL, Wilbert Ray 430
STEGER, Clara Walton Wheeler
    490 Clementine F. Hadnell 32
    Clyde Eugene 491 Humphrey A.
    491 James Robert 32 Nora J.
    246 Ruth Hardiman 491
STEPHANS, Georgia Ann (Swann)
    144
STERNE, Alice C. 170 James M.
    170
STEVENS, Annie Bocock 449
    Elizabeth Taylor 449 Estelle
    Kitchen 304 Lucy 449 Mary
    Branch 312 Susanah 449
    Thomas 449 Wm. (Billy) 449-
    450
STINSON, Ada M. (Ada Pear
    Mason) 453-455 Alexander Sr.
    450 Brown 523 Cary 457
    Catherine Eagle 454 Charles
    (T.) Jr. 100 Charles T. 100-101
    Charles Thomas 454 Christine
    Elizabeth 451 Christopher Don
    100 David W. 394 Dillard 455
    Earnest L. (Levi) 453 Edward M.
    453 Elizabeth 89 93-94 455 457
    Elizabeth A. 451 Elizabeth Vest
    455 Elliot Lee 100

STINSON, (continued)
    Ester Mae (Stinson) 101 Eva
    Roberta 110 Flossie May 453
    Garland P. 101 George (David)
    455-457 George (W.) 92 101
    George Curfit 101 Gertrude
    100-101 Gloria E. 110 Howard
    454 Irene 454 James 101 456
    James Wesley 103-104 456
    Jennetta 523 Joseph Morgan
    452 Leslie Mitchell 101 Lester
    456 Letiia Via 101 Letitia Via 92
    455-457 Lillie 91-92 Linda 454
    Linda Bryant 100 102-103 Lloyd
    Earl 101 Lloyd W. 101 456
    Lorene 93 Mamie (Florence)
    101-102 Martha A. Bryant 456-
    457 Martha Bryant 102 Mary
    101 456 Mary Bryant 110 Mary
    Lee 394 Mildred F. 430 Minnie
    (Elizabeth) Bryant 100 102
    Minnie J. 246 Nancy Eagle 103-
    104 456 Nannie S. 457 Neely F.
    (Cornelia) 89 98 100 102-103
    Odessa Reid 100 102-103 Paul
    Jefferson 110 Ressie 454 Riley
    H. 102 Robert J. (Jackson) 456-
    457 Robert Jackson 102 Robert
    Lee 100 102 Roger 454 Rosa
    Bell 103 456 Sam 457 Sarah
    (Elizabeth Via) 101 103 Shane
    Douglas 103 Sue Harris 451-
    452 Susan 455-456 458
    Thomas 455-458 Tom Henry
    452 Tom. M. (Thomas Matthew)
    101-103 456 Tommy 457 Viola
    B. 89 102-103 Wert 111 Wiliam
    Archie 451-452 William Etta 104
    William H. (Henry) 453-454
    Willie 102-103 Wilton D. 103
    Wm (William) C. (Carrington)
    455 457-458
STORM, Bill 104 William Etta
    Stinson 104
STOUT, Ercel Wayne 458
STOVALLE, Gerldin A. 417

STRANGE, John 449 Lucy Stevens 449
STRATTON, Nina Belle 20
STUART, Tom C. 458 William J. 458
SUDSBERRY, Mary J. 491 William 491
SUTTON, Diane Yvonne Haynes 576 Otho M (Mills) 576 Ressie R. (Ragland) 576 Winifred Mills 576
SWAN, Alexander Hugh 73 Alma Ethelle 72 Carrie Ragland 73-74 Cora Berkeley 73 Frederick Winston Jr. 73-74 Frederick Winston Sr. 72-73 Gary S. 81 Gracie T. 577 Mary Ann Davis 73 Melva Carrie Kitchen 304 Melva Kitchen 73-74 Renaldo 81 Walter M. 609 William Wilson 73-74
SWANN, Annie Leah 609 Eddie 144 Edith P. 81 Edward C. 609 Eliza V 144 Ely David 609 Georgia Ann 144 Gertrude B. 609 James E. 144 Janie 144 Lee 62 Linwood J. 144 M. Effie 144 Mack 609 Mark 609 Pearline W. 609 Shirley 139 Stanley 610 Victoria 610 Virginia 145 Willie P. 62
SWARTZ, Edith T. (Troyer) 211 Harold Franklin 491 John Franklin 491 Louise Morriss 491 Noah 211
SWOOPE, C. Howard 459 Dr. Wm. M. 458-460 E. Mildred 459 Eliza S. (Kyle) 459 Elizabeth M. (McCraw) 458-460 George W. 459 Julia T. 459 Mabel Mcdowell 460 Nettie C. 460 Sarah 460
TAYLOR, A. M. 76 A.C. 461 Alma 417 Annie 579 Arthur Jerome 516 B.L. 188 Bessie Wilkerson 577-578 Carrie 576 Charles Bernard 330

TAYLOR, (continued)
Charlie Lee 577-578 Christopher T. 577-578 Christopher T. Jr. 577 Cordelia D. 461 Dallas 330 E. Ruth 63 Earl Lee 577 Edwood 610 Fannie 462 Florence Lee 562 Harry J. 4 Horace A. 461 Ida B. 372 J. M. 516 James 391 James Allen 563 577 James H. 582 James Thomas 562 578 Jerden 462 John A 461 John C. 461 Josephine Allen 322 330 L.B. Jr 458 L.D. 461 Leslie Wilson 578 Lila Tyree 577-578 Louise E. 461 Lynn 577 M. (Matthew) J. 37 Mahala 460 Margaret 460 Mathew J. Sgt 462 Mattie 460 Minnie Branch 562 577-578 Minnie Chambers 339 Minnie M. 578 Nannie Cora 578 Noah 356 463 Ophelia Booker 63 Pattie W. 20 Pauline 563 Rev. William H. 20 Rosa Ayres 492 Ruby D. (Davis) 577-578 Sallie E. Miles 544 Sallie G. 356 Stafford 4 Virginia Banton 37 Walker 544 Walker E. 372 Walter 201 Wiley Haskins 578 262
TERRELL, Elizabeth J. 229
TERRY, Amanda A. 464 Bill A. 464 Cecil T. 464 Howell G. (Sr.) 464 Mare E. 464 Maria Donna Lynn 464 Robert L. 464 William A. Sr. (Bill) 463-464 William R. 464
THACKER, Edna Mae (Storm Bryant) 93 104 Wesley F. 104
THOMAS, Bernard 366 Dee A. 391 Elizabeth 63 Garfield P. 351 Julia B. 351 Marion (Wright) 585 Robert 585 Sallie Jamerson 282-283 William 351
THOMPSON, Ada Wright 585 Carolyn 312 Daniel 351 James Drew 145 Mary 539 Sherwood 312

THORNHILL, Carlton 298
THORNTON, Elisha 30
THROCKMORTON, Richard Lee 74
TIGGER, Wiss 132
TINDALL, Charlie 626 John E. 132 Mary 626 William 626
TONEY, Angie P. 119 Annie H. 465-466 Cirus 465 David A. Deacon 202 Edmond 465 Emma 351 George 351 George M. (Maryland) 462-463 George R. 351 Harry 465 Jane 202 John M. 330 Joseph Lee Rev. 202 Julia (Price) 202 Louise Shoemaker 462-463 Lucy A. 351 Mahlon 466 Marion L. 464 Mary 465 Mary Virginia 466 Mattie 486 Mildred F. 463 Nellie 462 Pearl M. 202 Samuel Lee 133 Susan E. 464 Thomas A. 119 William P. (Pleasant) 464-465 William S. 465-466
TONY, Jessie E. 202
TOOLE, Gertrude L. Cunningham 28
TOWNSEND, Ardean C. 171 C. Howard 171 Cora T. Norwood 171 Evert James 171 Homer H. 171-172 Homer Michael 171 James Sherman 171 John W. Jay 171-172 John Wesley 172 Katherine T. 171-172 Margie M. 171-172 Melvin C. 172 Rosa Hayes 172 Ruth T. 172 Troy L. 172 Vaden Dare 171
TRENT, Buster 610 Edna 441 Jerry 610 John R. 478 Julie 303 Mary Nelson 303 Mary S. 478 Mary W. 610 Matt Weldon 442 Wales W. 278 William M. 442
TROYER, Amanda 211 Edith 211 Ezra 211
TUCKER, Antonia M. 360-361 Eliza M. C. 361 George W. 361 Grant 202 Henry 361-362

TUCKER, (continued) Louisa A. Tucker 361 Martha A. 362 Rebecca W. 362
TURNER, Annie Booker 448 Barry M. 202 Caroline 202 Cornelius 330-331 Ellen 203 George W. 331 Hollis O. 63 James (Casey) 203 James D. 331 James Earl 331 James H. 203 James H. (Henry) 203 Julie 33 Mary (Willis) 203 Michael 203 Moses 330 Price Eldridge 492 Robert E. 331 Robert L. 33 Walker 203 William Howard Taft 492
TURNSTALL, Louise Agnes 618
TUTWYLER, Bernard 516 Robert Lee 133 Stanley 517
TYREE, Alexander 145 Alexander A. 145 Annie Elizabeth 88 90 94 Baby Boy 81 Benjamin 88 Charlie 145 Daniel 145 Daniel Benjamin 81 Deborah Colmore 610 Dolly 145 Doris B. 82 Earl L. 104 Echo L. 104 Edna Estelle 610 Hattie S.(Stinson) 104 James Edward 145 John E. Rev 146 John Randoph 611 Josie W. 146 Leroy 611 Lila 577-578 Louise 146 Maude 146 Roger Dale (Bubby) Jr. 258 Ruby 104 Susan Stinson 88 Vera Wade 82 Zenobie 146
TYREEE, Percy Phillp 146
TYRONE, Christian 391
UNDERWOOD, Eleanor Octavia 77 Jim 172 Lacie 172 Susan 172 Willie James 77
VANDERPOOL, Alice B. 108
VAUGHAN, Lucille Garrett 235
VAUGHN, Gertrude G. (Gordon) 539
VAUGHTERS, Henry Jr. 540 Robert Henry 540
VEST, Elizabeth 455 Nannie 93 Samuel 541 Thomas W. 541
VIA, Catherine R. (Becky) 542 Emeline (Emily) 542

VIA, (continued)
  Jenny Vest 103 John James Jr.
  541-542 John James Sr. 541-
  542 John L. 103 Leticia (Tish)
  642 Lucy 89 92 94 102 Lucy A.
  542 Martha J. 542 Mary
  Frances 542 Matthew 92 541-
  542 Sally 542 Sally Carter 92
  Sarah Carter 541-542 Sarah F.
  542 William M. 542
VOWELS, Mary Lee 63 Thelma C.
  63
WADE, Afred J. 543 Alfred Byron
  543 Alice 611 Bessie 266-268
  Beverly Louis 82 D.F. 543 Dan
  F. 543 Dan Henderson 611
  Frank T. 365 John Matthew 82
  Louise (Tyree) 146 Martha 82
  Mary E. 611 Mary Etta 82 Matt
  82 Mildred M. 365 Nancy 611
  Nannie E. 611 Nannie
  Mcfadden 544 Patrick 544
  Samuel Alfred 543 Sapah
  Elizabeth 543 Thomas Lee 365
  Vera 82 Willie 601
WAGNER, Julie Turner 33
WALKER, Ada Pear Mason 453-
  455 Burum E. 278 Charles D.
  401 Eva 500 Izetta 401-402
  J.W. 453 455 Johnny 402
  Joseph 402 Julia Brown 351
  Linsey 19 Minnie 400-401 Mittie
  W. 278 Monroe 400-402
  Susannah 249 Unice Adcock
  579 William Glenn Sr. 258
  William S. 579
WALLACE, Margie B. (Ballowe)
  239 258
WANN, Watt 612
WARNER, Calvin R. 173 John H.
  204 Louise A. 204 Mariah L.
  204 Mildred M. 173
WARREN, Mattie E. 444
WASHINGTON, Amanda
  Hedgeman 207-208 Emily 278
  Ethel L. (Jones) 278-279 Infant
  207 James 278 Lou 517

WASHINGTON, (continued)
  Mary 115 Mrs. Virgie 517
  Robert 278 Samuel 207
  Thomas 279 Tony 208 U. S. Sr.
  278-279
WATKINS, Baby (1) 63 Baby (2) 63
  Bennie 612 Charles L. 612
  Henry 612 Julia 63 Leatha B.
  612 Leslie R. 133 Lillian W. 612
  Maggie Elizabeth 64 Mattie 64
  Moses 612 Mrs. Daisy Anna
  517 Nannie B. 612 Robert J.
  613 Spencer (Buster) 64 T.
  Spencer 64
WATSON, Daniel Perrow 546 550-
  551 E.H. 552 Ethel 501 Fanny
  Wilkinson 549-552 George E.
  550-552 Isabel Day 502 James
  550 552 John B. (Bernard) 478
  Lucy Stevens 546 550-551
  Makey/Meekie Perrow 550-551
  Mary Ann Foster 550-551 Mary
  Spencer 550-551 Meekie Sue
  546 Nannie Elizabeth Pattie
  Walker Lucado 551 Powhatan
  552 Queen Elizabeth 478
  Robert 479 Roberta 552 Spicey
  Scott 396-397 Thomas Gal 396-
  397 552 W.L. 552 Wilkinson 552
  William Irvy 502 William Joseph
  551 William Jr. 550-552 William
  Sr. 549-552
WATTS, Bertha E. (Harris) 289
  Bertha Harris 7 Fountain 133
  George 7 289 Martha Coreene
  565 579 Robert Edwin 579
  Willie A. 133
WEBB, Eliza 567 569 Elizabeth
  552 Elnora 318-319 Mary Ana
  Perrow 552 Robert P. 552
WEEKLEY, Arietta S. 502 Arthur T.
  502
WELLS, Henry 64 Theodore 64
WEST, (sister Of Dorothy L. West)
  392 Agnes 390 Alonza 391
  Charles L. 442 Dorothy L. 391
  Ernest 391 553 Haywood L. 442

WEST, (continued)
Jack 391 James M. 442 Lelia E. 442 Mary Ann 442 Mary M. 391 553 Pauline 392 Solomon 392 W.S. (Solomon) Rev. 553 William M. 442

WHEELER, Alice B. 613 Clara Walton 490 Dorothy 479 J. Y. 553 John Robert Sr. 479 Leroy Lincoln 479 Nudie (Henley) 133 Percy J. 479 Robert Jr. 479

WHITE, Abe 626 Arthur Benjamin 64 Bobbie 64 Dora 64 Dorothy 624 Edmund Palmer 114 Eveline 65 Frank E. 352 Frank E. Jr. 479 Grace P. 65 H.A. 65 Henry A Jr. (Jiddy) 114 Henry A. Sr. (John Henry) 114 Hettie 538 540 John 65 Lana Francis 352 Laura Campbell 114 Lawrence Blackwell 626 Leitha 65 Lillie Woodson 626 Lucy 352 Mandy 626 Mariah 204 Mary Edna 65 Mary M. 133 P. (Patricia) H. 114 Rebecca 540 Rufus (Sr.) 627 Rufus J. (Jr.) 626 Shadrick M. 65 Susie Clementeen 479 Vivian Shadrach 65 William H. 65 Willie Sue 627

WHITLOW, Annie Richards 553-554 Nannie P. 554 Thomas Percy 554 William Johnson 553-554

WHORLEY, George Thomas 579 James L. (Shoemaker) 554-556 Jennie (Emily) W. (Whorley) 554-556 Jennie Rebecca 555 John B. 555 Kate Taylor 579 Lillian Lovings 555 Mable A. 554 William W. (Whitcomb) Sr. 556

WICKS, Christine M. (Jones Anderson) 302

WILEY, Lillie Wright 556 Paul 556

WILKERSON, Alma R. 579-580 Annie S. 173 Annie Taylor 579 Berta W. 173 Camm 579-580 Clearnce (Clarence) O. 579-580

WILKERSON, (continued)
Devin James (Chunkmunk) 579 Edward Camm 580 Floyd N. 173 Herbert. P. 173 J. Robert 173 James John 579-580 Jessee Herman 579-580 Lottie Ragland 579-580 Mattie R. (Ragland) 579-580 Ora L. 563 Ray Porter 173 Sallie E. 174 Samuel Cole 580 Shirley Lee 579-580 Wallace Herman 580 William Joel 579-580

WILKINS, Odessa J. 66

WILKINSON, Susan Toney 557 William 557

WILLIAM, Virginia H. 176

WILLIAMS, Agnes 248 Alexander 627 Anita L. 627 Annie D. (Daisy) 133 Birthiar Rev. 176 Chandra R. 627 Charles E. 176 Cynthia D. 627 Edna Cottrell 179 Elizabeth B. 174 Ellis 179 Emily (Harper) 540 Ervin Sr. 133 Ethel 483 Evelyn M. 229 George W. 134 Hollister Lamont 279 Jack 176 James 134 176 James A. 279 James Terry Dixon (Toby) 187 Janie F. (Forbes) 491 Jesse 134 Kevin E. 627 Lee E. 134 Lewis 491 Lucy H. 134 Margaret Lee 352 Maria 134 Mary 134 176 Mary Elizabeth 627 Mary Jane 627 Monroe 134 Odell Raymond 279 Percy 135 Robert 540 Sallie A. 177

WILLIS, Mary 203

WILLS, Lois Allen 8

WILSON, Adelaide 229 Nellie L. 66 Virginia 517

WINFREY, Baby 30 Egbert B. 30 Elisha Thornton 30 G. N. 30 George H. 30 James Allen 30 Judith C.R. 30 Sallie 380 Sallie Spencer 31 Sarah Y Holman 31 William Hill 31

WINGFIELD, Alice Scott 372 George 373 Harry S. 373 James H. 373 James H. Jr. 373 Lucy 373 Mabel Burton 373 Ophelia 517 Richard P. Sr. 373
WINN, Harold Raymond 66 James Randolph 66 Lillian J. 66 Thomas 66
WINSTON, Alice 115
WINTERS, Doris B. 313
WISDOM, Orville E. H. 482 491
WISE, M. Gormus 189 Mary Bryant 557 Missouria 557
WITHERS, Gertrude Laura 418
WITT, Edward Samuel 174 Goodwin Byrd 174
WOOD, Carrie 66 Dathleen 487 Gladys L. (Jackson) 540 Harold 540 Lillian Golladay 559 Minnie Lee 581 Nettie Lue Hackett 268 Ollie A. 268 W. A. (Pomp) 559 Westa Winn 66
WOOD(SON), (Jose)phine 628
WOODALL, Charles E. 174 George W. 174 Judith Ann 174
WOODARD, Johnnie L. 479
WOODFORD, Donna L. 392
WOODIE, R. Alfred 174 Thomas W. 174
WOODSON, Adline 582 Baby 66 Beulah 619 Callie 373 Cardozau Jr. 135 Catherine E. 135 Chambers C. 135 Charlie E. Sr. 230 Connie 613 Corine 135 Edith 619 Elbert 67 Elvira 135 Ernest 204 Florence 628 Glover T. 480 Gpa Elbert 67 Henry E. 135 Howard 613-614 James Edward 613 James P. 28 Janet Evelyn 135 Jennie F. 28 Jeter 352 John Early 67 John Edward 613 Joseph E. 480 Joseph L. 480 Lena 494 Lettie M. 136 Lillian W. (Saunders) 230 Lillie 626 Lillie L. 136

WOODSON, (continued) Margaret Jane 517 Marques 230 Martha 352 Mary Frances 613 Mary P. 83 Nancy Jean 628 Nannie 480 Norman E. 136 Obrey James 517 Olivia Susan 67 Pattie 628 Ralph 628 Ressie 136 Robert Frank 613-614 Robert W. 280 Rose 374 Ruby (Carey) 230 Rufus 628 Russell B. 280 Sarah Irene 230 Silvira 136 Sister Quinnie T. 624 Tarlton 628 Van D. 83 Walker Solomon 614 Wayne 67 Wiley G. 614 William 67 Willie Ann 67 Willie Brown B. 280
WOODY, Carl Gene 581 Lois L. 581 Otha Edward 581
WOOLDRIDGE, (Ann Elizabeth Jones) 582 (James) 582 A. L. 136 James Henry 583 John G. 583 William Louis 583
WOOLRIDGE, A. Lyle 175 Bessie C. 175 Nellie M. 442-443 Williard 442-443
WOOTEN, Albert Hayes 581 Anna P. 175 Charlie R. 502 Herman Sizer 581 Lorene W. 503 Shirley L. 175 Wayne Lee 581
WOOTTEN, George W. (Washington) 581
WOOTTON, J. W. 306
WORD, Carrie Burke Anderson 22 David Malloy Jr. 22 Marrie P. Caroline 267 Mary Elizabeth 267 Thomas Harrison 267
WRIGHT, Agnes V. 503 Annie Laura 503 Arthur 366 Ben 584 Charlie 366 585 Edward 443 Elisa 366 Estelle 585 Estelle N. 585 Frances 19 Harold I 443 Harry B. 585-586 Harry Jr. 586 Hubert 443 Irene (Bennett) 541 Irene L. 586 James Nickoles 443 James S.(Shirley) 586 John Henry 503 John Jr. 443 John Lee 443-444 John Willis 299

WRIGHT, (continued)
　Joseph Spencer 258 Lawton V.
　586 Maria R. 443 Marion 585
　Mary B. 87 Mary E. 280 Maud
　Gordon 443-444 Nettie Burnley
　258 Ola H. 444 Olanda
　Ambrose 258 Ollie Printess 258
　Richard 280 Robert 299 Rosa
　214 Sallie Allen 583-584
　Salomon 280 Seymore S. 503
　Vadney 427 Walter L. 503
　William J. 503 Willie 444

WYCHE, Pamelia E. 209
YANCEY, George G. 292 Sallie
　(Elizabeth Johnson) 292
YATES, F. D. Rev. 230 Hattie B. 28
YODER, Clara J. 211 Elvin 211
YOUNG, Ernest 628 Florence 586-
　587 George 587 Humphrey P.
　629 Isabel M. 587 Jordon 587
　Katherine 586-587 Nannie (f.)
　629 Willie 614

www.ingramcontent.com/pod-product-compliance
Lightning Source LLC
Chambersburg PA
CBHW071214290426
44108CB00013B/1179